YUSIF
SAYIGH

YUSIF SAYIGH

Arab Economist, Palestinian Patriot

A Fractured Life Story

Edited by
Rosemary Sayigh

The American University in Cairo Press
Cairo   New York

First published in 2015 by
The American University in Cairo Press
113 Sharia Kasr el Aini, Cairo, Egypt
420 Fifth Avenue, New York, NY 10018
www.aucpress.com

Dar el Kutub No. 2059/14
ISBN 978 977 416 671 6

Dar el Kutub Cataloging-in-Publication Data

Sayigh, Yasif, 1916-2004
        Yusif Sayigh: Arab Economist, Palestinian Patriot: A Fractured Life Story / Rosemary
    Sayigh – Cairo: The American University in Cairo Press, 2015
        p.   cm
        ISBN 978 977 416 671 6
        1 – Sayigh, Yusif, 1916-2004
        2 – Autobiography
        920

1 2 3 4 5   19 18 17 16 15

Designed by Adam el-Sehemy
Printed in Egypt

To Yezid, Joumana, Faris, Shona,
Yusif, Diyala, Jad, and Ayla

And with heartfelt gratitude to Hala Sayegh
for her help with Arabic words and family history

Contents

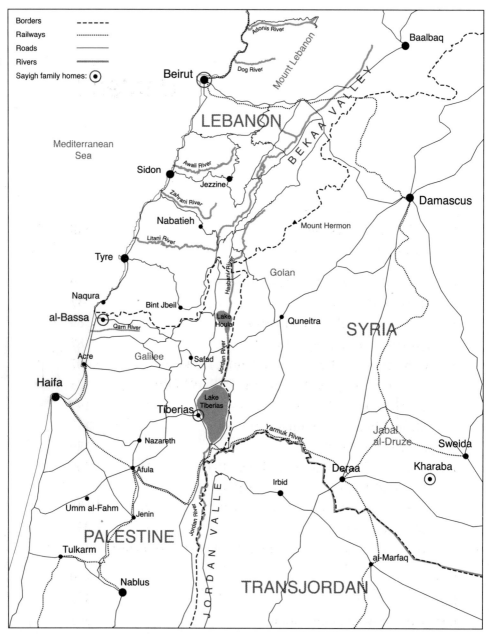

Map of Mandate Palestine, 1920–48 (Børre Ludvigsen)

Introduction

Rosemary Sayigh

The Man and the Family

Yusif was a great storyteller. The first of his stories to rivet my attention was the one about his capture by the Israelis in Jerusalem in 1948, and transfer to a prisoner-of-war camp where he spent almost a year. He told me this story in Beirut, when I stopped off on my way home from Baghdad to London, before we decided to marry. I also loved his stories of childhood, particularly those about al-Bassa, his mother's village in northern Palestine. His memories of his childhood in Syria and Palestine were like scenes from a film, separated from the time and place of narration, yet hyper-real. Characters from the past—Andraos the al-Bassa transvestite; Umm Rakkad who put the bishop of Haifa to flight when he attempted to shame her for adultery; Butros the blind Egyptian convert who took up interminable residence on the ground floor of the Sayigh family home; Abu Dakhlallah, the traveling seller of religious tracts whose itinerary always included a stay at the Sayigh home—were preserved in the memory of this curious and sensitive child. Yusif's descriptions of al-Bassa, spread between sea and mountain, endowed with rich water sources and luxuriant vegetation, formed a lost-Eden setting for these arresting figures.

Presiding over these picaresque scenes was the loving presence of Umm Yusif (Afifeh Sayigh, Yusif's mother), whom I only knew from a

1

framed family photograph. She was mysterious to me because of her premature death two years after the Nakba, and three years before our marriage, yet she was part of my life through Yusif's exceptional attachment to her. He had been her favorite son, but she was special not just in his recollection but also in that of everyone who had known her. 'Saintly' was a description often used of her. After her death, Yusif's brother Fayez said, "Life will never be the same without her." Abu Yusif (Abdallah Sayigh, Yusif's father) never changed his black tie though he outlived her by more than twenty years. That the essential scenes from Yusif's recollections should begin and end with his mother is entirely fitting.

Umm Yusif was highly educated for a woman of village background, having been sent as a boarder to the Gerard Institute in Sidon. She had worked as a schoolteacher before marriage and had looked after seven children, cooking, cleaning, and sewing for them. The first four children were raised in Kharaba, the village in Jabal al-Druze where Abu Yusif had property, and where he had built the Protestant church with support from an American missionary, Mary Ford. When the Druze uprising against the French began in 1925 Abu Yusif was in Damascus. Alone, Umm Yusif escaped with her four young children before the church was burnt. The family moved to Umm Yusif's home village, al-Bassa, in northern Palestine. After five years there, Abu Yusif's vocation as pastor took the family to Tiberias, still under the patronage of Miss Ford, to a rambling old house near the lake, close to the Scots Mission.[1] There they remained until the expulsions of 1948.

Though Yusif also admired and loved his father, and describes his many unpastor-like qualities, such as skill in carpentry and love of modern gadgets, he did not enjoy the stern Protestant discipline of their family life, focused around prayers and Bible readings. It is evident from the memoirs—and others who remember her confirm this—that the family revolved around Umm Yusif. A severe hemorrhage in 1931 at the time of the birth of Anis, her last child, brought on a heart attack nine years later, leaving her a semi-invalid.[2] War and expulsion from Tiberias in 1948, the move to Beirut, and anxiety over Yusif's fate as prisoner of war surely hastened her death in 1950.

The memoir or autobiography as the genre developed in the West was a record of the achievements of important men as movers of history, and has moreover always tended to focus on the individual. Family background would typically form the first chapter of the Great Man's memoirs but would be left behind as the subject proceeds toward his celebrated place in History. In Yusif's case, however, his parents and siblings are inextricably part of his memories. As eldest son he had 'fathered' his siblings, helping to eke out his father's meager salary as pastor to put them through college. His narrative, as a result, is full of stories about his family, including frequent references to the achievements of his brothers. This is as much a family story as it is the story of Yusif Sayigh.

Theirs is indeed a remarkable story, containing several elements that typify Palestinian and Arab families but others that are singular. Arab readers will recognize the struggle of the parents (particularly Umm Yusif) to get the children educated. Singular is the way Abdallah Sayigh and Afifi Batrouni met by accident in 1914, and fell in love and married; how Umm Yusif persisted in trying to persuade Abu Yusif to move somewhere where there were better schools than Kharaba; how he resisted because of his dedication to the church and ties to the village; and how Umm Yusif acted alone to save her children during the 1925 uprising. It was Umm Yusif who took Yusif across the border from al-Bassa to school in Sidon, and it was she who persuaded the school director to lower the fees.

Education marks Yusif's memories as theme, personal ambition, moral value, and source of family pride. Obtaining schooling was a constant struggle for the Sayigh family, given the extreme poverty of public education in Mandate Palestine and Abu Yusif's modest salary as a pastor. Kharaba had only one elementary school; al-Bassa had more schools but none at the secondary level; even in Tiberias the Sayigh children had to go elsewhere for secondary schooling. This meant that all seven children had to be sent away to private boarding schools to get high-school diplomas and qualify for college. Paying the fees wasn't easy. Scholarships, the generosity of friends, Yusif's contribution, and loans here and there enabled all six Sayigh boys to go through university. Four of them chose intellectual professions, one engineering, and one medicine. Four obtained PhDs. Yusif himself left university with only a BA in business administration. He didn't gain his doctorate in economics until 1957, at the age of 41.

Umm Yusif's weak heart seems to have been inherited by all her sons; all died from some form of heart failure, two of them while still in their fifties, all but the youngest, Anis, before Yusif himself. Combined with mourning for Palestine, these family tragedies cast a shadow over our family gatherings. Even so, Yusif's natural optimism and love of life color his recollections with joy rather than sadness.

I had long wanted to record Yusif's memories, partly because his background was so different from mine, partly also because we both came from middle-class families on the edge of poverty who valued education highly. But it wasn't just the difference in the landscape of our childhoods that made me want to record him; it was also that he had taken part in or lived through so many momentous events, and actively participated in many of them. I felt that his recollections must have value as part of the history of a region characterized by rapid political, social, and cultural change. People today can hardly remember how life was in villages in Jabal al-Druze and Galilee— what people wore and ate, what homes were like, how children were brought up, how they played, what were treats and punishments, what a missionary boarding school was like. Today there are few people left who lived through the Nakba.

Yusif did not share my enthusiasm for recording his memories. He would say that he wasn't important enough, it would be a sign of conceit, a trait he disliked. There were figures such as Abdel Nasser, al-Assad, Arafat, who created movements and made things happen; these were the proper subjects of memoirs. He did not accept the idea that ordinary people can contribute to a richer understanding of history through their memory and witness. Moreover, his work after leaving the American University of Beirut (AUB) in 1974 kept him continually on the move. It was impossible to pin him down to recording sessions.

Producing the Recordings

My chance came in April 1989, when he was forced to spend several weeks at home in bed recovering from an operation. He was my prisoner, and finally yielded to the tape recorder. Making the recording a joint project, something that we were doing together for our children and grandchildren, softened his opposition. Once started, he even began to enjoy the sessions. We didn't follow a strict chronology. His story of capture by the Israelis in May 1948 became the beginning for sentimental reasons. Then, since his presence in Qatamoun in mid-May 1948 needed explanation, we returned to his time in Jerusalem between October 1944 and his capture. From there we went back to his earliest memory, his mother weeping because her second baby had died.[3] Each evening we would plan what episodes to record the next day.

Between April 6 and 26, 1989, we filled twenty one-hour cassettes, covering his life up to the death of his mother in 1950. These twenty tapes form the bulk of the memoirs as they are presented in this book. But as soon as he was able to leave bed, Yusif was off on another professional trip, and became even harder to capture than before. It was during 1989 that his work began as advisor to Ahmad Qurei, director of the Palestine Liberation Organization's (PLO's) Economic Department, to construct an economic development plan for a future Palestinian state. From then until late 1993 he spent most of his time in Tunis, and although we continued to record from time to time in snatches between travel, these sessions were too far apart and too informal to achieve the focus of the first set.

It was only much later, after Yusif's death, when I came to edit the tapes, that I realized how much the quality of the recordings had declined between the first long, bedridden sessions and the later recordings snatched over a lunch or a weekend. From being mainly a monologue with occasional questions from me, they turned into reminiscences about our children, the homes we lived in, holidays, friends, domestic helpers . . . . This meant a marked decline in general interest after 1952, the moment when Yusif's professional career was just beginning to take off. Thus about two-thirds of the memoirs are about his formative years rather than the years of productivity. This is one of the senses in which this life story is incomplete: it doesn't cover what most readers would want to know about Yusif Sayigh the economist, teacher, writer, and conference speaker. However, we did manage to record a long set on Yusif's involvement in Palestinian politics, now the final chapter of this book.[4] In any case, politics and the personal are woven together in this account. We, his family, were always aware of the implications of Yusif's work: late-night meetings; having to poke a broom handle down the exhaust pipe of the car to make sure that there wasn't a bomb in it; an iron bar to place across the outer door at night; a Klashin[5] under the TV set; his bouts of stress and illness.

A more serious shortfall was our failure to record a full chapter on Yusif's career as an economist. In our early recording sessions we reached the crucial year 1952 when he completed an MA in economics and began working in AUB's Economic Research Institute, but we never fully covered the development of his career. Thus the final chapter of this book: "Bread with Dignity: Yusif Sayigh as an Arab Economist," is put together from fragments of the recorded memoirs, his writings, my recollections, and the tributes of colleagues.

Because I knew his stories so well, I played a more interventionist role in the recordings than a professional oral historian would have done, reminding him of anecdotes, or probing his account to get more details about points that interested me. In retrospect, I think this was a mistake because it deprived his recollections of full autonomy. It meant that my interest in social history directed him to topics that were not important to him, and away from others that were. A final listening and revising process would have corrected these mistakes.

Tunis: Challenge and Disappointment

The years 1989 to 1993 formed the peak of Yusif's career. His assignment to produce an economic plan for an independent Palestinian state fully mobilized his professional abilities as well as his Palestinian patriotism. In addition, he was working with the full support of Qurei, and with a large office staff. The inevitable delays, lapses in quality of the contributions, and the pressure he put upon himself to finish the plan on time, meant that he worked seven days a week, often until late at night. The strain was so severe that Qurei sent him to Paris for medical examinations after a bout of bad headaches. He had little contact with other PLO figures. His relations with Chairman Arafat had always been strained, and remained so in Tunis.

He completed the plan during the summer of 1993, as the Oslo Accords were being negotiated. In spite of his close association with Qurei, who was chief negotiator, Yusif had no inkling of the Oslo negotiations. Like many Palestinians he was unhappy that the Palestinians had gone to Oslo without legal advisors or map-makers. But he stayed on in Tunis for a few more months to negotiate with the World Bank about funding. His old dislike of Arafat's methods reached a peak in the aftermath of Oslo, as the president finagled the structure of the newly established Palestine Economic and Development Agency for Reconstruction (PECDAR) to ensure his own total control of development aid. Less than two months after Oslo, Yusif resigned from PECDAR's board and left Tunis. He returned to Beirut deeply disappointed by Arafat's ability to manipulate even the World Bank and international leaders simply because, at that point, the United States wanted the chairman 'on board.'

The Final Years

Back in Beirut, Yusif had to face the cold-shouldering of other Palestinians who wrongly associated him with Oslo. Now the stress of the Tunis years—symptoms that Yusif had suppressed in his eagerness to develop the plan—began to emerge. After Oslo all the health problems that had plagued him throughout his life—heart, ulcer, slipped discs—returned with a vengeance. At first a project with the Center for Arab Unity Studies kept him afloat. The idea was an interesting one: to carry out interviews with leaders of the European Economic Union to analyze what features could be applied to the Arab region. But open-heart surgery put this project out of the question, and with the loss of work, life lost much of its zest for him. The only times I saw him regain his old spirit was when giving interviews to journalists, especially about the Tunis debacle.

It was always our intention to go back over the tapes and review them. The memoirs are rich in what they give but I regret the loss of deeper reflections on his life and times that a second time around would have given. He might have taken the opportunity to analyze the reasons for failure—at least in our time—of secular Arab nationalism, and to reflect on the Arab governments in whose capacity to reform he kept faith almost to the end. A question he might have wanted to explore was the tension between the part played by American education in the formation of his character and intellect and U.S. policies in the region, especially the alliance with Israel. Time to revise would have encouraged him to reflect on these topics more deeply, but the last eight years of his life were so plagued by hospitalization and growing immobility that it would have been impossible to ask him to listen to the tapes.

In spite of their provisional quality I think the memoirs effectively convey an aspect of Yusif's character that I especially loved: his outspokenness. He was unusually courageous in speech and action, especially for a man who was far from being physically strong. The words he spoke to a Palestinian National Authority (PNA) official in 1994—"I argue things out with Abu Ammar himself, or with people even more important than Abu Ammar. I will never relinquish my right to argue"—could well stand as his epitaph. An Arab nationalist and Palestinian activist, a secularist and modernizer, he put his formidable brain, wit, and energy into the service of his people.

1

Earliest Memories, Kharaba, 1918–25

The earliest recollection I have comes from Kharaba.[1] My parents moved there after I was born in 1916 in the village of al-Bassa, near Acre in Palestine. I was about three years old. By then my mother had had another baby, Fuad, who died of some fever. I was lying with my head on my mother's leg, looking up into her face—I was *always* very attached to my mother, all through, until she died—I went on feeling toward her like a baby needing his mother's embrace. It was a very special relationship. So I was lying there, happy, looking into her face. Then I saw her tears falling. I said, "Mama, why?" and pointed to her tears. She said, "Because of your little brother Fuad who died." So I said, "What do you mean?" She said, "He went to heaven." That's my earliest recollection. She was expecting then, and a few months later she brought another boy into the world, and they gave him the same name, Fuad. It's unusual for families to give the same name of a child that has died. But my parents were both believers, and they felt that this was God's gift to them, to replace the loss they had suffered.

That was in Kharaba, the village where we were living then, where my father was a preacher. He was not an ordained pastor; he still had no theological training. But he was a very religious man. His brother-in-law was a pastor, and he had gone to school at the Gerard

Institute in Miyeh-Miyeh, near Sidon, where there was a great deal of religious teaching, since it was a mission school. It was his own decision to go there; he was an adult at the time and had his own means. He went to Sidon and asked about schools. Then he met the principal of the Gerard Institute, who was the same principal as when I went many years later, in 1929. He knew he wanted to be a pastor. Interestingly enough, my mother went to the girls' school in Ain al-Hilweh, between Sidon and Miyeh-Miyeh.[2] They overlapped in time, though my mother was several years younger than my father. It was because he was rather old for school, and she was rather young. They both graduated just before the war, I think, or in 1915. They married soon after.

They didn't meet in Sidon. They met through Miss Ford, an American missionary who had her own mission.[3] She had private means, and came to the region essentially to open schools, and to have preachers and pastors trying to convert people. She used to live in Safad. But it seems that she went to the Sidon School to recruit prospective teachers, and she met my father and my mother separately. My mother told me that Miss Ford—she was Mary Ford and my sister Mary was named after her—sent word to my mother to visit her in Safad. She had built herself a *beautiful* house in Safad, so beautiful that when the Israelis took over Safad, the military governor took it as his residence. It overlooks the Sea of Galilee and the beautiful hills around there.

So my mother visited Miss Ford, and Miss Ford said to her, "How about coming with me on a trip? I want to go to Hawran and see somebody called Abdullah Sayigh. I want to appoint him as preacher there." My mother went with her. It was remarkable that my mother had such freedom. Indeed, going to boarding school was quite unusual for a young village woman in those days. It was partly thanks to a cousin from al-Bassa who had gone to the boys' school there ahead of my mother—in fact, two cousins from different mothers, Wadi'a and Jiryis Khoury, and they both went to Sidon School. They knew there was a girls' school there, and here was a cousin who was likable and intelligent. They could tell that she could do well in school. So they encouraged her, and worked on her mother and father to let her go to school. It was amazing. I regret not having asked her for more details. All I know is that she went to school, and graduated the first in her class. My father was also the first of his class. He used to have such lovely presents that they gave him every year. The best present was an Elgin watch, one of those prestige watches, for being the first all through until the last year. Later he gave it to me when I went to Sidon School.

Miss Ford contacted my mother, and asked her to accompany her on this trip, and offered her a job as a teacher in a school she wanted to start up in Tiberias or Safad. As my mother had not yet accepted, she went with her to Hawran, and saw this man. She liked him, and he liked her very much. I don't know when he proposed but certainly they married soon, in 1915, because I was born in 1916, on March 26.

The amusing thing is that in al-Bassa there were two or three young men who wanted to marry my mother, and when they heard that she'd got engaged to a Hawrani—Hawranis were looked down on then as backward; they didn't wear western dress, people said they had lice—they tried to persuade my mother to change her mind. They also worked on my grandmother to influence her daughter. But either my grandmother was modern in outlook, or they did not succeed. So one of the cousins wrote a letter to my mother's brother, who had emigrated to America, saying, "Your sister, an educated girl, the first one in the village to go to boarding school and get a diploma, has accepted to get engaged to a one-eyed Hawrani!"—about my father, who was quite handsome! My uncle was very hot-tempered, and wrote an angry letter to his sister. They sent him a picture of my father to prove that he had two good eyes. But my uncle went on being angry, and for many years he didn't write to her. As for the man who wanted to marry her, I mean, I would commit suicide rather than be his son. Awful, almost illiterate. He had land. But my father was not without means.

Before my father was married he had two or three good horses, and one of them was coveted by a Hawrani from Busrah. This was in Kharaba. My father refused to sell it. One morning at dawn this man came and loosened the reins of the horse and led it out. My father heard the sound of its hooves and saw somebody going out of the gate, riding his own horse and leading the other horse by the reins. My father immediately got dressed. The man started galloping to get away from Kharaba as quickly as possible. My father took his rifle and ran to his other good horse, and galloped after him, shouting at him to stop. The man was ahead by a few hundred meters, and wouldn't stop. My father fired at him, but didn't hit him. Busrah wasn't very far from Kharaba, so the thief soon got there. Realizing it was the man who wanted his horse, my father went to the *mukhtar*'s house, and woke him, and told him the story. He said, "Come right away and you'll find my horse at this person's house." They went, and the man was brought to the *mukhtar*'s house and the elders of the village gathered there and apologized. My father got his horse back, and went home. It was my father who told me this story.

I was born in al-Bassa—this is moving back a little—because that is where they married. They were married there because my father wanted to escape conscription. He was caught in Hawran and made to join the Ottoman army, but he bought his way out—you could pay some gold coins and be released. But then he realized that they were coming back after a few months to grab people who had paid again. So he escaped and came to al-Bassa. He was already engaged to my mother at that point. They married in al-Bassa, and he stayed there. Then they grabbed him in al-Bassa. He hid but he was again caught and conscripted, and moved from one station to another until he ended up in Gaza. There he ran away again from his unit at night—apparently it was very cold—and he roamed about looking for a place to hide, until he found an oven. A big oven. Big households had large ovens, where you could throw in dozens of loaves at a time. There was no fire inside, but it was warm, so he slipped in. At dawn he heard some movement, and the moment he opened his eyes he saw a woman who was coming to light the fire and make bread. She was about to scream, but he said, "Sshh! Don't worry! I'm hiding from the Turks." She kept quiet, and I don't know how he managed to hide and make his way all the way back to al-Bassa—from Gaza in the south to al-Bassa in the north—walking, or taking trains.

Then in 1918, when I was two years old, the family went back to Kharaba, because Miss Ford wanted my father to be a preacher and a schoolteacher there. My mother taught very briefly with Miss Ford, around the period when she took her to Hawran, in a school for girls. My knowledge of that period is very sketchy. My mother told me that she was twenty-three when I was born. That's how I established that she was born in 1893. She used to say, "Your father was seven or eight years older than me," so I also established that he was born in 1885. Later, when my father was in his seventies and eighties, he began to challenge this, and say, "*La, immak heik* [Your mother was like that], she wanted to tease me, to make me sound much older than her."

In Kharaba my father became a preacher and we stayed there, near Deraa, which was within walking distance, even for a boy. Deraa was the seat of the emir of the Druze Atrash family. Kharaba in fact was more Hawran than Jabal al-Druze—there were two adjacent districts, Hawran and Jabal al-Druze.[4] The capital of Hawran was Deraa, and of Jabal al-Druze it was Sweida. Kharaba was in between, the last village to the north, and near to Deraa. And beyond Deraa there was Sweida. It was an all-Christian village, mainly Orthodox and Catholic, with some Protestants. The first Fuad was born in Kharaba, and then the second Fuad. Then Fayez was born at the time when my father was planning—with the help of Miss Ford—to go to Jerusalem and study theology. I think he stayed there for about two years. It was a college of theology. Because he had read many theology books, and was mature, his training took a little less than two years. We went to Jerusalem, and he was ordained in August 1923.[5]

My father wasn't from Kharaba originally; he was born in a village called Khirbet al-Sha'ar, not far from Damascus. That's where his father, my grandfather, Yusif Sayigh, had settled with his own father, Abdullah Sayigh. Abdullah came from Homs and he had been a goldsmith, a '*sayegh*,' but his real family name was Zakhour Kabbash. Because he was a goldsmith, it was simpler to refer to him as '*al-sayegh*,' and then he adopted it as his name. He had only one son, my grandfather, Yusif. My grandfather lived in Khirbet al-Sha'ar with his father until his father's death. Because he was well-to-do, my grandfather bought land—not much. My father's share was something like 130 *dunum*s, apart from the shares of his sisters—he had more land than them—and also sheep and horses. Then my father—I don't know at what stage—or maybe it was my grandfather—moved on to Kharaba. Three of my father's sisters were married in Kharaba. He had four sisters. One was married to a Christian in a Druze village called Salkhad, beyond Sweida.

So my father was ordained in 1923. On the way to Jerusalem, we passed by al-Bassa because my mother wanted to see her sister: she had a sister alive then, although she had lost two or three other sisters. She also had nephews, nieces, and friends. I don't remember my grandmother. I think she died when my mother was in her last year of school.[6] My grandfather died earlier. So we passed by al-Bassa and spent a few weeks there. It was there that I can first remember seeing a motorcar. There was a road from al-Bassa to Acre, and I remember a car coming, and everybody rushing to see it. Then in August, on our return to Hawran, we came back to al-Bassa, also for a visit, and from there we returned to Hawran via Lebanon. My father stopped in Sidon to see his teachers, and then on to Damascus, and then on to Kharaba. I don't remember much of that trip. By this time he was a pastor.

Ah, I remember the reason why he wanted to go back via Beirut: to meet the head of the Protestant Church in Beirut, al-Qassees Mufid Abdul Karim, who later became the father-in-law of the Reverend Awdeh. He was a very respected, venerable person, and my father wanted the church of Beirut to help Kharaba build a church of its own. My father was ambitious: he wanted to have a proper church. There was an Orthodox and a Catholic church but not a Protestant one, only a smallish room that served as a church. Miss Ford provided some of the money, and Beirut helped by giving money toward the making of the benches. What I remember very clearly is that they also contributed a set of cups for Communion. The Beirut church was getting a new set of its own. So they contributed a set of hymn books and twenty or thirty of these little cups.

When we returned from Jerusalem after my father's theology course, we happened to be in south Lebanon at the time when a census was taken. The people we were staying with in Sidon said, "Why don't we list you as Lebanese like us instead of Syrians?" My father laughed, and they seem to have put down our names. So my father was not telling a lie when years later, in 1958, he applied for Lebanese citizenship. It was open to people who had been in Lebanon in 1923 when the census took place.

My father went back triumphant with this help and set about immediately building. He knew nothing about cement fixing or building, but he learnt. He went to Deraa and learnt from some contractors building there. As he had taken carpentry in school for five years, he made all the church benches himself as well as the pulpit, the windows, the doors—all the wood work, everything. Alone. He was a fantastic person when he was determined to do something, especially for the Lord. We don't have any pictures of the church, but I remember it very, very clearly. There was a *hawsh*, an enclosed yard, around which were several rooms. That was where we lived, and also one of my aunts, the mother of Abu Victor, whose husband was a village doctor, *tubb 'arabi* [Arab medicine]. The church was built on top of these rooms because they had no money to buy land, especially for a church. So my father said, "Why not build it on top and have a stairway leading up?" I remember my father saying that some old-fashioned members of the church said, "But you can't build a church that is not on the ground floor." "Why not?" They said, "It's not decent." It turned out that the Hawranis didn't wear underpants—not even the women. This I discovered myself when I was a little boy, lying on the floor in our room, and the aunt who lived there came to visit, and stepped over me, and I could see that she had nothing on underneath. That's why they were afraid that somebody would look up. My father said, "Well, you'd all better be careful about the way you walk, or wear underpants."

So the church was built and equipped, and there was a big consecration. I think Miss Ford was there. But the completion of the church took time. I think that it wasn't completed until 1925. But then of course it was destroyed. So my poor father had to build it all over again. It was burnt when the Druze attacked the village in 1925.[7]

The Village and Its Surroundings

My aunt's husband read a lot, and it seems he was very effective as the village doctor. I remember him as a biblical figure with a long white beard and a hot temper like an Old Testament prophet. When I knew him he was already an old man, bent, with a stick. People would come to him from several villages for Arabic medicine. He had books about it. Every few months, his son Abu Victor would go to Sweida or Damascus and buy him powders and liquids from pharmacies. From them he composed liquids for coughs and powders for wounds or for stomach problems. He used one of those very tiny little scales, which he held with two fingers. He would put on one side grains of wheat for weights, and on the other the right proportion of the various powders. Or if he was mixing liquids he'd have a very small container, and put in the components in the right proportions. The powders were put in very thin cigarette papers and wrapped tightly as if molded, and people would swallow them.

There certainly wasn't a bank in the village—I didn't hear the word 'bank' until much, much later. There might have been one in Sweida, maybe a branch of the Agricultural Bank, an Ottoman bank, which had branches all over. The villagers used to borrow gold coins from each other. They would sometimes go to villages such as Busrah in Hawran, halfway between Kharaba and Deraa. Or if they needed a larger sum, it was usually from a merchant who supplied the borrower with seed, someone whom he knew and trusted. But of course there were guarantees and a very high rate of interest.

We went to those other places very seldom. I remember my mother used to nag about this. She felt imprisoned. My father had his work, his church, his congregation. Of course she had her children, but she wanted some breathing space, somewhere else to go besides Kharaba. She would say, "I wish we could go somewhere." I remember going once or twice to Deraa with the family. I think we went with two donkeys and a horse. My father rode the horse.

Every now and then my mother would say to my father, "I wish we could leave, and take the children somewhere where they can get an education. Maybe you can find a job in a town, in Syria, in Lebanon, or in Palestine?" This would lead to some questions from me about al-Bassa. I was the eldest so I was the readiest to ask questions: "What is al-Bassa like?" I'd seen it in 1923 of course. They took me all over the place, to the fig trees, the pomegranate trees, the *subbeir* [prickly pears]. My mother would tell me about al-Bassa at great length, about going to the sea, and having picnics. I used to think, "My God! What are we doing here?" It was like comparing Paris to Nabatieh.

There was no bus there at all, no railroad. My father had a bicycle—it's interesting how he learned to ride it. We had a threshing field, which was big and very flat, for doing the wheat. It was about ten minutes' walk from the house. So he'd take the bicycle there, and start riding and falling and riding and falling until he mastered it. It was the only bicycle as far as the eye could see. There was a dust road, not a car road: there were no car roads to Kharaba at all. Jubayb was another Christian village near to us, about twenty minutes away by bicycle. My father would go there to preach, after preaching in

Kharaba. He'd put on a pith helmet, one of those colonial things, because of the sun—there was no protection from the sun there, and it could be very hot in summer—and bicycle along. Every now and then he'd take me up behind him. I remember how annoyed he'd be when a thorn went into the tire, and he had to change it, and be late for the sermon. We always had to allow a bit of time for that.

"The Village Was Very Primitive"

After we returned from Jerusalem, I began going to the village school, where the teacher was my cousin, Abu Victor, who was at that time the only teacher. It was in one of the rooms below the church, just one room. He couldn't go very high—he taught us arithmetic and reading and a bit of English, but not French. The basics. A church school. I think after that a school was set up by the Orthodox. There was no government school at all.

The village was very primitive.[8] For instance, the water—there were two reservoirs: one for animals to drink from and for water to be brought home for washing, and the other that was dug deep in the rocks—we called it the pool. It received water from Ara', the village where the Atrash chieftain, Hassan al-Atrash, lived. This water came uncovered, not in a pipe, once or twice a week. I used to love watching the water coming when it got close to the village, how part of it would be absorbed by the soil, and the rest would make its way down to the pool, which was used for the animals and for washing, and was called *madkh*. The water went to it first because it would be muddy at the beginning; then, when it became a bit clearer, they would divert it to the *ayn* [spring] from which we drank. Women would go there and fill jars, and carry them on their heads all the way to their houses. The pool was on the outskirts, to the northeast of the village. Later on my aunt, who was married to the village doctor, moved out there; they built their own house there. The water would be brought and put in big earthenware jars, like the big oil jars you see in Lebanese villages. The villagers made them themselves, I don't know how—I don't remember seeing somebody actually making them—but I knew they were made in the neighborhood. We didn't drink directly from these jars; they were porous so the water dripped down, and that way it kept cool and was filtered. We'd keep a jug underneath and refill it. My mother didn't want us to drink the water as it came from the pool: it was open to the sky and anything could fall in it. The bottom was very dirty. It had tortoises in it.

I remember one day, a villager who worked our fields—because my father was too busy to do that—we called him *muraabi'*, a sharecropper—insisted that I should try to learn how to swim in the *madkh*. I had a fear of being touched by the tortoises, and there were leeches too, which were even more frightening. I used to see them because my aunt's husband, the village doctor, would fetch them to apply them to people who had a temperature or an infection—they were in the water, it was horrible! He put me on his back, and swam energetically from one end to the other. I clung to his neck, and when we reached the edge I said, "Please, please let me off." My father was watching; he said "All right, *ya Musa, bekaffi* [All right, Musa, enough]." From one side to the other was about twenty meters. They brought animals to drink from it: sheep, goats, plow oxen, donkeys . . . .

I felt that I was being kept away from the boys and their games. I noticed that I was different from them in some ways, especially in clothing. The boys of the village were barefooted and wore a *gallabiya*[9]—it was rare to find a boy who had shoes. I wanted to be like them, so I would hide my shoes behind the gate. I'd leave them there and run out to join them. The village roads were very dusty, and of course there was no public garden, no play house, nothing. But they played games like hide and seek. I'd come back all dusty, and my legs and feet dirty, and my mother would scold me. I said, "All right, if you don't want me to play barefooted, I'll put on shoes. But let me wear a *qumbaz* like them, or a *thawb*[10]—not my shorts." I felt so out of place in shorts with the boys. So she made me one or two *thawb*s to make me feel at ease.

We had a schoolteacher who wanted us to begin learning English. He suggested we should get together after school, and play any game but talk to each other in English. Anyone who slipped, his name would be written down, and later on there'd be some small penalty. It was a silly game. We didn't know enough English to play it, just a few words—maybe I knew more than the others. One of the boys—he was called Hani Shlaweet and became a preacher later—was always on the lookout to see if the pastor's sons did something unworthy of the pastor, just to annoy my father. His father was one of those fanatical Christians who believed the Bible from cover to cover. I remember that while we were playing, Hani shouted, "Yusif, you were speaking Arabic." I said, "No, that's not true." He went on repeating it, so I got very angry. I climbed a wall and in a low voice—but not so low he couldn't hear—I said, "*Yil'an abuk!* [Curse your father!]" He said, "At least now you spoke Arabic." He went and told his father, who immediately came to my father and said, "*Ibn al-assees bi'ool yil'an abuk?* [The pastor's son says 'Curse your father'?] Terrible!" I got a sound beating.

That's the first beating I remember. But the worst beating I had came later. Somebody in the village had hired a tractor to do the plowing. My father liked the idea and told the man who was our *muraabi'* that year that he wanted to hire the tractor. I got very excited about this machine that was moving on its own, not drawn by horses or cows. So I ran out to the fields. My mother said, "Don't go, Yusif!" I said, "Don't worry, Mama, I'll be careful. I won't stay long in the sun." I was wearing a *shursh*[11] that I had prevailed on my mother to make for me. The tractor was driven by a driver who came with it, not somebody from the village. So I walked by the tractor as it was moving, and he said, "Would you like to come up and sit next to me, and see how I run it?" I said, "Yes!" I was very excited. I tried to climb—I was very short when I was young, I remained short until the age of sixteen—I used to be very unhappy looking at myself in the mirror and thinking I was going to be a pygmy—I started to climb up. The wheels—it had metal wheels with diagonal bars jutting out—caught my *shursh*. Instead of climbing up and reaching the seat next to him, the driver saw me sliding down: down, down, down. I tried to extricate myself but couldn't: my *shursh* was caught. Then he noticed and stopped the machine and saved me. I was a bit scratched, because my thigh got gradually drawn down toward the wheel.

My father had noticed my absence, and was standing outside the door. It seems that word had got back to him about my robe being caught; somebody had seen it and told him. He started shouting, "Yusif! Yusif!" I guessed that he was very, very angry. I went back. By the time I reached the house, it was my mother who met me at the door. She said, "Your father is very angry; he's going to punish you. In fact he's going to flog you. I'll do what I can to make it as gentle as possible. I'm sorry for you, darling." She almost cried. But she couldn't sway him when he'd set his mind on something. He said, "Haven't I told you!" Instead of sympathizing with me—which I badly needed—he decided to flog me. He made me lie down on my back and raise my feet. He had two pieces of rope that he bound around each other. He beat me on my feet, on the soles, yes! It was the first and last time I got that. I cried of course. I cried in humiliation because I felt it was not fair, that instead of showing sympathy he flogged me. This was something that I always felt about my father. I would have liked to be able to go to him and hug him. You know, I loved him very much, but he always kept a distance. He was a patriarch; he frowned. I used to wish he would be more like my mother.

There was some social life. We would go visiting the relatives—my father had three sisters in the village. I used to go with my parents because I was the eldest, and the others were too young. By 1925, there were four of us: I was the eldest, then Fuad and Fayez, then Tawfiq. Our life was very dull. I remember feeling terribly imprisoned. I wanted to get out of there. I had seen a big city: I'd been to Jerusalem, to Damascus. There were trams in Damascus and in Beirut. There were trains; there were shops. In Kharaba, there were one or two little groceries, with *haloum* (Turkish delight), Marie biscuits, hummus [chickpeas], and *'adas* (lentils). I think the villagers were self-sufficient. We very rarely went to the shops. Things like *amariddeen* and *halaweh*[12] my father brought in quantity whenever he went to Deraa, or Sweida, or Damascus. He would go two or three times a year. Hummus, *fuul* [beans], and so on we had from our land. Meat of course we bought. Every now and then a sheep would be killed.

There wasn't much to do in Kharaba—we didn't have toys, or educational games, or music. There wasn't much to do outside either, in those dusty roads. I was horrified at the idea of getting lice—all the villagers had lice, you could see them scratching their heads, and finding a louse, and killing it between their two thumbs. Visitors, grown-ups, who came to visit us did that: it was horrible. People drank from the same cup. In our house at least we knew that we alone were sharing the central plate. But if we were invited out, or we invited people in, we would be sharing the same plate with them and digging into it with our hands, and drinking from the same big jug. It made my flesh creep. I used to accompany my father on his visits; it was part of his duties in Hawran, toward the end of our time there. I began to go with my parents, but I didn't enjoy these visits because I'm queasy about things that smell greasy. These houses had no water, and they weren't well cleaned. Frequently, I'd see lice in the hair of their kids, and it disgusted me. If I was thirsty I'd be forced to drink from the same dipper.

Traders used to come to the village to sell cloth. Sometimes they came with fruits from Jabal al-Druze, which had figs, apricots, pome-granates, and better grapes than Kharaba. In Kharaba there wasn't enough water for people to grow fruit around their houses; there was nothing but grapes, watermelons, and melons.[13] Rainfall was very, very scarce. There were no trees whatsoever—except one tree inside the yard of the church. It was all absolutely flat. Our house and the church were on a tiny hilltop, so we were the highest place in the village—from one of the bedrooms you could look for miles around. Everywhere you looked was absolutely flat, as far as the eye could see. Trees only began to come to life when one got to Deraa or Sweida.

Kharaba People

Among the people in Kharaba, the one I really liked was Yusif, Abu Victor's younger brother. He's a pastor now in Argentina. I liked him very much; he made me interested in literature. We had no books there at all, but when he got his hand on a book—he was quite a bit older than me— I would devour it. He used to write as well—prose and poetry. I got my interest in writing poetry through him. I liked Abu Victor a bit, but he was pompous. For instance, whenever a visitor would come from Deraa or anywhere, he'd turn to me and talk in English, to show off. I hated that.

I liked Anis, another cousin, the son of the pastor.[14] He was tall and handsome and had a presence; you could tell he thought things out. But he was much older than I. There was another aunt, whose husband was the *mukhtar* of the Catholics in Kharaba—she was the mother of Fareed Ghorayeb, who used to bring us produce from our land. There was another cousin, the daughter of an aunt who had married early, the sister of Anis, who had two boys. They were all teachers and pastors, except for Afif, who never had anything more than sub-elementary education. He went and settled in Jordan later on, in the village that was my father's, but that my wicked uncle and aunt bought with my father's money when he was still a child and registered in the name of my aunt's husband. Its name is Dibbiyeh. A whole village, yes![15]

A story I want to tell is when Huda, who was living with us and helping my mother, got married. She left our house on a horse, and I was asked—it was a big honor for me—to lead the horse to her husband's house. She had a white veil, something like a mosquito net that came down almost to her knees. I reached up and pulled it open and looked at her, out of curiosity, and saw that she was crying.

I asked her, "Why are you crying?" She didn't answer me. Afterward, when it was all over, I went back home and said to my mother, "Why was Huda crying? You told me that this is a happy day for her because she's marrying." She told me, "Don't worry. She'll be happy in due course."

Something happened in the period before we went to Jerusalem. I was aged between six and seven. We had someone who helped my mother, called Karma. She was very fond of me. Every time she came in the morning, she would pick me up, hug me very tightly, and kiss me many times on the cheek, then drop me. One day, my cousin Afif, who was ten or eleven years older than I, took me out of the house and said, "Do you like it when Karma kisses you like that?" I said, "Yes, I like it very much." He said, "If you want to enjoy it more, next time Karma picks you up, put your legs around her tightly, hug her, and kiss her on the mouth." I did this next time she lifted me up. I enjoyed it very much. Then suddenly she opened her eyes angrily and said, "Yusif, why did you do that?' I said, "It's nice, I like it." She said, "Never mind that! Who told you to do it?" I said, "Afif." She put me down, and went to my father and told him the story. My father, as I learned later, scolded Afif very severely. Afif didn't appear in our house for many weeks after that. And that ended my kissing sessions with Karma. It was my first sexual experience.

Life in the Family

My mother made us toys; she would bring cloths, rags, pieces of leftovers from shirts and underpants, and make a little ball by putting them around each other, and sewing it, and then adding a little more, and sewing again, until it had a little bit of bounce. If you threw it with all your strength from as high as you could reach, it might bounce five inches from the floor. And then my father would try to make something with wood, the semblance of a little house. I remember asking him to make a car with wheels, and he tried to make the wheels himself, and make them round. It was like a box, with four wheels. I used to drag it around; I liked it very much. And my mother made—although we were all boys—she made some dolls. We had to have something. But our main pastime was listening to the Bible and trying to read it when we started learning to read—every day, every morning and every evening. Grace was said three times before meals. There were no books in our house other than religious books.

The more of us there were in the family, the more we had an internal family life. We played; we also argued. My mother was the most influential factor in our life, because she was very gentle, very attentive, and always wanted to explain things to us rather than give orders. Whereas my father was the authoritarian type, and we were constrained. I was afraid of him, and my mother always had to be the mediator. When it was Fayez who was at the receiving end, or Fuad, it used to pain me very much and I would sulk, and I'd feel that he got angry if I sulked. It was a challenge to his authority, it showed disbelief in the righteousness of the punishment. In general I think he was not gentle enough with us, although—I knew this later on, not directly from him, but from my mother—he was very attached to us. But he was too much of a disciplinarian. He didn't hug us or put us on his knee. He remained rather distant. It was general among the Protestant community there in the village to be very rough and severe with children. They knew nothing about what religion meant except the verbal commands in the Gospels. They took literally what the Gospels say about Hell. They were strict with their children so that they would behave properly and not go to Hell.

My mother had to soften things a bit. She did this very gently because she didn't want him to feel that he was wrong. She had to influence him, but in a subliminal way. I was observant, and as I grew up I began to notice the cleverness with which she dealt with him. She felt that he was basically sterling silver, loving and good, but that the way he expressed his feelings, the way he concretized his principles and implemented them, was too literal, too strict, too scriptural.

He was very sure of his principles and his guidelines because they were from the Bible. And of course he hadn't had a happy family life himself as a child.[16]

Food Hates and Health[17]

The meat there was very fatty because it was mainly sheep—we ate mutton more than we ate goat, and the sheep were very fat. I didn't like the butter either; I used to see it being made in a goatskin. They would shake the goatskin filled with milk back and forth, back and forth, for hours. I didn't like milk or butter because they had a smell that made me uncomfortable. But I liked *laban*, and *labneh*, and *ayran*.[18] Then my cousin Abu Victor introduced us to café au lait—made from Arabic coffee with milk, not Nescafé. I used to like that. I was very fussy about milk and eggs too: I didn't like the white of eggs. I didn't like meat. Years later it turned out that it was good that I didn't like these things. In school in Sidon, Mr. Jessup, the vice principal, felt there must be something wrong with me. So he had me tested by the school doctor, Dr. Nabih al-Shabb, whose son now owns a hospital in Sidon, and they found that I had albumen in the urine, which meant I shouldn't eat the white of eggs or meat fat or drink much milk. It was as if nature was warning me. Later cholesterol came into the picture, so again I had to avoid all these things.

It was later, in al-Bassa, that my mother began bribing me to eat meat. By then, she began to notice that I was very thin. I didn't get colds but my stomach was weak. I always had to have it covered when I lay in bed. I was sensitive; it was easy to make me cry. For instance, somebody's death, even if they were not related to me at all, would make me cry. I would also cry if other boys teased me. That stayed with me until Sidon. It was a thing that annoyed me a great deal about myself; it took me time to overcome it.

There was a difference between the kind of food my mother cooked and the food of the Hawranis, which had a lot of *samneh* [fat from sheeps' tails] in it. Our food was very simple; there was very little variety. One thing that I used to like, though it had lots of *samneh* in it, was *lizza'yat*. They are a sort of pancake, made like bread, in layers. You put a layer of pancake, you pour some *samneh* on it while it is still hot, and sprinkle fine sugar on top, then you put another layer, and do the same, and a third, and so on. It wasn't especially for feasts—if we had guests we would make it. My mother mainly cooked al-Bassa dishes, for example *mjaddara*,[19] which was common to al-Bassa and Hawran. She would use rice and *yakhneh* [stew] more than the villagers in Kharaba: they used burghul more, because rice was a luxury for them. She'd make chicken, fried, or with rice. When there were vegetables, she would make *koosa mahshi* [stuffed zucchini] or something like that. Generally our house ate more vegetables and meat than other houses in the village. There would be meat at our house a few times a week. I think we drank more tea than the villagers; they depended more on coffee. Of course we had our coffee going all the time for visitors. One interesting feature of our food was *mansaf*, cooked whenever there was a big party, or an important person came to the village, or there was a marriage. The *mansaf* was the usual thing: a mound of rice with a whole sheep and heated *samneh* mixed with *laban* sprinkled on it. Now I begin to like this food but then it used to make my stomach turn, especially because it was eaten by hand the way it is in Jordan. At home we didn't eat with our hands, though the villagers did. I didn't like feeling the food directly, because of the richness in it. It was a complex I had about *samneh* and butter. The only *samneh* I liked was with the *lizza'yat*.

My mother made simple cakes, and she would give us cookies. And sweets, yes, we got sweets. *Haloum* was a staple. There were two kinds, exactly like the kinds you see now, the pink and the white. There was also *halaweh* and *dibs a'nab* [grape molasses]. For sweets to offer if people visited, there would be *bonboneh*s [candies] from the shop, unwrapped.

We didn't eat fruit every day. Even vegetables were not plentiful. Cucumbers were grown in the village, a few tomatoes, but nothing that needed water. We ate pulses mostly—'*adas* and hummus. Cooking was on primuses,[20] and sometimes in the oven where bread was made. My mother made our bread but she always had someone to help her. It was like what is called 'Iranian bread' in Iraq—flat bread that has bubbles in it, thicker than *khubz saj*,[21] in one piece, not two layers. It was delicious to eat because it was pure whole wheat with the husk of the wheat, nothing lost. That's the only thing I ever ate with real enjoyment.

Home

Our home was very simple by the standards of today. We didn't have much furniture. We had some chairs, but in the sitting room there were two mattresses on top of each other with a nice *bsat* [rug] on top. We ate on the floor, on a *tabliyeh*[22] that my father made. We didn't have beds, so the mattresses had to be moved every morning and placed on top of each other in an alcove. The covers were quilts and some lighter *bsut* [rugs] used on top in the winter. We depended heavily on the *taba'*— a beautiful *taba'* woven from straw.[23] We used it for food. Sometimes we put it on the floor, or on the *tabliyeh*. It was decorative, with beautiful patterns. The Druze were very good at making them, as were the villagers in Kharaba. Most people made their own. My mother didn't; we bought ours. We also used them as trays to offer things on, like sweets.

There wasn't a bathroom. One of the upper rooms was used as a WC. It had a hole that led to the outside of the house. The house had a wall all around: the waste just fell down, and the sun took care of it. For washing, my father—who was very ingenious—made two or three kerosene cans with a tap soldered at the bottom. These would be filled with water, and we would open the taps and wash ourselves out in the yard. That was for our hands and faces. For baths, water would be heated in a room next to the kitchen.

There was a room to which one of the primuses would be moved. We had two primuses, one for the kitchen and one for the bathroom.

The water was heated in those very heavy *tanajer* [saucepans]—we had to whiten them every year, otherwise they became poisonous. They were huge. The water would be heated, and then there'd be big, big basins for us to sit in cross-legged. When we were very little, my mother came and scrubbed us, and changed the water twice. I think we bathed once a week. But we didn't have toothbrushes, not then.

Clothing

Everyday clothing in the village was the *shirwal*.[24] Even the landowners wore it. But when the better-off people wanted to dress up, they would put on a *qumbaz*, with a belt around it. On their heads they would wear a *keffiyyeh* and *i'qal*,[25] not tarbooshes. Even my father wore a *keffiyyeh* and *i'qal* there, though in Palestine he wore a tarboosh. On top of the *qumbaz* they wore a simple *damer*, a sleeveless waistcoat of thick cloth. The better-off people would wear a better quality *damer*, with black braid around it and buttons covered with cloth. Usually for the men the *damer* was blue, and made from felt, or wool—some sort of *jukh* [velvet]. And again it would have a braid around it and also a braid at the end of the sleeves. There were two kinds of *damer*: the sleeveless kind that they wore under a jacket and also one with sleeves. If it was very cold, they'd put an ordinary European jacket on top, which they bought from Damascus or Sweida. The men wore sheepskin coats in the worst of winter, very simple, made locally by them. They wove wool to make very thick socks that they wore at home. The soles were leather, sewn onto the socks. I remember my mother wearing them inside the house in winter. But I don't remember people wearing woolen pullovers at all.

The poor men's shoes, especially farmers, were what we called *madas*. They were very coarse, homemade, loose, big things that had no laces. They slipped their feet into them, and they reached up to the ankle. The leather was the thickest you could think of. As they walked, their feet went in and out. I haven't seen them anywhere since. But often men went barefoot to the fields to plow. They wore these *madas*es when they were a little better off. They were so poorly thought of that there was a saying that if you had a lot of *samneh* you would oil your *madas* with it.

The women wore black robes, and under the neckline of the robe there was this black voile material that went around the neck and under the dress, so there was no danger of a woman's bosoms showing if she bent down. Christian, Muslim, they wore the same. The headwear of the women was a sort of scarf, all black. Sometimes if there was a feast or a wedding, it would be silk, in sober colors like dark red or blue. On top of it there would be a black headband, a piece of material folded around the head, with a bit falling down at the back. Their hair was usually braided, and they often had a bit of hair coming down in an arc, one arc toward the right ear and the other to the left. They kept their hair long, and sometimes they wore a string of gold coins. When the women wanted to dress up, they would wear the same black robe, but probably the material would be better. It was usually some sort of mercerized cotton, slightly shiny. But when they were dressing up, it might be a robe with a bit of soberly colored embroidery on the black. No white anywhere. If there was a wedding, they would have a headband with gold or silver coins attached to it. If you wanted to show off properly, it had to be gold, going around the head with the band. Or they would wear a necklace on top of the voile but under the robe, in the v-neck. If it was cold, they would wear a *damer* like the men. The women would wear this jacket on top of the *thawb* in winter. Their shoes were low-heeled and simple.

In our family we wore western clothes. We mostly wore boots that reached above the ankle—summer and winter. They had hooks that the laces went around, back and forth. My father loved boots: that's the one thing he spent money on. He would have two or three pairs at all times. He would take our measurements carefully—we would stand on a piece of paper, and he'd draw a line around our feet. Then he'd buy us the boots from Sweida or Damascus. He made two or three trips every year when he bought many things. He would come

home laden. At that time we still had one or two horses. He would
go to Busrah on horseback, taking both horses with the *muraabi'*. My
father would then hand him his horse and the man would come back
riding one horse and leading the other by its bridle. Then my father
would go on from there. Sometimes he would make definite arrangements that he'd be back at such-and-such a time, so he'd be met. He'd
be away for several days. Then he would come back laden with things,
and the man would be there with the horses again, to carry them.

I remember one trip especially. When Fayez was born, my father
was in Damascus. He knew that the birth was probably going to take
place in his absence. My mother managed somehow to send him a
cable from Busrah to tell him that a boy was born. He came back
with a beautiful gold watch. He got it for himself. He brought something else for my mother; I can't remember what. But I remember his
watch because I was fascinated by it: it was gold, with a lovely chain.
My mother laughed, and he was very happy—yet another boy—and
she said to him, "I see you've got yourself a prize!" He laughed and
said, "I've brought you a prize too!" He brought material, and she
made it into a dress. She was good at making simple dresses for herself—she couldn't have anything more than simple there.[26]

It was very cold in winter. The wind used to whistle and whine,
and I used to sit on the threshold of the outer gate, which faced
southwest, and listen to the wind at about sunset, and feel very sad.
The sun would be setting; I felt that was a saddening thing in itself,
and then this wind—often I would cry. And there were my own feelings of wanting to leave, to go somewhere else. I could see that the
school had nothing. I was very ambitious to learn. What added to
this was hearing my mother, every now and then, at night, when they
thought I was asleep—or sometimes in the afternoon—she'd be talking in a low voice to him, saying, "Let's begin thinking, Abu Yusif, of
going somewhere else." He'd say, "But going where, Afifeh? This is
my church, this is my life, this is my work, my congregation. How
can I live without them?" She'd say, "You would build up another

congregation. We have to think. We already have four boys; they need schooling. You wouldn't want them to have less schooling than you had in your days, or I had in my days." I used to be very happy when she said that, even though my father would resist the idea. But then fate took the decision out of their hands when we were forced to leave in 1925, when the church and our house were burnt. We saw them burning; we had to flee and come to Palestine. That started a new chapter in our life.

Flight from Kharaba

In the summer of 1925, around August, the Syrian revolt against the French was becoming quite strong. It started in Jabal al-Druze, and since Kharaba was a totally Christian village it was assumed to be against the Druze revolutionaries. At least people believed that that's how the Druzes thought of them. Word was coming of the expansion of the revolt under Sultan al-Atrash, and of the French bringing more troops, and beginning to use airplanes for machine-gunning.[27] We only were aware of the fighting if airplanes passed over the Druze villages in the distance; we'd hear the noise. Once or twice I saw airplanes from a distance, swooping down to machine-gun.

My father was in Damascus, on one of his trips.[28] The revolt hadn't been going on for very long; that's why he felt that he could leave. While he was in Damascus, somebody came with a message to my mother from Musa al-Kataani, the son of Oqla al-Kataani, a leader of the village. He was a village notable and also a national figure; later he became a member of the Syrian parliament. He spent most of his life in Sweida, among the Turshan. He was the only Christian leader with the Druze in their revolt. His son came to Kharaba—he had been with his father—and sent us word. Because my father wasn't around, my mother went to see him and stayed with him for quite a time. They had a big house, a mansion by village standards, on the outskirts of the village. She came back looking worried but determined. I said, "What's the matter? Why are you worried?" She said, "It's just that perhaps we have to leave, and go to Deraa." I said, "Leave?! But my father isn't here!" She said, "It's all right, we'll send him a message." With further questioning—I was nine and a half—she said that the revolt was spreading, and there might be some threat to Kharaba as a Christian village. I remember saying, "Why? We're not with the French." She said, "Well, people here think that's how they are thought of." I said, "How about Oqla Kataani? He's our friend." She said, "Yes, he is our friend, that's why he's warning us. But he cannot protect us, or stop anything happening. There are four of you"— Tawfik was born by then; he was a baby—"and I can't take risks."

At nine and a half I didn't understand much of what was going on. I knew that they were fighting, that the revolt was to get rid of the French. It wasn't really a war; the fighting was outside the villages, in the hilly part of Jabal al-Druze. From each village, occasionally, forty or fifty horsemen would come at night and shoot at a French soldiers' garrison. Sweida was the nearest place to us that had a French garrison. In fact, a French governor was located in Sweida, and of course there were soldiers around. I remember going there once and watching them taking down the flag at sunset and playing the special bugle—a dozen French soldiers lining up and saluting the flag. I remember feeling—perhaps it was my first political feeling—"That's a French flag and they are French, so why are they here?" My parents must have discussed things. Every now and then I would hear whispers, but they tried to shelter us, not to make us worry, especially because I was the worrying type. I was curious, and because I was curious I'd try to know more, and the knowledge would make me worried.

So my mother said, "We have to pack a few things, and I'm going to look for somebody with donkeys to take us to Busrah. From there we could go by train, if it's the day for trains to Deraa. If not, we'll have to go on by donkey to Deraa." But she could only find one person with one donkey. She said, "I know, they're going to say 'Hay al-shmaliyeh' [this foreigner]"[29]—I don't know why they called her that—"'look at her, she is running away at the slightest [danger]—not even waiting for her husband.' But you are my trust, and I have to protect you." Sure enough, later on we heard that even my aunts said about her, "Why should she leave? Is she any better than we are?" But it was only a matter of hours before they began running away too. Of course she told all the relatives, and asked them to come with us to help her.

There was a storage space under the floor of the yard, like an unused well. When the situation began to be worrying, my father put some valuables there, such as my mother's sewing machine and some rugs and *bsut* [mats]. When the rooms were built, years before my father was married, somebody thought of making this place. I don't know if they intended to make a well or a place to hide things—because the Christian villages always felt insecure. It had an opening that you couldn't see. The floor of the yard was flagstones, but my father knew which flagstone you could lift with the edge of an axe. Inside there was a hook or a handle, and you lifted that up. He managed to hide things there. My mother took the gold and she put it as a girdle around herself, under her clothes, and saved it all. She was a brave woman. I loved her.

We had this one donkey, so we put two bags on each side of the donkey, and my mother insisted that I ride and carry the baby. And I said, "No, you ride and carry the baby," but she wouldn't. In the end she accepted that we'd alternate, and when it wasn't Tawfiq and me, or her and Tawfiq, then it would be Fuad and Fayez to share the ride. When we weren't riding, either of us, we would walk by the donkey to make sure that Fuad and Fayez were steady and that the man was holding the rein of the donkey. Anyway, we had left the village by less than half an hour—we kept looking back—when we heard some shots, and later on we learned that one person was killed. The attack came from the north and northeast of the village, and the villagers began to move toward the south and southwest and also toward Busrah—to evacuate, to flee. I can't remember if the man who was shot had tried to shoot at the attackers. It wasn't a very big attack; there weren't many involved, because it was a small village. But soon after that—I kept looking back every other step—we saw a fire go up, and as our house and the church were on the top of the only hill in the village it was quite visible. It was very sad. I remember crying and my mother comforting us and saying, "*Allah bi'awwid, Allah bi'awwid* [God compensates]."

We went to Busrah. I can't really remember how we moved from Busrah to Deraa—that's a place where there's a gap in my memory. We got to Deraa, but we couldn't find room to sleep with the missionaries. They had a tiny house and they didn't have room for us. They said the French in Deraa were providing barracks for the refugees. There were many from other villages. So we went to these barracks, and there were low benches of stone or cement and higher up a wooden shelf, a second layer, like bunk beds, or for soldiers to put their bags or clothing on. I remember sleeping on the top one. Not much sleep. I kept turning around to see if my mother was awake—most of the time she was. My brothers were asleep on the floor. Maybe there was a *bsat*.

We managed to go early the next morning to the mission house, to see if they knew anything about my father. It seems he had managed to send word to them—I don't know if it was by cable—to ask if they knew anything about us. They managed to communicate with him, to tell him that we were safe. That was a day or two later. We stayed at least one night in the barracks, but I think we moved from there. I can't really remember. What is very vivid in my mind after all these years is the fire in our house and the church. Flames! The church had a lot of wood in it.

My father came to Deraa, and stayed three or four days—it was a very moving meeting with him, after he found his family safe. From there we went by train to Damascus. In Damascus there were two cousins of mine, children of my father's married sister who was living in Salkhad. We spent a few days with each of them. That was a relief because they met us with great warmth. But my father didn't want to stay much longer, so we pushed on to Beirut, by train. It was a long, long, long journey. We wanted to go to al-Bassa. My mother had a house there; she had a sister and nephews and nieces. We had our olives—something to live on. Nobody remained in Kharaba. Later on it was pillaged. My father had to go to Palestine to reach Miss Ford. There was no other way; there were no telephones. He couldn't just phone her and say, "Here I am, what shall I do?" She was in Safad.

From Damascus we went by train to Beirut, and my father made contact with church people, to tell them what had happened to us and to the church. Then we went to Sidon. We spent a day or two there to rest, because traveling in those days was not at all easy. From Sidon we went to Tyre and from Tyre we went up to Alma by car—a rickety car—and from there two villagers with their donkeys took us down the mountain to al-Bassa. We had to go that way because we didn't have passports. Nobody thought of making passports in those days. My mother brought away papers she knew were important, like identity cards. To have got a passport we would have had to go to Sweida, but Sweida was in turmoil—there was the revolt. I remember that we went very late in the day deliberately so that if there was a patrol, they would not catch us. Things were so easy then; you could cross by saying who you were and showing your identity card.

2

Al-Bassa, 1925–30

Arrival

We went down to al-Bassa from Alma.[1] Our relatives had somehow heard that we'd left Kharaba, so they were relieved to see us. There was rejoicing. They had vacated two or three rooms for us that had been let to somebody. As it was summer, we had two terraces up on the second floor—one terrace was in front of one of the bedrooms, which was a sitting room by day and a bedroom at night. It was a big terrace, the size of a room. It had a wooden railing, and we had mats there. We would have dinner on this terrace and spend evenings there, because it was summer. The other two rooms on that first floor, as well as the terrace in front, were taken by a Lebanese family from Tyre. It was unusual to rent out rooms but we had a very big house, and before we came, no one from the family was living in it.

There were four rooms on the ground floor, one of them a big room with an arch. One of the tiny rooms on the ground floor was let to a shopkeeper and then to a shoemaker. Because we didn't have enough rooms, we used the big room downstairs as a sitting room, and in winter we used it for sleeping in because it was warmer. So we had one room down there. My mother used one of the smaller rooms for laundry. The small room upstairs, we used as a kitchen, because it was close to us. For a while, all of us squeezed into one room to sleep, which in the daytime we turned into a sitting room by piling up the mattresses. A few weeks later we started using the room downstairs for sleeping. The other big room downstairs was used by the Lebanese family. They had made a corner on the terrace into a tiny kitchen—they had a bigger terrace than we had. We used a downstairs room as a bathroom. There was a wall around the house and a gate, and it had its own well. It was a big house that my uncle or my grandfather had built.

Our house was the largest in the village. My great-grandfather was a priest of the Catholic congregation, and he had land and money. My mother said her father was well off because he dealt in antiques. He was not from al-Bassa—he came from Lebanon to Palestine to sell little Phoenician statues. He would take them to Haifa to sell because there were rich people in Haifa—it had both a Jewish and an Arab community. When my grandfather first laid eyes on her, my grandmother was a nun, living at home. It seems that on his first trip to al-Bassa, my grandfather asked if there was an inn, or somewhere he could stay. They said, "No, but you can go to the priest's house." He stayed there, and his trips continued back and forth. He fell in love with this nun, and she fell in love with him, so she gave up her vow and her convent clothing to marry him.[2] Both her parents were dead before my mother married, though she may have been engaged before her mother died. Indeed, there was a photograph of my mother sitting sadly near her mother's body. My parents didn't tell us much about their parents. My father hardly knew his, but my mother certainly knew her mother, and she was especially attached to her, because her mother supported her in going to school. I don't know more than that.

My cousin, Mbadda',[3] lived in his father's house, on the other side of the road, a few meters from our house. He lived there with Elias, his brother, and his sister, Layya, Umm Joseph—none of them was married then—and my aunt, my mother's sister. There was no one else in our family. My uncle was in America. The house belonged to my mother, her sister, and my uncle. But in effect, the one who was getting all the benefit—there was quite a bit of land —was my cousin, Mbadda'. He got the rent, as the older male. Elias was much younger, and Mbadda' was authoritarian. Nobody dared challenge his authority. He put the money in his pocket, and anything that remained after his spending—he loved spending on drink and women—anything that remained, he would give to his mother and to his sister. But nothing to us in all those years!

When we got there, he realized that he had to do something, so he gave us olives and olive oil; and every time he went to the plots of land where he grew cucumbers, tomatoes, and *koosa* [zucchini], he'd bring us some. My mother began by being shy and not saying anything. Then when he didn't show enough sensitivity, she said, "Look, Mbadda', this is as much mine as yours. In fact, I'm an heir. You are only one of my sister's children, so you should have one-third. Deduct expenses and then we share." My uncle had said before that that he didn't want anything from the produce or the rent. This meant that the inheritance had to be shared by my aunt and my mother, half-half, and Mbadda' should get only his share as the *son* of my aunt. Instead of which, he was putting everything in his pocket.

My mother said to him, "Enough is enough." She began to make accounts with him. He always cheated, but it was useful to have the money because it was months before my father managed to establish contact with Miss Ford; and then she paid him a very small salary to start holding religious meetings in the village. There was a very small Protestant community there. Things became a bit better when a German mission in Haifa decided to open a school, and to hold services on Sunday, and to have a nurse or two in al-Bassa. They asked my father to help until they found their own preacher. My father would hold services, two or three times a month, and on the fourth week somebody would come from Haifa. They were Protestant like us, Lutheran I think. It wasn't a proper church; it was part of a ground floor that contained several rooms. One was big enough to be a school and another big enough to be a church holding twenty or thirty people. There were rooms for the nurses—they called them 'sisters.' One was German; another was American. I remember this because when Mary was born—she was born in al-Bassa—it was the first time my mother had a baby delivered by a trained midwife. All the others were by village midwives.

I began going to school there, and I think Fuad as well. It was a Catholic school, very close to us. The Germans started a school but it was far away, and we weren't sure that the level was very good. The Catholic school had just acquired a principal who was very dynamic. He was from Lebanon, and was thought of as highly educated because he had a baccalaureate. I began to go to school there and got a bit of French, more English and Arabic, and arithmetic. The school was happy with my progress; I was doing well and jumped a class. Then I began to complain that school wasn't giving me anything challenging. I was always ahead of my class. I read a great deal. My parents began to feel that something more had to be done about my education. When I went to Sidon School in 1929, they found I was good enough to be placed in the sixth elementary.[4]

Al-Bassa: Village and People

Even before arriving, I had formed a picture of al-Bassa in my mind from my mother talking about it. The place more than satisfied my expectations. It was attractive to look at; it had many trees. It was not 'closed': the people were liberal and loved fun. There was music in the coffee houses; you could hear the phonographs playing— this was before radios. People played instruments: the *mijwiz*—the double flute—and the single. You would hear people on their roofs in summer playing it and singing *'ataaba*.[5]

There were trees all round the village and, beyond it, on the west side, there were olive and fruit orchards and land for growing veg- etables that stretched to the sea. The al-Bassa people found it more remunerative to grow vegetables than wheat and barley. They grew them for their own consumption and for sale, partly to Akka and Haifa but more to south Lebanon—to Tyre and the villages between Tyre and al-Bassa. Near the sea there was another wide band of fruit trees: apricots, figs, pomegranates, and later on vineyards. Also, plums and apples. Later, people dug artesian wells in the plain and started *bayyara*s [plantations]. Most of the goods that were sent to Lebanon went through the mountains.[6] That way was cheaper and they didn't have to stop at the frontier for customs. That's what gave my father the idea of us buying land too.[7]

The village had wells. Right at the southern end of the village was a spring, and there the village had made a sort of reservoir into which the spring water came—it was clean—and they made a covering so that a man could sit there. He moved a wheel with his feet; attached to this wheel was a rope that went round it and ended with a bucket. He'd move the wheel until the bucket reached the water level, and it would fill. It was adjusted so that it would lean and fill, and when it filled it would straighten, and he would pull it up with his feet. When it came up it would pour into a small canal, and the women would line up down there with their jars, and would fill them one after another. Piped water came many years later, after we moved to Tiberias.

The village people were very industrious farmers. There were many seasons during the year. Most people had a bit of land for vegetables, and some olive trees, and some fig trees—this kept them busy. They also had carob trees, so they had to take time for the crushing of the pods. I think the *dibs* [molasses] was made in homes by people boiling the pods for hours and hours. *Dibs* was a staple— we didn't eat it with *taheeneh* [sesame paste] but by itself. The villagers also made grape molasses. For olives there were mills— they were motorized. The oil was produced, and it was graded as it flowed, from murky to clear. What was left of the crushed olives was used for *nareet*[8] for heating. The villagers made the murky oil into soap. My father learnt how to do it, and used to make enough for our laundry for a whole year.

I want to add to that the carob was an important tree, and the carob trees in al-Bassa were enormous. The tree I fell in love with first was a huge carob tree on the land of my mother's family going up toward the mountain. All around it were fig trees. But the carob was the center of our attention; we used to go there maybe twice a week with our *asraniyeh*, a sort of picnic. We'd sit underneath it. It was so large that you could sit in its shade any time of the day. Especially in summer it was delicious; you felt the coolness going through it. There was a huge branch that had fallen and was lying on the ground. We used to ride it, and pretend it was a train, and swing our feet. One day a sharp bit of branch scratched my left ankle, and the wound didn't heal for forty days. They had to take me to a doctor in Acre.

The main occupation was farming. Almost everybody owned a tract of land, big or small. The difference between large and small landowners was not as noticeable in Palestine as it was in Syria or Egypt. In Palestine, you could say that there was a class of prosperous landowners who had large tracts of land with trees; the trees were what made it more remunerative. In al-Bassa, there was also a small number of people who had no land at all, and who were available to be employed on other people's plantations. The Muslims in al-Bassa had their own land too. I think that the Christian community was more prosperous. This could have been because the Christians 'lived it'—they showed their money by drinking more than the Muslims and having more fun. But my impression is that there was more money on the Christian side.

Al-Bassa was a leading tobacco grower. The whole of Galilee was a tobacco-growing area, and al-Bassa was one of the leading villages for this product. Inspectors would come and assess the crop, and people paid a tax on the basis of the assessment. There were also two or three Arab cigarette-making companies that would come and make contracts for the purchase of the crop. I remember there was a period at the time of the picking of the leaves when everybody helped, because it had to be done quickly.[9] I spent many days every year helping my aunt's family, who grew tobacco, not just picking the leaves but—more interesting—after the leaves were picked, relatives and *shabab* [young people] from the quarter would gather together, boys and girls, and would put needles through the leaves with a string, *khayt massees* [strong thread], and then string them together. We'd string together something like a meter of leaves, and then we would tie the end of the strings so the leaves would not fall; this would be hung up like laundry ropes to dry. We also helped when the olives were picked—we helped to sort out the bad from the good. I used to enjoy helping with the carobs—I loved going to the carob trees—but I also helped when they made the molasses by carrying basketfuls to be put to boil in huge pots, with firewood to keep it going. And the soap making—I loved watching it and bringing them things they needed.

There were a few people in government service, maybe two or three policemen and three or four clerks in customs and excise. The elder son of a cousin of my mother's who had been mayor of al-Bassa worked in Acre in the district officer's office; he became the chief clerk there and would often be the acting district officer. Their family name was Freiwat. The younger son also worked with the government. They were Protestants like us.

The village was self-sufficient in most of the simple professions. There was a *sankari* [plumber], a tinsmith, and two or three carpenters. There were a few shoemakers, and several shopkeepers, groceries—the grocers had a mix of things, like flashlights, and shaving material, and sometimes cloth. The mill—there were two or three mills in the village, but the largest was multi-purpose: the olives were pressed there, it was a flour mill, and it produced ice blocks in summer. It belonged to a relative of my mother's, Tawfiq Jubran. He was very, very rich—probably the richest in land and crops in al-Bassa. He was not bad looking, but big and a bit simple, and so everybody was surprised when he found himself a beautiful young wife from Haifa. Her brothers were known in Haifa, but they were passing through a bad phase financially—probably that's why they let their sister marry this rich villager. There were other smaller mills, but they specialized either in olive crushing or flour milling. I think that somebody made *fukhar*, pottery.

Transport to Acre was by taxi. Most of the material that was sent to Lebanon went through the mountains. That way was cheaper and they didn't have to stop at the frontier for customs. There was actually a free trade agreement between Palestine and Lebanon. This I learned later on as a student of economics from [Sa'id] Himadeh's book. There were a few taxis at a time when you had to start a car by hand, by cranking. Every now and then there would be a trip to Tyre or Sidon—they would go that far—but usually it was Acre or Haifa. People could make a living driving a taxi, because many people had things to do, and they would carry boxes, *sahhara*s, of squash, cucumber, and tomatoes to sell. Later, when the road was paved, there were more cars in the village. I think that is when the buses began. And there were two or three small trucks. Because the buses were expensive to buy, people got together and formed a cooperative and owned shares in it. Abu Joseph[10] and about twenty others had two or three buses. There was quite a brisk movement. The buses would all go in the morning—there'd be, say, a hundred passengers going—and they would come back in the afternoon. There was no weekly market in al-Bassa. Each shop had its own fruit and vegetable stall.

There was a main street with shops. It ended at our gate, coming all the way from the bottom of the village in the south. Beyond us, to the north, the road branched off in different directions, becoming minor roads without any shops. But beginning with our gate and moving southward, there were three or four of these shops to the right and to the left within thirty or forty meters. Within a hundred meters, there were two cafés, a butcher's, and more grocery shops. That was the busy center of the village, the *saaha*. There were two smaller *saaha*s elsewhere: one in the Greek Orthodox quarter, which was to the southwest of us, and one in the Muslim quarter. A very rough car road led to Acre, and also connected with the Palestine–Lebanon road. If we wanted to go to Acre, there were small cars, taxis. To get a taxi we had to walk all the way to the bottom of the village because the roads weren't paved. But while we were there, the mayor—Abu Joseph's father—collected money from the whole village and paved all the main roads in the village. In the middle of the road there was a part that was lower than the rest, about half a meter wide. This was a channel for the rain to go down. It was also paved.

The part of the village where our house was located was sixty or seventy meters above sea level. The village was situated on the slope of a mountain, and ended where the ground became level. Parts of al-Bassa to the east and the north were on the upper slopes of the mountain. That's where our house was, at the top of the village—although later many people built beyond us, including Umm Joseph and her husband. With prosperity people wanted to move from smaller houses to bigger houses, and the bigger families broke up into smaller families.

The village was two-thirds Christian, one-third Muslim. The Muslims lived in the western part of the village. The Christians were mainly Catholic, but also Greek Orthodox, and there was a handful of Protestants. There were two churches, Greek Orthodox and Catholic, but my father's congregation met in rented rooms. Relations between the Muslims and the Christians were very good. Whenever there was a wedding party or a funeral the two communities participated together. Al-Bassa people were nationalistic, very pro–Hajj Amin, like the Muslims there. But what was special about al-Bassa was that it was very liberal. People drank a huge amount, not just the Christians, the Muslims as well, and gambled a great deal, and smuggled a great deal, into Lebanon and from Lebanon. There was adultery also, and lots of dancing, *dabkeh*s, and weddings, and *a'yaad* [feasts]. In the *dabkeh*s young men and women danced together, not separately. It was lovely to watch.

There were several cafés in al-Bassa, mostly in the Christian quarter because the Muslims did not sell as much arrack as we did, though they had their arrack too. And there were butchers around the neighborhood.

On Sunday, after church, people would have a lengthy sitting at one of the cafés in the *saaha*, and they'd spend the rest of the morning playing *dama* [checkers] or *tric-trac* [backgammon], drinking arrack, and eating pieces of meat—usually *kibdeh wa fasheh*, raw liver and lung—disgusting!—with bits of cucumber, to wash off the church service.

Al-Bassa was also culturally active. Every year two or three plays would be staged, Arabic translations of mainly French plays. The school led the way there. Everybody was a fan of a young woman about my age, called Evdokia. She was very good-looking, blonde, Scandinavian in looks. She was related to us somehow, from the Assad Khoury family. I took part in a play once—I said about three words—so as to see more of Evdokia. They used to perform in the churchyard. The church and the school were in one compound, and in the middle was a large space where the school children played in the daytime. They would construct a platform there, a stage. They had lux lamps[11]—there was no electricity—and the play would go on for three or four nights. It was the initiative of a new schoolmaster who'd come from Lebanon. He taught French and Arabic, and ran the school. Boys and girls acted together.

It's strange but I don't remember anybody from al-Bassa who was in university then. Other villages like Kafr Yasif already had university graduates, but I think Bassa people wanted to use their money for other things.

Doctors and Priests

The first doctor who came to al-Bassa was a Lebanese man from Joun, near Sidon. A Catholic by birth who had trained in France, Dr. Fadlallah Shami was a very amusing fellow, full of stories and provocation. He was an atheist and he'd start discussing religion with my father. He'd say, "Why do you think there is a God? Where is he?" Then they would enter into theology. He was a tease, but he had a light touch and didn't upset the beliefs of the other party. My father also liked teasing, so he teased back.

When this doctor came—perhaps because he was afraid people would not come to him in enough numbers—he interested the village in a health scheme whereby every family would pay an annual fee, a sort of insurance, and in return they would be examined free all through that year. It worked. He gave everything except the medicine. He'd write the prescription, and they'd ask somebody going to Acre to buy them the medicine. He stayed in al-Bassa for several years.

When Dr. Shami finally left, another doctor came from Alma Shaab near al-Bassa. He had trained either in the Egyptian University or the American University of Beirut. His wife was half Greek, half Egyptian. This second doctor was called Dr. Zu'rob. It was very strange: he fell in love with a blind young woman who used to help his wife with housework. He took her to be a receptionist in his clinic, to be closer to her. She was good looking. It was quite a scandal, but Bassa people were tolerant about scandals; they would laugh it off. When they heard his wife shouting, they would say, "Ah, she has caught him." Al-Bassa was wicked.

Before I tell you about the wickedness, let me tell you about the priest. A new Catholic priest came who was very fanatical. He came from Haifa. He was also Lebanese, though priests didn't necessarily come from outside Palestine—the Greek Orthodox priest was from the village. This priest hated Protestants from the bottom of his heart, unlike his bishop, Bishop Hajjar, who was also Lebanese. The bishop's seat was in Haifa, and whenever he came to al-Bassa he used to visit us and pray with the family. He used to say to my father, "I hope you don't mind a Catholic bishop praying with you?" My father would answer, "No," and he would pray to God to guide the bishop into the right course. It always ended happily. When he left, the bishop would turn to my mother and say, "Any time your husband decides to join our church, tell him that he's welcome. He can be a married priest."

But the new priest was quite a different type. He would start walking back and forth at sunset on his *ontosh*,[12] as we called it—his rooms were above the church and had a terrace. We were next door to the church compound. So the priest on his terrace heard my father's prayers at night, and we heard his prayers and his hymns—he had a beautiful voice. But then he began to say things in his prayers that were aimed at us, like asking God not to let innocent people slip into the heresy of Protestantism. Then one night he used the verse from the Gospel that goes, "You snakes, children of serpents, who told you how to escape the wrath of God?"[13]

Tales of Adultery

The priest was not at all successful at making the village virtuous. There were always stories about adultery, and men slipping at dawn from married women's houses when their husbands were away. Or even going to them when the husband was around if he was a sound sleeper. One such case was a neighbor of ours who lived on a ground floor, Umm Rakad. She lived behind our house. She was very attractive; I used to feel her appeal. Her husband was much older than she was—he was a carpenter who made benches and chicken coops. A young man—unmarried—from further down the village was in love with this woman. He used to come at night and slip into her bed, and sometimes Abu Rakad would hear them. We'd wake up at night with the noise, him shouting at his wife, and she shouting back defiantly. God! The beatings he gave her! But without any effect. The lover would just get up, put his shoes on, and walk away. This went on, and the priest tried to reason with this woman, and pray with her, and then rebuke her, and then threaten her with excommunication. But they didn't stop.

One day, when the bishop was visiting al-Bassa, the husband went to him and said, "Please, Bishop, she doesn't listen to the priest. But you're the bishop, she will listen to you." The bishop came—I think he felt challenged; everybody else had failed—he came with his big cross and his gilded stick, with the priest behind him and a few dignitaries—it was quite a procession. We knew he was coming; the news spread quickly. I remember kneeling on a little couch by the window that overlooked their house. The bishop talked to her in a low voice, but she was shouting at the top of her voice, "Why are you talking to me like this? You're coming to tell me that I'm an adulteress? My shoe is more honorable than the cheeks of your holy virgin!" The bishop lifted his robe, as though afraid the hem would touch the floor of this polluted house, and walked away quickly with the procession behind him. It was a complete retreat. We were able to see all this because we overlooked them; there was nothing but a narrow road between us. That was the end of the efforts to correct Umm Rakad.

The younger Freiwat son I mentioned before was not married, and he was in love with a widow. His father and mother were against the relationship, but they couldn't do anything about it, because it was such a liberal village. He didn't hide the relationship. I used to go to the compound where the widow lived—the top rooms became an American school, and I went there for a year before I moved to the Catholic school, which was closer to us. It was another one of those houses with rooms all the way round a yard and two or three rooms on the first floor. This woman owned this area and lived on the ground floor. When I was there in that building, I used to see Mikhail come to see Shams and close the door. We'd leave the school in the afternoon and the door would still be closed. One time—and the story of this record filled the village—he stayed in there for three days without leaving. Ultimately, partly due to his father's pressure, partly due to my father's pressure, he married her. It was my father who married them.

My cousin Mbadda', before he married—and even after he married—was in love with a young woman on the other side of the village. She was not married. I think she stayed unmarried—though she was good-looking—because she was in love with Mbadda'. She refused every suitor. They didn't marry because Mbadda's mother kept on after him, "You must marry your cousin." He married his first cousin, a cousin who was set for him from her birth, the way villagers used to do. Mbadda' went on going to this young woman, even though her brother was the tough man of the village. He'd killed one or two people in his day and spent a number of years in prison. Still—I could never figure it out—he somehow liked Mbadda' and didn't want to hurt his sister, so he let this go on. It was another sign of al-Bassa's permissiveness.

I remember one day, there was a stir in the village. People said, "British police are here!" They were looking for Mikhail Jabbour, the brother of this young woman. Of course they went first to his house. They didn't find him, so they came up to the café to see if he was there. I was standing there watching as three policemen went around with their revolvers in their hands—it was that serious; they were afraid he would shoot. He was the kind who shot first and asked for an explanation later. Anyway, they didn't find him.

"Let the Dark Young Man Sleep on My Arm"

The village didn't have its own police. If there was some trouble, then somebody would come and stay for a few weeks. They usually stayed in the police station up at the frontier. One of these policemen was a very handsome fellow from Nazareth. There was a wedding in our quarter in al-Bassa, not far from our house—I used to love weddings—I went there to listen to the singing and see the *dabkeh*. Everybody was calling out, "Evdoke! Evdoke!" wanting her to sing her favorite songs. She sang a song called '*Ya hnayina*'—"*Ya hnayina, ya hnayina,*[14] *laysh nawmek lil dhuhor, araytu hana.*" It goes, "Why do you sleep until midday? I hope it's all health for you." "*Nayyem al-asmar ala zindi ana*"—"Let the dark young man sleep on my arm." This policeman, who was in love with Evdokia, was dark. Of course she looked at him, and he looked at her, and the entire gathering clapped and asked for it again.

Eventually she married him. She was the belle of the quarter, but she didn't aim high; she didn't refuse an ordinary policeman. Maybe she thought there was no possibility of marrying somebody rich, because she lived in a village. She had brothers but they didn't mind, because she didn't do anything wrong. She flirted in words, but there was no kissing on street corners. She was intelligent and daring. Once she took part in one of these plays I told you about and appeared on the balcony during the intermission to shout to somebody below, in her petticoat, sleeveless, just like that, with the lux lamp shining on her.

Weddings and feasts generally were great fun. During the weddings—the ceremonies would go on for several days—there would be the march, when the *'aroos* [bride] was being brought to the church: there'd be a procession. Then the *'arees* [groom] would be brought to the house of the *'aroos*. There was always something to do. Apart from the *dabkeh*, there was also individual dancing. Then the *aroos* had to be *titjalla, yijallu al-aroos*, meaning 'to make her glitter.' She would carry candles in her hands and walk around slowly, with great dignity. If it was the season, she would have a crown of *zaher al-laymoun* (orange flowers) around her head. And she would change from one dress to another. This would go on for days. I think they took the bride walking to the bridegroom's house. There weren't many horses in al-Bassa. Two or three times people came from Zeeb, which was close by, only five kilometers from al-Bassa. There was a large area for threshing, south of the village. They'd race and play around on horses with their swords.

The storyteller would come, with the *sandook al-'ajab*, the 'box of wonders.'[15] We'd sit, two at a time, on a little bench. We'd look in, and he would turn something by hand—like a film—and he'd tell the story that we were seeing in a singsong voice: "*Undhur wa talla, wa shuf, shuf al-marakeh al-makshuf, Abu Zaid al-Hilali rakeb hisanu al-aswad.*"[16] We'd give him a *ta'reefeh*—half a piaster—or a couple of eggs. He would suddenly arrive in a bus or a taxi, carrying his box on his back, and stop in different places in the village, and people would come and watch. There were storytellers, and there were singers who would arrive every now and then with their *oud* [Arab lute]. Or they'd arrange it with the café owner—the big café owner in the *saaha*—that for several nights they would sit there and play the *oud* and sing Egyptian songs—"*Ya layli, ya layla*." I used to love to go down. My father didn't approve of it, but my mother would say, "*Khallee*, Abu Yusif, let him go." He didn't approve because there'd be a lot of drinking, and the songs would be love songs. He'd say, frowning, "All right, provided he comes back before prayers."

Family Life: Prayers and Picnics

Our family life in al-Bassa continued to have a very large component of prayers, morning and evening. What helped me put up with so much praying was the fact that, outside the house, al-Bassa was more interesting than Hawran. Al-Bassa was full of goings-on and gossip. There were people older than I, young men. I remember one specifically, who had a shop close to us. He was wicked; he used to tell me about women and how to get to them. I remember being introduced to 'French letters' through him—he encouraged me to sleep with someone. So it was painful to me to have to go through long, long, prayers every day, repeating the same things my father wanted to say to God, the same thanks, the same requests, the same prayers for the sinful village.

On the subject of family prayers, there's a story that happened later but I will tell it now. When we grew old enough to be able to read the Bible by ourselves and to memorize verses my father said, "Now children, tomorrow you"—and he would point to one of us— "will recite a verse at evening prayers from your reading of the Bible during the day." We did this. Whenever we came across something that looked like an appropriate verse, we'd learn it to recite it from memory. But one day, Fuad forgot to learn anything, and in the evening when his turn came, he said, "*Baka Yasu'* [Jesus wept]," from the story of Lazarus. My father looked at him and said, "Is that all?" Fuad said, "Yes, it's a whole verse." My father said, "Yes, you couldn't find a shorter one in the whole Bible. Perhaps you'll try for something longer next time." The following day, Fuad accidentally came across a longer one that goes, "And thus does man leave his father and mother

and cleave unto his wife, and the two become as one body." Fuad
recited it in the hour of prayer. He must have been ten or eleven. I
think it was just before we left al-Bassa for Tiberias. My father looked
at him, amused, but not wanting to show it. He said, "Need we jump
from '*Baka Yasu*' to this one? Is there nothing in between?"

Frequently I'd go to sleep while my father went on with his
prayers, and if I happened to be next to my mother she would nudge
me to wake me up when he was nearing the end.

Our family life in al-Bassa was quite happy. We didn't have many
fights or arguments among the children. That came later when Fuad
and Fayez were older, in Tiberias, when Fayez realized his own
intelligence and became a tease, and teased Fuad rather than me. In
al-Bassa we played outside a lot; we'd go together, especially in the
summer holidays, to pick figs in the early morning, when they are
fresh and cool. We also went for picnics to Bat al-Jabal, the place
where we picked our figs, and to a place called Ma'sub, a little higher
up, where the figs were even better. Sometimes, we'd go to the area
of olive trees between the village and the sea. We'd have a picnic
under the olive trees and pick watermelons from right there in front
of us, and cucumbers, and tomatoes. People didn't mind if you took a
few things, but anyway we had our own. Al-Bassa had such a variety
of places around it to go to.

We'd go on picnics to Musherfeh, at the sea. That was always a
big expedition; Layya would come with us, and later on there was a
cousin who lived next door to us with his family, Abu Ghassan, the
only person in al-Bassa with a university degree. He and his wife and
children would join us. We would be a big group, and we'd go in a
small bus or a car. Or we'd walk—it was a forty-five-minute walk.
We'd take a donkey to put all the picnic things on and rugs. We'd
spread the rugs under the trees. There was a café nearby which supplied us with cold drinks.[17] The ladies would have the food ready
– *kibbeh*[18] and whatever else they made—and the things for making
coffee. We children would go and swim in the sea before lunch and

come back all salty, and then we'd swim in the reservoir to get the salt off—it was close to where we picnicked. The reservoir belonged to Musherfeh. There were springs in that area, and the reservoir was made to irrigate the gardens and fruit groves.

My mother used to take her cousin Layya with us. When we went to al-Bassa in 1925, I was nine and she was sixteen, and she was still unmarried. The year after, she got engaged and married. After that, her husband Jad would come with us, and sometimes her brothers, Mbadda' and Elias. My father always came too. He had a pair of underpants made especially for swimming. The women swam too. About three hundred meters away from where we picnicked there were rocks, so they could hide behind them when they undressed. I don't think they had bathing costumes; they swam in petticoats. The beach was lovely—white, clean sand, no litter. The sea was rough there; it was a little dangerous, but we didn't go out far.

I learned to swim properly when I was twelve or thirteen, in the sea at al-Bassa. We went from school. One of the school teachers, a stupid man, went with us. He would take ten or twelve students at a time out swimming. There was quite a difference there between high and low tide. The floor of the sea was not all sand; there were also rocks, and there was one point where the rock was concave and had sand in the middle. When the tide was low you could walk there, but when the tide came in, it got quite deep. That day we were playing around, and I hadn't noticed that we were being driven out, and the water was getting deep. Suddenly I found myself in that sandy bit, but now the water was over my head by half a meter. I struggled to get up to the surface of the water. The teacher was swimming under-water near me—he was a good swimmer—so I signaled to him with my hands to come closer so I could hold on to him to rise. He knew I couldn't swim, but because he was stupid he thought I was playing a game and started imitating me, teasing me under the water. Finally he noticed that my eyes were going out of my head, and I was swallowing water. So he grabbed me, lifted me up, and took me straight out to the sand, where he laid me with my head down. He lifted my legs up so that I spat out lots of water from my lungs.

I rested in the sun for half an hour, to regain my calm. Then I went to him. He said, "No more swimming today." I said, "You're going to teach me how to swim." He said, "You have the nerve? After almost drowning?" I said, "Try me." He took me, and taught me that same afternoon how to swim. It was the dog paddle, not the breast stroke, but that was enough; I could keep afloat. A few days later, I went again with my cousins—Mbadda' was a sea lover, he went almost every day to swim. He taught me how to swim on my back, which gave me more confidence.

Our family grew by two members in al-Bassa. Mary was born in 1927. As I said, she was the first one in the family to be delivered by a trained nurse, one of the teachers who started the school in al-Bassa. Munir was born in al-Bassa too, six or seven months before we left for Tiberias. My mother was very happy to have a daughter. All the relatives and neighbors were happy for her too. They called her Mary after Miss Ford.

My father did all of the shopping, food and other things, because my mother had to cope with so many children at home. We always had help—in Hawran, we had Shafiq's mother, Huda; and then we had the Hawrani girl. But still my mother ended up with seven children to look after. She made all our clothes, shirts, shorts, and dresses for Mary. So she had a lot to do at home. And my father was better than my mother at bargaining. When my mother found something too expensive, she'd ask my father to buy it. She used to do *mooneh*,[19] the way village people did. In Hawran people on donkeys would come around and sell us *zebeeb* [raisins] and potatoes because the shops had nothing in them. In al-Bassa the shops were in a neighborhood and my father would go with a basket, and I would usually go with him, unless I was in school. I just went to be with him; I enjoyed it more than my brothers. I used to rush to him saying, "*Ana jayi ma'ak, baba* [I'm coming with you, Dad.]" I enjoyed going out, and I enjoyed being with my father.

Visits and Characters

Another component of family life was visiting. We visited our nearest relatives and friends in the village. I liked most going to visit Shukri Freiwat, the former mayor, a Protestant, and a cousin of my mother's, who lived at the other end of the village.[20] I liked to listen to him; he spoke very clearly and shrewdly. I remember noticing how every word he said was studied; it had a purpose. He was rather short, straight, and always fashionably dressed, except when relaxing at home.

I want to describe Hanna Boulos, the man who became mayor after Freiwat, the father of Abu Joseph. He wasn't shrewd at all. Though he was simple in character he was always very elegant in his Arabic dress. His baggy trousers were made of *sitte krozeh*, a silky material, with braid around the pockets here and there. He was always in shining black boots, and he wore a silk cummerbund, and lovely shirts, always neat, clean, and ironed. And a silk *keffiyyeh* and *i'qal*, always put on in the most elegant way; and he had a waxed mustache that he twirled. A very handsome man. He was elected mayor, which meant that he was popular. He was quite dynamic—he got the roads paved, and established a service to collect garbage. Although not a clever man like Freiwat, he was a doer. He had five sons, but none of them went to school beyond a few elementary classes. My father tried to persuade him to send them to school in Sidon, or somewhere else in Palestine, but of course the schools that my father knew were all Protestant, and Hanna Boulos refused because he was a pillar of the Catholic church in al-Bassa. He wouldn't send his children to a Protestant school.[21]

My mother had two uncles, brothers of her mother, who were still alive then. We would go to visit the uncles—I loved going to them. One had a beautiful house of old, used stone, and a room at the top like a tower, which you reached by an outside staircase. He had a very large garden with many kinds of fruits—pomegranates, grapes, figs, *subbeir*. But he was terribly stingy. My mother would send me to buy fruit from him, say a kilo of grapes. He had one of those old-fashioned scales; he'd lift the thing and make absolutely certain that the sides were equal. If the fruit side tipped down a little, he'd take five grapes off the bunch. This uncle's oldest son went to school in Sidon, to my father's school, because his mother came from there. He had two daughters—one of them had been married and divorced, and was known to be promiscuous. I remember that a few years later, when I was nearly seventeen, and we used to come to al-Bassa on visits from Tiberias, whenever this woman came to visit as well, if Abu Joseph happened to be there, he'd say, "Yusif, how many times could you sleep with Kaysani if you had the opportunity?" In her presence! She'd say to him, "Don't corrupt the boy!" He'd say, "Let him be corrupted. You're an ideal opportunity, you're a relative, you're clean. Why not?" She'd say, "No, Abu Joseph, stop it."

The other uncle was a village doctor—a very shrewd man and respected in the village even after a proper doctor came. Like Abu Victor's father, he wasn't a trained physician. People would go to him with eye trouble, or trachoma, and he'd have drops to give them. I remember he did a bit of surgery on my finger when I got a swelling with pus inside; he lanced it for me. He made some medicines; others he bought. He also did *tajbeer*, bone-setting. He had a few books.

There were many people to visit in al-Bassa—not just Protestants; we visited Catholics too. My father's congregation was not all Protestant—for instance, Abu Michel[22] and Abu Joseph were officially Catholic but they would come to our church to be sociable. I used to like visits, though there were some visits that weren't so interesting, for instance to my mother's cousins. Her mother had had three or four sisters, so she had many cousins. All of them were married and had children, but their children hadn't had much education, except for one who was my classmate, and another who went to Sidon at the same time as me. But unlike my parents, his mother said, "Why should you go to college?" Instead she told him, "Find a job in Palestine." So he took a job as a policeman during the Strike—it must have been in 1936, two years after he finished school. He worked in Acre, as a policeman. He certainly had a future in the police; he could have ended as a major, like Munir Abu Fadel.[23] He had rooms there in Acre, and one day his mother was visiting him, and he was standing chatting with her. As he was standing there, leaning against the window, facing his mother, somebody put a bullet in him and it killed him straightaway.

There were three faithful members of my father's congregation who were all blind. There was Musa Jubran Khoury, who was the son of a cousin of my mother's. Musa was blinded when he was less than ten years old. There was smallpox in the village, and he and his sister were sleeping next to each other, both ill with smallpox. His sister got up one night to go to the toilet. There was no light. She put out a hand to lift herself, and it went into her brother's eyes and blinded him—he already had smallpox in his eyes.

Another blind person was an Egyptian who appeared suddenly one day, guided to our house. It seems he'd come to the village and asked, "Is there a Protestant pastor here?" They said, "Yes, there is Qassees Abdullah Sayigh." "Can anybody tell me where his house is?" They brought him to us. He said, "I'm an Egyptian. I was born a Muslim. I grew up as a Muslim. I was a sheikh, but I converted . . . ." He had a good voice and used to be a muezzin before his conversion. So the family put him in a small room on the ground floor that wasn't rented out. He said he was coming for a few days, but the few days turned out to be a few years. He was terrible! Even now when I think of it, it makes my stomach turn, because he was so filthy, and the way he ate wasn't neat like the other blind people, who often ate at our place. He was with us all the time; he lived with us. My poor mother had to take him down his food and take away his plates, all messy. For some reason, his throat was very fertile; he'd always have lots of mucus to spit out, and he always spat it very far.

At one point he left us briefly, and during that period we went to Tiberias. But he found us there, in Tiberias. He stayed a year or more. One day I got so fed up I waited until my parents were out on a visit, and I said to him, "If you don't leave in so many days, I'm going to make you leave. Don't ask me how; it won't be pleasant. My mother has had enough." He called himself Boutros, as a convert. He was so full of Christian enthusiasm that he would almost try to convert my father. He sat there; he would take part in the prayers. He prayed a lot—my God! This is the most awful of my memories of the village. He would sit there praying and shaking his head back and forth. Tawfiq was a tease and very funny—though he had his moments of unaccountable sadness—and when we prayed, he would look around to see how each of us was praying. He would call poor Munir 'Boutros Munir,' because he would close his eyes very hard, the way Boutros closed his eyes. My father never expressed discontent with Boutros. He and my mother would say, "*Yusif, malayshi habibi, hadha ajr andkun* [doing charity will protect you children from evil]."[24] "What is brotherhood otherwise? He's a convert; he's a poor man." All very noble, but why should it be on us?

Another village character was the transvestite. He was a grandson of the midwife who brought me into this world—a lovely woman. I remember her visiting us for many years, whenever we went to al-Bassa. This transvestite was in love with women's dresses. He wore high heels and make-up, he shaved his face very close and took the hair off his legs, he powdered his face, and put lipstick on. I never saw him except in women's clothes. In the square, especially on Sundays, there'd be dozens of people there in the cafés, drinking and smoking an *argileh* [water pipe] and chatting. They'd all shout greetings to him, "Andraos! How about me tonight?" He'd laugh. Tolerance was the word for al-Bassa.

A pleasant part of life in al-Bassa was our relationship with Abu Ghassan and his family, who were close neighbors. Abu Ghassan was an intelligent and well-educated man, who had traveled and lived in South America. He liked my mother very much—in fact, earlier on it seems that he'd had his eye on her. But he decided not to marry early, instead emigrating with his brother to America to make money there. He made some money, but he had to leave his business because of poor health, and come back to al-Bassa. For a few years he lived without a job; then he became a schoolteacher in the Catholic school. That's what made me move to it. I had been one year in the American mission school, but he said that their curriculum was much better, and since he was well-educated himself, I moved to the Catholic school with him. Abu Ghassan had three children. Ghassan, the eldest, was about five years younger than me. There was a girl younger than him by about two years, and another girl. All three of them were very good looking. Their mother was beautiful. He met her in South America; she was a Lebanese or Syrian immigrant, born there. Her Arabic was second-generation immigrant; she learned some from her family, but she wasn't very fluent.

Then there was Hanneh. She was very good-looking: slim, brunette, bright eyes with a smile in them when she wanted to be nice. She was married to one of Abu Joseph's older brothers. To begin with, the oldest brother was in love with her, his own brother's wife. He had an affair with her. This older brother, before Hanneh became his favorite, was late in marrying, and when did, he married the daughter of a woman he'd been having an affair with. Then he shifted to Hanneh. She was really wicked, at least according to Umm Joseph, who accused her of having put a scorpion in the crib of her first son Jamil. Somehow they had quarreled—I don't know if Umm Joseph suspected that Abu Joseph had been looking at Hanneh too closely—but there was mutual suspicion between them. Umm Joseph had given birth to a girl, and then another girl, and then had two or three miscarriages, and so she was eager to have a boy. When at last she got one, she called him Jamil. And indeed he was a lovely baby. One day Umm Joseph was doing something outside the house. When she went in she found him shrieking. She lifted him out of his crib, and he died in her hands. In the crib she found a scorpion. She always accused Hanneh of putting it there, because Hanneh was seen passing near the crib just before this happened. Their house was built on what had formerly been a threshing ground, so you could imagine there would be scorpions there. But Umm Joseph was convinced; one couldn't argue with her about it.

Abu Michel also lost a son. Abu Michel's loss was even more painful because his son was older than Jamil had been. He was called Salim. Abu Michel had been painting, and he had put turpentine in a glass in case he needed it for his brush. The boy was playing outside. It was hot, he rushed in and saw this glass of what he thought was water, and gulped it down. Immediately he began to shriek because of the pain. When Abu Michel went to see what was the matter, he saw that the glass was empty. They rushed him to Acre, but nothing could be done for him; he died.

To go back to Hanneh. For years I used to hope that she would notice me, but I was too young for her; nothing ever happened between us. But one day, Elias and I went to visit Umm Joseph. At that time Umm Joseph was still living in her father-in-law's house with Hanneh, and her husband, and all the brothers. It was late afternoon, after sunset, almost dark, but not dark enough for a light to be lit. Umm Joseph was not at home, so Hanneh said, "Can I offer you a *haloum* [Turkish delight]?" We said, "Yes." She squatted to open a low drawer to get the tin that had *haloum* in it. She was wearing a short dress, and to make her movement easier she pulled her dress up and, as she squatted, her legs opened. Elias and I both looked at her legs, and Elias shone the flashlight he was holding on them. She said, "*Yihrik deenak, shu mista'jil! Shway shway! Khud nafas!*"[25] That was all; she wasn't really angry.

In the late 1930s my parents decided that they did not want to go to al-Bassa any more for the summer. It was because we began to have trouble with Mbadda', Abu Michel. He was a crook. The property was my uncle's and my mother's and his mother's, but he took all the oil, including the share of the two sisters and the brother. If we wanted some oil, my mother had to ask him for it, although it was our right. We would see him coming back with kilos of beautiful cucumbers, still dewy from the field. He never thought that they were grown on our joint land. He would come to my mother to say, "The cultivation costs so much, your share of the cost is so much." But when it came to the produce, we had to ask for it. Then he was always quarrelling with his wife and beating her, and it was my mother who had to reconcile them. His wife would come to my mother to invoke her support. And then she was always quarreling with Layya, so my mother had to arbitrate between them. Especially after she had her heart attack, my father felt that it was a shame that this should be imposed on her. She should relax, instead of having this continuous tension.[26]

Growing Up

I lived in al-Bassa from the age of nine and a half to thirteen before going to school in Sidon. These were important years for me. I don't think I developed intellectually—probably if we had been in a town with a library I would have developed more. But I think I developed within myself, because I was left to my own resources. I thought about things. I used to try to write: prose pieces, ideas, and impressions. I kept these pieces. Later, when my cousin Yusif Azzam—the brother of Abu Victor—came to stay with us, while he was preparing to go to Jerusalem to study theology, I showed him my writings, because he was interested in literature and wrote poetry himself. He would correct my writing, and we'd sit and discuss things. He had a few books with him, so I began to read Arabic literature. I became interested in becoming a writer because of that time with him. But it was a short-lived desire.

Another kind of development was that I stopped feeling shy in al-Bassa, because people there were extroverts, and drew me into their extrovert world. One of the ways in which the young men tried to 'develop' me was to talk about women and urge me to try. I remember somebody saying to me, "You're thirteen, why wait? Why don't you try to sleep with somebody?" But the development of that trend came later when we used to return to al-Bassa from Tiberias for visits. This pattern went on all through my college years; we always went back to al-Bassa in summer, except for the first year in Tiberias. That summer we went up to Safad and from there to Kafr Bir'em. Even after Tiberias became our home, al-Bassa was home with a special flavor—because of the relatives there and because of incidents related to my awakening to sex. It was my mother's village; we had many relatives, some of whom I liked. As far as outings were concerned, Tiberias was restricted to the lake in front of our house. But al-Bassa had all those picnic places, by the sea and in the hills.

The beginning of my sex awareness in al-Bassa was with Wardeh. Wardeh was a second cousin of Yusif Azzam. She had her eye on Yusif to marry him, but she had little hope because he was much more educated than she was. So she decided to go to school. Her mother arranged for her to come to us at al-Bassa and for us to arrange for her to go to school. She stayed with us in al-Bassa, and also went with us to Tiberias. She came when the weather was changing; it wasn't summer any more, and we were sleeping in the ground floor room, the big room with the vault. We all slept in that room, but I happened by chance to be sleeping at the far end before she came, with my parents at the other end. Possibly they chose to be nearest to the baby, and I'd be the farthest, so I would not hear anything.

So when this girl came, they put a mattress on the floor for her, at right angles to mine. I noticed her, I noticed her breasts, and two or three times during the day, I noticed her looking at me meaningfully. I understood that there was something that was drawing me to her. So one night, I went to bed but did not go to sleep right away. I kept myself awake until I was sure everybody was asleep, and then I crawled for about a meter to get close to her. I put out my hand and touched her cheek. She said nothing but stroked my hand to tell me she was awake. So I got even closer and put my hand on her neck; then she led my hand down to her breasts, and I stroked them for about half an hour. And then of course I had to go back and sleep. I didn't dare get into bed with her; it was too risky. This happened several times.

Nothing else of this kind happened in al-Bassa until the time when Abu Ghassan came back. His wife was very, very good looking. To begin with, I just noticed that she was good looking. There was a rumor that the principal of the school was having an affair with her. He lived in a house very far from the school, one of the farthest houses in the village. He was not married then. Every now and then he would come and have lunch at Abu Ghassan's, and Abu Ghassan had an early class after lunch—the rumor was that it was assigned deliberately. His health was not good; he'd suffered some mysterious disease in South America that affected his virility. He could not satisfy Umm Ghassan, who was a very hot woman. The school principal used to come frequently to Abu Ghassan's for lunch. He would stay after lunch, and I could see him from our house having his nap in the bedroom, lying there in his vest and underpants, with Umm Ghassan in one bed and him in the other. But while I noticed Umm Ghassan's attractiveness, it had no practical significance for me at that stage.

I was sixteen or seventeen then, and a friend had an air gun that he suggested I borrow when he wasn't using it. I would take it every now and then to the Ma'sub or to Bat al-Jabal, the area where there were fig trees, because the birds loved fig trees. Every time I went Ghassan would say, "Let me come with you." So I would let him. One day, I noticed that he had a sexual interest in me. He was five years younger than I, and he did and said some things that were openly suggestive of a homosexual relationship. To be honest, it excited me a little, but we never carried it far. Sometimes I would go swimming by myself because my brothers were not as eager as I was about the sea. I would borrow a horse from another cousin—a very tame horse— and I'd go to the sea on horseback. Ghassan would come with me. We'd go to the beach, and we'd be by ourselves, swimming naked, and of course, that meant a bit of playfulness.

Soon after this, I began to notice that Umm Ghassan herself was becoming quite open in the inviting looks she gave me. The first time I noticed this was on one of our picnics, when the two families were together. She and my mother were sitting next to each other on building stones that were set in a circle around the trunk of a huge carob tree. We were playing around, and I happened to pass in front of Umm Ghassan and my mother. I noticed that Umm Ghassan was looking at me in a very pointed way, and opening her legs so I could see up to her thighs. While being careful that my mother wouldn't notice where my eyes were directed, I went around again, and every time the same thing was repeated, with Umm Ghassan opening and closing her thighs.

Then one day I was up on the terrace of our house, looking down on to the ground floor, where my mother and Umm Ghassan happened to be washing clothes together. Umm Ghassan was sitting in such a way that if she looked up she would see me, whereas my mother had her back to the wall and could not. When Umm Ghassan saw me, she started slowly pulling her dress all the way up until her legs were bare to her knickers. She would look up and smile, pretending that she was just looking and smiling while talking to my mother. Every time I looked, she would close and open her legs.

One day I was feeling a bit unwell, and she got to know of it while visiting us. She said, "You ought to rest after lunch like me. Why don't you come and rest in our house? Your brothers won't disturb you there"—in front of my mother! My mother said, "What a good idea! Thank you very much, Umm Ghassan." She didn't realize that she was trying to seduce me. I went there and lay on the bed where the headmaster used to lie. She lay on the other bed, and turned her head to look at me very pointedly. She said, "Oof! It's so hot, I must cover my stomach with a towel." But as she was pulling the towel over her body, she was also drawing her dress up from her knees to bare her legs. Then she started opening her legs all the way and closing them, pushing the towel further and further up. It was very tempting. She just kept looking and smiling—what more could she do?—she couldn't send me a written invitation. But I didn't dare; I was afraid.

The final incident happened one day when her children were playing somewhere, and my parents had gone visiting with her husband and none of my brothers were at home. We were alone. It was getting near sunset, and we were standing on a little porch between their house and our house, chatting. I felt thirsty, so I bent and picked up the pitcher to drink. It was nearly empty so I said, "I'll go and fill it." She said, "No, no, I'll fill it." We started struggling for the pitcher, but she pulled my hand toward her bosom and started rubbing my hand against it. At last I found the courage: I said, "Let's go inside." She said, "No, no." She was panting, excited but afraid. I said, "Why not?" She said, "They might come any minute." I said, "We'll hear their voices downstairs." "No, no, I daren't." That was the last time there was any such approach. That was the last opportunity.

Leaving Home for School in Sidon

In 1928 my parents decided that I should go to school somewhere else. There was nothing more I could learn in al-Bassa. The boarding schools in Palestine were far away, in Jerusalem and Jaffa. We were not in contact with them, and they would have cost a lot. My parents had both been to school in Sidon, so they decided to send me there to the Gerard Institute. My father knew the principal, and my mother had an old schoolteacher there who was still teaching. She said, "She'll treat you like a grandson." They wrote to Sidon and found out that I should improve my French. At home they helped me with English, my mother mainly. So my vocabulary was good, and I had a feel for languages, for forming sentences. My father said, "Well, the only way I can help you with French is for me to take you to Kharaba in the summer."

After the stay in Kharaba, toward the end of the summer, my father and I returned to al-Bassa. There was enough time for my mother to make me some shirts and shorts and underpants—she sewed them herself. When she had prepared everything, and it was time to go, she said to my father, "Abdullah, you are too proud to ask the principal to give Yusif a scholarship. If he suggests it, you'll say thank you, but if he doesn't you won't ask for it. I'll do better at that than you." It was painful saying goodbye to my brothers and sister—all of them except Anis were born by then. Munir must have been six months old. My mother was going to be away for only a week. It was very sad; we all cried, except my father, who prayed for me.

We hired a donkey and climbed up the mountain again to Alma, and from Alma to Alma Sha'b in Lebanon, where we spent the night with some close friends. The owner of the donkey came with us to take the donkey back—he was somebody from al-Bassa whom we had known for years. The following morning, early, we went to Nakoura by car—to Nakoura village, not the police post. But still a gendarme met us and asked us for our papers. My mother said, "We're coming from Alma." He said, "But from where before Alma?" She said, "From al-Bassa," and asked him, "Since when do people going between al-Bassa and Alma have to have passports? I'm taking my son to school in Sidon; I'll be back in a few days." He said, "Pass!"

Postscript: Al-Bassa was occupied on May 14, 1948, soon after the fall of Acre, during Operation Ben-Ami. Most of the population fled before the attack on the village, after hearing about the massacre of Deir Yassin; most went directly to Lebanon, where they ended up in the refugee camp of Dbeyeh, north of Beirut. Al-Bassa people who did not leave say that the day after the village fell there was a massacre outside the church: see Nafez Nazzal, The Palestinian Exodus from Galilee *(Beirut: Institute for Palestine Studies, 1978, 1948), 57–58; also Yusif Ayoub Haddad,* al-Mujtama' wa-l-turath fi Filastin: qaryat al-Bassa, *n.d.*

The website palestineremembered.com has photos of al-Bassa taken soon after 1948, when the semi-ruined village was briefly occupied by Jewish immigrants from Romania and Yugoslavia. Today the development town of Shelomi stands over al-Bassa, and only two or three of the original build-ings remain.

3

Boarding School, Sidon, 1929–34

From Nakoura we went to Sidon by car, and then up to Miyeh-Miyeh with the school bus. My mother visited the principal of the school.[1] She told him who she was and how she had studied at the girls' school in Ain al-Hilweh. Mr. Nasim al-Helou was very welcoming—"How is the pastor?" He was a short, solid man who wore his tarboosh all the time, even when he was taking the Sunday service. He was from North Syria, so his 'r' was like an 'l'. Another encouraging thing was that I had two cousins who were teachers there, Ibraham Murqus and his brother Sami. In fact they were sons of a cousin of my mother's from al-Bassa who had married into Lebanon. They said, "Don't worry, we'll look after him. We'll examine him and see what class he will fit into." My mother was worried that they would put me in second or third elementary—I was thirteen years old by then. We had brought my grades from school. I had been first for the three years I was in school in al-Bassa, but this didn't mean much to them. They said, "With a little effort, he'll be all right in sixth elementary."

My mother said, "Now we come to the question of the fees." We were visiting the principal first in his home. He said, "I have to see what the fees are and what we can give him as a scholarship. His grades are good. His father was our student, and he is a pastor." We went to his office. I can't remember how much the fees were, but my mother said, "What! That much!" The principal said, "Well, let's see what we can give him." He began thinking of figures out loud. My mother said, "You're still too high for us"—she brought him down. If they didn't give me enough of a scholarship, we would have had to borrow. But my mother had brought with her a bag of gold coins hidden under her dress. She said, "I'll sell as many of these as necessary." I was amazed. Finally they agreed. Then they examined me, and put me in sixth elementary.

My mother stayed three or four days with me, just before the beginning of term. Then she said, "I won't say goodbye to you up here. We'll go to Sidon; I'll hug you there. Then I'll take the car." The crying! I cried a great deal. My teacher cousin came down with us; he said he'd take me back. But first he took me to the city and gave me cake and lemonade. When I went to bed that night, it took me hours to go to sleep. Even in my second and third year, I would cry a little at the beginning of term, although not as much. By then I was happy as a student—I had friends; we played games.

I came first in the class in the midterm tests. There was a general meeting of the whole school, and the principal stood up and said, "I'm going to begin with the lowest class. Yusif Sayigh got the highest grade. We have decided to promote him straightaway." So I moved up to the first intermediate where there were students whom I had known from the beginning of the term: Rushdi Maalouf, Beshara Trabulsi, and Izzat Zein.

When I first came to the Gerard Institute, I was surprised to find how moved the students of my age group were by the hanging of Fuad Hejazi and the other two young men by the British.[2] I remember how Rushdi Maalouf, with whom I became friends in the first few weeks of school, began talking politics for the first time, and he immediately talked about those three and how heroic they were. That established an added bond between us as friends. The Sidon boys were all very nationalistic, very pro-Palestinian.

Rushdi Maalouf was first in the intermediate class, but I overtook him. He was always good in Arabic literature and grammar—he became a poet later on; he had a flair for language.[3] I wrote well, but he had more flourish.

Service for the Scholarship

Soon after the beginning of term, after I'd received the scholarship, the principal called me in and said, "Yusif, we want you to work. Don't think us hard; it will make more of a man of you." I remember saying to him, "You didn't say that when my mother was here." Even at that age I was outspoken. He said, "Everybody here works." The first year I had to fill the water pitchers of the teachers who lived on the second and third floors of the school, because they had no running water. I checked on them every day in the afternoon and evening. The second year they increased my scholarship and told me they wanted me to do more work. This was to serve at table. By then I was established as bright; I was the first in every subject except geometry. Outside the dining room I was helping my classmates, explaining algebra to them, and in the dining room I was serving them food. I found serving painful. There must have been about two hundred full boarders, and the teachers had another table of their own. That meant about ten tables, and there were five or six of us who served. We servers got our food afterward, when everyone else had finished.

For the remaining three years, they made me a librarian, and that was a great pleasure. I read every single novel in the library. Fortunately the boys were not great readers, so I wasn't disturbed—they didn't come up there even to do their homework. I loved stories and novels. The first novel I read was *A Tale of Two Cities*. I was thrilled by it, so I began picking one novel after the other. The library was organized, so I knew where the novels were, and I read every single one.[4] A few new books were added every year; the rest were old.

The School Regime

We would be woken up at five-thirty in the morning, with half an hour to wash and get ready for breakfast. From six o'clock until a quarter to seven we'd prepare for the morning session. At quarter to seven we'd go and play for fifteen minutes, and then have break-fast. Classes began at eight. In the evening, after supper and a play break, we would have another hour's study. These morning and evening study hours were difficult for me—I was such a lover of sleep. I needed somebody to come and shake me to wake me up in the morning, to make me get out of bed. I just couldn't leave bed, especially in winter. It was terribly cold. In the evening study period, invariably, after fifteen minutes, I'd put my head on my arm and go to sleep. The supervisor would come and shake me and say, "You have to prepare your lessons."

I stayed at the Gerard Institute for five years as a boarder before I got my diploma—two intermediate years and three high-school years. As in my father's days, the school was not just academic. I had to take a craft. The first three years, I took carpentry. The fourth year I took chicken breeding. This involved a machine: we had to light gas to heat the hundreds of eggs and the chicks. The fifth year, we took mechanics. There was an old Ford in the school that belonged to the American teacher who taught us mechanics. We dismantled this car to the last screw and then rebuilt it under the supervision of the teacher. I loved that class. I'm the only one in the family who had that opportunity. Anis went to the same school for his last two years of high school, but by then they had stopped teaching this subject.

The Teachers

The teachers were a mixture. There were two Americans. One of them, Mr. Weeks, later became a pastor. Maybe he taught us scripture. There was a French teacher who taught French, a very amusing teacher called Monsieur Bost. The two Murquses, Shehadeh and Monsieur Sroor, were Lebanese. There was an Armenian who taught us algebra, who had graduated from AUB; he taught us European history as well. The principal, Nasim al-Helou, taught us Arabic grammar. Mr. Jessup taught us English language and literature—his wife taught some sections but he covered the basics. I owe him four-fifths of the English that I knew on entering university. Another Lebanese teacher taught us bookkeeping because they thought that some of us would go into business. The only thing the school program lacked was art and music—there was nothing of that sort, no chance to learn a musical instrument. We sang hymns, but there were no music lessons. We had science, but only a very miserable laboratory.

We had a Lebanese teacher, who also taught us French, who came from a village near Jbayl. He was the bragging type. Apparently he'd been in Belgium during the First World War, and he was caught in the war there. He boasted to us about his courage, how one day a German soldier threw a grenade at him, and how he caught it before it exploded, and threw it back, and it killed a dozen German soldiers—that kind of story. We used to tease him a great deal—"Monsieur Sroor, tell us about another battle. Did you fire shells from a gun?"

The teacher who taught us mathematics, algebra, and plane geometry was from the Shehadeh family. He was always a bit eccentric, but after I left school it seems he became almost mad, and his madness took the form of extreme religiosity. When I went to teach in Iraq, years later, I got a letter from this teacher telling me that he'd also moved to Iraq to teach there. He wasn't writing just to give me news, but to tell me that the time had come for the army of God to be mobilized. He hoped that I would be among the first to join and become an officer in the army of God, serving the will of Lord Jesus Christ. He was a Protestant. I wrote back saying that I'd always been a pacifist and didn't want to join any army.

An item of gossip was that a wife of a teacher, who was herself a teacher, used to like handsome, athletic boys. Either the heroes themselves talked, or people observed that some students would go frequently to the house of this lady, which was separated from the school by a long driveway lined with cypress trees. Presumably they went for tea and help with their English, but some people were wiser than to think that. I also had tea there once, and not for English tutoring.

An important part of school life was the English speech-making competition. One of the American teachers used to like to coach the participants. He wanted me to train with him. The woman teacher was also interested in coaching students. She was an enemy of the American teacher because he was intelligent and handsome, and she had hoped he would marry her daughter. But after one summer holiday, he came back with an American wife. Anyway, this woman teacher wanted to coach me, since I was likely to win the contest. She must have been forty-five, possibly fifty.

A competition started between them, each of them taking me for a walk, each trying to persuade me to take one piece rather than another as my speech. We didn't write the speeches ourselves; we'd take a well-known piece of oratory. One day she saw me and said, "I want to talk to you. Come and have tea. I want to show you a lovely piece I've found." Being coached by her meant going to her house every day for weeks. I went there for tea. She was dressed in a low-cut black dress, and I knew that her husband was teaching at that time. It was my last year; I was seventeen or eighteen. She said, "Just give me a minute to make the tea because I'm all by myself today, I gave the maid the afternoon off." I registered this even though I didn't put the knowledge to good use. She came and sat on the couch next to me, quite close, put the tea down there and said, "We can have tea and cookies from this table." As she sat, she leaned sideways, and her dress slipped, and her shoulder next to me was bare. There was no bra strap or anything. Very tempting. She looked at me significantly. I was torn between a feeling of physical desire and fear of making a wrong step—supposing I had misunderstood and she had no intention of seducing me? If I made an approach, she could use it to ruin my school career. So I didn't do anything. She asked me when I would make up my mind about the speech. Later I went to her and apologized. She showed me a different face after that.

We had lectures every now and then. One lecture was by a former student who had gone to AUB and got a BA. He got a job with an American press in Beirut that printed holy books, Bibles, and hymn books. This made him act as if he'd become a Nobel Prize winner. When he came to the school he made them arrange for him to give a lecture. He was the kind of person who shaves twice a day, and his face still looks blue. He stood there speaking banalities. Rushdi and I sat next to each other, giggling: "Shit, what does he think he's telling us?"

The school doctor gave us four or five talks a year—sensible subjects like appendicitis, food, and diet. The only lecture on sex we ever had was by a bishop, an English bishop, who came to visit the school. This bishop went up to the platform with an English lady who introduced him and sat there while he gave his talk. He was supposed to pray and then give his talk. He finished praying. There was a small table in front of him. He said, "I'm going to move this table; I don't need it here." We were surprised. Then he started saying, "You are young, your life is ahead of you, and you're going to be tempted by pleasure, by going out with women. But let me warn you that pleasure can be dangerous. There are venereal diseases." He went into a discussion of venereal diseases, and it became clear that the reason he moved the table was because he wanted to be able to point to his penis. The lady got red with embarrassment, poor thing.

The moral tone of the school was very religious. There was a lot of praying, and a service before classes every day. We had to go to Sidon church on Sunday, whether we were Muslim, Druze, or Christian.

Our school was among the best in sports. There was football, basketball, tennis, and volleyball. I wasn't great at games—I used to borrow a racket from a friend and play a bit of tennis. I played a little volleyball. No track and field—we had it but I didn't do it. We had to do athletics; we had to play some sport. I chose football, but I wasn't on the school team.[5]

The Students

Most of the boys came from Lebanon, many from Sidon and the south. They were a cross-section socially, but several were from influential families. For instance Abdel Latif al-Zein, a member of parliament now, was a son of Yusif al-Zein, who was once speaker of the parliament, I think—or if not that, always an MP.[6] He would come twice a term to visit his sons in his huge chauffeur-driven Buick. In winter he'd be wearing boots with a white fur-like lining, which was fashionable then. We had the Abu Dahers from Sidon and Nazih al-Bizri, who was two years ahead of me. Maarouf Saad was a student as well; he was an athlete, a shot-put thrower, rather badly off.[7] In Sidon, the elite went to one of two schools: to our school if they wanted an English education, or to the Frères if they wanted French. Most came to us, especially if they wanted to go to university later on—they needed English to go to AUB, and AUB was more prestigious than Saint Joseph. We had students from Beirut and also from the Lebanese mountains, for instance Rushdi. But most students were from the south, from Marjayoun and Rashayya. We had a number of students from Damour. Not from Tripoli because it had its own American school. Broumana had its own school, which attracted boys from the neighborhood. We and Broumana were top in academic standards—the International College didn't exist then—and in athletics. But in athletics, Aley began to compete. The school in Aley was a national school run according to American standards; Souk al-Gharb had another mission school, which later became a national school.

There was no sectarian feeling in the school. Most of the students were Muslim, I think, but a good number were Christian.[8] Most of our students were from Sidon, which is a mainly Muslim city. The atmosphere was very nationalistic, anti-French, and pro- independence. This was on the part of the students, not the administration. Nasim al-Helou, the principal, was highly respected by the Muslim religious leaders in Sidon. He was a great friend of Sheikh Aref al-Zein, the publisher of the magazine *al-Urfan*. He was loved and respected because he was an excellent scholar in Arabic, as well known as the Bustanis in their day, a student of the Bustanis and the Yazijis.[9] He was a very warm-hearted man with a stern exterior and a sense of humor. He taught us Arabic language, grammar, and literature. One day he called on me to talk about *kana* and its sisters. He caught me unprepared; I had been whispering to my neighbor. He said, "Yusif! Analyze this sentence." It had *kana* in it. I said, "*Kana* is such and such, the noun after the main major subject is *marfu'*, and the object is *mansoob*." Instead of shutting up and stopping there, I went on, "And its sisters do the same." He asked, "What sisters does it have?" I said, "*Kana, sara*, and its younger sisters."[10] He said, "I'm interested in the younger sisters, name them for me." I was at a loss; I didn't know what to say. Yes, he caught me out on things like that. I wasn't always first.

I don't remember that we fought—there were no collective fights, none at all. There were some individual fights. I got into one, and Rushdi got into a very nasty one that could have led to a crime. There was one very tough boy who tried to use a knife. I was not at all a 'tough guy.' There were two instances when I was threatened. Once it was by a student who used to be friends with me and then, for some reason, became very challenging. The other time was by a Beirut boy who was a boxer, young but with a very mature body, athletic, very tough—from the Ka'ki family, a Sunni. He was expelled by one school after another. The family came and begged the Sidon School to accept him and they did—with some hesitation—because the family was rich and paid the full fees. This boy would be very friendly with me, and come to ask me to help him with a lesson, and then another day he would be very aggressive. Possibly because he was so strong and I was so thin, so unmuscular, the bully in him would come out. Fortunately, Beshara Trabulsi was there and Beshara was much stronger than him. Once or twice he would say, "Let's box," or "Let's wrestle." I would say, "Look, I'm not a boxer, I admit it. But there are things in which I'm superior to you," to make him angry. He would have killed me. Fortunately on both occasions Beshara happened to be close. Once I called him, when the Beirut boy was about to finish me off, using me like a bag to box against. Beshara came and threw him to the floor, and said, "If you do it again, I'll strangle you."[11]

We were a group of friends there, five or six, very close—Rushdi and I, Labib Abu Daher, Beshara Trabulsi, and Izzat Zein. This was the nucleus, all from the same class. Kamel Mroueh was in a higher class—he was very amusing and quick-witted.[12] His friendship with Rushdi was closer than his friendship with me. They both had an inclination toward journalism. The school put out a journal every one or two months, and they alternated as editors. Hassan Zein was another warm friend. He became a lawyer after finishing college, and died in the Israeli invasion of 1982—he and his whole family, wife and children, all together. They were going into a shelter when a bomb hit them, a direct hit.

Beshara was very good-hearted, though he didn't have much intelligence, poor boy. He used to get lots of presents from his family. They would visit him frequently and bring him *baklawa*. He would give some to Rushdi and Izzat and me, but not all at once; he rationed it, just on Wednesday afternoons. Every other Wednesday, we used to have something like a debating club. We would stand up and make a statement about a subject, and the others would challenge it. Then they would decide who won. Beshara, with his *baklawa*, would make us wait until after the debating meeting on Wednesday. One Wednesday after he had given us one *baklawa* each from a big box of about three kilos, we asked him, "When are we going to have the next one?" He said, "Next Wednesday." I said, "That's very hard on us; they are such lovely *baklawa*s." I prepared a plan, and the next day I called him, Beshara, and Rushdi together. I said, "Beshara, yesterday you said that we must learn to be democratic and that we should practice Robert's Rules of Order. You objected to anyone trying to get something without a majority. I move that Beshara opens his cupboard and gives us a round of *baklawa*. Anybody second the motion?" Rushdi said, "I second the motion." I said, "Two to one." He said, "Two to one, democracy." He opened the cupboard and gave us each a *baklawa*.

Domestic Concerns

We had a matron, Emile Bustani's mother.[13] Emile had been a student at the school, ahead of me. His mother attended to the laundry and the needs of the students. She was very motherly to all of us, and if a student couldn't manage his ironing she would do it for him. We had to do our own ironing—we used to put charcoal into the iron—it was very primitive. I learned to iron from Umm Emile. I decided to do it because I didn't feel it was right to let her; she was older than my mother. It wasn't included in the bill. I think she did ironing for several students, maybe the rich ones. But I had no money to pay her.

I had very little pocket money—we were poor. Even later on in college I didn't have much. The only thing I spent money on was a little bar of Nestlé chocolate, about two inches long, and very thin—one mouthful, like a wafer—every two weeks or so. A stamp from Lebanon to Palestine cost two and a half Lebanese piasters. I would wait until I was down to my last five or ten piasters before I wrote to my father asking him to send me money. He would send me a quarter of a pound inside a letter. I'd think, "It will take two weeks for my letter to go and money to come back, so ten piasters must last me until then."

I was very thin and yellow in those days, and they were worried about my health. They had me examined and found I had albumen, so I had to give up a few things, like egg whites. One day, as I was going down the steps of the school from the dormitory, the American vice principal of the school, Mr. Jessup, met me going up. He said, "I was just going up to see where you were. You weren't playing downstairs." He went on, "Wait a minute." He pulled my lower eyelid down, and looked at both my eyes. I didn't attach any importance to it then, but later, when I was in university, I was told that if one masturbates it shows in the eyes. He must have suspected me. Every year, three or four boys would be kicked out for homosexuality. I think they did a check-up every night, to make sure that we were all asleep in our own beds.

Outings

The school was well balanced; it was good academically, it was good in craftwork, and it provided us with many opportunities for recreation. First was the Sunday walk—every Sunday, unless it was raining heavily, we would go down from the school and up the hills to one village or another, until we knew all the villages around—Darb al-Sim, Maghdoushi, and so on. On the way, we'd buy prickly pears or hummus, whatever was in season.

Once or twice a month we'd go down to Sidon, in small groups. We'd leave after lunch and would have to be back by dinnertime. We'd amuse ourselves down there, maybe do some shopping. The school also took us for picnics three or four times a year. For instance, the whole school would go as far as Nahr al-Kalb in buses, and we would cook barbecued meat under the trees there.

We were invited a few times, I remember, to the houses of friends. Our class was invited to the Abu Dahers for lunch one Sunday, and Izzat Zein and his father invited us to their village, Kafr Roman, for the night. Not the whole school, just the upper classes, about fifty of us in two buses. We spent a night there and went around the fruit trees, picking anything we wanted.

In summer on Saturdays we sometimes went swimming—the school would take us. We also went to other schools to compete with them in track and field, or basketball, or football. We and Broumana used to be best in these games.

In brief holidays like mid-term or Ramadan, groups of us could get permission to do something special. Once seven of us wanted to go to Beirut by bicycle, and then on up to Broumana by bus—it was a steep climb—and then stay as guests in the school there, before coming back by bicycle. It was Joe Bustani and Rushdi's idea. My teacher cousins tried to stop me. Because I was thin they thought I didn't have the muscles for it, but I said to them, "Please don't stop me; it's something I've set my heart on." In the end they gave in, but they made me promise that when we reached Beirut, if I was too tired to go further, I would wait for the boys coming down from Broumana and come back with them.

It was afternoon when we started, and it was getting dark when we reached Beirut. I remember that it was quite difficult because the cars coming toward us made a glare—I was at the end of the line of cyclists, and that was what gave me greatest trouble. In Beirut, Rushdi and I went to the home of Rushdi's uncle, who was a physician at the girls' school down by the Protestant church.[14] We had a good dinner and spent the night there. We were so tired we almost fell asleep at the dinner table. The other cyclists went to different relatives. The following morning, we went up by bus to Broumana, putting our bicycles on top of the bus. We spent two nights there, and they treated us royally—we were students from a sister school, and we had Joe Bustani, the star athlete, with us. Then we went back by bicycle, downhill from Broumana, which was quite tough because you had to depend on your brakes. We spent another night in Beirut so as to start the next morning early, but this time as guests of the Maqasid school. They put us up in their gymnasium—they had thick mattresses for jumping on that filled the whole gymnasium floor. They gave us blankets and pillows, and we all slept there. It was fun. They gave us a good dinner and breakfast too. The following morning we went back to school triumphant; especially me, because they thought I couldn't make it.

Girls

Relations between boys and girls were very restricted. Four times a year we met the girls in the girls' school down the hill. It always excited us—we felt a flutter in our hearts when we walked down to Sidon. We'd always direct our walk to pass over a little bridge there in front of the girls' school, near Ain al-Hilweh, so we'd see them running around in their skirts. We'd smile at each other from a distance.

The only contact I had with a girl in those school years was with a girl from Sidon, two or three years older than I, who came up—I presume with her parents—to a carpentry exhibition that was held annually. I had a piece in it which she liked; she came and looked at it—it was a holder for letters and envelopes, fret work, carved like lace. She said, "That's too expensive for me." I said, "If you decide to buy it, we can talk about the price." I thought that if it meant giving up my share of the price—because after expenses were paid to the school, the rest was given to the students who made the pieces—I'd sacrifice it to be able to talk to her a bit, maybe touch her hand. I said, "Pay me the price that is fixed to the piece, and I will see what I can return to you." So she stretched her hand out with the money, and I stretched out my hand, and then with my other hand I drew her hand to rest on my open palm so I could feel the softness of her hand. She smiled; she got the message. I dragged out the talking about the price a little longer, and then I said, "I've decided to pay you something back. But first go and show the piece to anyone you want. Then come back and I'll give you the rest." She came back and we did the same again, she stretching her hand, and then me stretching my hand with the change, and holding her hand and stroking it a bit, and feeling very moved by that. But naturally it couldn't go any further. I knew she lived in Sidon. I remember asking her, "Do you come when there are functions here?" She said, "It's the first time my parents come and bring me with them." I was looking round apprehensively and yet proudly—apprehensive in case her parents should notice and proud if any of my group saw me holding a girl's hand. I was sixteen. I wanted to concentrate on the feel of her hand rather than on getting to know her name. What chance would I have had of meeting her in Sidon?

Sex

In our last year, the Lebanese teacher who taught us French took five students to sit the baccalaureate exam in Beirut. I was one of them. He took us to a hotel on the eastern side of the Saahat al-Burj. We didn't know what that meant in those days.[15] After supper he said, "Now, you can either go to your rooms, or you can sit together and go over your literature"—that was the first examination the following day. "You won't need me. If you do, knock on the door, don't just dash in." We went to a room, and as we began to review, one of us—I think it was Izzat Zein—stood by the window. It was a very hot evening, at the beginning of summer. His eyes began to bulge. He said, "Come and see." We all went to the window, and he said, "Turn the light off." We turned the light off. We were opposite what we later found out was the 'red light' district. There was a room there, with a prostitute lying on the bed and somebody making love to her. I can't remember who it was who said, "Do you think Monsieur Sroor is also looking?" Another mischievous one said, "I bet he is. Why did he bring us to this hotel otherwise? Let's go, and walk softly, and open his door without knocking." He was there without his light on, watching by the window. He said, "I was having a breath of fresh air, because the light makes the room very hot."

In the last two years in school, we used to talk about how to approach girls. Izzat Zein was the best informed about these things; it was he who'd make suggestions. He'd already had sexual experience in the village, because his father was the grand seigneur there, and they had farmers. He noticed that his father, in addition to his four wives, would also avail himself of the opportunity to have relations with girls. It was dangerous, but he must have been careful. Izzat himself had also had some experience. Sometimes it was with girls who worked for them in the house, and sometimes under the trees. More often it was in the three or four sheds they had in their big garden, for workers to live in, or for implements, or storage. I can't remember the details. But whenever we talked about girls—we were seventeen or eighteen then—he would say, "When we're in university we'll have the opportunity. There will be girls with us, and we'll be in Beirut."

Farewell to School

In my final year I got the first prize in English composition, Arabic composition, French composition, Arabic speech-making, English speech-making, and French speech-making. When I graduated I went up to the platform I don't know how many times to receive a prize. I got the prize for the highest average, then a special prize because I was the first student in any American mission school in Lebanon to pass the first baccalaureate. Finally, the first in the class gives a speech to say goodbye to the school. My mother and father were sitting there in front—they'd come from Palestine. They were so proud.

I didn't think they would come to the ceremony, but they came. They were so overjoyed to see me, so happy about my prizes, and they expressed it in their warmth. They said, "Here is a gold pound as a gift. What do you want to buy?" I used the gold coin to buy a violin. I had heard somebody give a recital in Sidon, and I got excited about the idea of playing the violin. This used to compete in me with the desire to play the organ, because I loved the organ music in the church in Tiberias. I had no idea how I would learn to play the violin, but I was sure that if I went to university, there'd be a chance to take lessons. Even in Tiberias, if I ended up there, there might be some Jewish violinist who would teach me. I thought that I'd get a job and earn an income. As for AUB, my parents said, "We won't allow you to start working. We'll borrow money to see you through college."

It's strange but even in my last year at school I didn't think of a career. Even in regard to university, I didn't really plan to go because I knew how difficult it would be. I thought that my richer classmates would go, even though their grades were not as good as mine, and that I wouldn't be able to. I didn't even try to find out about scholarships. Some time in the last two months of the last school year, somebody came from the AUB registrar's office and talked to the graduating class about AUB. I think he mentioned the fees, which sounded like a lot of money, and he distributed application forms. He said, "Anybody who thinks he might come, there's no harm in filling out the application so you won't be late." We all filled them out and sent them over. My teachers all said to me, "You must apply." Two teachers who had graduated recently from AUB said they would try to help me. Mr. Jessup was very practical. He said, "The best help the school and I can give you is our recommendation." I remember writing to my parents to tell them about the representative from the registrar's office coming, and saying, "I understand how difficult— perhaps impossible—it would be for you to send me, but it would be lovely if you could. I promise you I'll work hard. I'll do very well." I told them that the school would give me a first-class recommendation that would perhaps help me get a small scholarship.

After that I went back with my family to Tiberias. My parents gave a party for me to which they invited the hospital doctors and the nurses, as well as friends of the family, like a neighbor who had a rowing boat in which he took tourists on the lake, and who used to give us free excursions. The party was simple; it was tea and lemonade and things that my mother made, like *klaysheh* (pastry with dates), and *fatayer bi-s-sabanikh* (pastry with spinach), and of course *tabooleh* (parsley and crushed wheat salad). There was something we called *macaron*, which was not the Italian macaroni but sweet. It was June; we had the party outside, in front of the house. The house had a wide area around it—I'll come to Tiberias later—and we had flowerbeds around the place where we sat and put chairs, and we also sat on stones. It was very pleasant.

While we were still in Tiberias, before going to Lebanon for the summer, Habib Kourani, the registrar of AUB, came on an annual trip he used to make to Palestine. At that time Palestinians were better off than Syrians or Lebanese and AUB depended heavily on students from Palestine, because they could pay the whole fee. He came to Tiberias, and he made it a point to visit us. He had received the application that I had sent from Sidon, and also the recommendation from the school. And being a Protestant, he wanted to visit my father, and to say how eager he was for me to go. He assured us that I would get a scholarship. He didn't say how much, but he said, "Somehow or other, we'll make it possible for you to send Yusif to college." I remember how happy my parents were. They hugged me, and one of my father's rare long-lasting smiles appeared on his face, poor man.

4

Tiberias, as a Boy, 1930–38

The family moved to Tiberias during the Christmas holidays, in a sort of station wagon that could take us all plus clothing, with a small truck behind carrying extra bags. It was the first day of 1930. My father had gone to Tiberias beforehand, to see to it that there were beds and chairs. It was my first trip to Tiberias. We arrived there early in the afternoon. It was gorgeous. It wasn't yet spring, but it was sunny, and as we descended the hills, Lake Tiberias was like a mirror at the bottom, encircled by the Safad and Golan mountains, and the hills of Galilee to the west. As we went down, the colors of the lake began to change. The fields had received some rain, and they were grassy and green. Wildflowers would come later.

The houses of Tiberias were built of very dark gray stones, almost black, that were volcanic and very hard. When we reached our house, I was happy that it was large. Miss Ford had a wing, the part that was by the wall of the convent, to the south of the house. We shared the kitchen for a few years. The house was one and a half levels; it was built on a slope. We had the big room on the ground floor, which one entered either from the gate to the house, or from an internal stairway that went down from the dining room on the upper level. Beyond the dining room we had a room in which we slept. Then there were two other rooms, one that we used as a sitting room, and a long rectangular room that my father turned into a study. He made himself a desk with a small folding table—on which to write his sermons—as well as some bookshelves. A door led from the sitting room to a bedroom. In the corridor outside, a tiny place was turned into a bathroom, just a shower. The toilets were separate from the house. There were two of them; one had to walk to them. Later, a room was added to give us a bathroom inside.

As one entered through the gate there was a garden. My mother soon began gardening, and prepared a long U-shaped flower bed. I remember she liked long stretches of the same plant—two meters of carnations, then two meters of *otra*.[1] One went up ten steps from the lower level to reach the upper rooms, which was the real house. Above the house there was a vast area of land, a good four or five thousand square meters, with a lot of eucalyptus trees and space in between. Later on, a sort of barracks was built there in which a Bedouin family lived. They looked after the church; the wife did some cleaning in the mission hospital, and the husband attended to the church grounds. There were plantations and trees that had to be watered. The [Scottish Mission] church was on the other side of the hospital but farther down, between the road and the lake. It had big grounds.

Up on the level of the main rooms, my mother also planted flowers, all around the house. She loved watering them and digging here and there. There was plenty of water. I was thrilled by the fact that this was a proper house, with proper bathrooms. Our house in al-Bassa was large, but it had no amenities. The toilet was an outside room with a deep hole— you could see all the way down; there was no seat, you had to squat, whereas in Tiberias there were proper toilet seats. And there was electricity—it was such a thrill to switch it on. In Tiberias there was a proper shower. It was I who put pressure on my father to put a pipe high up, and attach a shower head to it, and a tap to open it. In Tiberias it got very hot even before real summer came, but we could go out in bathing suits and cool ourselves under the shower.

The kitchen was quite big. It had a floor of cement, not tiles, and a worktable and sink of smooth cement—but no hot water. There wasn't a stove; we cooked by primus. There was no heating system. Heating for the bathroom was done in the corridor, with *nareet*. There was a shower, and a little room next to it that had the water heater. There was a tub there with a tap. I rarely used it because Tiberias was so warm that even in winter I could use the shower. We didn't have a fridge; we had an icebox. There was an ice factory half a kilometer away toward Safad, and the truck would stop—my father placed an order every day—and leave half a block of ice for us. We put the food that needed to be cool there, as well as the *bateekh* [watermelon], and water. It was warm in Tiberias even in winter; it's more than two hundred meters below sea level. Rain was very rare.

I didn't stay long after we moved from al-Bassa because I had to go back to school; I had already started school in Sidon the October before. But when the holidays came—the Easter holidays and then the summer holidays—I began to enjoy the swimming. I loved swimming, and my swimming improved there. I also started rowing, borrowing a boat from a family near by. I would exercise that way, and began building up some muscles. I was less than fourteen when we moved. To go back to school, I went via Haifa, and I felt very important to be going by myself. I went by taxi because my father wanted the taxi driver, an Arab, to show me the cars going to Beirut. It could easily be done in the same day. Tiberias to Haifa was about fifty kilometers, which was nothing; and then from Haifa to Sidon was less than three hours.

Above our house there was a steep slope to a road higher up, beyond which the Khouri and Sabbagh families lived. Beyond them lived the Tabaris, the leading Muslim family in Tiberias. The mufti was a Tabari.[2] Sidqi Tabari was a leading figure; he was general manager of the Arab National Bank in Tiberias. And there was a younger generation of Tabaris, two of whom became very close friends of mine—Yusif, who was a little older than me, and Khalil, who was a few years younger. They were cousins. Khalil Tabari was a nephew of Sidqi

Tabari. He was an orphan. His father had died when he was a baby, and his family consisted of just his mother and himself.[3] They lived with his uncle. Sidqi was very dynamic and strong-headed—when he wanted something he would go ahead and do it even if it meant trouble for himself and others. Khalil was more diplomatic; he got things through diplomacy. He was extremely political. Later when he and I became close friends we would sit for long hours in the lido—this was a swimming place with tennis courts, a dance floor, and a restaurant, right opposite our house, on the shore of the lake—and talk about politics. Khalil was very much with the mufti.[4] Actually, I think our friendship started when I was about to finish school in Sidon, maybe three or four years later.

My life in Tiberias was divided into two parts: the first part was from 1930, when we first came from al-Bassa, to the summer of 1938, when I graduated from AUB. In this stage I only knew Tiberias during the holidays, and not even all the holidays. Every summer we went away for a couple of months, usually to al-Bassa, but one year to Kafr Bir'em.[5] Later we began to go to Lebanon, the first time to Ain Qabu, the village of the Maaloufs, the second to Faraya in 1939, just before I went to Iraq to teach. The Second World War broke out while we were there. So my first acquaintance with Tiberias was limited to these brief spells of Christmas and Easter holidays and the beginnings and ends of summer holidays.

The second part was when I worked there, after I came back from Iraq in 1940. That's when I took the job in Himmeh. While I was in Himmeh I only visited Tiberias at weekends, every now and then, and for a month in summer. The longest stretch I had in Tiberias was from 1943 to 1944, when I became manager of Hotel Tiberias. By then I was playing tennis in the lido.

Tiberias as Place and Population

Old Tiberias, the lower part, was mixed. Most of the Arabs lived there, and also a number of Jews who had lived there from decades before. Tiberias was one of the towns in Palestine in which Jews had congregated in Turkish times, even before the entry of the British. As you moved uphill, into the northern part of the town, you came across a quarter with many Arabs and the more expensive houses. The Tabaris lived there, also the Khartabils and the town doctor. As you went further up still it became all Jewish, new Jewish.

By 1948 Tiberias had a population of eleven or twelve thousand, of whom at least eight thousand were Jewish. Arabs were a minority. Of the Arabs, between five hundred and seven hundred were Christian, no more. Many of the Arab population were fishermen. Agriculture was not an important activity. Some worked in building—there were two or three families of masons: one was Protestant and the others were Catholic. It was one of them who added rooms to our house; his sons were friends of ours. A large number of Tiberias's Arab population had cafés and little shops along the lake; and of course there were craftsmen—shoemakers, plumbers, carpenters, and so on. There were also small fishermen. The best-stocked shops were Jewish.

Many of the Arab population were caterers, or tourist guides, or had rowing boats to take people on the lake. Tourism was a big thing in Tiberias. There were people who sold mother-of-pearl handwork from Bethlehem or Jerusalem. At the northern tip of the lake was Tabka, the place where Christ was supposed to have done the miracle of feeding the five thousand out of a few loaves and fishes. They actually found a church there in Tabka where the floor had mosaics that showed the fishes and the loaves. It was made into a rest house—people went there to spend weekends. I went there several times later, when I was in university, and when I was working around Tiberias.

The water of Lake Tiberias is fresh; it's the meeting place of the Jordan and the Hasbani rivers. Where the water comes out from the southern end of Tiberias, where it becomes the River Jordan, it's joined by a river coming from Syria called the Yarmouk. At the meeting point there, there was a bridge called Jisr al-Mujama' (The Unifying Bridge), which in fact joined Syria, Jordan, and Palestine.

The central electricity works for Palestine was there, because there was a waterfall. It was called the Rutenberg Concession—a Jewish concession.[6] Another point of interest about Tiberias was its hot water springs. They were not as famous as the Himmeh mineral springs, or as diversified. There was just one spring that came out on land, and there was an establishment there for people to go just for the day, and take the baths—it was good for rheumatism. But people didn't sleep there. The better-off people would come to Hotel Tiberias. Most of the clients in Hotel Tiberias were Jewish. That was my hunting ground, because they were mostly women by themselves.[7] Tiberias had many hotels because it was a winter resort. The Arab hotels were all very primitive except for Hotel Tiberias. That was the best hotel, and the best known, when we first went to Tiberias. Later on Jewish hotels were built, much further up the hill, with more amenities. Though it was as famous as the Baron Hotel, the rooms in Hotel Tiberias didn't have showers or baths. Every floor had bathrooms, three or four at each end.

Most of the professions and the big businesses in Tiberias were in the hands of the Jews. Khartabil was big, but he was just in real estate. There were several Jewish pharmacies. The cinemas were all Jewish. Apart from the lido that belonged to Hotel Tiberias, which was owned by Germans, the hotels and cafés where there was dancing and drinking were all Jewish, also the restaurants, though there were a few Arab restaurants along the lake that specialized in fish, *lahm mishwi*, and hummus. Fish was fried rather than grilled. It was so fresh that the fish would still be jumping around when they were about to be fried.

The Jewish community had many professionals, and they had their own football teams. They would come and have swimming contests at the lido—among themselves—like the Maccabi team against some other team. We'd simply watch. I think one or two Arabs became members of the Maccabi football team, those who were good players.[8] The school in Tiberias had only a very small football ground, and no basketball, whereas the Jewish community had all these things in their schools. Jewish children didn't go to government schools.

Being Part of the Protestant Community

An important center in lower Tiberias was the Scots Mission hospital, which had been built in the late nineteenth century—of course with expansions as the years went by—and attached to it was the Scots Mission. There was a Scottish pastor there all the time and a church as well. The church and pastor's house, which was on top of the church, were on the other side of the street from the hospital, between the road that goes to Safad and the lake. The hospital was a small one—when we went there there was only one doctor, Dr. Torrance.[9] I think his wife had been the matron. In about 1938 a lady doctor was brought from Beirut, Dr. Bekamjian. Then another doctor came, Dr. Zakheh, or something like that, a converted Jew from central Europe—a very nice man, very cultured. The hospital had around ten nurses. Most were from Tiberias, but there was one from Jerusalem, and one from Nazareth. They were all Palestinian girls, four of them Jewish, and the others Christian Arab.

The hospital was an important center because it also catered to patients from outside Tiberias, from villages like Samakh, and further away. Dr. Torrance was very well known as a good surgeon. Like his father before him, he did not believe in giving people much medicine. He believed in the body adjusting itself, and in herbs, and natural treatment.

The Mission was a mission for the Jews—essentially they were interested in converting Jews to Christianity, not Muslims, and they were very Zionist. That was one thing that annoyed me about our association with them. They were never explicit about it, but you could feel that their sympathies were with the Jews. Almost all their patients were Arab—the Jews had their own hospital uphill. The Scots Mission hospital was almost free. All the staff—like the head nurse, the matron, the pharmacist, and the few other nurses—were Scottish. What I liked about the hospital community was the Sunday afternoon service in English, because they had a choir, and most Sundays the nurses sang a hymn or two to organ music. All the time that I knew the mission and the church, the pastor was the organist too; he was quite a character in the hospital.

There were two or three interesting people in the Mission. One of them was half Armenian, half Scottish. We always knew her as Miss Vartan; she was a retired matron. Years later, when I was in university and Fuad and Fayez were about to enter, and my parents could not finance three of us in university at the same time, she came to our help, and lent us money from her savings. Another person who lent us money was Dr. Hart. He had been the head of the YMCA in Jerusalem, and it was he who built the new YMCA opposite the King David Hotel. Then he retired to Tiberias. He lived about a kilometer outside, to the north of the road to Safad, where he had built a beautiful house on a promontory that jutted out into the lake. One went down by steps to the lake, and there was a hot-water spring bubbling up at that point, as you got to the water. He liked me, and used to lend me books. His presence opened cultural opportunities for me because he was educated. I think his doctorate was either in literature or political science. He was a converted Jew as well, a Presbyterian.

Miss Ford was also Presbyterian; she and the Scots Mission worked very harmoniously together. She didn't have her own mission. She wanted all her property to go eventually to the Scots Mission. In fact when my father moved to Tiberias, she was paying only a small part of his salary, and the Mission paid the rest. He was the Arab pastor. There was a congregation there, and my father went around visiting the congregation. We shared the same church.

Miss Ford was a very old woman then. She spoke Arabic—she had been in Palestine for decades—but her Arabic was not very good. She would join us most evenings for prayers, before going to bed. On top of my father's long prayers, she would also usually say a prayer. Sometimes she would start in English and end up in Arabic, or the other way round. She'd get stuck with words, and would stop and say—if she remembered my father's name—"Reverend Abdallah, what does so-and-so mean in Arabic?" He would tell her, and she would go back to where she was, if she remembered where she was. She was in her eighties—she was ninety when she died—and getting a bit forgetful. The funniest thing was when she would say at the end of her long prayers, "Please, God, be with this good family, the family of—" and she would forget my father's name. She'd say, "Afifeh"—my mother's name she never forgot—"Afifeh, what's the name of your husband?" whispering as though my father wouldn't hear. My mother would say, "Abdallah." She would say, "Yes, Abdallah, and his family, and his sons and his daughter."

She always said "his sons and his daughter" until an incident happened one day before prayers. She often told us things about America—she came from the state of Tennessee, and was very racist, she would talk about 'the blacks' in a racist way. Fayez was already alert as a teenager, very sharp. One day he said to her, "I haven't seen a 'black.' Are their hearts black like their skins?" He was teasing her. She said, "How stupid you are!" And to my father she said, "How stupid your son is! You must teach him to understand things better." She had told us that in America blacks were not allowed to go into white restaurants; and she often talked about heaven. Once Fayez said to her, "Miss Ford, is there a heaven for the blacks separate from the whites?" That night when she said her prayers, she asked God to look after the Reverend Abdallah and added, "Please, God, put some intelligence into the head of that son of his who thinks that there is one heaven for blacks and another for whites!"

I respected my father very much and I felt very warm toward him, but I rarely expressed my feelings for him because he inhibited me. He had a frown; he was so reserved and dignified. But deep down, I loved him so much I wanted to be with him and to imitate him. For instance, my fussiness about putting things in one place, even if it's the wrong place, but always in the same place—I took that from him. I'm the handiest in the family in the sense that I can mend things and do carpentry; that's from him. He had a workshop in Tiberias, a room downstairs where he kept his tools. He made cupboards, tables, bookshelves—he did much of the woodwork for the house. He learnt carpentry in school, just as I did. As he saw my interest, he'd come and give me hints—how to hit a nail, how to plane wood, how to design things before beginning to build them. He wasn't very good on electrical things, but the installations were so good in Palestine that we never had a problem with them. The most we had to do was to change a bulb.

My father was very good at practical things. He'd find a problem and then design something to suit it that was simple but effective. He did a bit of metalwork as well—he'd bring tin and solder things to make containers. If water was being wasted—as happened in al-Bassa in the orchards—when an owner wanted to change the water's flow to use it for irrigation, there was often a gap where the water dropped into the irrigation channels. I remember my father designing a wood thing slanting inward for the water to flow in, like a trough. That way he stopped the waste of about one-third of the water. He would think of these things. He had the kind of hands they call useful—broad and strong. I think his masterpiece of design was a bookshelf in the room he used as a study in Tiberias. It was composed of bookshelves, but in the middle there was what looked like a drawer, a wide drawer. You pulled it out, and as it pulled out it brought out supports under it, so that it became a desk. That's where he always prepared his sermons. He would lift the top, which he had covered with glass, and under it, in the drawer, he would have his papers and pens. At the level of his legs, the cupboard had drawers to file things in.

There was something else that he bought that was interesting, the only piece of woodwork that he hadn't made himself. It was a book-shelf that rested on an axis, with four metal legs coming out, and the top was a six-sided set of shelves for books that rotated. My father used two of the sides, and he would turn them toward him when he wanted to check something theological. He organized these things around himself. It was very effective. Eventually Fayez began to use it for his many philosophy books.

My father got himself a camera in Tiberias, and I inherited it. He used to go for things like that—buying a bicycle and learning how to ride it, and having a very old typewriter and learning how to touch type. That's how I learned typing to begin with. One day he came home with a camera, one of these things you open and pull out, an old-fashioned Kodak. Not only did he want to learn about photography, and had bought a book about it, but he also wanted to develop his films. There was a room outside the basement room that he used for his carpentry, to make cupboards and bookcases. He turned a corner of that room, which was quite spacious, into a darkroom. He built a wood thing around it and lined it inside so that it would be a real darkroom; he began developing his films there. He didn't take many pictures because he found that it was too expensive. So he gave up and I took the camera.

Siblings, Schools, Friends

There was an elementary school in Tiberias; it didn't go beyond the sixth class. All but one of the teachers came from outside Tiberias. My brothers went to the boys' school and there was a girls' school, a government school, which was near our house, and Mary went to it. There was no secondary school. The British were very mean with schools for the Arabs, and the Jews had their own system. That's why Fuad and Fayez, when they finished elementary school in Tiberias, went up to Safad, to the Semple school, a foreign school called after its headmaster Mr. Semple, who was a very good mathematician and scientist. Tawfiq, when he finished elementary, went to the Arab College in Jerusalem, headed by Ahmad Samih al-Khalidi. My parents sent him there and not to Safad because he was accepted free; he had very high grades in school. Munir went through the same process;

he had very high grades, and he went to the Arab College too. They both graduated from it with matriculation.[10] When it came to Anis, Tawfiq said, "Don't send him to that school [the Arab College], or he will never smile again." We sent him to Bishop Gobat's school, another English school in Jerusalem.[11] By then, in 1947, things were becoming quite dangerous. After he had been there a few months the fighting got so bad that, after telephoning the family, I took him to Sidon to the school where my father and I had been. He graduated from there. But that is moving ahead.

The years when I was in school in Sidon, and went back for holidays, were the years when I began to make friendships—with Khalil and Yusif Tabari mainly. They were also the years when we became teenagers, and began to think of college and careers. It was at this time that tensions began to build up between my brothers, especially between Fuad and Fayez. I got on well with both of them, but I used to take Fuad's side because he was bullied by Fayez, almost persecuted, because of Fayez's greater cleverness. I admired Fayez, but I felt sympathy for Fuad. Tawfiq was the one who would go through fits of misery.[12] Right from when he was a little boy he would say, "I'm going to die at thirty." Years later, he began to say, "No, it will be forty." In fact, he didn't go much beyond that; he was only forty-six when he died. Tawfiq was very close to Mary; he liked Munir very much and then Anis. He was very warm; he had good relations with everybody. But I think his relations were closer with the younger ones than the older. To some extent our family was cut in half; we three older children formed a sort of unit, and the four younger ones were another unit. This was exemplified by the way that Fuad, Fayez, and I were in university at the same time; they graduated a few years after me, Fuad in 1940 or 1941, and Fayez in 1942. At that time Tawfiq hadn't yet come to university. When he came, I was already working and helping with his education, as well as that of Fuad and Fayez.[13]

In spite of these tensions it was a happy life because we had space, we could go out; it was a town, we'd go to the marketplace. We had friendships outside the house. My father's income was a bit better; we could enjoy more things. The church and church services provided some interest. For instance, at Christmas time, in the holidays, on the religious feasts, there would be several activities; the nurses would come at dawn to sing Christmas carols on the steps of our house and there would be a church service with a Christmas tree. These were things that we didn't know before. It was more diversified. The school had a small library, and I could use it.

Fayez was a tease from very early. He teased everybody. Once we came into the room, and there was a travel bag—it was mine, I was about to go to school. He closed it quickly as though he had taken something out of it. I said, "Fayez, have you taken something out of my bag? I packed it very carefully." He said, "Yes, I've taken something out." "Where is it? Put it back!" He said, "I can't put it back." "What do you mean, you can't put it back?" He said, "I can't find it; I can't identify it." "Fayez, be reasonable." He said, "I am being reasonable." He wouldn't budge. So I had to take the thing to my mother and then to my father. When it came to the point where my father said, "You'll get a beating if you don't come out and say what it is," he said, "I opened Yusif's bag, and took out a handful of air. Can I identify it? Can you identify it?" We always thought of him as being silly—teasing and silly. How could anybody but a silly person think of something like that? But he was logical all through. Just like later, the cornerstone of his arguments was always logic. He used logic in his debates with the Zionists, many years later in America.[14]

It's true that I used to beat my younger brothers; I was like another father to them. It wasn't my father who put me in that role. In fact when my parents learnt about it, they were upset. My mother, who always took the role of mercy, said to me, "You are the elder brother, you feel responsibility, you want to help us. But you shouldn't beat your brothers." It was more slapping than beating. It was mostly Fayez and Fuad who quarreled with each other. Their quarrels went on even when they came to college; every now and then there would

be a misunderstanding between them. But by then they were beginning to grow out of it. It was quite serious when they were at the
Safad school as boarders. They were in the same class, and Fayez was
the first in the class, while Fuad was second or third.

The Safad school was a very good school, especially in science
and mathematics, the best in Palestine. But Fuad and Fayez didn't do
the matriculation there. They didn't want to take the risk, because
matriculation was like the baccalaureate; if you didn't pass you
would have to wait another year to take it again. So they left before
matriculation to enter AUB as freshmen. The Arab College was a
government school; Ahmad Khalidi was the headmaster. He was very
tough. Tawfiq was excellent in literature and language, but hopeless in physics and geometry and algebra. Khalidi terrorized him. He
was a boarder; he must have been twelve when he first went—too
young to be away from home. But it was the same with Fuad and
Fayez and Munir. And Anis later. Mary went to school in Lebanon,
to the American School for Girls, as a boarder, just like the rest of
us. Tawfiq got his matriculation at his first attempt, in spite of giving
in a blank paper for science. This was because he was so good in all
the other subjects, particularly Latin. He had the highest grade in
Latin in the whole of Palestine in the exams, as well as in English and
Arabic language and history. It was just in science and mathematics
that he did poorly.

In the early thirties, I can't remember which year exactly, my
mother had to go to al-Bassa. There was a strike, and the schools in
Tiberias were closed, so she had to take the younger children with
her. In al-Bassa, Fuad caught measles, and Fayez caught it from him,
and then it went all the way down the family as far as Munir—only
Anis didn't catch it. With Munir, the measles rash didn't appear on
the skin, but under it. Apparently this happens in very rare cases, and
it's very bad for the system. When my mother came back weeks later,
after she had to nurse one child after another through the measles,
Dr. Torrance told her that measles would leave its mark on Munir's

health. He needed to breathe fresh air to regain his health, but he was too weak to walk. We had no car, and we couldn't afford to take him by taxi. So I would carry him on my back, for a kilometer and a half, to a point near to Dr. Hart's house, talking to him as I walked, to keep him amused and laughing. We would rest there for a little while, and then I'd carry him back home. I did this for weeks.

Abu Dakhlallah

There was somebody who was a feature of our life in Hawran, al-Bassa, and Tiberias—a constant. This was an old man who would suddenly appear out of the blue, on his shaggy horse, with a *khuruj*, a saddle with two sides in which you put things. This saddle would be filled with religious pamphlets and gospels, which he sold almost for free. People would buy them out of curiosity; they were very cheap. He was a Protestant and distributing the pamphlets was his entrée. He re-stocked from every city he went to where there was a mission. Everybody knew him. He was called Abu Dakhlallah; I forget his family name. He was very neat and clean, not like Boutros, the Egyptian convert. He would stay with us for two or three days to recuperate after his long horseback trips, and for his horse to rest as well. Then one morning at dawn he'd be gone and six months later, a year later, suddenly we'd see him again. When we left Hawran and came to al-Bassa, one day Abu Dakhlallah appeared with his horse. He had a rather high-pitched voice. He said, "I found out where you were, here I am." We said, "*Ahla wa sahla* [Welcome]." He'd stay three or four days, then disappear, and then come back again. When we moved to Tiberias, sure enough, a few months later, Abu Dakhlallah entered through our gate and tied his horse to it. We always welcomed him, because he was *khafeef al-damm*.[15] I think we used to put him in the sitting room because we didn't have a guest room. We were a bit squeezed for space. We used to split up: some of us would sleep in the room downstairs, and sometimes the maid would sleep in it. If the weather was warm, some of us could sleep outside.

The Cloudburst

In the spring one year—I can't remember which—a cloudburst poured over Tiberias as much rain as it normally received in a whole year. There was a flood. Old Tiberias houses all had underground rooms to sit in in summer—they were cooler—and when the flood came it filled many basements. About forty or fifty people were swept into the lake by the flood and drowned. I was in Sidon when it happened, but my father wrote me a long letter describing it all in detail. It frightened me when I began reading it. But right from the beginning he said, "We're all safe." He described the details. My brothers were in school when this cloudburst happened. My father hardly had time to put his shoes on, find his umbrella, and dash to the school, which was at the other end of the town, high up above the hot-water springs. It was about twenty minutes' walk normally, if there wasn't rain pouring on one's head. He got there and found them safe. Before leaving he reassured my mother, saying, "Don't worry, I'll stay with them until the rain stops. If we are late don't think that something has happened." It took hours of waiting. When they finally got back, the rain was less, but they were drenched. I don't think any houses collapsed, because they were built of stone and very strong. But people drowned in the streets as they were running from one place to another. Tiberias is at the foot of very steep hills, and the rain water came down in torrents from the hills. It must have been frightening.

Friends and Acquaintances

Tiberias was the seat of a sub-district; the district officer was there. The Arab community had a contingent of educated people, professionals, and we came to know them gradually. My familiarity with the community developed over two or three years, not immediately when we arrived in Tiberias. There were government officials. There were two people in irrigation. We had an Arab bank, a pharmacy, and two or three Arab lawyers. There were the Khourys—Tawfiq and Shehadeh Khoury—two brothers. The son of one of them is Sa'id

Khoury, a partner with Haseeb Sabbagh.[16] These Khourys were a rich
Safad family. They would spend the summer in Safad, and the rest of
the year in Tiberias. The reason they lived in Tiberias was because
they had a concession from government, a monopoly of fishing in
the lake. They had shared capital with a Jew; it was a partnership.
Another leading Arab family, not from Tiberias but who lived there,
was a lawyer, Anabtawi—very shrewd and clever—who had three
sons. The whole family was very ostentatious in their clothing, and
they had a beautiful car, and the boys had beautiful bicycles with
decorations on them, until they got old enough to drive their car.
The government physician in Tiberias was an Arab. First it was Dr.
Mikhael, an uncle of Hanan Mikhael,[17] and then Dr. Barnikh. They
lived in the same area as the Tabaris.

There were also the Khartabils. They had three or four sons. The
eldest was a doctor, the husband of Wadi'a Khartabil.[18] Two younger
brothers also became doctors, one an MD, and another a veterinary
doctor. Their father Khalil Khartabil was rich, not just the richest
Arab but possibly the richest man in Tiberias. Whatever he touched
turned into money. He was not in trade but in real estate—houses
and lands. There's a story about him that one day he was walking up
from lower Tiberias, up toward the government building that used
to be called Tegart.[19] During the 1936–39 rebellion the government
built a stronghold in every town, where all government offices were
grouped, and police stayed there, so that it would withstand attack.
Khartabil was going to the tax office to pay some taxes. Ahead of him
a couple of men were talking animatedly. As they told the story later,
they were talking about a deal they were trying to clinch to buy some
property, involving tens of thousands of [Palestinian] pounds. One
of them heard footsteps behind, and looked around and saw Khartabil. He said to his companion, "God, this man is going to take the
deal away from us." Khartabil caught up with them, and they said,
'Hajj Khalil, there is no need for us to compete. We will give you
something." He said, "Ah! You have to satisfy me with something

worthwhile." "What would it take to satisfy you?" He knew it must be big money, so he said, "Ten thousand pounds." They said, "No, that's too much." In the end he settled for seven thousand. There and then they gave him a check. He decided to go to the bank and deposit it— he wanted to make sure of the money. They waited for him. He went inside, deposited the check, came out, and asked them, "Now, what's this deal you're talking about?" They were amazed. "You mean you got seven thousand pounds without knowing what the deal was?" He told them, "Sooner or later I would have known about it."[20]

Our friends the Georges were not Tiberias people. The father was an engineer, not really a degree holder in engineering—they called them clerk of works. It was a phrase used for practicing engineers who had some education, but not a full engineering degree. He was an interesting man. He'd been in Africa for years—in Dar es Salaam, and other places. He was the first in the community to have a radio. He was a Protestant, a member of the congregation. He wasn't religious himself, but his wife was the daughter of the pastor. They were both Lebanese. Their children and my brothers were great friends, very close to us. Their eldest son George became very political later in the PPS.[21]

Another friend of the family, who also happened to be Protestant, was the head of the tax department in Tiberias, Antoun Khabbaz, from Jerusalem, formerly from Homs. His wife was from the Salah family in Jerusalem. He was assassinated sometime around 1939. He was going home to his house after visiting somebody, with a young son of his, a boy of ten or twelve, when suddenly, before he reached his house, somebody waiting in ambush fired shots at him. The boy was killed immediately, and when people came and found Khabbaz, he could just pronounce words that sounded like 'Kh— Tabari'. He died without saying any more. The British head of police was very anti-Khalil, so they grabbed him. He was arrested for a week for interrogation, but managed to establish an alibi. Everybody else thought it was Khair Tabari, the son of the mufti, who was impulsive and hot-headed, and always carried a revolver. Khair was hostile to Khabbaz because he insisted on collecting taxes from the Tabaris, and wouldn't be swayed by intimidation.

Later, in 1948, after his father had left Tiberias to become the mufti of Nazareth, as the Israelis passed under his balcony while taking over Nazareth, Khair Tabari emptied his submachine gun into them, leaving a few bullets to put into his own head.

5

At the American University of Beirut, 1934–38

When the registrar of AUB came to Tiberias, he told my parents not to worry, they would somehow manage for me to enter university. It wasn't until the day I was to leave, as my father was about to pray for me, that he asked me what I was planning to study. I told him that I wanted to do architecture. He said, "All right, *mwafak, mabrook.* [May you succeed, congratulations!]." I was impressed by his modern attitude, giving me my independence of choice. Any other father would have said, "Why that? Choose something else!" Perhaps he did not try to influence me because he hadn't been to a secular university; he didn't know what fields were open to me. He asked God to protect me, then gave me a quarter of an English pound as pocket money, and said, "When it's nearly finished send for more. You know it isn't easy for us." I understood that this had to last beyond the trip.

They bought me a new suit in Tiberias. I still remember it; I wouldn't wear it now. I don't know how I picked that color, a sort of dark salmon. I said goodbye and left with a heavy heart. I went to Haifa, and from Haifa took a taxi to Beirut.

In AUB, after settling in a dormitory, I started the process of registration. The system then was that there would be three or four hundred chairs stretching from the door of the registrar's office all the way out into the campus. One had to spend hours registering. You just took your turn, you sat down, and as one person left the registrar, everybody moved up one chair. In those days there was just one man to do the registration, the registrar himself—you had to see him. The newcomers, especially, had to see him to decide on what to study. After waiting a couple of hours my turn came. The registrar recognized me; he said, "Yusif, what do you want to go into?" I answered, "Architecture." He said, "We don't have architecture, you'll have to choose something else." I said, "Law"—I had already decided that law would be my next choice. He said, "We don't have law. Hurry up, you're holding up the line." I said, "What shall I take?" He said, "Why don't you take business administration? Look at me! I took a BA in business administration, and here I am." I looked at him, and said, "All right." My career was chosen that easily, without any proper preparation or thought.

He just initialed a card, and I went on to pick courses, because specialization began then in the freshman year itself, not in the sophomore year. Then for payment, I found out that the registrar had already made arrangements with the head of the finance department, an American called Archie Crawford, and they had allocated me a fellowship to help me with tuition. They said, "We will consider adjusting it after the first term, when we see what your grades are like." The first term my grades were very good, so I went and saw Crawford, and asked him, "Mr. Crawford, is there any chance of increasing my scholarship?" I already had heard that an Armenian student who was about sixty places behind me in grades was getting more help than I. He said, "I'm afraid we can't do anything about it." I said, "But so-and-so has twice the amount of scholarship although his grades are way below mine." He raised his spectacles up to his forehead, and looked me in the eye, and said, "Do you seriously expect to be given as much as an Armenian?" I said, "Yes, in my country"—I was very nationalistic—"I expect that he should be getting half what I get, not the other way round."

That meant that I didn't get any more that year, but we managed—the fees were low and I lived very modestly. The second term I got a small job in the canteen. I sat at a table, and the students who were boarders had slips for every meal. We'd take their tickets and make sure they were theirs—just a simple clerical job that helped me get a little more money.

Each year I picked courses, and tried to select a variety. During my four years for the BA in business administration, I took all the requirements for a BA in economics as well, and so it was like having two BAs. I graduated in 1938 with distinction. In the whole graduating class of four hundred students who got their BA, there were four of us who got distinction. There was Rushdi Maalouf and I, living in the same house. He got his in Arabic literature. The third was Munir Ba'albaki. He is a publisher now, at Dar al-'Ilm li-l-Malayin; he also publishes an English–Arabic dictionary. The fourth was Badr al-Fahoum—now president of the Arabian Insurance Company—who studied political science.

What was more important than classes was just being at AUB. It was such a great thing for me, coming from a small school, from a small town, from a village. Here there were three or four thousand students from all over the Arab world, as well as from Ethiopia, America, and other places. The Arab students came from all over the place—not from the Maghreb, but there were several from Sudan, three or four from Egypt, many Iraqis, many Syrians, many, many Palestinians, and of course many Lebanese. And many came from Transjordan. I don't remember any from the Gulf. The intellectual ferment was very strong, especially in its political aspect. But there were other issues. Charles Malek was in the university then, teaching philosophy, and there was a great deal of talk about philosophical questions. But it was political science and politics that were the main subjects of discussion—what should we do in the Arab world?

At that time there were four professors in the university and one figure who was not in the university but close to it, who had a huge influence on my whole subsequent life, intellectually and politically. These were Charles Malek in philosophy, but also representing the Lebanese nationalist and humanist view—I audited two courses with Malek.[1] But it was not in the classroom that Charles Malek was at his most interesting; it was at the house of the Maaloufs. He was a friend of Fakhri's, the eldest Maalouf brother, who was in physics but also had an interest in philosophy, and later took theology and became a Catholic. Charles Malek was interested in bright young students, to win them over to Catholicism—Albert Hourani came to the university later, and was influenced by Charles Malek along those lines. Hourani returned to teach after graduating in history.[2] The other two professors who influenced me were Arab nationalists, Constantine Zurayk[3] and a junior assistant professor, Fuad Mufarrej, who was exceptionally intelligent. He only had his master's then, but he was already teaching. These two upheld views of Arab nationalism and Arab unity. George Hakim, who had just got his master's, and was already teaching courses in my department, was the Marxist in the group. He taught a course on Marx, which I took, and a course on the history of doctrines. He got interested in me, and gave me a lot of things to read, like some of Laski's work, and Joan Robinson. I read Marx's *Capital* then for the first time, though I didn't understand it. That makes four. The fifth person, outside the university, was Antoun Sa'adeh.[4] He taught German—some people studied German with him, some people studied Spanish, and one or two studied Russian—he was fantastic in languages.

Joining the PPS

I came to know Sa'adeh toward the end of my first year. He was friends with the Maaloufs, and also with Charles Malek. Imagine sessions when there would be all these five mentors having arguments for five or six hours! It was fantastic. My inclination was toward Sa'adeh, because of the five Sa'adeh was the only one who was doing something, not just talking. He was building an organization, building the party—the party was secret then. I joined it at the beginning of 1936 when it was still secret. Rushdi and I joined together, and Sa'adeh himself conducted the ceremony when we took the oath.

We were indoctrinated by Sa'adeh himself. It seems he felt that the two of us had promise for the party. He was interested in the Maaloufs, and I was living with them. He wanted us to be his immediate disciples, not to be taught through somebody else. That took months. He always spent five or six months talking to people, testing them intellectually, testing their fiber, before in the end saying, "You are ready to join." The secrecy of the party was well maintained through the cell system. Nobody knew about the others. In the university, the unit was the *mudiriyyeh*, which was larger than a cell; at any one time there would be twenty or thirty members in the meeting. Later on we became many more than that, so they had to divide it between faculties. The secrecy worried me a bit—it reassured me because it meant that there was protection; but on the other hand if it became known—the party was illegal, it had no license—there would be prison. The French were extremely hostile. This was because the party was opposed to a narrow Lebanese entity. But their hostility was more because the party was against the French occupation. It wasn't undertaking active resistance, not then. But it took part in every movement after it was disclosed.

After the party became legalized, we had many, many arguments with Arab nationalist students. The one I argued most with, who was a classmate of mine then, was Muhammad Shuqair, who was killed when he was advisor to Amin Gemayel. He was very much an Arab nationalist in those days, an acolyte of Riad al-Solh.[5] In fact, when Riad al-Solh was assassinated on his way to the airport in Amman— he was leaving after visiting King Abdullah—Muhammad Shuqair was with him. Muhammad was sitting next to Riad al-Solh in the car when a military vehicle overtook them, and somebody stretched out his hand with a revolver into the window of the car—the window was open—and said, "This is from Sa'adeh"—al-Solh was prime minister when Sa'adeh was executed. He was killed on the spot, and fell into the arms of Muhammad Shuqair. Years later Shuqair became a friend of the PPS, and a critic of the Arab nationalists.

The main trends then among students were Arab nationalism and Syrian nationalism. Not Lebanese nationalism—in those days at AUB nobody took Lebanese nationalism seriously. The Phalanges were viewed as just a boy scout movement with uniforms. It was Arab nationalists against Syrian nationalists. The arguments were very hot. Not physically hot, there were no fights in those days. We, the Syrian nationalists, managed all right because we were more aggressive than the Arab nationalists. Zurayk, their mentor, was a mild person. Fuad Mufarrej took everything as a joke. He was an Arab nationalist, but he never carried his arguments to a serious level where there would be friction. He left for the States to study for a doctorate, and died in a car accident soon after he got there—a great loss. Albert Hourani was interested in the Palestine cause. He knew Sa'adeh and respected him. He was very close to Charles Malek of course, and to Zurayk. He wasn't somebody who took sides.

On campus the activity was intellectual and political—arguments and discussions, a great deal of that. We in the party were busy converting students, and we were growing very fast. We were sheltered because we were inside the campus. But there was a lot of recruiting outside as well. So long as it was done without contravening any laws it was okay; the university did not block it. There was nothing against people joining, but we were not supposed to hold meetings inside. We held them secretly. I remember one time when I was *mudir fira' al-jam'a* [director of the university branch], we were holding a meeting inside the university in a room in West Hall. Hassan Qaedbey came into that room, which was on the second floor, with his back to the wall, sliding like a burglar, and slipping inside the door. Munir Taqqedin, the brother of Sa'id, came in a similar way.[6] I said to them, "What a pair you are, coming scared like that!" I don't think we would have been expelled if we were caught, just given a written warning.

"The Day Didn't Have Enough Hours in It . . ."

In AUB, I worked very, very, very hard. I had no social life. Every month or so Rushdi and I, or Beshara and I, would go to the cinema. But at the beginning I was very hard up. I would wait until I was down to my last Lebanese pound, or half pound, and then write a letter to my father, and he would send me another quarter of a [Palestinian] pound. Things became better in my sophomore year because I began to get university employment. First, I lived as a boarder in West Hall. It had no dormitories, but Rushdi and I and two other students were allowed to live there in return for moving chairs down from the attic into West Hall for film showings. There were four hundred chairs in the attic and we had to carry them down before a cinema show, and then take them back the same night. The first year I slept in the dormitory, the second year we moved to West Hall. The third and fourth years I lived with the Maaloufs.[7] In the third and fourth years I was given a job—two jobs in fact—one was to help in the library, to bring books for students and teachers, and return books to the stacks. The other was in the office of Grounds and Buildings, with Aziz Nahhas, where I did some accounting for the department. I made enough money to finance a trip to Switzerland, but never went because I felt I should give the money to my brothers.

After my second year in college, it was time for Fuad and Fayez to come. Fayez was not admitted because he was too young, but Fuad was supposed to come when I'd be in the junior year. I felt that maybe I should leave university and take a job for a year or two, to help my father. Just at that time, I learned that the registrar's office was losing an assistant. So I applied for the job, and they took me, and I started working in the summer. When my parents heard of this they were angry. They said, "We won't let you interrupt your studies. We're making arrangements for the money." So I worked for two months and then resigned and went home to Tiberias. I found that my parents had borrowed money from Dr. Hart and Miss Vartan. That was on the one hand; on the other was the fact that I was costing them hardly anything because of the jobs I was getting. So I went back to studying. I was a junior, and Fuad was a freshman.

In university we had to be in class by seven-thirty for most classes. I didn't have the same difficulty waking up as I had had in school because I was more interested in my classes. The whole atmosphere was invigorating. To students coming like me from traditional high schools, university was new and exciting. AUB had its own mystique—we used to sing "*Nahna awlad al-kulliyeh* [We are the children of the university]" when we went down to the cinema, filling the tram. We felt that we were a special breed. I used to wake up early, and either I did Swedish exercises in my room, or I'd go to the gymnasium in AUB and do some gym and rope climbing—we used to have a gym in Bliss Hall that was scrapped later because they needed the space for other things. I'd do exercises for twenty minutes, run back from the campus to the Maaloufs on Jeanne d'Arc street, close by the Taqqoush flower shop, then wash or shower, depending on the season, dress, shave, eat, and be on the campus by seven-thirty. It didn't take me as long then as it does now to get ready in the morning.

In my second or third year I started taking violin lessons. I couldn't start before because of my work with the PPS, and my courses, and my job. When I began to earn more money, I started taking lessons. It was a regular course, but one student at a time. The teacher was a French Lebanese Jew. I think I took the class for two years, but I didn't practice much. By then I had moved to the Maaloufs, and was embarrassed about making a noise. In the end I gave it up.

I did two kinds of sport. I entered contests such as the body improvement contest, and got the silver medal. In the first year we had to have some physical training, and I took gym. But the thing I did most was swimming. I loved swimming, so I took life saver training. In my sophomore year I got the junior life saver badge, and in my junior year the senior badge. Because I wasn't known as a bad character, the director of physical education asked me to go early mornings once or twice a week, when the junior college girls came to our beach to swim, to be a lifeguard. I remember that a student from Haifa, a Jewish girl, very attractive, came to me and said, "I'm interested in life saving. Would you like to teach me?" I told her what it involved theoretically. She said, "But suppose somebody is drowning, and hangs on to your neck like this"—and she clasped my neck and pressed against me—"What do you do?" When she repeated this two or three times, I realized that she was pulling my leg. So I said, "If it's a girl like you I'd drown with her." Then she said, "Let's swim together, I'd feel more secure if you were there." I asked somebody who was a junior lifeguard to keep an eye on things, and I went out swimming with her. She was such a strong swimmer that in no time she was ahead of me. She had managed to pull my leg twice. This pleasurable task ended by giving me a bad cold. I would go there at five-thirty every morning, and I didn't have a pullover. I stopped going after that.

The day didn't have enough hours in it for all the things I wanted to do. I attended every lecture that sounded interesting. I went to all the concerts and organ recitals. I managed the things one had to pay for by becoming an usher—that gave me a free ticket for myself, and an extra ticket for a friend. This period in university was full of activity. I was taking more courses than the regular load. There was the work I did to earn money. There was my PPS activity. Then I had friendships—I was making new friends in AUB, as well as the friends who had been with me in Sidon, like Beshara, Izzat Zein, Adel Karam, and Labib Abu Dahar. Now there were also the 'friend-opponents,' the people with whom I always argued, like Muhammad Shuqair and Ramez Shehadeh. We were very good friends but we always argued about Arab nationalism versus Syrian nationalism. Things were never dull. Whenever our throats got dry with discussion, we'd dash out for coffee at Faisal's. Faisal's was an institution in itself—the owner was a character, and his place was a 'salon politique.' Fuad Mufarrej went there, and Muhammad Shuqair, and Mahmoud Sa'eb; Munah al-Solh went there later on. Faisal's was mainly the Arab nationalist meeting place but we went in there too to argue with them. We had a café of our own, a tiny room run by Ajaj Mukhtar, who was a solid party member, as well as a well-known Lebanese *zajal* poet. We used to go there simply out of loyalty to him. There was another restaurant near Faisal's, another PPS faithful. We went to these two cafés because they were cheap, and also to support them. For snacks we went to the *mana'eesh*[8] bakeries. But what I loved more was *dibs kharoub bi taheeneh*[9] spread on a loaf with butter. It was cheap and a very nutritious meal for somebody who didn't have much money. They had it in the AUB cafeteria. As a boarder, you had to eat there; otherwise you'd lose what you had already paid for.

While I was at university, they had to take me to hospital for a thorough check-up by the specialist in internal medicine. The man who was the leading figure in this was Dr. Khayyat. He did x-rays, and told me, "You don't have an ulcer but you are the ulcer type. You get excited, and then your gastric juices flow." He said, "If you don't relax and decompress, you will certainly get an ulcer." All my life I've suffered from my stomach.

The friendships were very lively. I remember one year I lived in the hall near the IC [International College]. That's where we used to look out, Izzat Zein and I, at the pasha's wife. This Pasha Arslan was an old man married to a young woman. They lived over where the Socrates restaurant is now, on the first floor. There was a very light curtain, silky white net, that enhanced what we saw rather than hid it, with the light behind her. She used to undress in a very leisurely way. It was the same almost every night. Izzat Zein managed to make signals to her. She couldn't join him, but her younger sister who lived with her went for a walk with him a few times. They flirted and kissed, nothing more serious. Izzat did not go further. In those days it wasn't easy to have a real affair.

I remember that near the Maaloufs' house, in a building opposite where we lived, there was a woman who must have been over fifty, who would invite in young men, mainly students. She said that she wanted a child, and her husband couldn't give her one. But she was far past conceiving children by then. One day in the summer of 1938, a friend of mine who lived in that neighborhood was sleeping on the balcony. At dawn he heard sounds. He opened his eyes, and saw that this woman was throwing things onto his balcony from her window on the other side of the alley. He picked them up and found Turkish delight and biscuit sandwiches, wrapped in paper. They agreed on a time—he went to her in the morning because he was afraid that her husband might come—a Moroccan, ferocious looking, who worked with the army.

I went to church every Sunday; that's an activity I never missed. I remember once there was Communion, and I was there with Fayez. After leaving church, we reached a certain point in Ras Beirut where I said to him, "I'll leave you here." He asked where I was going. I said, "I'm going to my friend." It wasn't a girlfriend in the proper sense of the term; it was a woman I was hoping to get some favor from. Fayez was furious. He said, "You've just had Communion!" I told him, "That's one thing, this is another. Maybe Communion will give me advance forgiveness." I was just trying to be clever but he got really angry with me. Fayez was quite religious.

Fayez rose very quickly in the PPS. He joined perhaps two years after me, and in no time he became assistant to the *amid*[10] of culture and information. He would stay in Beirut for the summers, and not go to Tiberias, because he wanted to do party work all the time—speeches, mobilization, writing. This annoyed my parents very much. He was the editor of the party newspaper; he was a full-time student for a master's; he was doing this party work; and he was madly in love.

There were two people he argued with most: Burhan Dajani, an Arab nationalist, and Wasfi Tal, who later became prime minister of Jordan. The animosity between him and Wasfi Tal reached a point where one day Wasfi Tal went to the university with a cut in his throat, and complained that Fayez had tried to kill him. Of course they interrogated Fayez, and Fayez denied it completely. The university appointed Albert Badr to investigate the accusation. He found it was not true, but nonetheless he told Fayez, "I know it's untrue, and I'm going to recommend the university to expel Wasfi Tal. But I cannot let you go scot-free." Fayez said, "But if I had nothing to do with the cut, which he inflicted on himself while shaving, why should I be punished?" Albert Badr said, "It will be just a small punishment." They expelled Wasfi Tal, and they made Fayez leave the university for one year. During that year Fayez went and worked, first in Nazareth and then in Tiberias, as director of food rationing. He did an enormous amount of reading during that year. Every day he would come home from his job, have lunch, rest a little, and then go to the lido with some philosophy book. He would read until it got dark, and then come home.

Teachers

In the university, I liked Sa'id Himadeh very much, although he was a difficult teacher, difficult to satisfy with one's answers to his questions. I liked his character, he was honest, and he was a teacher in the full sense of the word, someone who tried to guide students along certain lines of moral principle and methods of work. He was a hardworking researcher himself, and he injected that interest in research into us, at least in me. He taught us courses on the economic organization of the Arab world. By 1936 or 1937, he had already covered this subject in books—he edited these books and had chapters in them himself—on Syria, Lebanon, Iraq, Palestine—'Dimashq' (Damascus)— he was a pioneer in that field.[11] He'd been well trained at Columbia University in 1934.

Then I liked Husni Sawwaf, a Syrian teacher who only had a master's. He was not very demanding—I liked his easy attitude. George Hakim had a sharp mind. I think he had the sharpest mind of the department. He taught us one course that I hated, commercial law, and also the history of economic doctrines. He interested me in reading. I don't think I did any reading in economics other than the books assigned in the courses, except with Hakim. He opened my eyes to a number of books on socialism. I was being influenced by the PPS toward national socialism rather than scientific socialism, and I felt that I wanted to understand both better. Sa'adeh suggested things for me to read on national socialism and power politics, the 'game of nations,' how policy is made; and he also asked me to translate a couple of books.

Outside the department itself, in our freshman year, we took some courses that were given to everybody, like the cultural studies program now. There was a course on history, for instance. Several people taught this course, among them Assad Rustum, who was very brilliant. I took a course on the sociology of the Middle East with Afif Tannous, who had been a student of Stewart Dodd—in fact Dodd taught part of that course. History at AUB was better than the history I took in high school. The book had been prepared by a team of professors headed by Rustum, who had just got a PhD with distinction from Princeton.

Outside the department and the regular courses I was taking, there were two professors who were very popular on campus, Zurayk with his new doctorate from Princeton, and Charles Malek from Harvard. Zurayk also gave some of the lectures in the history course. Zurayk said sensible things, but there was no fire in him, whereas Malek had a physical presence, his voice and his imagery were impressive. We Arabs are impressed by philosophy. I read the whole of the *The Dialogues of Plato* on top of everything else I was reading in my classwork, though I was only auditing this course.

Off- and On-campus Cultural Activities

I attended lectures downtown as well. When the Cenacle Libanais came into being, I used to go to their lectures. Many years later I was invited to give a few lectures there. It was downtown in the Burj somewhere, near the Roxy cinema.

Through Rushdi, and as a young poet, I came to know several poets outside the university, like Salah Labaki and Sa'id Akl. Sa'id was a friend of the Maaloufs; he came frequently to visit them, and to argue with Sa'adeh. Hot arguments! But it was Sa'id Akl who wrote the national anthem of the PPS. He was greatly impressed with Sa'adeh as a person, and with his ideas. But to him, Syria was really Lebanon. In other words, Lebanon wasn't just this little bit of land along the coast, but the whole of Syria. It was an inversion of Sa'adeh's idea. I came to know several writers too: Fuad Suleiman, who was a critic with a sharp pen; and Tawfiq Awwad, who was older than me by a few years. I would go to salons for discussions of poetry and literature—to Salah Labaki's house, where people went and drank coffee and smoked. It was usually Rushdi and me from the university. Salah Labaki became the vice president of the party, so Fuad Suleiman and other young writers would go. In literary journalism, there was *al-Makshuf*, an avant-garde weekly or bi-monthly, which published short stories and literary criticism, edited by Fuad Suleiman. It was liberal. I came to know, but didn't like, someone who published a popular sex journal, almost like pornography, called *Alf layla wa layla*. It was all to excite young men and to sell. I read some of his stories and found they were trash. I didn't go on reading them.

I myself wrote a few things, and published them in the university magazine that was put out by al-Urwa al-Wuthka.[12] One day I wrote a story and gave it to them, and they liked it. I published two or three short stories with them. In my last year I wrote a poem to a French girl I was in love with, just seven verses. Sa'id Aql liked them, but Rushdi criticized them hotly. I read a lot of literature—Dickens, Daphne du Maurier, *The Brothers Karamazov*, *Crime and Punishment*—classics like that. I've always loved novels, and I still do. There was a brief period when there was a literary club, and I joined it, but it began to have fewer and fewer meetings and then died.

I went to poetry readings as well. These were very popular. Many such events were held in West Hall—poetry readings by old-fashioned poets like Dr. Niqula Fayyad, who was also a famous orator. I remember the joint session he had with May Ziadeh.[13] It was her first appearance after being released from a mental hospital. She gave a speech in West Hall based on her personal experience. Niqula Fayyad introduced her. He wrote a poem for the occasion. I remember the first verse, '*Ya Mayu! Hadhihi sa'tu miyadi/Fa sa'li fuadaki 'an khufuk fuadi*'—'May, this is the hour of the rendezvous between us. Ask your heart about the trembling of my heart.' It was a feast to attend events like this.

May Ziadeh's story is an interesting one. She was declared mad by her family, because they wanted her money. She wasn't married. They brought a mental doctor to visit her, and she made fun of the questions he asked her. He went out saying, "Of course she is mad. I asked her so-and-so and she answered this way." But it was tongue-in-cheek. She said later, "The session proved that he is mad, not I." They managed to put her in a mental hospital for a while, by force, through the court. But there was immense pressure by writers in the region, by everybody, and she was freed.

One other very important event was when Habib Bourguiba came and gave a lecture, with his high tarboosh. We had several such lectures and literary events. There were also concerts. There was this White Russian musician, whose wife was a pianist. He formed a symphonic orchestra and trained it, and when I came to university he was already giving concerts. The orchestra must have consisted of about twenty musicians. Later on there was a photography club, but it was not very active. There was no art department in those days. As regards my social life, my intellectual life, and artistic interests, I had a foot inside and a foot outside the university.

I didn't often go to the cinema—I didn't have enough money. But I loved the cinema, so when I began earning money, I went more frequently. I went to films that had Orson Welles or James Mason in them, films like *Mutiny on the Bounty* and *Gilda*— films with Rita Hayworth and Charles Boyer. I didn't like Robert Taylor; I found him too effeminate. I was keen on women stars like Greta Garbo and Rita Hayworth . . . I'd be keen on someone for a few months and then I would shift to somebody else. But this was later when I began doing those extra jobs. Rushdi's and my lack of liquidity is illustrated by a story. We went one day to the college store, in the basement of West Hall. Rushdi saw a pocketbook for keeping banknotes. It was attractive, and he said to the storeowner, "Mr. Naseef, how much is this pocket book?" Naseef said, "Only five pounds." Rushdi thought and thought. Mr. Naseef said, "What's so serious about it?" Rushdi answered, "I have a problem I can't solve. I have five pounds on me. If I buy the pocketbook I'll have nothing to put in it. But if I don't buy it, I don't know where to put the five pounds."

When I was in my last year in college, Rushdi and I went to the cinema. It was terribly cold, the rain was torrential, and the cinema was almost underground. The rain came in, and our feet were in water all through the show. The following day we both had a temperature. We thought it was a cold, but the temperature went on, and Rushdi's uncle, the physician, came and examined us. He said, "There is every sign that this is measles." So I went to George Salibi, whom I knew from the party, he was a very active PPS member. He said, "I'll get you into hospital." I said, "I can't pay for the hospital." He said, "No, no, you're a student, you're covered for this." I went to hospital and stayed there in the isolation section on the top floor of the old building. They treated me in the modern way, with ice cream. But Rushdi stayed at home with his mother who, supported by her doctor brother, forced him to put a wool pullover next to his skin. They told him he should stay like that for a month. By the month's end he had got used to it, so that all his life, if he took the jersey off, he would start a cold.

Last Days at University

The finals consisted of the written exams and the comprehensive— a written comprehensive, and then an oral comprehensive. That was the peak of difficulty, the main hurdle. The written exam was a three-hour exam; I did all right in that. I went to the oral exam, and the chairman of the examining board was Sa'id Himadeh. He had prepared a number of questions, written them on separate sheets of paper, folded them, and put them inside his tarboosh, which he put upside down on the table. He asked each of the other professors to ask a question, and I did well with all of them. But with him, I always had—and still have—a block with regard to Ricardo's theory of rent. I kept saying to myself, "My God, I hope I don't get that question"— because every year, in every exam, he always put that question. I put my hand in the tarboosh, and it came out: "What is Ricardo's theory of rent?" I decided to make a joke to ease the situation for myself. I said, "Professor Himadeh, perhaps all the questions you put in there are the same—what is Ricardo's theory of rent—so nobody can escape it?" He laughed and said, "No, no." I tried to answer, and he squeezed me; he went on and on. My answer was passable, but he wanted me to give a better answer. I went out sweating.

Waiting out there I began to worry that they were discussing whether I would pass or fail. Although my overall average was high, the comprehensive could just tip the balance. Perhaps I would have to come and sit it again at the end of summer? Then the door opened and Himadeh came out, followed by the other professors with smiles on their faces. So I knew that I had passed. He said, "Yusif, you still stumble on Ricardo." I said, "But I passed?" He looked me in the face with wide-open eyes and said, "Yes, you passed . . . with distinction." He had his hand in his pocket. I exclaimed, "With distinction! And you're taking your time to tell me!?" I pulled his hand out of his pocket and shook it—like that. Everybody laughed at my excitement. That was the end of my time as a student at AUB.

Toward the end of that year, 1938, my graduating year, the university got a scholarship to give to somebody to go to America and study for a doctorate. Everything would be covered. The university offered the scholarship to me. I apologized because I wanted to work and help my brothers. They offered it to Eva Badr, later to be Eva Malek. Her family said, "No. You, a girl, going by herself to America!" She was studying political science and philosophy, and graduated with distinction the year after me.

My parents came for the commencement exercises. We stayed together in the Hotel America, in Saahat al-Burj—not the east side! The manager was a Protestant; he gave my parents special rates because my father was a pastor, so we were able to stay about a week. My father had trimmed his mustache nicely, and had a new haircut. My mother had a new dress. I was cheered by their happiness, especially after they got the news that I had passed with distinction. They were very proud, of course, because only four out of four hundred students graduated with distinction, and we received long applause.

By then I had already been offered a job through Elia Ibrahim, who had taken a short course in commerce and left two years ahead of me. He was working as a junior accountant with Socony. The chief accountant said to him one day, "People are finishing AUB with degrees in business administration. Is there anybody special you can think of?" He said, "Yes, Yusif Sayigh. He graduated with distinction." The chief accountant said, "Bring him over." Elia took me there, and this man interviewed me, and gave me a firm offer right away, which I accepted. The salary was fifty pounds, with a twenty-pound living allowance, altogether seventy pounds, which was quite something in those days in Lebanon, when things were really cheap. I told him that I wouldn't start right away because I wanted a summer holiday.

6

Ain Qabu, First Job, Work for the PPS, 1938–39

The Maaloufs—Rushdi and his mother—had invited me to spend part of the summer with them in the mountains at Ain al-Qabu, near Baskinta. My parents were thinking of bringing the whole family to spend the summer in Lebanon, and the Maaloufs said, "If you all come, we'll find you a house near ours, at a reasonable price. Things are very cheap."

We hired a car, a six-seater, to carry the whole family to Beirut. By then we all had passports. I went ahead of them to spend a week or so with the Maaloufs before they came. I knew what day they would arrive, and I met them with Rushdi in Beirut. We all went by bus up to Ain Qabu. They had found a lovely house for us. But we never imagined, in this lovely red roof house, with its many windows and the garden around it, that the moment we put our heads on the pillows, an expedition of bugs would come out of the woodwork. We couldn't sleep that night.

The following morning we went and saw the landlord, whose house was not far away. We said, "What's this? Look at our skin." He said, "*Baseeta*. Tonight you won't feel a single bug." He came with a basket full of vine leaves, which he placed around the beds, bed by bed. The vine leaves have little hairs, and you have to place them in such a way that the hairs point outward from the bed, so when the bug comes it gets caught in them. He said, "Don't go to sleep straightaway. Have ready two or three lumps of dough. An hour after you go to bed, get up, and you'll find the bugs all stuck to the leaves. Put the dough on them, and pick them one by one." It was too much trouble doing that every night, so Umm Fakhri, Rushdi's mother, told us about something we could spray. Another way of getting rid of them was to boil water and put hot peppers in the *tanjara*, and then pour this stuff in the crevices of wood, the doors, and the bed frames, after lifting the mattresses from the beds. We killed hundreds of these bugs, and we managed to stay there.

Whatever wasn't available in the house was supplied by a very kind uncle of Rushdi's, Dr. Shukri Maalouf—his family owned a beautiful house, which Rushdi bought years later. He also offered us the use of his garden, with its figs, *anab*, and pomegranates. My father insisted that we should rent three or four trees of figs and grapes, so as to feel at ease. It was a battle until Dr. Shukri accepted a few Lebanese pounds. We spent a very happy summer there in the mountains. Dr. Shehadeh Ghussain, who became the first consul general of Lebanon in Palestine, was there with his family. There were several other Maalouf households.

That was the summer when I walked to the top of Mount Sannin. There was Antoun Sa'adeh, Charles Malek, Rushdi and I, and one or two others. We met for lunch at the Maaloufs', and decided to climb Sannin. The weather was right. We went to Baskinta at night, and slept at a little inn at the foot of the mountain, and had supper there—*labneh*, fried eggs, mountain bread, and lots of fruit. Charles Malek didn't come on the walk, but Sa'adeh did, and Fakhri, Rushdi's brother. The following morning at dawn we climbed and reached the top, and saw the sea. They say that in the afternoon you can see the shadow of the Cyprus mountains in the sea.

Going down was interesting because people competed to see who could do it faster. We slid. Rushdi said to me, "I want to beat *al-za'eem*." Sa'adeh was very competitive too. I finished later than the others because I was cautious; I'm not used to mountains. I didn't dare slide the way the others did. Each step would take them two meters.

Those times in summer when I spent weeks with the Maaloufs, Sa'adeh would be there too. We would sleep in the *arzal*, a tree house—there were two tree houses there. Rushdi never slept in the *arzal* because he was afraid for his stomach.

In the summer of 1948, after leaving Tiberias, my parents went to Ain Ar. They spent a few months there and then they came down to Beirut, to a small house at the end of the tramline on Bliss Street, overlooking the sea. It was enough for them because only Tawfiq, Mary, and Munir were at home with my parents. Anis was in his last year in high school in Sidon. When I came back from POW camp, and they were expecting Fuad to marry and to come to them, they moved to the house in Ain Mreisseh where they are now.

All this is a prelude to describing my relationship with my father and how it changed during those summers in Lebanon. It was as if leaving his parish, the place where he had duties, released him from something. He became relaxed, told jokes, laughed. He had a great time with Rushdi's uncle, Dr. Shukri Maalouf. They met every day, at least once, the two of them. He wasn't trying to convert anybody to Protestantism, since Dr. Maalouf was Protestant already. Lebanon has a thing about it; people there have a wider range of interests. My father gradually became more accessible. Graduating from Sidon School had been a landmark in our relationship; my graduation from AUB was another. This series of trips to Lebanon marked a period when there was another big transition. I began to be able to influence my father a little. For example, if I saw him being angry about things, or too serious, or when his sermons became all fire and brimstone, I would say to him, "Baba, *khafifha* [lighten up], or they'll take it as a joke." He would laugh and say, "Do you think they're not sinful enough to deserve my sermon?" I said, "Even if they deserve it, they're not going to take them seriously if you give them such a big dose." I began to talk to him like this, and he would smile indulgently.

First Job

I went back with my family at the end of summer for two weeks more swimming in Tiberias, before going to Beirut to start working at Socony. I worked there almost until the following summer. Then I resigned because I was bored stiff with accounting. I was in charge of the accounts of lubricants; all the stations in Lebanon sent their accounting forms, and I had to consolidate these forms and make a balance sheet and a trial balance. This meant that there were two sources of accounts, so one would be a cross-check on the other. If I made a mistake of one pound out of millions of pounds, it could not be ignored. It could be a difference between 2 million and 1,999,999, but I would have to go over the whole work again. Most months, I got the thing straight from the first go. But I hated the job.

One night I had a strange dream. I used to add up these long accounts with a manual adding machine—there were no electric adding machines in those days. You made up the accounts, and clicked the machine, and it printed. I dreamt that there was a huge roll of paper, all in one piece, meters and meters long. I was adding up with the manual machine, and the paper started going down, down from the machine from the table to the floor, from the floor to the wall, and then climbing up to the window sill, and over the window sill, and down to the street, and on to the tram line. Then I heard the bell of the tram, so I began pulling the paper back, back, back up. I woke in a panic. I thought that this was a sign from heaven that I must leave the job. The following day, I went into the office of Mr. Khoury, the chief accountant, and told him that I wanted to submit my resignation. He said, "What! Aren't you satisfied with your salary? I can raise it." I said, "No, it's not a matter of salary." "Anybody bothering you? I was hoping that one day you will take my place when I retire." I said, "That's exactly what I'm afraid of, the prospect of ending my life as a chief accountant!" His face got red as a beetroot—he was a very fair-skinned person—he could have thrown a bottle of ink at my face. He said, "That will do. It's almost the end of the month; stay until you make the final balance sheet, then leave."

Years later I met him swimming at the St. George's. Bahjat Khawli, Sami Korban, and I—three or four of us—went swimming from AUB all the way to the St. George's beach, with a football in our hands. We didn't touch ground at all. I think it was when I had started work with UNRWA, and was already studying at AUB for a master's. We met at the beach, and he asked what I was doing. I told him that I was studying for a master's in economics. A few years later we met again—by then I was a professor at AUB. I asked him, "Did I make a mistake?" He laughed and said, "No."

Social and Sentimental Life

We were lodgers—at one time Fuad, Fayez, and I were all three of us lodgers in the Maalouf house. They had a large house with five or six bedrooms, and they offered us a room at a reasonable rate because they needed the money, and we needed to save money, too. Even after I started working, I stayed there—I doubled with Fuad and Fayez when they were students. They stayed on after I left for Iraq. The Maaloufs were four sons and two daughters. The mother was by herself in a room, with the maid I think, and two rooms for the boys, two each in a room, and one room for the girls. The fifth room we took. They had a full-time maid; she did the washing and ironing for us. The food was good. Mrs. Maalouf, God bless her soul, had a notion of a balanced diet. The mountain food she gave us had a lot of healthy ingredients.

Life at the Maaloufs' was interesting. Rushdi's brother Fakhri, the oldest, was very dynamic; he wanted to do a number of things. He had graduated in physics with very good grades. After Charles Malek became influential, Fakhri went back and took a year or two of philosophy under Malek. He also took it into his head to start playing the violin—I was already practicing in their house—so he bought a violin and started playing it. In addition, he joined the party, and became a very fanatical party member. Then when he went to America, to Boston—he got a scholarship to do a PhD—and met a Catholic girl, and fell in love with her. He'd already been half converted to Catholicism by Malek, and his conversion was completed by this woman. He became a married priest. One day Fayez and I got letters from him, on violet paper. He wrote, "I'm writing to you on violet paper because it is the color of the heart of the Virgin. When you get this letter, go down on your knees and pray God for forgiveness for still being Protestants. If you do that, write and tell me, so that we can continue corresponding. If I don't hear from you in a month's time, I'll know that the grace of God hasn't fallen on you." It didn't. He was the only one in his family who became Catholic, though Rushdi became Maronite later in the hope of becoming a member of parliament. The only people who escaped Charles Malek's influence, and did not become Catholic, were Ghassan Tueni and Fayez.

In the floor below us in the Maaloufs' building lived this French family, the Roederers, Louis Roederer and his attractive sister Noelle, with whom I fell in love. He loved swimming and playing tennis. He came up one day—I had never said hello to him or her; I was very shy—and said, "*Voila, nous sommes des voisins*. Do you speak French?" I said, "Yes, a bit." He said, "Why don't you come down and have a cup of coffee?" He was a student in the French section of International College, and then in St. Joseph's University. There was just his mother and an aunt. His parents were divorced—his father had been a consul. His mother was Armenian. They loved it here; they had very little money, but Louis could go to St. Joseph's and study law. He had two very close friends, and he invited me to a small party, a dancing party. So I went down, and these friends were Paul and Marcel Carton—the Marcel Carton who later became ambassador of France in Kuwait and was kidnapped.[1] They also lived here because their mother was Lebanese and their father was French, and they didn't have much money. They both spoke Arabic. I started moving in this circle, a French-speaking set—dancing, mainly at the Roederers', but sometimes in other houses.

There was a very attractive brunette, Nadia Sourati, who was Lebanese. I always had mixed feelings about whether I should be in love with her or with Noelle. Paul Carton had a better approach with Noelle because of language, and she had known him for a longer time. With me she was never at ease, I don't know why. One day, she asked me, "Do you listen to Radio Liban?" I said, "No, very rarely." She said, "Listen on such-and-such a day to a song, and notice who asked for that song"—it was a request program. The song was, '*Ya hubb min gheer amal*,' 'Oh, love without hope,' and it was requested by Yvette Aoun, a friend of Noelle's. Noelle wanted me to realize that this girl was in love with me, so that I would look in her direction.

Mrs. Maalouf used to make me feel that she disapproved of my infatuation with Noelle. One day she said, "Yusif"—there was nobody else at home except she and I—"I would like to talk to you about something personal. I've noticed that you are inclined toward Noelle. She's a fine girl and good-looking, but she's a foreigner, and ultimately your culture and hers differ. You're a nationalist, there's the language barrier . . . ." I told her, "I'm not thinking of marrying; I'm just interested in her." She said, "I was hoping you would fall in love with my daughter, Kamal." Kamal was well brought up, good-looking, educated, young, but I wasn't attracted to her. I had to pull out of this quickly, so I said, "I wouldn't dream of that. I'm not good enough for her. She's a jewel; you want a really steady person who knows what he wants to do. I'm still groping for my career." She said, "Well, you should seize the opportunity because somebody else is interested." I said, "I know, he's fine, he suits her perfectly. If you searched the whole Middle East you wouldn't find somebody as suitable as Charles Abu Shaer." Later they married.

There was another daughter, Fayzeh, who was between Fakhri and Rushdi. An instructor of physics at the university, Fadel Antippa, fell in love with her and married her. Fadel had a very powerful motorcycle. I remember when I visited the Maaloufs in the mountains he would come up from Beirut on his motorcycle with Fayzeh riding behind him.

We used to go swimming as a group, at a place called al-Jamal, at the end of Ain al-Mreiseh, the little bay where you turn left to go to the American embassy. It was very cheap. Then someone said, "There's French property behind the Collège Protestant. We should make a tennis court." There was an empty space there, like a big parking area, with eucalyptus trees and cactuses. They told us, "Get permission from the consul"—because the property was French. The consul said that if we leveled the ground with a stone roller, and bought the net ourselves, and made the wire netting, we could use it as long as we realized that it wasn't our property. We did that, and we used to go and play up there. We also used to go swimming at Ramlet al-Bayda—it was dangerous, but we were young and daring and strong. Sometimes I went swimming with Sa'adeh. He was a sports lover, very muscular, handsome, and impressive. We used to go to the rocks below al-Mataam Ghalayini, and jump from a rock there. I was not much of a diver, but when he jumped I had to jump after him; I couldn't appear to be a coward.

Fayez's Escape from Death

During that period, Fayez was in hiding for almost a year; the French wanted him because of his fiery speeches. He grew a beard and put on a monk's habit. That's why his master's took longer than it should. He lived in the mountains, in the houses of party members. In 1939, when we were in Faraya, a group of friends, including Fayez, Fawzi Maalouf, and Musa Beshouti—who later became the top sportcaster on the Arabic program of the BBC—decided to walk all the way to the cedars on the mountain tops. They went over one way and came back another. They had lost so much weight by the time they got back that my poor mother insisted on them staying three days with us, to feed them up.

While Fayez was studying for his master's, and doing a lot of work for the PPS, there was an attack on him that could have been fatal. He wrote a great deal of criticism of the Arab communists because of their position on Palestine. He was riding on a motorbike behind a friend of his, who also had some high responsibility in the PPS. They were going to this person's home. On the road to Jal al-Deeb and Antalias, they were ambushed by three or four men with sticks. The men hit the rider of the motorcycle, and he fell; the motorcycle spun round, and Fayez fell off. They concentrated on beating Fayez until he was unconscious. The young man who was with Fayez was wounded too, but the blows that Fayez got were mostly to his head—in fact they thought he was dead, that's why they left him; we knew this later because there was some jubilation in their circle over his death. But the other young man, the owner of the motorcycle, managed to get a lift, and reached Jal al-Deeb, and got the word out so that people would go and help Fayez. A couple who were very loyal PPS members—I think his name was Khalil Abu Jawdeh and his wife Linda—rushed in a car, and picked Fayez up. When he woke up he was in their home; he didn't know what had happened to him, because he was still concussed. He refused to go to hospital because he was hiding from the authorities. He stayed there for two or three weeks until he recovered. It left no visible scar, and I don't think it affected his head.

With the PPS

Since his membership in the PPS was an important part of Yusif's early adult life, most of what he said about the party has been assembled in this chapter, including events that happened later, like Antoun Sa'adeh's execution in 1947, and Yusif's gradual withdrawal in the 1950s.

As I said, I first joined the PPS while I was a student at AUB.[2] Joining involved an oath, and the oath had a preamble, which said, in effect, that joining the party was like signing a contract; the contract has two parties to it; the founder of the party, Sa'adeh, and the member, or the candidate to become a member. All the power rested in the hands of the leader. He could change his mind about things, he could change the constitution—in fact he did that more than once. He changed the principles of the party, like expanding it in the early forties to include Iraq; then later he said that Cyprus was also part of 'natural Syria.' That was when he became over-confident and thought himself infallible. We were told that the party was not just principles and ideas, it was discipline; and the discipline had to be expressed through certain manifestations, like salutes, and taking semi-military training—not with arms, but lining up, and knowing how to march. Later on he had a special guard, but I wasn't part of it.

One misgiving that I had right from the beginning, and it grew over time, arose because of my background, coming from Palestine, and always thinking of Palestine as an Arab problem. But the PPS considered the salvation of Palestine as a Syrian affair—Syrian within the notion of Syrian nationalism. We had been brought up praising everything Arab— Arabic bread, Arabic music . . . . Now we had to shift and say Syrian bread, and Syrian music, and Syrian culture. For instance one of his ideas was that *al-nafs al-suriya*, the Syrian soul, contains everything needed in philosophy, thought, art, and culture. I felt embarrassed and ill at ease with this idea. But I considered that this was only a minor part of being a member of the party. The more important thing for me was that here was an organized party with a large membership, yet it was still secret, which meant that it was well-organized and well-disciplined. Sa'adeh believed that we should look into whatever capabilities we have as a nation and that individually each of us has to look inside and mobilize all his capabilities, rather than seek aid from a foreign country. This was totally the contrary of what people accused Sa'adeh of doing, of hoping to get help from the Germans. They accused him of being a fascist, following the Nazi line, saluting with the right arm bent while his followers said, "*Yahya al-za'eem*! [Long live the leader!]." He also spoke of himself in the third person as 'the leader' the way Hitler did. I felt embarrassed about these things. Whenever we were in a group, for example if we were at a lecture, and the leader came in, we had to stand up and salute him. I remember that my arm could never make the salute properly; it was always a little bit lower than it should be. I didn't enjoy these manifestations.

Before becoming a member of the PPS, we spent months listening to lectures, and were made to read intensively about Syrian history, particularly about why Syrian nationalism is right, how 'natural Syria' is an entity in itself, and how that is substantiated by its history—past history and modern history—and by its geography. Sa'adeh always wanted us to realize that our history did not begin in 672, when Islam and the Arabs came, but that it went back to Biblical days and before. He was very knowledgeable about history; he knew about the excavations that revealed Syrian culture, Syrian laws, and Syrian irrigation works, things that show there was something to be proud of, and that Syria could constitute an entity in itself. It should cooperate with other Arab entities like Egypt, but as a separate nation. For Sa'adeh there was no Arab nationalism. I remember once Zurayk saying to him that Arab nationalism is something in the making, and Sa'adeh replying sarcastically, "Isn't something that's already there, that has been there for many centuries, more credible than something 'in the making,' which may or may not materialize?"

Intellectually Sa'adeh was very capable, powerful, and articulate; his thoughts were well organized, the points came crystal clear from him, and the relationship between the points, the causality, was very clear. Though he was self-educated, he was so well read that he could argue with Charles Malek on philosophy, quoting one source after another, and do the same thing with Zurayk.[3] He knew more languages than they did; he could quote from German and Russian. His father was a doctor and an intellectual, well known in the region. He too emphasized Syrian nationalism. He had produced an English–Arabic dictionary that is still considered one of the best— certainly the best dictionary produced by one person. Sa'adeh the father had gone to South America when Antoun was about fifteen years old. He stayed many years outside the region, but traveled a lot, and spent the time after finishing school until he was thirty, when he emerged in Lebanon, in the wilderness as it were, like Christ, studying, reading, and thinking.

From what origins and sources did he put his ideas together and form the party? I think the ideas were his essentially, though influenced by his father, and by his readings about Syria, the role of Syria in history, and its cultural history. But as far as the party's organization is concerned, he must have been influenced by the phalangists and the Nazis— the idea of discipline and salutes and the leader business—that must have been from the Nazis. But in those many sessions, before I joined the party and all through until 1939 when I left Beirut, never once did I feel that Sa'adeh was defeated in the arguments that he had with Zurayk, Charles Malek, Fuad Mufarrej, or George Hakim. Sa'adeh always stood his ground; I never felt that he was defeated by them. At most they would reach a position where neither party would give in to the other. But it always ended smoothly; there was no ill feeling.

George Hakim, in the meantime, was converted, and joined the party, representing a radical wing within it. George thought that there could be a marriage between his socialist ideas and the party's ideas on nationalism and organization, since Sa'adeh himself attached a great deal of importance to economics and to labor. But I think Sa'adeh was not permissive in his attitude to unionization. Labor would not have had a free hand with him; it would be allowed to organize, but there would always be control because of his belief in a strong state that had to have important socioeconomic functions. By insisting that the state should provide education and social security for everyone, he felt that he could justify a strong state.

The party intended to come into the open at a certain moment. It planned to ask for a license when it had reached a certain size. When you applied for a licence you had to say, for example, that you had six members who want to form a party. Sa'adeh wanted to say that we had six thousand who wanted to form a party and to appear in strength rather than to beg for a license. But it didn't work that way; information about the party was passed on to the French before it reached that point. The source of the leak was known later. This took place just before Sa'adeh's arrest. After the party came into the open, after the prison sentences, there were many clashes. The final clash was the one that ended in Sa'adeh declaring a revolt against the government. But that was after independence. The Kata'eb Party were used by the government as a 'provocateur'—first by the French government, then by the independent government. This was a period of very strong activity for the PPS.

I used to write for the party paper under a pseudonym—'Yezid Jawahiri.' 'Yezid' means 'may he add' in Arabic, and 'Yusif' has the same meaning in Hebrew. 'Sayigh' means goldsmith, 'Jawahiri' means jeweler. I thought that it was a nice way of making the name; it was close, yet people would not guess it because few people know that 'Yezid' and 'Yusif' have the same meaning. I used to prepare position papers on Palestine. Later on I began to write on economic matters, especially after I got my BA, during the year I spent here in 1938–39. I worked on economics—especially a series of articles on labor, and what lines of production the Syrian national movement should encourage, and how it should direct the economy—that was the kind of thing that the party was preaching.

Fayez's Resignation–Expulsion from the PPS

Fayez's involvement with the party ended in 1947, when he went to America to study for his PhD. There's a story to tell about how he managed to go to America. He was sent by the party to make a tour in Africa, essentially of Ghana. There were a number of party members there, and he spent a few weeks lecturing in one place and another, and collected a large sum of money for the party. A very rich member, who knew that Fayez wanted to go to America to study if he had the money, said to him, "Don't worry, I'll finance this trip." I think he put at his disposal five hundred or six hundred sterling for him personally, aside from his contribution to the party. It wasn't a loan that this rich Lebanese offered Fayez; it was a gift. He was a millionaire, and Fayez was brilliant, and this man loved his speeches.

After the visit to Africa, Fayez came back to Beirut. By then Sa'adeh was becoming quite eccentric and over-confident in himself. For instance, he issued a directive, almost a decree, that the party should adopt a philosophy he called *al-madrahiya*. What was *al-madrahiya*? It was a play on words—*maddiya ruhiya*—materialism-spiritualism—an Irish stew of philosophy. By then Fayez had had enough. The leader had spent the war in South America, for fear of being arrested if he stayed in the region. In his absence, Fayez had kept the party alive, and resisted those who were trying to move it toward becoming a Lebanese party. Fayez fought that, and Sa'adeh was happy that Fayez had stood his ground and resisted them. But Fayez felt uneasy about adding Iraq and Cyprus to the territorial claims of 'natural Syria.' Sa'adeh said that the two together, Iraq and Syria, should be called 'Suraq,' again a play on words. So Fayez called for a meeting in which he took the absolutely unusual step of contradicting the party leader. It was a meeting of the *umada* [plural of *amid*], the leadership, the council of the party. He made a long presentation of schools of thought in philosophy, and asked where would *al-madrahiya* fit? You can't just create a school of thought by decree. The leader's intention was that we must neither adopt materialism nor spiritualism but try to make a combination of the two. But his way of approaching the problem was very superficial.

Then Fayez wrote an article on the subject, and the leader got mad with anger. There were articles being published by party people, all praising the concept of *madrahiya*. Fayez's critique was to say, "Wait a minute, let's analyze this concept and see what content it has." When he realized that he was going to be kicked out of the party, he decided to leave before that happened. He wrote a letter of resignation listing his reasons and disagreements— all of an intellectual nature. The party then published a dismissal of Fayez in terms like "this conceited fellow whose only intellectual capability is what stuck to him of the leader's brilliance." When Fayez pulled out of the party, the leader said, "You don't pull out of this party, you are expelled." He expelled him, and there was a 'cause célèbre.'

When they published this, Fayez felt that it was his right to defend himself. He wrote a couple of booklets on why he had left, and challenged the leader on ideological and philosophical grounds. He said that he had not been kicked out but had resigned. Right after that he went to the United States together with Hisham Sharabi.[4] Hisham was still a member of the party and loyal. He and Fayez kept their friendship for the duration of their journey together, but then there was a froideur between them. Their relationship only improved in the late 1970s.

I stayed hanging on. I didn't want people to think that I would leave because my brother left, in 'tribal' fashion. But I began to distance myself from the party, partly because of the clash between Fayez and Sa'adeh, partly because the position of the party toward Arab nationalism was to my mind extreme. I felt that though Syria was great in the past, new realities were different. Now there was an Arab League, why not move and help the maturing of Arab nationalist ideas?

I stayed on, but I began to find more and more that I couldn't belong. First of all, I always felt embarrassed in meetings when I had to stand up like a soldier and do the salute of the party. When Sa'adeh came into a meeting, he would be ushered in with a salute: *"Hadara al-za'eem! Yahya al-za'eem!"* and we'd have to say, *"Yahya! Yahya al-za'eem! Yahya! Yahya! Yahya! Yibni al-hayah li Suriya! Wa huwa qa'idna! Yahya al-za'eem, yahya, yahya* . . . ."[5] I used to shrink inside my clothes. That was before I went to Palestine. Later I used to come continuously from Palestine to Lebanon. Then there was a revolt by the party [against the Lebanese government], and Sa'adeh was arrested.[6]

Sa'adeh's Execution

When Sa'adeh returned to Lebanon in March 1947, by plane, from Argentina, his arrival drew an enormous crowd. We came from Jerusalem—Fareed Ataya, George Salameh, and I—to be there at the airport, to wait with the others. When we got there, there were tens of thousands of people. The news had spread that Sa'adeh was returning. The whole of Lebanon was electrified. When word reached the government that thousands of people were waiting there, hours before the arrival of the plane, two ministers and some Sûreté officials went up in a small plane. They circled around the airport, and saw the tens of thousands of people. The government got panicky. They feared a coup, later on if not on the spot, because of so much popularity.

From that moment they began to plan to get rid of him. They arranged with the Phalange for the attack on the press where the party's paper was printed. Then the government arrested party people, pretending that they had started the attack on the Phalange [Kata'eb]. Sa'adeh decided that the time had come. He declared a revolt, and went to the mountains, to the Dhour al-Choueir area, in upper Matn. Hundreds of PPS people took up arms. The government began to narrow the circle around him. Husni al-Za'im in Syria had just staged his coup.[7] He sent word to Sa'adeh that he would give him refuge. Sa'adeh went there, and Husni Za'im offered him his personal revolver as a token of friendship.

Then one day Husni Za'im invited Sa'adeh to a meeting. As he sat with him in his office, from behind the curtains there emerged three or four officers of the Lebanese Sûreté, with the director of the Sûreté, the emir Fareed Chehab. Of course Sa'adeh understood that it was a trap. Husni Za'im said, "*Baseeta*, go with them, *dabbir halak ma'hum.* [It's okay, go with them, work something out with them]." So Sa'adeh took out the revolver Za'im had given him, and gave it back, saying, "I'm returning the revolver to you so that you will be able to face yourself the next time you look in the mirror." He went with the Sûreté. He was tried, and sentenced. His appeal was refused, his papers went to the prime minister, who approved the death sentence, and he was executed—all within twenty-four hours, though he had a team of top-notch lawyers representing him. The head of the team was Hamid Franjieh, the brother of Suleiman, helped by Habib Abu Shahla and Emile Lahoud, all of them Maronite lawyers, well known and well respected. But they couldn't do anything; the decision had been taken to get rid of him. They wouldn't even let his wife and three daughters say goodbye to him. They took him to execution, along with twelve others who were caught in the fighting. The awful thing was that, since in Lebanon everything is confessional, they selected those to be executed to represent every sect, though many more were sentenced to death. They were executed by shooting.

I was in Jordan when this happened. I went there to buy a car, a Vauxhall, because I could get it at a reduced price from the Tannous company, and on installment. During my absence in Jordan, Sa'adeh was sentenced to death and executed. I got word from my family saying, "Don't be in a hurry to return"—because they were going around arresting people. They came and arrested my cousin Elias from our house, and held him until they found he had no connection with the PPS. My family thought that if Elias who had no connection was taken for questioning—in fact he might have slept one night in detention— then surely I would be in trouble. I spent a month and a half in Amman. That was in 1949.

When I got back to Lebanon I found that the party was in trouble. First of all, many people had gone to prison. Confusion and divisions set in because now that Sa'adeh was dead, there was rivalry over who would be head of the party—the very fundamentalist George Abdel Massih or Na'mi Tabet, who, in the absence of Sa'adeh in Brazil after the war, took a permit for the party and changed its name from 'al-Hizb al-Suri al-Qawmi' [Syrian National Party] to 'al-Hizb al-Qawmi al-Ijtima'i' [National Social Party]. Even within the mainstream that Na'meh Tabet led there were rivalries. There was somebody from the family of Kaddoura, and somebody from the family of Fakhouri, Jraij . . . They were not as intelligent and present-able as Na'meh Tabet, who was a cousin of Zelfa Chamoun, and a very clever, articulate person. But I disliked the whole atmosphere.

Many years later, after I was released from prisoner-of-war camp, and came to Lebanon to work, I was drawn again into party activity through my appointment to head a team to prepare an economic plan or blueprint, setting out what the party's position would be with regard to labor, investment, distribution of income, property—issues involved in ideologies like socialism and capitalism. They still con-sidered me a member. I remember saying, "But I'm not a practicing member"—I'd only lapsed, I hadn't resigned. They said, "Never mind. You might become one at the end of this exercise." I admit that this work was rather primitive, because my economics was still undeveloped; I hadn't read much about economic systems, or on controversies between socialism and capitalism. I was still trying to see if the two couldn't be reconciled in some way. Two people helped me, Bahjat Khawli and Fuad Badr—Bahjat was my classmate in busi-ness administration. Sa'adeh had already written a series of thirty articles on what the economy should be like. The 'old guard' like George Abdel Massih, who by then was chairman of the party, felt there was no need for anything to be done except put what Sa'adeh had said into some detail. Economics wasn't Sa'adeh's field but he was widely read; he had read Marxist literature and works on capitalism. I remember him citing Sombert, Tawney, and Weber. He had a fan-tastic memory. By then the head of the party was Abdel Massih, who was a literalist who believed in every word that the leader said—not one comma should be changed. He felt that I was almost blasphe-mous in the program we drafted—where was the control of the labor unions? Where was 'dirigisme'? He said, "We cannot accept this; it sounds like communism." Later, when I got the scholarship to go to America to do my doctorate, word came to me that Abdel Massih said, "Maybe after getting a doctorate in economics, Yusif Sayigh will begin to be able to understand Sa'adeh's economics."

I began to feel more and more out of place. I left, but not with a bang like Fayez. It was an accumulation. It started when I began to feel that the leader was going mad. After he was executed, the party leaders who came after him became even more determined to preserve the philosophy that he invented and to propagate it, without having the intellectual capability that he had. So what was I staying for? I just passed it on verbally that I didn't want to attend meetings any more. I told people to consider me out of the party. In this way my relations with party people remained passable; they respected me because I didn't make a big issue, I didn't throw mud at them.

By 1956 Abdel Nasser had emerged. It was the dividing line. I began to feel that no activity could interest me unless it was pan-Arab and had Palestine in it. Concern with Palestine had to be there because I was getting more and more convinced that we could not liberate Palestine alone. Throughout the fifties the main issue for the Palestinians was where was the leadership of the Arab world going to be? Egypt or Syria? Usually people decided on the basis of who was the leader in country Y or Z. It was all personalized. For example, when Nasser emerged, everyone said Egypt is [the leader]. People rationalized it; they said it's the largest [Arab] country. Syria always used to be called the heart of the Arab world, but the many coups showed that it was not stable.[8] Shishakli was promising when his turn came to lead a coup, but then he was dethroned. The Ba'th came, and the Ba'th had very hostile relations with the Arab National Movement, because it was more aligned with Nasser, and the Ba'th were competitors. The PPS was out of that altogether because it was not Arab nationalist. For me that whole period was one of political confusion in the Arab world. I just hibernated until Nasser came in 1956. Then I began to be more involved, but intellectually at first, in writings and lectures. Then I was away in America for a year and a half for my graduate work, and when I came back I was very busy with the university, as director of the Economic Research Institute and chairman of the department. And I had my research project with

Rockefeller. And after that I went to America again for two years. So this period was filled with other things; I had a family, yes, that depoliticized me. Then I was drawn back into politics, after becoming a member of the [Palestine] National Council.

During that period Kamal Sha'er invited me to dinner at his house to meet Michel Aflaq.⁹ That evening stretched till three in the morning. Knowing that I was an economist, Aflaq said, "We need someone like you with us, because all we have are very broad general ideas, we don't have an economic system around our economic ideas. We are socialists, our name is socialist, but we don't have socialism. Why don't you join us, and design what you think Arab socialism should be? You would be in charge of that." I said, "You're asking me to design a system, and on the basis of that system I will be eligible to be part of the leadership? This is really like nepotism. As if I'm cutting a suit for myself. Anyway I don't think I can do that—a system initially designed by Karl Marx can't be redesigned by an Arab and called Arab Socialism." Though I did write an article called "Arab Socialism" in which I tried to humanize the basic ideas of socialism to avoid the mistakes of totalitarianism and the Soviet Union. It was published in the late fifties, I think, in *Abhath*, a journal that Fuad Sarrouf edited.

Iraq: "Room for Hundreds of Teachers"

I didn't start another job straightaway. The summer was coming, so I waited for the family to come, and went up with them to Faraya. That was the summer of 1939. While we were in Faraya, in September, the Second World War was declared.

My parents weren't upset about my job. They said, "If you want to be an accountant, come and be an accountant in Palestine, the salaries are much higher there." But I already had a job by the time the family came. Abdul Karim Dandasheh, a classmate from Syria who took political science, and later became a member of parliament, came with Rushdi Maalouf, and told us that in Iraq there was room for hundreds of teachers; they had a very dynamic program of education, and wanted AUB graduates. The salaries they were offering were very good—eighteen Iraqi dinars a month for someone with a BA, but for me and Rushdi, "since you two rascals have distinction, it's twenty-one dinars." That was much better than Beirut, and anyway I was game to try something else.

He gave us the address of the man who was the principal of the school, a Lebanese from Shoueifat, someone from the Sa'b family. We contacted him, and he welcomed us, and immediately got us confirmation from the head of the mission. It was a private institution, like the Maqasid, called al-Tafayud al-Ahliya. They had several schools in Iraq. They sent us a letter of appointment to teach in Tikrit. Rushdi too, but Rushdi pulled out. So I had a job to start in the autumn.

7

Teacher in Iraq, 1939–40

At the end of the summer of 1939 I started this job in Iraq teaching in a private school. I went there by Nairn bus.¹ I reached Baghdad, and found the headquarters of the school administration, and got my first shock. My salary was not going to be twenty-one dinars a month, but only eighteen. The three dinars' difference they promised me in Beirut because I graduated with distinction was simply canceled. I tried to fight it but they said, "Nothing doing. You can return if you wish"—but of course I didn't want to do that. I went by train to Tikrit.²

The head of the school, a Lebanese from Shoueifat, Maarouf Saab, had made all the arrangements for me in Tikrit. He found me a two-story house, and somebody to cook for me, whose wife would do my washing and ironing. When I first got there, I spent a night or two at the house of the principal, because my house had no furniture. One of the only two Jews in Tikrit was a shopkeeper—I think his name was Victor. He got me basic things that I needed for the kitchen, and a few chairs, and a mattress. He brought me a bed from Baghdad a week or two later, and spoons and knives. I think he found a couple of forks too.

Tikrit was a very small place. Its streets and roads were not asphalted. When they caught a big fish from the river, the fisherman would take it to the square, right down from my house—I saw this happening many times, until I decided not to look—they'd just throw it on the earth, and bring a huge knife, a *satora*, like a meat hacker, and cut it in pieces. People would buy the fish by the piece; nobody would buy it all, except maybe Mawloud Basha Mukhlas, who used to be a speaker of parliament, a famous figure from Tikrit. He would buy one or two fish because he always had guests. But ordinary folk bought chunks of fish. Every time they made a cut, hundreds of flies rose from the fish. I decided almost from the first day that I was not going to spend another year in Iraq. I missed Beirut, I missed my family very much; they were so far away. And the place was terribly primitive. I would sit there and compare it with Tiberias, or even al-Bassa.

Another thing I noticed was that women in their black robes all the way down to the soles of their feet would suddenly squat in the middle of the square, or anywhere, and then walk away leaving a little black area of wet. Only urine, not more than that—but to do it like animals, without being embarrassed! I haven't seen that anywhere else in the Arab world. When they were outside the house, there was nowhere they could go. The sun looked after it.

I was given history and geography courses to teach. It was a boys' school, up to the end of the intermediate level, but not to the baccalaureate or matric. It was called *mutawassita*. I was also asked to teach algebra and geometry. I wasn't happy about that because I hadn't taken these subjects in university, only in high school. Now I had to teach high-school algebra and geometry in Arabic. This meant I had to study harder than the students, to stay a little ahead of them. I didn't teach English because English was the territory of Maarouf Saab, the head of the school.

Iraq then was in a political fever of nationalism and regeneration. It was just before the Rashid Ali Gailani uprising.[3] The teachers were given officer rank, and had to wear military uniforms. I had three pips as a captain, and if I passed a soldier or a policeman they saluted me; and I had to salute if I passed someone of higher rank. We had to wear this Iraqi *sidara* or *sidra*, a kind of cap.

Social life was rather restricted. There was the shopkeeper, who was very amusing and very sociable. Though he was a Jew, every house was open to him—probably because he was a Jew. The whole town was Sunni except for two or three families. One of the teachers in our school was Shi'i. There was the government doctor, who was also a Jew. In our circle of teachers, we had two Iraqi teachers; one taught religion and Arabic language and grammar, and the other taught arithmetic. This one was the Shi'i. We teachers would meet alternately, sometimes in my house, sometimes in Haseeb's house, sometimes in Maarouf's house. But we were never invited to the houses of the Iraqis. They were embarrassed to invite us to their houses and not have their women appear. Maybe once we were invited to a meal at Salah's, the Shi'i teacher. There were no women visible.

One day Salah didn't come to class. The next day when he came, I said, "You didn't come yesterday. I hope everything is all right?" He said, "Well, not really. *Ajallak hurmti kanat mareeda.*"[4] *Ajallak* is a word we use meaning 'may your dignity be kept.' If you want to mention a donkey you say "*ajallak al-himar.*" They used it for their wives. It was like saying, "Excuse me for mentioning it."

A month later I got a letter saying that my mother was ill, she had had a heart attack. I was very upset, and it must have showed on my face. They said, "What's the matter?" I spoke openly, I said, "*Immi mareeda* [My mother is ill]." They all just bent their heads without saying anything. Later I told Maarouf Saab about this. He said, "Well, it was sympathy, but it was also embarrassment because you said '*immi.*'" As if saying "my mother," who is a female, is this and that. So social life consisted of evenings at the houses of the non-Iraqi teachers. Sometimes we would go to the coffee shop, and listen to the news there. It had a radio that ran on batteries; there was no electricity. There were two coffee shops in Tikrit. The bigger one had a radio and lux lamps; we'd sit there and drink coffee or tea. Some nights I would just spend at home reading by lux light. I had brought with me a few books from Beirut—I had been advised to do so—and every time I went to Baghdad I would buy a few Arabic books. It wasn't until much later that I found a bookshop that had some English books. In the daytime we often went to Victor's shop, and sat there in the afternoons.

The only family that opened its doors to us, and gave us a lot of hospitality, was the mayor's family. They had several boys, two of whom were my students, both very intelligent and pleasant. For two or three years after I left Iraq they kept on sending me presents, to Palestine. A few years ago, on one of my trips to Iraq, I heard one of these former students mentioned, so I made inquiries, and he turned out to have been an assistant professor of economics in the Baghdad university, but had died through some illness. I made more inquiries, and found the address of the family, and went and visited them. They had moved to Baghdad. The father was still alive, a very old man, and two of the children were there. They gave me a lovely meal. This family was 'home away from home' for us in Tikrit; they invited us very frequently. We didn't see the women, but we found a table full of lovely dishes, and the father was a very fine person. His education was limited, but he was really sensitive and honest, very genuine. You felt it was genuine hospitality, wanting to help these foreigners.

Tikrit was where so many Ba'th party leaders came from, but I didn't teach any of them. Ahmad Hassan al-Bakr's age group would have made him one of my students, but the others were too young. Saddam Hussein would have been a baby.

My awareness of differences between Shi'is and Sunnis came from that period spent in Iraq. The evenings we spent in different houses—except in my house—were spent in gambling. I didn't gamble; I just watched the others. The two most serious gamblers were Haseeb Abdullah, a Shi'i from south Lebanon, and Salah, the Iraqi Shi'i. There were also two teachers from the government school who used to come and play with us. One evening there was an argument between Haseeb and Salah about the game, and the argument became very hot. As we left the house where we were playing to go home—the game had ended—Haseeb hissed to Salah, "'Istihi 'ala halak'—shame on you—you and I are the only Shi'is here, and you make a scene?" Salah answered crudely, "I don't care two hoots if all the Sunnis know about our quarrel." That's when I began to find out more about this division in Iraq, through asking questions. The animosity didn't appear on the surface; it was hidden, it was an undercurrent.

We used to drink arrack with the gambling—Iraqi arrack and beer. I wasn't a connoisseur then, but I remember noticing that it was good beer. I went to the cinema once or twice when I was in Baghdad. There was no cinema in Tikrit, of course, because there was no electricity. Once I went to Samara to see the winding minaret, but never to Kurdistan. I went up by train to Suleimaniyeh and Mosul years later with Hikmat Nabulsi. He came with me to help me with some research.

Food!—the food was terrible. The only thing that the husband and wife knew how to make was *yakhneh* [stew]. By the time it reached me it was cold; he carried it from his house, next door to mine, in *tanjara*s [saucepans]—I never saw his wife. What I couldn't eat, he would take and eat himself—in fact I was feeding two families. The things I wanted to eat—the meat I could tolerate—he didn't know how to cook. They could do kebabs but they were very rich and fatty. I couldn't eat fish every day so chicken was something I depended on. At least once a week I had a meal at Maarouf Saab's house.

One day I made the serious mistake of checking on the cleanliness of the knife, fork, and spoon. I found they were smeared. I told Uhayyeb—that was the cook's name—"Look!" He said, "*Baseeta*," lifted his robe, and rubbed the knife, fork, and spoon on the inside of it. I had seen that robe on him for two weeks. I said, "The other times things came clean. How did you clean them?" He said, "This way, with cloth. Cloth is very good for cleaning." I said, "From now on you clean them with soap, in front of me."

There was this sheikh who first visited me in Ramadan, Sheikh Abdul Karim. The first or second day of Ramadan, somebody knocked at the door. Uhayyeb went out, and said, "Sheikh Abdul

Karim." I said, "*Ahla wa sahla, tfaddal* [Welcome, please come in]." I was having my lunch, it was an odd time to visit. I didn't invite him to share my lunch, because I thought it would be an insult to him. Certainly a sheikh, an Iraqi sheikh, must be fasting. So we talked at length, and then he left. The next day the same thing, and the same response from me. The third day he came, but this time I was prepared for him because before the lunch break I had told Maarouf Saab about these visits, "How come I have been here for two or three months, and the first time that Sheikh Abdul Karim visits me is now? He's coming at lunchtime, it's very embarrassing. I can't invite him to lunch because for sure he's fasting." He said, "For sure he's not fasting, that's why he's coming to you. When will you remember your politeness and say, '*Tfaddal sharikna* [Please share (lunch)]'?" I said, "How about Uhayyeb?" He said, "I think Uhayyeb realizes why the sheikh is there." So from that day Sheikh Abdul Karim came to me every second or third day. He would go one day to the Maaroufs, and one day to Haseeb, and one day to me. The first time I invited him, he said, "*Akheeran! Khallasna! Emta rah tgool hal kilmeh* [At last! Let's finish with it. When are you going to say this word]?"

Being very bored, I seized every opportunity to go to Baghdad. This cost money but every now and then I had to go beyond the four-dinar budget I had set myself—four dinars out of my eighteen dinars a month. The rest I sent to my family. But when there was a month ahead with a holiday, I kept a couple of dinars more, as a reserve to be able to go to Baghdad. The train cost hardly anything, and the hotels and food were very cheap. I could live a whole month on four dinars.

I liked Baghdad; it was a city. I had a couple of friends there. One of them had been with me in high school, Sa'id Abu Ulwan; he also went there to teach. The other was Abdul Karim Dandasheh, a Syrian, also a teacher. I didn't know any Iraqis then. There was no home I could go to in Baghdad. When I went there I stayed in a very simple hotel. I never spent long there, just two or three days. But I went every time there was a holiday like Ramadan, or Eid al-Adha, or Christmas, because there was nothing to do in Tikrit. I'd take the train from Samara.

One day I felt so miserable—I wanted badly to talk to a woman. I hadn't done that at all—except for Maarouf Saab's wife, and Haseeb Abdullah's wife, after he married and his wife joined him. He married her by proxy (*'aqd kitab*). She was his first cousin, a very good-looking young woman; you could tell from the first look that she was going to be promiscuous. Given the slightest encouragement she would have let me, or anybody, sleep with her, if the opportunity arose. She didn't hide herself. Haseeb had his eye on the wife of the principal, a petite Druze, rather lively and amusing. These were the only two women I could even say hello to. In Baghdad I met a friend as I was leaving the train, somebody who had been with me in university. I asked him, "What can I do?! I want to dance." I couldn't afford a cabaret. He said, "The only thing I can suggest is a dancing school. You can go and pretend to join a class. Dance with the wife of the owner of the school—they are both foreigners."

It was a big house, with a second floor upstairs that had an internal balcony around it. The man would go up frequently and look at the people who were dancing below. I headed straight for his wife and said, "Will you dance with me? I know some dances, but in others I'd like to improve." Without losing any time I tightened my grip on her. Two or three dances like that, then suddenly the husband came down, and said, "Now you dance with me!" Not at all what I wanted! I danced one dance with him and said, "If you are going to insist, I won't dance any more, I won't come again, I don't feel natural." He was punishing me; he saw me from up there holding on a bit too tight.

We went around to a few restaurants and cafés. We spent two days, three days there, doing nothing really but just changing the atmosphere. I swam in the river, both in Baghdad and in Tikrit. I thought myself a powerful swimmer; I swam with the flow for a hundred meters, and I did it in no time. When I decided to go back to my clothes, I realized how difficult it was, swimming against the current. I could do it, but I got really tired.

The climate was very harsh—I suffered from the cold more than the heat, possibly because I was used to Tiberias's heat. The cold was terrible because the uniform that I had was lightweight. That's one of the reasons I decided not to spend another year there—I didn't have a thick winter uniform. When we got there it was still very hot so we wore summer uniforms, just cotton khaki. I stayed in that—not only me, everybody else around me. Of course I could put on a coat, and luckily I had a coat that was camel hair, so it went with the uniform— we were supposed to wear army clothing, but I didn't want to buy a winter army overcoat. Between one class and another, I used to dash outside to stand for five minutes in the sun, just to get some warmth, to be able to talk without my teeth chattering. We had no heating, absolutely nothing. I had a simple charcoal fire in my house.

One holiday I stayed in Tikrit and invited Sa'id Abu Ulwan to stay with me. We had fun; we talked a great deal. We talked about things we should be doing instead of being there. He was already tuned to the idea of converting to Christianity. He was a Druze who became a monk, and lived in Paris, and died there. He read a great deal of good, solid literature, like Russian literature, so we had a lot to talk about. He spent two days with me and then went back—it was a nice change. He was a Druze like Maarouf Saab, so they liked him.

Iraqi politics at that time was very nationalistic; it was all one line—Arab nationalism.[5] And there was a military attitude to things— everybody was a soldier, every teacher was an officer, and the pupils wore uniforms as if they were recruits. I don't know if this was due to the influence of al-Madfa'i or al-Askari, who had all been officers in the army.[6] It must have been somebody who was a great believer in discipline, the outer appearance of discipline. It could have been the Ottoman influence. All the older people liked it. But also it was the attitude of those times, 1939–1940, only a year after Ghazi's death.[7] He was greatly loved and admired because of his anti-British feeling.

Iraqi politics was a change from what I was used to in Beirut, at least from Ras Beirut, which was a mixture of Lebanese nationalism, Syrian nationalism, and Arab nationalism. In Beirut there was room for different lines of thought, whereas in Iraq, I don't think anybody would have dared to speak of Kurdish nationalism then, or any nationalism other than Arab nationalism. It was all around one, and in the newspapers. But I didn't like the expression of it that I had to live through, namely wearing a uniform. It was just putting on a uniform; there was no indoctrination with it, no training, no philosophy. I read the papers almost every day, but they were very poor. Even now they are very poor. Of course I heard a lot about Iraqi politics during those evenings when we went to the house of the mayor.

Another person who was intelligent, and had a BA from AUB, was the district officer, the *kaymakam*. He was there most of the year that I spent there, and we often met in one of our houses, or in the coffee shop. We talked politics—what the British were doing, our anger at Great Power politics. Because I was Palestinian, they often asked me about the Zionists. They were very pro-Palestinian. I was the only Palestinian there. This *kaymakam* turned out to be the brother of somebody I had known at AUB, who had subsequently gone to the United States to finish his studies, and died there in a car accident. This immediately established a rapport with him, that I had known his brother.

By the spring I had heard about my mother's illness, and I decided definitely not to renew my contract. When I was engaged, we were told that for every nine months of teaching we would have a paid summer holiday. But when I notified the head administrator of the Tafayud al-Ahliya in Baghdad that I was not going back to the school for a second year, he refused to pay my summer salary. I told him that this was contrary to the contract. He said, "We don't say in the contract that if you don't come back you won't receive a summer salary because we assume that people know." I said, "But I didn't know, you ought to have told me. Supposing I change my mind, and come back?" He said, "No, you are only saying this to fool me. And then you won't show up." In Beirut I went to the consulate—there was no embassy then—and complained. I said, "If I don't get my salary, I'm going to write articles warning other teachers who might want to go to Iraq." Ultimately I got half the salary that they owed me. Later, I got a letter from the principal with a postal order—I had left my bed, and sheets, and blankets—they sold them and sent me the few dinars they fetched. They sold them to the same shopkeeper who had sold them to me.

8

Life in Tiberias as an Adult, 1940–44

My association with Tiberias stretched from the first day we went there, the first time I ever saw it, January 1, 1930, all the way to 1948. But during this period I sometimes stayed weeks or months, and sometimes I made very brief stays.

Political events in Tiberias as far as I remember were minimal. There wasn't a debating or cultural club like there was in Jaffa for instance, where educated people met and discussed politics and resistance. Of course Tiberias took part in the strike and rebellion, from 1936 to 1939—even Tawfiq wore a tarboosh to school. Taking part meant not going to Jewish shops, or having economic dealings with them—social dealings were minimal anyway. Our family was not involved except that we boycotted like the others. I remember feeling a tension with the Scots Mission hospital people. They realized that my father had all these sons who were wearing tarbooshes. This was a sign of support for the rebellion. My father had always worn a tarboosh anyway. Older people put on *keffiyyeh*s. My brothers didn't want to wear the *keffiyyeh* and *i'qal*[1] so when Fuad and Fayez came to Tiberias from Safad, they would wear the tarboosh. It was to differentiate Arabs. If you went bareheaded you would be like the Jews. It was a question of identity. If somebody wanted to shoot at a Jew, he would not shoot at you if you were wearing a tarboosh. But also it meant exposure, because the Jews would know whom to shoot at.

Most political activity in Tiberias was just talk. But sometime around 1937, when I was in university, Antoun Sa'adeh suddenly appeared in Tiberias. He came and stayed with us for a few days. I was already in the PPS; that's why he came. We were thrilled to receive him. My parents had heard a great deal about him—we would host him again when we spent the summer in Ain Qabu; he came and stayed with us there. When he came to Tiberias I invited a few friends, including Khalil Tabari, to meet him. He came because he was again in a clash with the authorities. The French first arrested him in 1936, so it must have been soon after he was released from prison that he came. He traveled for a few months to Lebanon and Palestine, and I think to Transjordan, to convert people to the cause, or to get away from the French.

A political activity worth noting in Tiberias was that a lawyer from the Tabari family, and Sidqi Tabari himself, were very active in trying to block the sale of Arab land to Jews. There wasn't much of this in Tiberias; it was more in the village area around. Sidqi came into this matter through the bank that he managed—it was called the Arab National Bank. It had been instrumental in building up a fund, not very large, for the purchase of threatened lands. They would pay something to people who were about to sell their land because of shortage of liquidity. This was an activity which Sidqi and other Tabaris were active in. They saved land in Mkhaybeh, on the road to Himmeh, and around Samakh.

Of course the Jewish community in Tiberias was aware of this activity. If there was a foreclosure that threatened the land, a lawyer would be paid to go to court to defend it. Sidqi was a banker, so they knew that the money was obtained through him. But they didn't attack any of the Tabaris, because this would have had ramifications beyond Tiberias. Sidqi was very influential with the Arab Higher Committee, and had relations in Nazareth, and in Safad and Jerusalem, so it would have meant a larger confrontation.

I was away in Beirut during the years 1936–39, so I don't really know if there was support action for the *mujahideen* [freedom fighters] in Tiberias. There must have been. But I think that not much happened in Tiberias because Arabs were a minority there. The Jews were physically above us, so just by rolling rocks down the hill they would have killed many. The rebellion was happening in other areas, in the Nablus mountains, in the Hebron mountains, and areas of Galilee where Palestinians were concentrated. I think there were some *mujahideen* from Tiberias. There were rumors that one or two Tabaris took part, but no one really knew. Certainly the professionals, the bourgeoisie of Tiberias, were not involved. I think the son of a barber I knew got wounded. Of course I knew what was happening, I read about it, but it was distant. We were electrified by the strike, and by the harshness of the British reaction—that used to shock me more than Zionist actions. I expected the Zionists to act that way, but somehow I thought that a mandate power would be more neutral, rather than side totally with the Zionists.

Soon after the end of the Second World War, when tension was rising between Arabs and Jews, there was an operation carried out by a driver from the American consulate. He used to take parcels—books, literature—from the consulate to the Jewish Agency. This driver took his pickup—he was known to the guards after weeks and weeks of doing this—and drove it into the yard of the Jewish Agency. There were pillars under the first floor; the driver put the pickup between the pillars, and walked away after saying to the guards, "I'm just going to get a sandwich." A few minutes later the car exploded. This was in Jerusalem. The driver disappeared, but he reappeared a year or two later as the driver of Dr. Hart in Tiberias. Nobody knew except me. I came to know it, because we became friends. Another person who is dead now so I can tell his story, Gaby Deeb, also did something very daring. Through collusion he managed to get an armored police car, drive it into Ben Yahooda Street in Jerusalem, and leave it there. I suppose people thought that there was a policeman inside it. It exploded, and killed a few people. It was a completely individual act. He may have bribed a policeman. The police said that the car had been stolen.

One incident I remember is the sudden disappearance of a taxi driver–owner who drove inside the town, taking people from one street to another. Suddenly, this young man—Fawzi—disappeared. Two weeks later, they found his body in an irrigation canal, in a Jewish agricultural area south of Tiberias, with a meat skewer through his head, going in one ear and coming out the other. Later I learned from Khalil, who was a great source of information, that Fawzi was an informer for the Zionists. They [the Palestinians] found out that he was a double agent, pretending to give them information so as to able to get information from them. Because of his treachery, they gave him that awful death.

The first armed operations in Tiberias in 1948 were against the Palestinians. I remember one against a small village called Nasr al-Din, about three kilometers southwest of Tiberias. The Jewish terrorists— they'd call them "freedom fighters" of course—went there and killed several people.[2] In Tiberias itself, very close to our house, where there were steps, one of the owners of the ice factory was walking toward the factory when somebody who was sitting on the lowest step of that long staircase shot him dead. It may have been in revenge for something; the man who was killed was influential in the community.

Return from Iraq, Family Pressure to Marry

In the summer of 1940, I gave up my job in Iraq and returned to Tiberias, with a job as assistant general manager of the Himmeh mineral springs. Himmeh was a large spa located at the meeting point of Syria, Jordan, and Palestine, fifteen or twenty kilometers southeast of Tiberias. It was a more popular place than the Tiberias mineral springs, because of the quality of the water. It had three types of springs, with varying temperatures; the chemical composition of the water was much richer and more effective for arthritis, and generally very strengthening. I used to swim in the pools every day, and I think my health benefited a great deal from the three years I spent there. Ahmad Abdel Khalek and I—he was a clerk there, and we became friends—would go very early before the pools were open to the public. We'd have them all to ourselves, the water bubbling under our feet. The very hot one was called 'al-Hammam al-Mi'li' [literally 'the frying bath']. The intermediate one was quite hot for me, but people would even dive into the hot one, which was fifty-six degrees centigrade. The cooler one was called 'Masbah al-Reeh' or 'Naba' al-Reeh' ['the windy pool' or 'the windy spring']; it was light and gentle, the water was fresh. People drank this *reeh* water every day while they were there. The drinking water also had some radioactivity, a tolerable level that was apparently very healthy. We sent samples of the water for testing to the Hebrew University and to AUB, and we got reports from both, praising the water for its qualities.

The doctor who was in Himmeh when I first went there was Dr. Shami, the same doctor who had been in al-Bassa earlier. It was very amusing meeting him there again. He was an old man then, but full of life. He was fond of me, and one day he said, "Yusif, you're a young man. I realize you're having sex. When you want, in the afternoon, you can use my clinic." That solved my problem.

I had contradictory feelings about sex. I had a hunger for sex, possibly as a release from so much piety in my younger days, so much praying, so much Bible reading. But I also had feelings of guilt. At the beginning, the first time I knew a woman, for a while I would come back and pray every time after I had been with her, and ask for forgiveness. But then I repeated the same sin again. And when I moved later to Tiberias, and had opportunities there in Hotel Tiberias, I felt not just internal guilt, but also social pressure, because the hotel was only two hundred meters from my parents' home. I didn't want to cause my parents embarrassment or distress.

My mother suggested that I should marry. Twice there were suggestions that she was aware that I was 'carrying on,' and very gently—poor thing, she didn't want to embarrass me, she was embarrassed herself by mentioning it—she talked about marriage. She was very hopeful that I would marry a young doctor who had just graduated from AUB and had come to work in the hospital. She thought that as we were both from AUB we would get on well. This doctor used to visit my mother almost daily and have tea with us. Then when I took the job in Himmeh, and came to spend a weekend, we began going out for walks, and I would visit her in her room in the hospital. We became friends. My mother was hoping—in fact praying, as she told me more than once—that we would marry. But I was determined not to marry so soon. Though I was very, very fond of my mother, I didn't want to fall in with her marriage plans.

My love for my mother didn't mean that I agreed with everything she suggested, least of all marriage. I would say to her, "Mama, times have changed, it's not like your day. Now there is room for friendships. Until I find a career that I like I won't think of marriage." She used to say—because by then, in 1940, she had had a very serious heart attack—"But I want to see you married before I die." I would say, "Come on, you're using blackmail on me"—that's the phrase I used—"You're going to live for many more years." Poor thing, she lived only ten years after that. She didn't see me married.

The things that made me not want to marry then were important to me. I remember one night not being able to sleep because I was trying to work out the conflicting pressures. There was the pressure of my love for my mother, which made me feel that it was impermissible to cause her pain. On the other hand I didn't want to suffer the pain that I would have suffered if I had given in. I wasn't ready to marry with the salary I was getting then, and face having children. I only raised that issue once, when she said, "If you marry V., she has a good job here, and you have your job." I said, "But if I marry her, do you expect me to stay in Himmeh? And if I come to Tiberias, there is nothing I can do here." That's when she came up with the idea of a shop. I said, "Mama! Me a shopkeeper!" I used as an argument that if I stayed unmarried I could help with my brothers' education. She said, "God will provide. I'll sell everything that is not essential to help your brothers. I know that you will always help them."

My mother's pressure on me to marry is a general trait of Arab mothers, but it was also special. I was the oldest, and she was very, very fond of me. Maybe I was her favorite. She wanted to see grandchildren; she wanted to see my children. My father almost never mentioned the subject; it was a division of labor. My mother would start the discussion, and if he was around he would take it up, smiling gently, saying in the end, "Well, my son, of course it's up to you, but we'd love to see you married." He never put more pressure than that. He never said a word about the life I was leading. I knew that he knew that I was going to . . . dances. There would be sometimes two weeks before I would come and visit the family.

Himmeh Mineral Springs

My job in Himmeh was very interesting. It was new to me, and it was exciting to be running this big establishment, a concession from the government. It covered a large area, two hundred *dunum*s, which was fifty acres. There were six villas, four big and two small, which had the mineral water running into them, from the coolest of the three springs. People could sit in the mineral water in their own bathtub, and they could do their own cooking. In addition there must have been seventy to a hundred rooms—from singles all the way up to four-people rooms. There was a restaurant, which was commissioned out, and a café. But the bulk of the visitors, those who couldn't afford the rooms or the villas, stayed in tents that we rented out. We had so many tents that we might have two thousand people on any one night. I had quite a staff: three people helping me in the office and a telephonist; and about ten people who went round collecting rents from the people who stayed in the tents—they paid daily because we were afraid that they would slip out early in the morning. The collection was done through tickets, so I had to devise a system that would stop those who went round with the tickets from just putting the money in their pockets, or from giving a reduction—I caught two or three of them. The reason I couldn't go home more than once every two or three weeks was because you couldn't leave that place. I had to be alert. Ahmad Abdel Khalek was the clerk who dealt with accounts, and there was another clerk. But the thing that really needed careful attention was this mobile staff that went round collecting money. They could put a family in a tent, or ten families in a tent, without registering them. I had to devise a system that would be foolproof. Every now and then I did spot checks.

This Abu Iskandar from Damour, I caught him once, twice, and then I said, "The next time I catch you, either you resign or I kick you out." He said, "Kick me out? I'm the favorite of Suleiman Bek." I said, "So you want Suleiman Bek to know of this?" When Suleiman Naseef came, I told him this story in front of Abu Iskandar. I said, "Anybody who cheats you in your absence is likely to cheat you when you are here"—because he used to give him money to buy things. That put the fear of God in him.

Ahmad Abdel Khalek worked with me in Himmeh, and then in Tiberias when I became manager of the hotel there, and on to the Arab National Treasury in Jerusalem in 1946. We were taken prisoner by the Israelis together.

Suleiman Naseef was a remarkable person.[3] He was seventy-six when I first met him, and he could out-walk me in speed and duration. He came from Lebanon, from the Deir al-Qamar area. He had worked with the British in Sudan and again in Egypt. He was Protestant. His wife was the aunt of Camille Chamoun's wife, Zelfa; she was half British or Irish. Suleiman Naseef was very intelligent, political, shrewd. His politics had been pro-British, and people thought that in Egypt he must have been working for the Intelligence. He was in the administration—he might have been with the Intelligence, I don't know.[4] He knew so much and was full of stories. He would tell me of his past experiences. He became rich, and owned large tracts of land.

He had decorations; he was a Bek from King Fuad, Farouk's father, for services to Egypt. In Sudan he was with the English. He had an *izba*, a country house, in Egypt, and of course a city house. He lived to the age of a hundred and six, or maybe a hundred and ten.

The waters of Himmeh had been known for centuries. Naseef asked for the concession. They said, "Only if you form a limited-share company." He formed the company; the capital was small at the beginning, thirty thousand sterling. Most of the shares went to his family, but in order to be able to 'guard his back,' as we say in Arabic, he brought in Sidqi Tabari as a shareholder, and as a member of the board with him. He also brought in a leading nationalist from Haifa, Rashid al-Hajj Ibrahim, for the same reason. When I was there, I thought of promoting something bigger. I interested Fuad Saba, the head of Saba and Company, the auditors in Jerusalem, in the idea of bringing in a number of people who could work smoothly together, honest and enterprising like Fuad Saba himself, and Bassem Fares, to expand the capital. If I remember correctly, the capital of Himmeh was expanded to two hundred thousand pounds.

We had just begun to do this when everything ended—it was toward the end of the mandate. The plan was to build a proper hotel to replace rooms that were in a line: they were not even chalets, just rooms strung one next to the other, without bathrooms. The only thing that was acceptable was the villas, but there were only six of these. The plan was to do away with the tents; or to keep the tents, but to have proper baths and WCs attached to them because people used to go out to the fields, and washed the following morning in the bathtubs. Luckily the baths were clean because the springs were very strong; the water ran like a river. If you went beyond Himmeh a few hundred meters you could see the three springs joining together into a strong stream, which joined the Yarmouk River.

I was given a very substantial cash bonus and a hundred shares free for my efforts in promoting the company and influencing and persuading the other financiers. I've still got those shares. When

Himmeh was overrun by the Israelis, when they took the Golan Heights [in 1967], I received a letter from the Himmeh office in Damascus, signed by the grandson of Suleiman Naseef, saying, "We found in our records that you have a hundred shares, but there is no record of your having paid for them." Fortunately I have a habit of never throwing anything away. I found the agreement in Fuad Saba's handwriting, with the clause that said that "in appreciation of what he has done to promote the expansion of the company, Yusif Sayigh will get a bonus from the existing company, and a hundred shares free from the expanded company." So I xeroxed it and sent it to him. I didn't hear anything after that. The legal aspects of the new company were finished before the end of the mandate, and it was registered with the Registrar of Companies. It was a big thing to have achieved.

I was very active in those years, getting up at six to be ready to have a swim of half an hour, come back, shave, eat, run to the office, and then make a tour to see that the cleanliness of the whole place was adequate. Besides the baths there were the tents, the rooms, the restaurants, a couple of shops, and the clinic. There was a citrus grove, which produced oranges and grapefruit the like of which I have never tasted in my life. Everybody guessed, and this was confirmed through examination of the soil, that it was because of the water—all the water in the area had some radioactivity in it. I attribute the fact that my eyes are still good to my three years in Himmeh.

I was enterprising. The best thing was that Suleiman Naseef had faith in me. When I took over from the general manager of the company before me, I went over the books to make a trial balance of the ledger, and prepare a balance sheet and a profit–loss account. Then I was supposed to take the books to Haifa, to an English auditors' firm. Before taking the books, I was curious to look at the months before I joined the company, and being sharp in accounting, I discovered discrepancies. I dug more carefully, and found that the man before me, another Protestant whom Suleiman Naseef had trusted totally, had put in his pocket the odd twenty pounds here, thirty pounds there—nothing very big. I had to show this to Suleiman Naseef, because the auditors would have found it anyway. I didn't want him to think that I was stupid or that I was covering up. I showed it to him, and he wrote a letter to his former secretary, whom he liked, saying, "My feeling is just distress that somebody I trusted should do this. *Allah yisamhak* [God forgive you]." He bore the loss himself, from his share in the dividends.

At the end of each year I received an extra bonus, other than the big bonus I mentioned, because the whole accounting system and management was so neat. In the whole year Suleiman Naseef would come there for only six weeks or eight weeks. He would come and stay a couple of weeks, and then go to Egypt—he loved staying in Egypt—or else to an elegant German hotel in Haifa. He could do this because he knew the company was in good hands. The other members of the board would visit too. Most times the board meetings were in Himmeh; once they were in Tiberias, and I think once or twice in Haifa. I conducted dealings with the government, because the secretary of any limited-share company was supposed himself to submit returns and reports to the Registrar of Companies and to the Finance Department. I did all that work, and every time that Suleiman Naseef came I would have two or three hundred documents for him to sign. I was empowered to sign, but every time money was deposited in the bank, or large sums drawn from the bank for current expenses, the voucher that went to the account books had to be signed by him, as general manager.

He would come and sit there for days, signing, and then spend two or three weeks just enjoying the baths. He didn't go to the springs to swim, he had a tub in his room; he had two or three rooms of his own, with his companion. He always brought a young companion, good-looking nurses, one after the other—he reminded me of King David who, in his old age, couldn't feel warmth in his thighs, so they brought him a girl of seventeen. Workers would bring him water—there was this very strong worker of Bedouin origin who carried two kerosene tins on a pole across his shoulder. Two of these men would come and go, carrying kerosene tins full of water from his favorite spring to his tub, and he would have his bath there, in his room. At times when he didn't have a water bath, he'd have a 'bed bath.' Sometimes I would go to see him early, at nine o'clock, and he would still be rubbing himself with a flannel. He had a very elaborate silver thing in which he kept Yardley water; he'd put some in his hand and rub himself on the groin. He still had an eye for attractive ladies—he was seventy-six in 1940, but I knew him for years after that.

Suleiman Naseef had an extremely intelligent and beautiful daughter called Widad, married to his nephew, Antoine Naseef. Antoine worked for a while in Himmeh, before I went there, but then left to work in Jaffa. He and Widad were separated. Widad and her mother, who didn't get on with Suleiman Naseef after she became religious, lived together at Himmeh because that meant free accommodation and food. She could count on me to give her pocket money. Suleiman Naseef said, "Yes, give them up to so much, no more." Every time they came I would tell them where they had reached with respect to that ceiling. There was nothing to buy in Himmeh, but Widad would sometimes go to Tiberias or Haifa to shop.

Widad was very political; she was close to Antoun Sa'adeh in Lebanon. She had been educated in England, at one of those fancy schools. She spoke beautiful English and French. A fantastic woman. She was the only person who did not leave Quneitra when the Israelis blew it up in 1973, when they withdrew. They said then that she was seventy-three years old, and it was the year 1973, so I realized then that she must be sixteen years older than me, although I would never have guessed it. A terrific woman, she had a great deal of influence on Sa'adeh. Her home in the Sana'yeh area in Beirut was a sort of a salon for the PPS. When she stayed in Himmeh, I would spend every other evening with her, talking politics—PPS politics, the French and British mandates, the revolution, the rebellions—everything.

One day she said, "Soon there is going to be a visitor here. I'm not going to say anything about him, just listen. But don't enter into the conversation because it would be dangerous for you." She wouldn't say more than that. A few days later he came to Himmeh. He was the head of a police station about two kilometers away, on a hilltop overlooking Himmeh. He came; he wanted to draw me into the discussion. Every now and then he'd throw me a word. But I was on my guard. Widad controlled the conversation; she tore him to pieces with her sarcasm. She'd turn it all into jokes, as if to show him, "You think you're clever? All right, if you want cleverness, here's a sample." She showed him what a child he was compared with her. He used to come once a week, and spend three or four hours there, never getting anything out of her. After he left, she said, "You see why I told you not to say anything? I wanted you to find out for yourself what this man is after." He wanted to know whether she was active in politics. They had a file on her that she was active in Lebanon—was she coming to Palestine for the party? Was she recruiting? What was she doing there? That was the war period, 1940 to 1943. Eventually she left, she couldn't take Himmeh any more. She rented an apartment on her own in Jerusalem. When I left Tiberias in 1944 and went to work in Jerusalem, I used to visit her there. Her father would come and we'd have tea together.

An event I remember was the arrival of the Nabulsi family, who are still an influential family in Nablus, and very rich. They would send us a cable saying, "We are arriving at such-and-such a time, we want three villas." They always took villas. They would usually arrive in the early afternoon, and come and register and greet us. Then they would go to the villas. An hour or so later—I suppose they would have had a bath in the mineral water—they would come to the café for an *argileh*, five or six of them, dressed in silk pajamas, with their tarbooshes on, *ub'abs*[5] on their feet, and shirts still on with ties under their pajama jackets. All silk and all rich. Not the women. They would be preparing supper, and having their own beautifying bath.

The people who came to Himmeh were a cross-section of Palestinian society. But they were not only Palestinian—Lebanese people also came. One day two ladies came in a private car, a huge Buick, like the Buicks of the Nablus people. They had come all the way from Lebanon in their own car, a mother and a daughter, French. Another person came from further away. This was an Iraqi who came leaning heavily on a stick, with his very attractive young daughter. He turned out to be Hassan Zekki, who had been a minister in Iraq thirteen times. His daughter later became well known in Iraq as a writer, Sameeha Zekki. This man would come and stay two or three weeks in Tiberias, at the Tiberias springs, and two or three weeks in Himmeh. He also came the year that I became manager of Hotel Tiberias; I became friends with his daughter, and he became friends with my father. They came several times to have tea with us, and my father and I went to them, because by then my mother couldn't do much walking. He was very modern in attitude. I remember sitting with him in his room, when he was in Tiberias, and he said, "Why do you young people stay with me all the time? Go out! Take Sameeha to the pictures, do something together." She was very attached to him; she wouldn't leave him. She said, "We'll go out to the balcony and sit there." So we went out, and there was a double-seated cane chair there. We sat there talking until about one in the morning, not quite flirting but on the edge.

An odd story from that time relates to a man who was with the Customs Department in Tiberias. His job was to go around the lake in a motorboat to see if there was any smuggling, because we were close by the Syrian frontier, the Golan mountains. Usually he'd spend hours there, almost until dawn, before coming home. He was a Christian from Haifa and his wife was also Christian. This woman had a lover who was also Christian, from Acre, in the Food Rationing Department, a very funny person, very witty and quite good looking. That evening, for the bad luck of this couple, the lake was very rough—Lake Tiberias can be quite choppy—and the husband decided that it was too risky, so he went back home much earlier than expected, walked in, and found—let's say George—in his wife's bed. He started abusing them, "You unfaithful wife! You disloyal friend! I'll show you!" Of course he usually had a gun. George sat up in the bed, his chest naked, and said to him, "Careful what you say! It seems you have no sense of propriety. Would it be better if you came and found a Muslim in bed with your wife? Here I am, a Christian, and you say this to me?" The husband began apologizing, upon which George got up, put on his clothes, and walked away.

Hotel Tiberias

In the summer of 1943 I got a much better-paying job as manager of Hotel Tiberias. The salary was three times more than my salary in Himmeh, plus ten percent of the profits. The hotel belonged to Germans, so it was under the Custodian of Enemy Property. The manager before me, a Lebanese, decided to go back to Lebanon. He contacted me, and at the same time told the custodian's office that he was leaving, and that he had a candidate with a degree in business administration, who had been running a spa, where during the season there would be two thousand people staying every night. He also won over to my camp the lawyer of the hotel, an Englishman. So I received a formal offer from the lawyer of the hotel, the lawyer who represented the owners—they couldn't send letters themselves because they were 'enemies.'

The owners at that time were an old German lady and her daughter-in-law, who had been married to this German lady's elder son. He had committed suicide because his wife was in love with an Armenian doctor. One night the Armenian doctor was visiting Tiberias, and they all—the doctor, the husband, and the wife—went out for a trip in a boat, and drank a lot. That night, when they got back from their rowing trip, the German husband went into the bathroom and shot himself.[6] I was in Tiberias then. This German was much loved by the Arabs because he spoke Arabic like a Bedouin—he was born in Tiberias. There was another brother in the family who was taken prisoner of war, and he was in Canada at the time, a prisoner. The owners were not allowed to take any managerial decisions. The lawyer wrote me a letter giving me a formal offer, which I accepted, and resigned from my job in Himmeh.

In Hotel Tiberias, my job was to manage the hotel, and look after the lido, which had a restaurant, dancing floors, a bar, a couple of tennis courts, and of course swimming. I wasn't prepared either in training or in temperament to run a hotel. I never went to the kitchen, to see what was being cooked. I'm sure there was a lot of money being made in the kitchen by the cook, because he also bought the meat and the vegetables. I concentrated on the guests. There were three receptionists, and they looked after the registration of the guests, but I looked after the social side, entertaining them. If they were agreeable I'd invite them to drinks, or to have tea with me. There was always a favorite guest or two who would sit at my table for meals. I ate there, and I lived there. I had two rooms. I didn't go to our house for meals. I had to be at the hotel all the time; there might be telephone calls, or things to decide on. I liked it too, I enjoyed the atmosphere, and, well, I was a young man then, and most of the visitors were ladies coming for holidays. So that was an attraction. It paid very well. That year I made eight hundred English pounds and, in addition, ten percent of net profits. This made it possible for me to help with my brothers' education, and to buy a car. The car was a Mini Morris, one month old, my first. I bought it in 1945, as soon as I went to Jerusalem. I gave the bulk of the money to my family to help with my brothers' and sister's education, but there was still enough for me, because when I went to Jerusalem I went straight to another job, I didn't lose a day's income.

A Glamorous Visitor

The singer Asmahan used to come and spend weeks in Hotel Tiberias when I was manager. When she first came, she had her lover with her, an Egyptian, who was the first man to become a pilot in Egypt, Ahmad Salem. He was handsome, but very ungroomed. When you looked at him you felt that he hadn't showered or shaved for several days. I think they quarreled, and he went away, and she stayed there by herself. She would leave Tiberias very early in the morning with bags of gold coins, not huge bags but hundreds of them, and go for two or three days. She would have people with her, British guides, to lead the way, and then later perhaps people from Jabal al-Druze itself.

In the early forties, when the British wanted to enter Syria and Lebanon and expel the Vichyists, one of the things they did was to work on the Druzes. The Druzes owed the British something because they had supported them during the revolt of the Turshan, of Sultan al-Atrash. They sent them arms, and when the rebellion of 1925 was crushed by the French, the British allowed hundreds of Druze fighters to come to Transjordan and settle there. They stayed for several years before they were allowed back. By way of repayment for what they had done for the Druzes, the British decided to send a respected Druze to go to buy the chieftains there so that they would help the British when they entered, if they were to enter from the Tiberias side.[7] The person they brought for this purpose was Asmahan, the singer, a Druze and an Atrash, who had been married to the Emir Hassan al-Atrash. By then she had left him and become a singer of great renown in Egypt.[8]

We had living in the hotel a British major; I think he was head of Intelligence, very well dressed and elegant. He would arrange for her to be accompanied to the frontier, and from there she'd be met by people from Jabal al-Druze; they would take her over the frontier through the Druze Golan, and then probably to Jabal al-Druze. When she had spent all the money she had, she'd come back. It was obvious but nobody cared. After all, the French were not our bosom friends. And the British made a statement that they wanted to remove this Fascist regime and to give Syria and Lebanon their freedom and independence.

Asmahan was extremely attractive, very striking, with green, green eyes. Looking into her eyes was like looking at a clear sea, the bottom of which you can't reach. She must have been in her late twenties or early thirties. Very slim and handsome. Every now and then the officer would invite a few people—including me and Khalil Tabari—into his suite in the hotel, and drinks would flow, and she would sing for us. I don't know what they did after we left. It was a sensation having her there. Once I sat next to her—I couldn't move my eyes from her face. She is the Arab singer whose voice I love the most.

Family Life

Our family life was happy except for the sadness we always felt that my mother was almost an invalid. In those days—I don't know if it was the way heart trouble generally was treated—but the hospital there forced her to stay in bed, instead of telling her to walk a little. My mother had had a major heart attack in the spring of 1940, when I was in Iraq teaching. It seems that at night she felt she had an upset stomach, she needed to vomit, but she couldn't. Her heart began fluttering, so my father took her to the hospital next door. They realized it was a heart attack. She stayed there for several weeks. After that they told her to stay in bed and take it easy. The letter made me cry for days, because a heart attack in those days meant almost immediate death. I was terribly afraid that she might die in my absence. I couldn't get leave to go back. By then it was close to the summer holidays.

She stayed most of the rest of her life in bed, really. When I had my heart attack, I was urged to walk, a bit more every day. She was not advised that way, and as a result I think she got weaker. She would get up a little and move around the house but she didn't do much gardening any more. She became the center of the house. When we were there for holidays, we stayed at home with her. She stopped visiting but many, many visitors would come. The rare times when she felt strong enough, she and my father would go by taxi to pay a visit. Sometimes she would go to church, even though it was on the lower road, and she had to go down twenty-five or thirty steps to get there. This meant climbing up these steps on the way back. She'd put her arm on mine, or my father's. And every four or five steps she would stop and rest a little, talking. Church gave her the motivation and the strength.

By late 1943, I was twenty-seven years old. Fuad had just graduated from AUB in engineering. He found a job with the government in the department of public works in Tiberias. He was appointed clerk of works, to look after roads and public buildings in the town and in the neighborhood. He didn't stay there long. During our last years in Tiberias, he worked briefly in Haifa, then in Jerusalem, and then went to Gaza.

Fayez was doing philosophy and needed one more year to finish. He wasn't admitted to AUB the same year as Fuad because he was only fifteen years old when he finished school. He spent a year in Tiberias working in a pharmacy there, and then entered AUB in October 1937, got his BA in June 1941, and registered for a master's. It took him four years to get his MA because he had his work for the party, and he was wanted by the French.

In 1943 Tawfiq was in university, doing Arabic literature. He had obtained his matric in June 1940 from the Arab College. After school he didn't go straight to university but taught for a year in al-Bassa and then Tiberias, and entered AUB in October 1941, and got his BA in June 1945. After getting his BA, he came back to Palestine to teach, and then worked in a government department of information, news, and translation for a year. In 1946–47 he went back to Beirut.

By 1945 Mary was in her last two years of high school, in the Ahliyyeh school in Beirut. Munir was in the Arab College in Jerusalem; because of his record they took him without any fees. He got his matric in Jerusalem in June 1946 and entered AUB in October. Until the end of the mandate his fees were paid by the British government. After that Munir, like Tawfiq, Fuad, and Fayez, got a loan from the Alumni Association.

Anis went to Jerusalem in June 1946 to Bishop Gobat's school, and he stayed there until February 1947. By then things were becoming very hot, so I contacted Sidon boys' school and arranged for him to go there, after discussing it with my father over the telephone. On the 4th of February I drove him to Tiberias; we spent a few days there with my parents, and then drove to Sidon where he was admitted to school.

So by the summer of 1945 we had Fayez getting a master's, Tawfiq getting a BA, and Mary getting a high-school diploma. When they went back to Tiberias my parents gave a big tea party for the three of them, to which they invited members of the congregation. Then, some days later, they gave another party for the hospital doctors and staff. And then, later, another party for personal friends of our generation like the Tabaris, Ahmad Abdel Khalek, Fareed Ataya, and Munir Samaha.

Last Days in Tiberias

I spent about ten months as manager of Hotel Tiberias. Then a couple of government officials—the head of government laboratories, an Armenian doctor, and a Lebanese friend of his who was an engineer with the public works department in Jerusalem—they were close friends—applied to the Custodian of Enemy Property to run the hotel, instead of the custodian having a manager. They took over the hotel, paid my salary down to the last penny and my share in profits, and I left the hotel and went to Jerusalem.

Those last ten months at Hotel Tiberias were the longest stretch that I spent in Tiberias. I was very happy there. I loved the lake; I loved the swimming. I began playing tennis more actively than before, especially with Yusif Tabari, Khalil's cousin, who was a very good player. I had an active social life in the hotel. I started drinking a little—I have never been a drinker, I might have taken two or three drinks a week, that's all. I hadn't got to whiskey then—it would be wine, and beer in summer, and sherry, due to the influence of the

British. I did a lot of dancing there. We had an orchestra; we took one on contract for the winter season. The year I was there I got a new one, a singer with four musicians. It was European-style music: tango and fox trots, the slow waltz. The floor would be crowded every night.

Every now and then I would take my brothers and parents out on the lake in a large rowing boat. I loved rowing. If my brothers weren't there, the son of the man who leased us the boat would help, so there'd be four hands rowing. We'd make a long stretch from our house all the way to the mineral springs south of Tiberias and back, to give my mother an outing.

This last period in Tiberias was especially rich politically, because my two brothers and I had all joined the PPS by then. We talked a lot about the party, and politics, and Palestine, and organization within the PPS, and its ideology, and its expansion. Outside the family, my friendship with Khalil Tabari intensified at that time. We talked about the Arab Higher Committee—I wasn't very hopeful that it would be able to lead the struggle for the protection of Palestine, if not the total defeat of Zionism. He had more faith in what the Palestinians could do from the villages, because he was in contact with them. The Tabaris had land in the countryside; he came into contact with people who were working on the land, and he knew about their activities, and their readiness to fight. But Khalil wasn't always in Tiberias.

I got the job in Jerusalem while I was still in Tiberias. The job was with the campaign for the formation of savings' cooperatives, which Keith-Roach Pasha was head of.[9] He had been in Tiberias and had offered me the job there. I told him I'd think it over. Then I decided that rather than go to Jerusalem and spend money looking for a job, I would accept it, and look for another one from there. That's what happened, except that the job looked for me, I didn't look for it—with Saba and Company. In late summer or early autumn, 1944, I went to Jerusalem where a new chapter started.

9

Jerusalem, 1944–48

My first job in Jerusalem was with this organization involved in saving companies and cooperatives, and fighting inflation. It worked with chambers of commerce. There was a Jewish section and an Arab section. I was the head of the Palestinian section, and there was a Jewish head for the Jewish section, a Jew who was a writer, who didn't care two hoots about savings or cooperatives. We were about the same age; we talked about things. He was a creative writer, and politics didn't seem to be a priority for him. The first secretary they gave me was Jewish and turned out to be somebody I'd known at Himmeh. I passed her on to the Jew, and got an Arab woman secretary. But I only stayed in that job a few months.

Fuad Saba[1] contacted me, and said, "What are you doing there?! Savings? Come and work with me." Right away he appointed me as manager of the Jerusalem branch of Saba and Company, and assistant general manager for the whole Arab world—he had branches from Egypt to Syria. There wasn't one in Lebanon, so I came and started the office in Lebanon for him, and found somebody to run it. It was a much better job in every way.

I stayed with Saba for about ten months, until Izzat Tannous[2] sent for me to work for the Arab National Treasury. This ten-month period was the most active one for me as representative of the PPS in Palestine. Most of our work then was recruitment, getting young people to become members, and spreading the ideas of the PPS, which were not well known in Palestine. Indeed there wasn't great readiness to accept the ideas of the PPS because it emphasized the Syrianness of Palestine, that Palestine was southern Syria, whereas the Palestinians always called themselves Arabs, and thought of the Palestine problem as an Arab problem. There were a few individuals—like Awni Abdel Hadi[3]—who had taken part in congresses in Damascus and France, in 1919 or 1921. But by that time nobody thought that Greater Syria could save Palestine, because it consisted of Lebanon, which was controlled by France and divided denominationally, Syria, which was not strong though its heart was in the right place, and Transjordan, which was totally British. What we needed was countries like Iraq, which was outside the 'dish' of the PPS, and Egypt, and the Maghreb, and the 'Land of Islam'—Saudi Arabia and the rest. So it was an uphill fight.

There was also the issue that the PPS had its own leader, who was Christian, rather than Hajj Amin al-Husseini. There were attempts by some people of an older generation to draw us into fusion with the mufti. In fact, somebody said, "The mufti has no organization behind him, why doesn't the PPS become his organization? We must just make a few changes in the dogma." But Sa'adeh was such a fanatic about dogma, he considered his decision was inspired; nobody could change his mind about things. Besides, fusion would have meant that the mufti was the leader rather than Sa'adeh. It couldn't work.

We worked on a few well-known figures who were not very political—that's why they were willing to join us. For some time we cultivated a lawyer from Haifa called Fuad Atallah. He was very dynamic, but I knew from the start that he wanted to become a political figure, and we would have been his base. We wanted somebody who was pure, indoctrinated, and who believed in everything the party said. We asked Sami Taha to join us.[4] Khalil Tabari used to be a regular visitor at our meetings, especially social events like the commemoration of the founding of the party. We had one in Haifa at which Khalil spoke for about six hours, and then said, "This is the introduction; we have reached 1918." Six hours! I went on for a long time teasing him about that.

There were cells in Jaffa, in Haifa, and Jerusalem—these are the ones I'm sure of. We had a very small cell, not enough to be officially a cell, in Jenin. Later there was somebody who had been converted on his own to the party, through his readings. He was a fantastic person, a lawyer—I think his name was Mustafa Arsheid, from Jenin, the Nablus area. Later he became head of the whole PPS in Lebanon. Arsheid was strong, articulate, thoughtful, and disciplined. He had everything that I didn't have; he should have been head of the branch, but he wasn't known to the party then.

So the PPS restricted itself to proselytizing. It was mainly young people who joined. Not peasants, they had to have some education, because the things we talked about were intellectual. There was a great deal about the definition of a nation, the difference between the nation and the state, and the separation between state and church, things like that. Our gospel was the book that Sa'adeh wrote in prison, *Nushu' al-umam* (The Emergence of Nations). Our members were not all students, but they were politicized and had read something. We had some fine members, very tough.

Toward the end of '47 we decided to have military training. But by then it was becoming difficult, we didn't have grounds that were open and easy to reach, for training in shooting for example. The PPS had military training and instructors in Lebanon by that time, but in Palestine we didn't have that.

My activity with the PPS was strongest before I joined the Arab National Treasury. I remained active afterward but joining the Treasury was a form of compensation. In the PPS our activity was mainly cerebral—meetings and indoctrination and political education. I didn't feel that we were really doing something. There were village groups that got together every now and then, especially in '47 when there were clashes with the Zionists, but the PPS was out of these things. For me the opportunity to be director of the Arab National Treasury was a higher form of action. I could serve the cause in a way I knew something about, organization and economics.

Palestinian Political Figures

My acquaintance with political figures until I joined the National Treasury was very restricted. I knew a few younger elements like Anwar Nusseibeh,[5] whom I met in the early days of the Arab National Treasury. Maybe I met him a little before in the YMCA. He was a very good tennis player. I used to watch him, and then we became friends. I knew Anwar al-Khatib,[6] another lawyer, who was maybe with the Istiqlal. There were three or four people from Jaffa who were nationalists, whom I met in Jerusalem through attending meetings and lectures. But I only began to meet members of the political leadership after I joined the Arab National Treasury.

Joint meetings held between the board of trustees of the Arab National Treasury and the Arab Higher Committee brought me in touch with Jamal al-Husseini,[7] the vice chairman of the Arab Higher Committee—Hajj Amin al-Husseini was chairman in absentia—and Emil Ghoury, who was secretary general. I used to see Jamal al-Husseini frequently, and I came to know Musa Alami[8] after Fayez and I had written a memorandum giving the PPS ideas on how the Arab League should be formed, and where Palestine should fit, and what the League's priorities ought to be, and its strategy. He liked this memorandum, so I began to visit him.

When the Arab League was being founded, each Arab country sent representatives to Alexandria, and then to Cairo, for the preparation of the protocol which established the League. In Palestine meetings were held and Musa Alami was chosen by all the leaders in Palestine as sole representative of the Palestinians in these preparatory meetings, because he didn't belong to any one group. He contacted the various political groups, and me, as representing the PPS. Immediately I sent a message—I think I sent somebody all the way to Lebanon because I didn't trust cables or mail—to the leadership of the party. Fayez was then, if I'm not mistaken, the *'amid li-l-thaqafa wa-l-idha'a* (head of culture and radio). Anyway, he was high up in the party, so he came to Jerusalem, and we sat for a few days together drafting the memorandum to send to the Arab League. It was such interesting work that a year or two later, when we looked at the memorandum, we couldn't remember who wrote which part. Our thoughts moved in the same direction. Musa Alami was very happy with our memorandum because it was well organized, logical, clear. It was rooted in principles of patriotism and nationhood, but we tried to be as realistic as possible.

I was already quite known by then because I was publishing things in Jerusalem and in a magazine in Jaffa. Most of my writings, I must admit, were polemics against the Communist Party, which took a line that was almost identical with the Soviet line. That was before the Partition resolution, but you could tell that they took their cue from Russia, not from their own history—very Zionist. The Communist Party in Russia acknowledged the right of the Jews to a state in Palestine. Their message was that the Palestinian proletariat should cooperate with the Jewish proletariat to fight the landlords and the bourgeoisie on both sides. My response was, "Find me ten Jews who are willing to fight against their nation-class in cooperation with us, and I will change my opinion." Both Fayez and I were heavily indoctrinated by Sa'adeh and the PPS in that respect. The PPS had a newsletter, which appeared on and off. It was mostly written by hand and then stencilled.

Musa Alami was a magnet to younger people like me, first because of his character, as someone who was absolutely honest, committed, and anxious for Palestinians to organize, though I think he was a bit too aloof to start an organization himself. He had hopes in our generation, but he didn't tell us how, he didn't want to dirty his hands with politics. He was one of those people who believed that politics are essential but dirty. The second thing that attracted our generation to him was his foundation of the Arab Office, which had branches in Jerusalem, London, and Washington. He drew to it older-generation people like Darwish Mikdadi[9] and Ahmad Shuqeiri,[10] and then the generation of Albert and Cecil Hourani,[11] and younger people like Walid Khalidi and Burhan Dajani.[12] The other thing he established was a fund—he aimed at a capital of one million Palestine pounds—to save lands threatened by Zionist purchase. He was highly respected in the Arab countries; Iraq supported him, but I don't think he succeeded in getting all the money he needed.

My greater involvement [in Palestinian politics] came when I joined the Treasury. I didn't join any of the parties that were active in Palestine then because I was already a member of a party, and I was disciplined, I wouldn't join two groups. If Musa Alami had had an organization, I would have been tempted to join it. But I wasn't tempted by any of the so-called parties [in Palestine], because they were not true parties. They had no structure, no organization. They were a few notables who met now and then and spoke generalities, who had some influence in the countryside, more because the country people were dynamic and ready to do something than because they were inspired by these people. Moreover I wasn't impressed by most of them. Jamal al-Husseini, for instance, was pleasant but didn't do much. The natural leader would have been the descendant of Musa Kazim Pasha al-Husseini. But Musa Kazem died in the thirties, I think, and his son, Abdul Qader, was young then.[13] There were leaders like Dr. Ruhi al-Khalidi, whom I liked as a person, he seemed to be intelligent; but he was mayor, and not directly active in politics.[14] There was Awni Abdel Hadi, whom we didn't see much because he was in Nablus. He had his own party. There were the Nashashibis whom I didn't like at all because of their connection with King Abdullah and the British. Emil Ghoury, a Christian, could never become the leader of a big party. Besides, he was very loyal to the mufti. These are the people I remember now. None of them impressed me a great deal.

Afifeh Batrouni (Umm Yusif), probably before her marriage.

Abu Yusif, Umm Yusif, Yusif, Fuad, and Fayez, probably taken in Sweida, early 1920s.

Left to right: Fayez, Yusif, Tawfiq, Fuad. Probably taken in Sweida, early 1920s.

Yusif, probably in al-Bassa.

The Sayighs: back row from left: Fayez, Abu Yusif, Yusif, Umm Yusif, Fuad; front row from left: Anis, Munir, Mary, Tawfiq. Probably in Tiberias.

Pastor Abdallah Sayigh (back row) with nurses from the Scottish Mission Hospital, Tiberias.

A family album page arranged to show that all the Sayigh family had cleft chins.

Yusif as a teacher in Tikrit, Iraq (1939–40). In Iraq all teachers wore uniforms.

Yusif (second from left), as *homme de confiance* in an Israeli prisoner-of-war camp, 1948 or 1949, with Israeli officials.

The Sayigh home in Tiberias.

Mary Ford, the American missionary
who employed Pastor Abdallah.

The Sayigh family in Tiberias, perhaps shortly before 1948.

Marriage, October 1953.

Abu Yusif, Beirut, probably mid-1950s.

Yusif with Yezid, Baltimore, 1955.

Yusif with Fayez, Baltimore, 1955.

Yusif at a conference.

Yusif with Chairman Arafat.

One of the last photographs of Yusif.

Later on there were movements to establish grass-roots organizations, for instance the Najjadeh, established by Hawari in Nazareth, a sort of a youth group. But it was thought to be encouraged by the British in order to take people away from Hajj Amin. They had some kind of uniform; they must have been influenced by Nazi traditions. Another group was encouraged to emerge to counteract the Najjadeh, under Kamel Uraykat, who subsequently became a member of the House of Notables in Jordan. Nobody like me would seriously consider joining them because their motivation was suspicious, and they had no ideas. As for the Communist Party, I was very far from them on ideological grounds, because of their attitude to the Palestine problem. I wrote a number of articles putting the PPS point of view on this, criticizing the Communist Party. They were published once or twice in *al-Difa'* and also in weeklies. There was a weekly published by Hanna Sweida in Jerusalem, in which Salim al-Louzi was a writer—he was living in Palestine then. I also published one or two things in a Jaffa weekly.

Outside the PPS, my political activity was mostly with young people whom I met at the YMCA, because I used to eat most of my meals there. The new YMCA building, right opposite the King David, was a hundred meters from the Saba offices, so I would come from there and have my meal. Many of these young men were students of law in the law school in Jerusalem. That was my group. We always talked politics.

I also wrote two or three stories when I was in Palestine. It must have been in '45 or '46. I remember meeting Jabra Jabra,[15] who was very active culturally, through the YMCA in Jerusalem—it was a gathering place for many people. One day he heard that I had written a short story, and I showed him my latest. We met again and he insisted that I should read it at the next meeting. He liked it very much and the group did too. I can't remember anything about it; I can't even remember its title. I think the stories I wrote were very sentimental, not much action but lots of thinking and feeling.

I also built quite a library. I had begun reading in high school and continued in Beirut. I especially liked novels. I used to go to the Sa'id bookshop to buy books, the Standard Stationery, owned by the fathers of Edward and George Sa'id. Ultimately I had to leave this library behind. It included, among other things, the Encyclopaedia Britannica of 1934. Before I was taken prisoner of war I managed to store my collection with the YMCA. Years later, when I was working with UNRWA, I got in touch with Labib Nasser, then head of the YMCA. He wrote back saying that the novels had got old and worn by then, but that he would send the encyclopedia.

I didn't see my family very often during that period. I used to pass by Tiberias when I went to Galilee to form committees for the Treasury. Tiberias was on the way to Safad, not many kilometers from Nazareth, less than half an hour's drive. Every few weeks I'd go for a weekend. But I always felt guilty because I was not really paying them enough attention. I made it up to some extent by telephone. I put pressure on them, and one day my father wrote to say they had a telephone. That made it easier, we began to communicate.

The *Arab Land Hunger Report*

My concern was essentially that we were slipping on two grounds: land was going to the Jews, and immigrants were coming in much larger numbers than officially admitted by the British. I followed the statistics, and thanks to Sami Hadawi[16] I was kept informed about land transfers, because he was the highest official on land taxation and land ownership, maybe the highest Arab official in the mandate government. Under the mandate there were no ministries. There were secretaries, a chief secretary, and secretaries under him. I think it was the Secretariat for Land Ownership and Settlement that Sami directed, and he was in charge of taxation records and statistics. Anything that I wanted was available to me through him. That's how I got all the information I needed for my paper on Arab land hunger.

The Arab Office asked me to write this paper on the suggestion of Albert Hourani, when the Arab Office was asked by the Arab
Higher Committee to prepare the Arab case for the Anglo-American
Committee of Inquiry into the Palestine problem. The Arab Higher
Committee realized it didn't have the intellectual skills among its
members. Indeed it had no structure at all. When Jamal al-Husseini
left the office in the afternoon, he locked the door and put the key
in his pocket. There was no secretariat, just one or two people to
make coffee— not even a secretary to take notes or type. Luckily they
recognized their shortcomings, so they asked the Arab Office—Musa
Alami, assisted by his lieutenants Ahmad Shuqeiri and Darwish al-
Mikdadi—to prepare the case. In fact the whole burden fell on Albert
Hourani, to design an outline and decide what to include. There were
several papers and several people took part in preparing them.

So I wrote this paper. I got the basic information from Sami
Hadawi; he gave me sources and put at my disposal all the reports
of the commissions of inquiry that had come to Palestine, from the
twenties all the way down to that time—the Peel report, the King–
Crane report, the Shaw report, all of them. He was in charge of the
preparation of the village statistics, that wonderful reference work
which contains breakdowns of ownership—Arab, Jewish, state—not
only town by town and village by village, but also hamlet by hamlet.
What was equally important was not simply the area each group had,
but also the breakdown into categories of land. There were sixteen
categories, divided according to its fertility. Sami had to have that
because taxation was based on fertility.

In this paper I did something that I think was an innovation—I
must have it published one day. Until then the argument had gone,
"The Arabs have so many million *dunum*s, the Jews have only so many
million *dunum*s, and therefore the Arabs are much better off. They
can afford to lose land." What I did was to say, "Let's look at the quality of the land." The first seven or eight categories were taxable, if I
remember correctly, because they were assumed to have a high net

return per *dunum*. If you put so many pounds a year into that *dunum* for production, you will get so much. The highest rating was for citrus, the next was for banana plantations, and then for other fruit trees, and so on down until you reached a level where the margin was almost zero. Categories below this level were not taxed. So I took the land owned by Palestinian Arabs, district by district, sub-district by sub-district, to see in which category it lay. Then I made a weight by taking the lowest taxable *dunum* as the standard *dunum*. That was one; the next one higher up was two by this standard; the next three; and so on. In this way I converted the ownership of Arabs and Jews into standard *dunum*s. This method showed that the discrepancy between the two in land value was much greater than the raw figures showed. The Jews had taken Esdraelon, and the Haifa lands, which got most rainfall. Of course they bought land for strategic purposes too, but productivity was a high consideration. This finding was the core of the *Arab Land Hunger Report*.

I don't know how much my manuscript was edited. They never published the Palestine case report because by then things were moving too fast. But I remember Albert Hourani telling me that they prepared an overall report integrating the various papers—political, historical, economic, social, and so on—all into one mother paper, and attached the individual papers as appendices. I must acknowledge the man who edited my paper, John Cook. My English wasn't all that good then. He removed everything that showed anger or emotion. As I worked I discovered so much that was unjust, such as the eviction of hundreds of families from the Esdraelon plain—twenty-three villages in all. My feelings appeared in my writing. John said, "Calm down, you're writing for Britishers and Americans. You'll lose the strength of your argument." He went on talking until he persuaded me to tone things down here and there. He spent several days working on it.

I wrote other reports, a few on political economy—although I wasn't familiar with the concept then—relating to the struggle and the financing of the struggle, and passed them on to Jamal al-Husseini. These were parallel products to the organizational work I was doing for the Arab National Treasury. For example, I had to justify what taxes we were going to levy, so I wrote memoranda justifying them, and the principles underlying them, and also justifying the categories of taxation we were going to charge. To do that I had to go back to statistics on income distribution. Luckily a number of new studies had appeared in those last two or three years. One of the most important to my mind was a very detailed socioeconomic study of five villages. There was also the *Survey on Palestine*, also produced for the Anglo-American Committee of Inquiry, and the *National Income of Palestine*, put out yearly by Loftus, the government statistician. I began to be aware of it, and of the national accounts of 1944, 1945, and 1946—I think that's the last one that appeared. On the basis of these things, I would write brief memoranda of a few pages each, thinking that there was somebody to read them, and absorb them, and use them as inputs in their political decisions. The fact that people did not make adequate use of these things never stopped me from writing them. I was excitable and full of energy.

Another thing that I wrote in that period was a study on the foreign trade of Palestine, to show how much of it was with England and with western countries. That wasn't for Jamal al-Husseini. While I was preparing it, the father of Riad Khouri, publisher of a monthly in Jaffa, who was preparing an economic directory for Palestine, heard of it and said, "When you finish it, give it to me and I'll publish it in the directory." It appeared there, a long study. There was a lot of talk of boycott in those days, and I wanted to see what would be involved in this boycott. How much trade did we have in Palestine, how much of it came from England, how much came from America? I wanted it published, and I was sure I would find an outlet for it.

Directing the Arab National Fund

I was with Saba and Company as manager of their Jerusalem branch, when Dr. Izzat Tannous contacted me. I knew and respected Dr.

Tannous as a person who had given up his medical practice and his partnership in a very lucrative business with his brother Kamal, a big car agency in Palestine, to devote his time to the national cause. He used on me the formula that I heard from him a hundred times in the next year and a half—"When you came to see me, did you come by car?" I said, "No, I came by bus." He said, "Well, that bus had to have petrol. What is our petrol? We need money for the struggle. That's why I've called you to come and see me." It turned out that a group of notables, about ten or fifteen people, had got together and decided that we needed to collect money from the Palestinians. This ought to be done even though Palestine was not a rich country, and Palestinians were not rich. We ought to see how much we could collect. They envisaged this being done through an autonomous body, not directly under the Arab Higher Committee, because the Committee was not known for efficiency, and nobody would have had faith that the money collected would be used in the right way.

This group decided that the first thing was to establish a board of trustees. The president of the board of trustees was, if I remember correctly, al-Hajj Taher Qaraman, and the executive trustee was Dr. Izzat Tannous. The job he was offering me was to be the director general of the Arab National Treasury. I immediately accepted, before we even talked about terms. It was a little before I wrote the *Arab Land Hunger Report*, but by then I was quite well known because I had had several articles published. And all of them knew I was the commissioner general of the PPS for Palestine.

In Arabic the Treasury was called Beit al-Mal al-Arabi. In those days people didn't use the word 'Palestinian' so much. There were many things that were called Palestinian, but official names usually had the word 'Arab'—for instance al-Hay'a al-Arabiya al-Ulya, the Arab Higher Committee, not the Palestinian Higher Committee. Because the Jews were Palestinian too. *Beit al-mal* is a term from Islamic days, to indicate a treasury or fund.

I accepted the job, but insisted that it should not be run on the basis of *faza'a*. This means when a village rushes to the rescue of another village, or suddenly five people feel generous and they each pay a hundred pounds—the Treasury had to be managed scientifically. I asked them for a few days to prepare a brief memorandum setting out my ideas on the subject, then immediately went back and resigned from Saba and Company. I was very excited and enthusiastic about this new job. Tannous and the president of the board both assured me that I'd have a free hand in the administration, within the broad lines of the articles of association. They accepted my memorandum and proposed structure.

I started with something very small. Though it grew, at no time did the head office in Jerusalem have more than twelve people for the whole of Palestine. But we had people in each of the towns in Palestine, whether they were districts like Nablus, or sub-districts like Jenin and Tulkarm. There was a budget—they only gave us enough to start with because I said the preparations would take at least six months. So they gave us a budget for that period, and they said, "When you begin collecting, we will reconsider the budget." They were very small salaries. I remember my salary ended up being sixty Palestine pounds. At Saba's I got much the same, but at Saba I had many benefits. Within a year or two I could have become a partner and got a share in profits.

The period of preparation involved essentially two things: preparing ideas as to how we could legitimize what we would ask people to pay. I thought of two ways: a tax that every Palestinian would pay, whether rich or poor, male or female, young or old. That would be one shilling a year. The second type of tax should reflect ability to pay, a sort of income tax. But as we were not a government, and had no access to people's actual income, we had to divide people into categories according to occupations—physicians, lawyers, engineers, carpenters, electricians, cobblers, barbers . . . . Then within each occupation, we had a lower and upper limit, to relate that occupation to other occupations. That took a lot of work, and some research. I had to make use of the statistics of the government on income distribution. It was a thorough job that I'm still very proud of. The only remnant of it now is the memorandum that Dr. Sa'id Hammoud wrote when he was with me in the Planning Centre.[17] He interviewed me at great length, and wrote a thirty- or forty-page study of the Arab National Treasury experience.

That was the ideas side. The other thing that had to be prepared was the administrative structure. I decided that the best thing would be to involve as many people as possible in the effort. This could only happen if we had committees in every single town and large village. We had dozens of these committees, and I traveled to all of them. I remember at the beginning I used to be away from Jerusalem about twenty days a month, if not more, just going around from one sub-district to another. Alone. Of course letters were sent beforehand to leaders in each of these towns saying, "Soon the director general or one of his assistants will be visiting you to form a committee which will determine who is taxable, and to get these people together in accordance with occupation, and see how much tax each of them will have to pay."

So every time I went to a place, they already knew that I was coming. Invariably there would be a big meeting arranged, never less than fifty people in a town of six or seven thousand. That would be the Lajneh al-Wataniyeh [National Committee].[18] But I would stay on for a few days and meet with the barbers, the carpenters, the teachers, and so on. To each group, I'd say, "Now, teachers are paying between two and six pounds. You know each other's salaries, who should be paying two pounds?" They would say this, that, and the other person. We'd make lists, and the lists would be signed by two or three of them, who were sort of chairmen for each occupational group. I'd bring copies of these lists back with me.

In the districts themselves, in the seat of the districts, like Nazareth in Galilee, Nablus for the Nablus district, or Gaza for the southern district, we had a manager or director for the Treasury, a salaried person, who followed up the occupational committees to see to it that the collections were made. They also went to the groceries that were collecting the shilling tax for us, because this tax was collected separately through the groceries that were officially charged with the distribution of rationed foodstuffs. There were tickets of a shilling each, in three perforated sections. They would tear one part and give it to the head of the family when he would go to collect his flour and sugar at the beginning of the month. I don't remember anybody ever saying, "No, I can't pay." People just paid it in one go and forgot about it. For every shilling the grocers took the money from the family and issued a ticket. He would attach the second part of the perforated paper—each had the same number and the same wording—on a string, because they amounted to quite a bundle, and go to the bank and remit the money with what we called the *bordereau*, a covering notice saying 'Remitted by So-and-so, forty-five pounds,' let's say, 'to the Arab National Treasury, account number so-and-so, in Jerusalem.' They did it right away, after every collection. The grocers collected once a month, because the distribution of foodstuffs was once a month. Whereas with the occupation tax they would send us a remittance every month or so.

The preparations took more than six months, because though Palestine did not have many large towns, it had very many small towns and large villages. So going round establishing the committees and finding managers to run things took a great deal of time. Sami Alami was our manager in Gaza, in Jaffa it was Ali Shaath, the father of Nabil Shaath,[19] a very nice man. The manager in Nazareth was Khaled Fahoum, later president of the Palestine National Council. It was a full-time job in the cities; you had to go around to people, collecting. The managers of the districts had to go to the sub-districts too. They had hardly any assistants, because we told them we had to be careful with money. There I was, director general of the Arab National Treasury. I was not yet thirty. Well, at thirty Napoleon was already an emperor!

We began collecting money seriously early in 1947. Unfortunately we didn't have much time, because by then tension had risen and some areas were very risky to travel to. For instance, going to Galilee through the plain of Esdraelon was a very frightening experience, always, because there were many settlements there. Every time I had to think of somewhere to hide the papers in the car. The settlers would stop people. Going to Haifa was the same. They didn't have the right to set up checkpoints; it was like Beirut in the civil war. If the British were not physically standing by, they [the settlers] did what they wanted. I adopted a useful trick: whenever I saw people near a settlement looking out for a lift—generally Jewish young men and women—I would stop and say, "Hello! Where are you going? I'll take you." I would stop to unload the passengers, and they would wave me through.

The only time I was really frightened was when suddenly, between Jenin and Nazareth, I remembered that I had my revolver on me. Where could I put a revolver? They didn't usually do body searches, but in case they did, I wanted to be prepared. I stopped after Jenin, and suddenly it dawned on me that my new Studebaker had a mechanism whereby you pressed a button from inside, and the cap of the place where you put petrol into the tank opened. It didn't have a key from outside. I found that it could take the revolver; it could go in there and the cap would close. I thought that the worst they would do would be to take the revolver, but not hurt me. But they only looked under the seats, and signaled me through. Going to Haifa from Jerusalem was also very tricky.

Once I was going to Nablus, which I always thought was safe. But there was a Jewish settlement on the way, which later was destroyed by our people. Suddenly there was a bang and a hole in the glass this much above my head. I stopped, and looked round, and saw a young man on a rising bit of terrain. I thought it could only be he who had shot at me. I took my revolver and fired two shots in his direction. I had had no military training. When I first got the revolver, which the Fund gave me to carry around in my travels, I went to Jericho for a week with Ahmad, and we aimed at telephone posts. So I fired two shots in the direction of that young man. They were the only shots I aimed at a human being in my life. He ducked and disappeared, and that was it. He knew I must be an Arab because no Jew would be traveling in such a fancy car at that time.

The job was very tiring—there was much traveling to make sure there would not be the slightest whiff of scandal that money was mis-allocated. We were only responsible for the collection of the money, not for the spending of it. I insisted that the money should go to the highest authority possible, and at the same time the mufti decided that he wanted to get the checks. So every two or three months I used to go and see him, once in Aley, and once or twice in Cairo, in Helmiyat al-Zaytun, on the road to the airport. With the Arab Higher Committee, there was inefficiency but not dishonesty. People always thought that money went 'around' [that is, into people's pockets]. But there was no money. People didn't realize this; they thought that the Arab Higher Committee must have masses of money from the Arab League. Nonsense! I became a favorite of the mufti; he appreci-ated my work very much, especially that in the few months that we worked we succeeded in collecting 176,000 pounds sterling. From a poor country like Palestine! And we had only just begun.

Then Izzat Tannous, carried away by the success of the work, and against my advice, began to make endless statements to the press. I kept saying to him, "For God's sake, be discreet! The British will bother us, the Zionists will threaten us."

In fact, the Zionists twice tried to attack our head office, in a Tannous building in Jerusalem, very near the Old City, near Wadi Sultan. We had guards, and I made sure that they were well trained. I made them come after dark, so that if six or seven Zionists crept up the hill to get to our office to dynamite it, they wouldn't realize that there were guards until suddenly there would be a line of fire facing them. Twice they tried that. The guards just shot; we don't know whether they hit anybody. We began to get translations of news items in the Jewish press saying, "The Palestinians are collecting money for buying arms"—which we were. We gave the money to the mufti to use for buying arms. But it didn't have time to go very far. I remember in one of the statements [to the press], at the very end, probably toward the last week of our operations, Izzat Tannous gave the figure of £176,000, bragging about it. A day later, an old Jewish widow from South Africa, already living in Palestine, donated a million sterling. I felt the futility of all our work.

The work went on until it became impossible to travel without very serious risk to one's life. At that point the Arab Higher Committee said to me, "Look, you can't collect money now, when anybody who has a few extra pounds wants to keep them to buy bread for his family in case prices go up." They wanted me to do something else, to be a liaison officer between the Arab Higher Committee and the British army, which was beginning to vacate camps. I met with the commanding officer in Jerusalem. He said, "This is our policy: Where a camp falls in a predominantly Jewish area, we give it to the Haganah. Where it falls in a predominantly Arab area, we give it to you. But where it is fifty-fifty, a mixed area, we leave it and you run for it."

It was a camp in this mixed category, which we got to ahead of the Jews, that led to me becoming a prisoner of war. It was a camp east of Bekaa where the Jaysh al-Inqadh[20] said it had sent a hundred and fifty men. They arrived but then they withdrew. I waited and waited and waited for reinforcements, but they never came, and then the road to the Old City was closed, and we were trapped. At the beginning I didn't want to leave because they kept saying that they were sending troops. By the last two or three days, we could have left by walking down the Wadi Sultan road to get through one of the gates of the Old City, though it would only be possible at night.

The Mufti[21]

I must say that I had a great respect for Hajj Amin al-Husseini, whom I came to know in 1946, a few months after I took over the directorship of the Palestine National Fund. At that time I had nothing to say to him about the Fund, because we hadn't collected any money yet, but I had things to tell him on the basis of information given to me by people who were militarily knowledgeable about what we ought to do, what kind of training we ought to have, what kind of arms we ought to buy. I collected all this information and organized it, and brought it up in points. I went to Cairo, where he was living then. He was living somewhere near to Gamal Abdel Nasser's house, on the road to the airport.

The mufti was in Iraq when the Rashid Ali Keylani revolt took place. Then when it collapsed he went to Iran. When Iran collapsed he went to Germany. And then I'm not sure whether he came to Lebanon first or to Egypt, because I visited him in both places. The first time I met him, he had with him Jamal al-Husseini and Munif al-Husseini, his son-in-law. I didn't care for Munif. Later I discovered that he was very anti-Christian.

I talked at great length to the mufti, about how important it was to organize. I also told him about the PPS, and he indicated that he would welcome any group; he wouldn't stop at ideological differences, like the PPS talking about Syrian nationalism rather than Arab nationalism. He was a pragmatist. He didn't want to be bothered with all these theological differences. I didn't find the same readiness to cooperate in Sa'adeh later on. He [the mufti] saw the point of organization, and saw the point of putting arms in the hands of these young men that were to be organized. But where was the money? I remember him saying, "My hope is that you'll find money through the Arab National Fund." Soon after that I began to have money and to send it to him.

He also was very much in favor of the cities organizing guerrilla groups or fighters, to defend their own homes and quarters rather than depend on the villagers. I must say that I liked him very much; I liked the way he made me feel that he trusted me, even though I was unknown to him. Of course those who organized my trip had sent him information about me. Judging by the references he made to the Arab Higher Committee in Jerusalem, I don't think he had a high opinion of them, or their ability to organize and to mobilize people. He was very sad; you could tell that he felt that he could do a great deal if he were in Palestine, but he wasn't able to be there. I felt that if he were in Palestine his presence would have a mobilizing effect but not an organizing one. He couldn't form brigades.

One thing about the mufti that impressed me greatly was the way he listened. He was very attentive when I talked, and you could see his mind was working, preparing questions, seeing the significance of points made. He would ask many questions. I think he asked more questions than he made statements about the things I told him. Every now and then I would press some point to see whether he was going to do something about it, especially ideas related to two kinds of organization. One was to form a group of young men to be trained as saboteurs in case Palestine fell, because I was convinced by then, after having talked to some military people, that we had no chance of holding on. We needed young men who would stay behind as civilians, carpenters and plumbers and so on, but who knew how to blow up a bridge or cut a telephone line.

The other kind of organization was more ambitious, that is, to have a fighting force even if Palestine fell, whether outside or in secluded parts of Palestine, the way the Jews used to train in areas inside Palestine. Of course they had protection; they could work with the police and nobody would surprise them. It would not be as easy for us as it had been for the Zionists.

When I made such suggestions, he would agree wholeheartedly but say, "I don't have the money." He would talk bitterly of the Arabs, and how they were not helping, although he was not asking them for much. It was not a question of millions but of hundreds of thousands of pounds. I also felt that he was compassionate, although people thought of him as ruthless. Whenever he knew of a case of hardship, he would try to help; and he would ask about specific people, how were they doing? Were they able to manage? My relationship with him was sporadic but I found him a likable person. You couldn't tell from what he said how capable he was as a leader—he must have had some leadership qualities, but he did not advertise them.

I think his essential weakness was that he always thought that the purity of the cause he was working for—the setting up of an independent Palestine, saving Palestine from a takeover by the Zionists—was enough in itself, to the point where he did not build a fighting force in the modern sense—well organized and well trained—to face the situation, and depended on the spirit of the villagers and their willingness to rush into battle when it was needed.

Maybe part of it was that he feared a big organization, because he wouldn't be able to control it. He could control an entourage, people to whom he whispered and who whispered to him. He'd be aware of details, of what was happening. He'd have his finger on the pulse. A big organization would have to be decentralized to a certain degree, and he would lose touch. Perhaps he would have to depend on them, and they would depend less on him. Perhaps he was afraid that some charismatic young fighter would emerge who would take away some of the loyalty and support that was his, the mufti's, at that point.

He was very traditional. It's true that he didn't stuff his statements with Qur'anic verses as many politicians do today. He understood the struggle as a national struggle involving Christians and Muslims. But that was the extent of his modernity. You didn't feel that he had any notion of a socioeconomic content in the call to arms. He only pointed in broad terms to the stake that all Palestinians had in protecting Palestine from the Zionists, who were trying to take it over. He was not more specific, perhaps because he realized what every little fellah [peasant] was aware of, that the danger was dual, or rather triple: loss of land, loss of our numerical majority, and the predominance of Zionist institutions. Perhaps he did not need to say more than that.

He was successful as a magnet in attracting the loyalty and devotion of the vast majority of Palestinian Arabs, partly because of his name, partly because of his position as Grand Mufti of Jerusalem, and partly because of his persistence. He went on with the struggle whether forced into flight or banished or whatever. He went on. To the best of my knowledge, nobody every seriously or credibly accused him of deviating from his national stand, or of serving somebody else's interests.

If he had connections with Germany, he did that for the service of the Palestinian cause. If he fought the British it was for that. If he made friends with the French briefly it was to counterbalance the hostility of the British toward him. I think to that extent he had points in his favor that supported his leadership. But he had many odds against him. People today judge him by the endowments of the present Resistance movement. People say, "Why didn't he do what the PLO is doing now?" He didn't have the money that the PLO has. And the historical moment he worked in was different from the historical moment that we are in now.

As to ending the revolt in 1939, I think at no point did the mufti trust the British, or trust that they would keep their word. But the British made an offer he could not refuse. And the Arab governments said to him: "If you want us to say one word in your favor, you must break the impasse. Stop the general strike, and let's see what the British have to say." After a long strike, the country was in great hardship. And the British had brought in a huge number of soldiers. To have refused a settlement then, on the eve of the Second World War, would have meant that the British would have been even more ferocious in their repression.

Once the mufti was no longer in Palestine, the British managed to freeze everything. They said it was wartime, and that they would not allow anything to weaken the war effort. At the same time the economic situation in Palestine improved because there was full employment. Inflation always produces an illusion of prosperity in the beginning. People think that because they're getting more wages, things are good. Many businesses and economic institutions were started by Arabs. People became more occupied with economic than with political affairs. The Arab Higher Committee had no mobilizing power to get people to arm or to attack settlements. And the British would have hanged people for anything then. The emergency rules were a strong instrument in their hands. If somebody was caught with a penknife with a blade longer than five centimeters, he could be sentenced to death.

Last Days in Jerusalem

Part of the reason for the despair of the Palestinians in 1947–48 was the fact that the Zionists were undertaking successful terrorist acts against the British, such as the hanging of the sergeants, after an Irgun or Stern member was hanged. The incident that I witnessed that was extremely effective—because it showed the British and the Palestinians how well equipped and organized the Jews were—was the blowing up of the King David Hotel. I was standing with Fuad Saba on the balcony in the Bible Building, opposite the Maskoubieh. The King David was south of us. As I was talking to him, before I heard the explosion, I saw a wing of the King David rise a few meters in the air, and then collapse and crumble into pieces. Then the noise of the explosion reached me—it must have been about two hundred meters away. I said, "Mr. Saba! Look! The King David has gone up." He thought I was out of my mind—he had his back to the window. Ninety-five people were killed in that operation— British, Jewish, and Arab.

The combativeness of the villagers was proven over and over again in confrontations with the Haganah, and in the countryside. I can't remember how many well-armed, well-guarded convoys were destroyed in Bab al-Wad, the road down the wadi from Jerusalem toward Jaffa and Lydda. Tens of Zionists were killed in every single confrontation, and there were many such confrontations, especially in the hill country. These attacks were carried out mainly by villagers from the Bab al-Wad neighborhood. But the toughest were from the Nablus and Hebron areas.

The villagers in those areas were already there, in the hills, mobile, more or less full-time fighters. Though the peasant commanders of the 1936 revolt had mostly been killed, by 1947–48 there were new commanders, another generation. And there were many fighters who fought in the late twenties and early thirties and again in 1947–48, for instance Bahjat Abu Gharbiyeh, who was a colleague of mine in the PLO executive. These local commanders who had been active before worked with Abdel Qadir al-Husseini and the Jaysh al-Muqaddas. There was a degree of coordination and exchange of information between them—the confrontations demonstrated that. There must have been prior knowledge of a convoy being prepared at such and such a time to go down or to come up from Tel Aviv to Jerusalem.

I think it was in 1947 that I began hearing the words 'Jaysh al-Jihad al-Muqaddas.' Abdel Qader was appointed commander in that period. It was nominally under the command of the Arab Higher Committee, but the conduct of the fighting was Abdel Qader's decision, or that of his état-major.[22] The Jaysh al-Muqaddas cost the Israelis considerable losses. Its recruits were peasants rather than townspeople. There were some city recruits, without doubt, but nothing to speak of in terms of their proportion to the total. West Jerusalem where I lived, modern Jerusalem, did not contribute much, though there were certainly more volunteers from the Old City. Towns like Hebron, Nablus, Jenin, and Safad contributed more.

The more modern and westernized the town or city the less its contribution. Though the coastal cities were all modernized in comparison with the inland cities, there were differences between them. Haifa was more modern than Jaffa. It was also more mixed than Jaffa; it had a large Jewish community, and there were more business connections between the two communities than in Jaffa. Jaffa was an Arab city face to face with Tel Aviv, so it had to keep its 'Arab purity.' There were fighters in Jaffa, but they fought in their yards and quarters, whereas fighters from places like Safad, Hebron, Nablus, and Jenin took part in battles outside their own cities and the towns. They weren't permanent fighters, with regular leave every third week, but they were permanent in the sense that most of what they did was fighting. Even Tiberias had a few young men who took part. But it was all very disjointed. There was no General Command. Abdel Qadir al-Husseini may have been the commander, but his orders certainly didn't reach as far as Tiberias and Safad. There was no way of communicating, no staff, no telephones, no field radios. We didn't have time. The Jews were prepared for it—they had been preparing from the time the first settlements were attacked, even before the mandate was established, within the first few years of the British entry into Palestine.

After the mufti was banished, there was a noticeable drop in morale. There was a feeling that top leadership was missing. When the mufti was there, other elements like the Nashashibis and the Istiqlal people could not defy him openly. When he was outside, their prominence—or defiance—became relatively greater. Their voices were more conciliatory. They could be heard saying, "Let's see what the British will do" or "Let's see what King Abdullah will do." There was a certain envy of the mufti's supremacy among other politicians.

Holding Out in Qatamoun

Between late 1946 and the spring of 1948 when I was taken prisoner, I had the opportunity to talk to many people in the Qatamoun area. Every now and then you'd hear that five or six young men had spent a night or two with Ibrahim Abu Dayyeh's men, protecting Qatamoun. But that was not a line of defense. A few days later you'd ask about these five or six young men and find that three had left. By the end, when I was taken prisoner of war, there were just twenty-three young men in the whole of that part of west Jerusalem. We were not really fighters. Three of us had revolvers, but to be honest they were ornaments. What training had I had? Nothing.

I began to notice people leaving soon after the Partition Plan. But departures accelerated a great deal after the Qastal battle, in which

Abdel Qadir al-Husseini was killed, and after the Deir Yassin massacre a few days later. It was then that the flow of people moving out
became a flood. By the end of April you couldn't meet anybody in the
part of west Jerusalem I lived in.

You could divide the young men I talked with into three categories:
one was people who felt that this bad situation, this utter unprepared-
ness, should make us do something even at the twelfth hour. I think
I was in that group, and possibly we were not realistic, because what
could we do? But honestly—there is no dramatics in this at all—I felt
that I would rather die than run away with the others. That's why I
insisted on staying on until I was taken prisoner of war. Most of my
friends thought that I was a fool. But I still justify it to myself, and I still
feel I would have been better dead than among those who ran away.

The second category was people who felt they must do something. So they would rush out and buy a revolver at a very high price,
and put it on their hip, ostentatiously. Then they too would run away.

The third group said, "*Ya hasirti* [my grief], what can we do?"
They would recite chapters of Jeremiah to you, expressing their
frustration and helplessness, but they wouldn't do anything positive.
These were the majority of the people, especially in the cities.

By April morale was very low. Yet at the same time, the Arab
Higher Committee was broadcasting from Ramallah and, contrary
to what the Zionists claimed later, all their messages were, "Stay
put!" I know this for a fact because we prepared the text of several
of the calls that Anwar Nusseibeh read on the radio. Anwar wasn't
a fighter, but he was very active politically. He was the secretary of
the Lajneh al-Qawmiyeh. Every city had its Lajneh al-Qawmiyeh to
look after provisions and arms, urging people to stay put, and if the
Jaysh al-Inqadh came, telling it where to go. These committees were
under the umbrella of the Arab Higher Committee, but generally
they were formed by self-motivated people.

Qatamoun, the area I was living in, was empty by the end. Almost
everybody I knew left when the area became dangerous because of

Jewish infiltrators. One morning I woke up and found a paper stuck to my car in Hebrew. It was from some Jewish organization that had come at night, and stuck notices to cars saying, "If you don't leave you have only yourself to blame." Later they went beyond my house to the Semiramis hotel in Qatamoun and blew it up. Eleven people were killed. It was a small hotel near a flour mill and an ice factory. They said it was being used by our fighters and commanders from the villages for meetings. At that point I moved a few hundred yards down from there, to the house of William Hadawi, an architect, the brother of Sami Hadawi.

When that area became 'hot'—the Jews were gradually moving in everywhere—I took over the house of an Armenian dentist in Baq'a. All these houses were empty. People were begging us to live in them, Ahmad and I. Everyone said, "Why don't you take my house?" All of them went to Amman; most had relatives there. Poor loyal Ahmad wouldn't leave me. He said, "You're obstinate but I'm going to stay with you, no matter what."

By that time the whole of Qatamoun probably contained no more than a hundred and fifty people. The Qatamoun battle was very stiff. I remember reading somewhere that the Zionists lost eight hundred people trying to take West Jerusalem, and that the hardest area to crack was Qatamoun. It was defended at first by the Jaysh al-Jihad al-Muqaddas under Abdel Qadir al-Husseini, but later it was defended by little groups led by their own tough fighters. In our area the leader was Ibrahim Abu Dayyeh, a little man, very brave and very likable, a very tough fighter.[23] I was in the habit of helping him by carrying rifles and ammunition from the Old City in the trunk of my car—I had a big Studebaker with a lot of room in the trunk. I was able to do this, though there was a wire fence around the area, guarded by British soldiers, because I had a letter from Ghassan Tweini, son of the owner of the *an-Nahar* newspaper in Beirut, and a friend, saying that I was their correspondent. This enabled me to have a sign stuck to my car from the official Information Office, with the word 'press' on it, in Arabic and English. So they never opened the trunk. That's how I got to know Abu Dayyeh. There was an atmosphere of familiarity and friendliness between us. At a certain point he told me the situation was hopeless unless we had help from outside, essentially from the Arab Legion.

A Last-minute Attempt to Save Arab Jerusalem

This story means going back a bit. Several people were involved in the attempt, including Abu Dayyeh and Darwish Mikdadi, then director of the Arab Office in Jerusalem. Mikdadi said to me, "Why don't you go and describe the situation to King Abdullah? He might be able to give us some help." I gladly agreed to do this, but before going to Amman, I talked to Colonel Abdullah al-Tal, head of the Arab Legion force in Jerusalem. They were nominally there to protect the Jordan consulate and other Arab consulates, but in fact he and the small number of soldiers with him were providing essential help to the Palestinian fighters. He liked the idea, and he told me about the military situation in detail.

Darwish Mikdadi arranged a meeting for me with King Abdullah. We went to Amman together, but on the way Mikdadi said, "I'm not going to say anything except introduce you; you're going to do the talking." I had never talked to a king and, besides, it wasn't going to be easy to get him to send more men to support us and to defend West Jerusalem. We all felt that he would let West Jerusalem fall because it was being protected by Hajj Amin al-Husseini's men. We went in, and Mikdadi made the introduction.

I said, "Your Majesty, the situation is very tough. We have good terrain in our hands but we are short of men and arms. If we can resist this final assault by the Zionists, we can save Qatamoun, and that would be crucial in saving West Jerusalem. It's a matter of days." He said, "Why do you say that West Jerusalem is in danger? I don't understand how." I said, "May I draw you a map, Your Majesty?" I went around and squatted next to him—there was no chair—and drew him a very rough sketch. I said "This is Jerusalem, and this hilltop here is Qatamoun. It commands the areas that are in Jewish hands. If they attack us, they'll be exposed." There was a no-man's-land between Qatamoun and the Jewish areas. I couldn't quote Abdullah al-Tal because he asked me not to. I said I had it from military sources.

The king looked at the map and said, "Let me see if our consul in Jerusalem confirms what you are saying, that help is urgently needed." When he said this my heart sank because the consul was having an affair with the daughter of the Latin American consul general, and we knew that she was in contact with the Jewish Agency. She was a very attractive young woman, and in normal times I would have envied the consul. In any case, the king asked for the Jerusalem consulate by telephone, and talked to the consul. I could hear him saying, "Your Majesty! Who is telling you these stories that Jerusalem is about to fall to the Zionists? Nonsense!" The king turned to me and said, "Of course I believe what my consul says; he knows the situation better than you." I tried to argue with the king within limits, but he said, "Nothing doing, I will not send any men." I said, "Even if they take off the uniform of the Arab Legion and put on just a militia uniform?" He said, "I won't let them go either as military men or civilians. What kind of city is this, and what kind of defense, if you cannot wait for a few days? In a matter of days, my victorious army will liberate the whole of Jerusalem." On that confident note we had to thank him and leave, Darwish and myself.

I went back to Jerusalem and relayed the information to Abdullah al-Tal and the Lajneh al-Qawmiyeh. This Lajneh was stationed in East Jerusalem, inside the wall, and our telephones were certainly tapped. Anyway, I contacted them by telephone. I talked first of all to Anwar Nusseibeh, and he said, "Stay where you are, we'll see what we can do." When the situation got more dangerous, I talked to the head of the Lajneh al-Qawmiyeh, Ahmad Hilmi Basha—who became the prime minister of the All-Palestine Government in Gaza[24]—and he gave me the same assurances.

The job given me by the National Treasury at the end, as I mentioned earlier, was to take responsibility for any military camps that the British left in the neighborhood of West Jerusalem. One of these military camps was near the area where I lived, and we were ahead of the Jews in taking control of it. The Jaysh al-Inqadh managed to send a hundred and fifty soldiers there. I don't know if that was the real number but that's what the Lajneh told me. They were headed by an Iraqi major called Fadel Bek; that's the only name he was known by. One day, just two or three days before I was caught, word came that these hundred and fifty men had disappeared, melted away. I started again, not asking for arms to protect Qatamoun, but for a replacement for the camp, because this was a crucial position that we had to maintain. I was assured about five times every day, every time I telephoned, that the men were on their way, any minute now they would arrive. They never came.

Yusif's parents with his sister Mary stayed in Tiberias until April 17, a few days after the massacre of Deir Yassin. Mary remembers that they packed everything, including furniture, and had it taken down to the road to be taken away by truck. Someone from the Scots Mission saw them and said, "Why take all those things? You'll be back in a few days. We'll take care of them." Abu Yusif planned to accompany Umm Yusif and Mary to Lebanon and then return, but on the way to Nazareth they heard that Tiberias had fallen. They stayed for a few days in Nazareth, and during that time Abu Yusif disappeared for several hours. When he rejoined Umm Yusif, she asked him if he had gone home to get her jewelry, which they had hidden under a threshold between two rooms before leaving. He said no, he had been in church praying for Palestine. For an account of Tiberias and the expulsions of 1948 see Mustafa Abbasi, "The End of Arab Tiberias: The Arabs of Tiberias and the Battle for the City in 1948," Journal of Palestine Studies 47, no. 3 (2008).

10

Prisoner of War,
May 1948–Spring 1949

I was taken prisoner of war four or five days after the state of Israel was established. I had realized that I was going to be taken prisoner because I could see that the Zionists were advancing on Qatamoun, and closing the roads out of it one after the other. I felt like a bird with a snake circling around its head; it can't move, but waits to be grabbed by the snake and swallowed.

At the same time I didn't want to leave. At the beginning my friend Ahmad Abdel Khalek and I could have left. We were together with a few others in Baq'a, in the Greek colony area, and we could still have made it if we walked down hill into the back of the Old City. But I felt that if a young man like me left, I couldn't blame somebody who was older, with a family and children, if they ran away. So I stayed on.

When we were told by people in the area that the Zionists were closing in, Ahmad and I and about twenty other young men from the quarter decided to go and register in the German Hospice, where people could stay as paying guests. It had already been placed under International Red Cross protection.

The nuns were very kind, and registered us as bona fide guests who had been there before the time of our arrival. They told us that there were others who had come with their families. In all, there might have been a hundred and fifty people there. By then the whole of West Jerusalem, west of the German Hospice, had already fallen to the Jews.

The more daring of the young men who went out saw the Zionists were already occupying the Arab Higher Committee Office, a bit to the west. What surprised me was that they were throwing sheaves of paper from the windows by the kilogram, not caring to collect and study them—I had assumed that they would systematically collect every scrap of paper. They were not shooting at us, just closing in, moving a building at a time.

Then one afternoon somebody who was acting as a scout came to say that it would be an hour at most before they reached the hospice. I rushed to the mother superior of the convent and said to her, "We are going to be encircled, and soon they'll take the young men, God knows where, maybe to shoot us. Since you are under Red Cross protection, please pass sheets of paper around so that everybody will fill in their names." It was dinnertime; we were in one dining room. I took over as though I were already elected leader of the group, and said, "The Jews are outside; soon they'll be here. We'd better give our names to the sisters here so there will be a record of who has been taken. They won't take women, children, or older men, but for us young men this is essential." They took our names. A few weeks later, when the mother superior managed to have access to the Red Cross, she passed the lists to them. That's when the Israelis acknowledged our existence as prisoners.

Another thing that we did—the few of us who had pistols—was to bury them in the garden. The nuns didn't say a word. I also brought my car inside the walls of the hospice. It was a Studebaker, a beautiful car, almost brand new.

Then one of the nuns came into the dining room and said, "Please stay calm. The officer in charge is going to come in with his soldiers, and he'll tell you what to do next." In came a number of soldiers carrying submachine guns. They were very nervous and edgy; they went all around with their backs to the wall, facing us with their guns in their hands.

One of them, whom I took to be an officer, started talking in Hebrew. I said, "We don't speak Hebrew. Will you address us in Arabic or in English?" One of our young men, a smart aleck, stood up and turned to us beaming as though he had scored a great achievement, and said, "*Ana bihki 'ebrani* [I speak Hebrew]." Later we found out that he was Lebanese and worked as a cook somewhere. I said to him, "Shut up! We want our language to be used or English." I turned to the officer and said, "I'm sure you speak English. We don't trust this man's translation." So he spoke to us in English.

The officer said, "You're going to be called in for interrogation over the next few days. After that we'll see what we will do with you." But the first thing they did was to separate us into two groups: women and everybody below fifteen or above fifty-five were allowed to go to their rooms—I never saw them after that. That left twenty or thirty young men, among whom were Ahmad and I. They began taking us to be interrogated in an upper room in the hospice.

We had all thrown away our identification papers. I for instance threw away my Syrian passport because they were extremely hostile to Syria, as well as to anybody who had taken part in the 1936 Intifada, or in the fighting under Abu Dayyeh, or Abdel Qadir al-Husseini.

Interrogation

When my turn came, much later that night, they put me in a chair, and the guard stood behind me with a revolver at my neck. In front of me sat a smallish young man with a smile on his face. I noticed that on the floor there was a blanket covering two mounds; I couldn't see what was under them. The officer had a long stick in his hand, like the one that teachers use to point at maps. He said, "Tell me about yourself." I said, "What do you want me to tell you?" He said, "What do you do?" I said, "I'm an accountant, the manager of the head office of Saba and Company, the auditors." He said, "What does your job consist of?" I explained it. He said, "Let's be a little more honest. Tell me about your real activity. You may have been with Saba and Company before. But what are you doing now?" At that point I assumed that he knew that I had left Saba and Company more than a year before, and that I was the director of the Arab National Fund. But I didn't want to collapse and tell him everything. So I said, "Well, Saba and Company's work has almost ended, so I have an assignment as a journalist with *al-Nahar* newspaper. My car is out in the garden, and it has a press sticker on it."

He said, "If so, why do you have all this material on the . . ." he tried to translate PPS—"in the trunk of your car?" I had forgotten all about it. For weeks I had been collecting all the documents I had on the PPS in Palestine, and all this material, including the seal of the party, was in a big parcel in the trunk of the car.

He lifted one side of the blanket, and I could see the material there. So there was no hiding it. He asked if we had trained and mobilized people. I said, "No, we were too small a group for that. We just wrote articles." He went on asking about the PPS, and its attitude to the establishment of Israel. I spoke frankly, because all along I thought that I wasn't going to get out alive, so I might as well be brave, and say what I felt as a young Palestinian Arab. It went on for several hours. He didn't mention the Arab National Fund. This made me relax a little. I felt that if their records were good, he would have got a report about me from some central office, and would have asked, "What about your work with the mufti?" That would have been the most serious thing for me to face. But he didn't say that.

Three or four hours after the start of the interrogation, he smiled broadly and lifted the blanket from the other mound. I saw that it contained love letters exchanged with the woman I was in love with for years, tied in a string. He had obviously looked at one or two of them. He said, "As to this literature, it would make very interesting reading, but I'll have to have more leisure." I was terrified to death that something in these letters would reveal the identity of the woman. We never used names except on the envelope, and I had destroyed the envelopes, but I thought that if they had good intelligence they might find out who she was. That would be a problem.

It took two or three days for the interrogations to finish. By then the number of young men had increased, because other people had been caught from other areas, such as the YMCA, and brought to the hospice.

Soon after, they told us to collect our belongings, and to go out in line. We had practically nothing with us—not even pajamas or a toothbrush—because we were just pretending to be living there. They had brought armored buses with no windows in them. They crowded us in with guards who locked the door from inside. We started moving in a convoy. Of course we couldn't see outside.

About fifteen minutes after we started, the bus suddenly stopped. The door opened a little bit, and a soldier put his head in and asked, "Who does the Studebaker number so-and-so belong to?" I said, "Me. My name is so and so." He said, "I'm not interested in your name. How does the radio work? The officer is driving it and he can't run the radio." I said, "Let him find out for himself." I foolishly thought that regular armies would register property they seized and return it after the armistice.

We drove on and on—it felt like hours. Later, those who knew Jerusalem well realized that they must have driven round and round so that we wouldn't know where we were going. From our first prison camp we could see Bethlehem far to the south, though we couldn't see much of Jerusalem. On the way to the camp, there was very little talking among the prisoners. The guards kept saying "Shut up! Shut up!" if anybody opened his mouth— they were afraid we might be inciting each other. But if the prisoners said anything at all it was "May God protect us!" or "My poor family!"

The First Camp

Eventually we stopped and they opened the doors—"Come down!" The place turned out to be a new settlement. Only the foundations of the houses were laid, there were no walls at all. It was called Nabi Shaalan. There was some scaffolding on which guards sat with their submachine guns pointing at us. There was no fence around us, but we were heavily guarded. They made us squat, and put our hands behind our necks.

Somebody spoke to us in English, "I'm the commander of this camp, and you'll have to obey my orders and the orders of any sergeant or soldier. We have to see what we'll do with you. We consider you saboteurs. According to international law we are allowed to shoot you. But because Israel is a state now, we want to be correct. Before shooting you we need to make sure that you are really saboteurs and under what article of the law you will be shot."

I said, "No, we are prisoners of war." A few months before Palestine fell I had looked up the international war conventions—the Geneva Conventions had not been signed yet but there were conventions from earlier wars—so I knew what the rights of prisoners of war were. When I said that we were prisoners of war, he said, "Huh! A prisoner of war is a soldier, he's in uniform, he has arms, he has a number. You have none of these things. What army are you with?" We couldn't pretend that we belonged to any army. They weren't much of an army either. They all had different uniforms; some were in khaki trousers, others had gray flannel trousers; most had a jacket or trousers that were quasi-military in color and shape.

That night we were divided into three or four of the room foundations. We slept without food or water, in the open, on the bare ground. Some of us wanted to bring flat stones or tiles to put as a pillow under our heads, but they wouldn't let us. I had a pair of gray flannels and a zip jacket. Luckily it was warm. All my life, I've suffered from a weak stomach, and there I was near Jerusalem, thousands of feet above sea level. I unzipped my jacket, folded it and put it on top of my stomach, and slept like that on the cement, with my shoes under my head. I had very nice crêpe shoes, with a thick sole that provided some comfort. We stayed there for about six weeks, until the siege of Jerusalem was lifted. No blanket, no pillow, nothing!

Next day they began giving us food, but what food! The guards made their own tea, in saucepans over firewood. When they had finished it, they sent us the saucepans with the leftover tea and told us to make a fire with wood from the immediate neighborhood. They gave us used tuna fish or jam cans to use as cups. There weren't enough, so each six of us had to use the same can. And I am fussy about using other people's cups. We had to cook the tea over and over again. For many days that's all the food we got. It was terrible. But the interesting thing is that I didn't have any pain in my stomach at all, not once, though before I would get a stomach pain if ever I slept uncovered.

They said, "You will get three liters of water each every twenty-four hours for drinking, washing yourselves, and washing the utensils." But we got much less than three liters; it was more like three Coca-Cola bottles. We had to be very, very careful with water. As to food, all we got was one hundred grams of bread per person per day, no more than a quarter of an Arab loaf. There was nothing else—no jam, no butter, no margarine, no olives, nothing—just bread and tea. There was no sugar—they didn't have sugar either, because Jerusalem was still under siege.

After the tea had been cooked three or four times, I would dry it out and use it as tobacco. The greatest thing was getting the first food parcel, which contained some tobacco for my pipe. But that was much later when we were taken to a proper POW camp by the sea, two or three months after I was first taken prisoner.

Some days after we had settled into this routine, the officer came, lined us up, and said to me, "Since you are acting the brave fellow, I'll talk to you as the leader of the camp. Tell these dogs that they must dig cesspits that you will use as toilets" (before that they allowed us to go a short distance away and do our business in the open). So I looked around and I said, "I don't see any dogs here." He said, "Don't try to be clever. I am the officer here; I'm ordering you to tell these dogs to dig three toilets. The sergeant will tell you where to dig them." I said, "Unless you say, 'Tell your men, or your colleagues, or your friends, or the other prisoners of war . . . .'" I always tried to bring in the words 'prisoners of war'—we were scared because they kept saying to us, "You are saboteurs, you ought to be shot. When the order comes . . . !"

He said, "First we haven't decided that you are prisoners of war. But all right, tell your men to—." He was so angry by that time that he fired three shots between my feet. I was standing in front of him, and he was shaking with anger. He did not aim at me; he shot at the ground very close between my legs. It was the first time in my life that a bullet came that close to me. So I shut up.

We started digging. They gave us some kerosene tins with *kils* (lime) in them; every few days we had to throw some in. Then they brought us wood, and asked if somebody knew carpentry. It wasn't difficult to make a frame, and to nail some jute sacks to the frame. But when we went in we had to leave the flap open, and the guards would stand or sit in front of us, watching us. There was nothing except stones to clean our bottoms. We weren't allowed to use big stones in case we threw them at the guards.

The First Red Cross Visit

Then one day a Red Cross car came. God, what a relief it was! I almost fainted. Out of the car came a civilian, short, speaking English with a French accent. He said "I'm Dr. So-and-so, I represent the Red Cross. I'm coming to tell you that you are under Red Cross protection."[1] He was so good, that man. He remained a friend for two or three years after I was released; we corresponded with each other. He was Swiss. It was thanks to the nuns that he got our names. They went to some minister or other, and said, "We know that you have these people. We want to know their location, their numbers, their names, everything." The Israelis denied our existence at first. When they were squeezed they said, "We only have some saboteurs." The nuns said, "No, you took them from the German Hospice, which is under Red Cross protection." In the end the Israelis had to admit our existence and our numbers.

A couple of weeks later, parcels came from families. Five or six of us got parcels the first time, no letters to begin with. Ahmad got a parcel, and I got a parcel prepared by friends in Amman who had heard that we had been taken prisoner. When we disappeared they assumed that we'd either been killed or taken prisoner. They sent me sardines, jam, cheese like Picon, chocolates, tobacco, and another pipe. God! I'll never forget that.

The guards began to envy us, and smile at us hoping that we would give them something. They were almost as afraid of us as we were of them. There were about ten guards at any one time, and we were around 123 prisoners, but they were armed and we weren't. When we wanted to open the cans we had to be nice to them because we had no knives. We had to give them a bit of something as a bribe.

I remember how mean hunger makes one. When my parcel came and I opened the jam—I longed for something sweet—I called Ahmad and a young boy from the Sakkab family, who must have been only sixteen or seventeen. I called these three or four around me in a conspiratorial manner. The majority hadn't received anything, and yet it didn't occur to me to share with them. Greed, self-preservation—I wanted to fill myself, to have mouthfuls of something sweet: jam, chocolate . . . . After that those of us who had received parcels began to feel ashamed, so we got together—one of the people we invited to share was Rassem al-Husseini, a very good friend in later years. We gathered and said, "We must share. Now that we have begun to receive parcels, more will come." So we distributed a little to everybody.

Parcels began to come to others as well, so the food situation became a little easier. But the bread remained little, and they gave us only five grams of sugar per person per day, a teaspoonful. Later I started receiving parcels from my family in Beirut.

One day while we were still near Jerusalem, a civilian car arrived, and out came two soldiers and a priest, the father of one of the prisoners.

When he saw his son, he started crying, poor man, and hugged him, "My son, what have you done to me?" It seems he had contacted the Israeli authorities, I don't know who, and said, "Since these people are prisoners of war, they must be allowed to have a priest to pray for them." He claimed that most of us were Christian, because we had been in the German Hospice. He said a few words of prayer but really he wanted to talk to his son.

We began to feel more at ease as more people knew of our existence. The officer who shot between my feet was removed later on. Then the good Red Cross doctor lined us up, and said, "Under international law you are allowed to have a camp leader. Who do you want?" Everybody shouted "Yusif Sayigh!" because I had stood up to that officer.

Transfer to Jleel

Around the end of June, we were put on buses again, closed like before, without windows, and we started on a very long journey. As we discovered later, Jerusalem was still under siege, but the Israelis had managed to find a route to the coast that avoided the cordon around it. Hours later we stopped at a place called Jleel, somewhere near Jaffa or Herzliya. It was a five-thousand-man camp by the sea. All the young men in Palestine were brought there, as well as eight hundred Egyptian soldiers, and thirty or forty Syrians, but no Iraqis as far as I remember. The Iraqi army had made a thrust reaching to the sea and cutting Palestine in two. After that they got orders from Baghdad to withdraw to Jenin, and this withdrawal cost them more casualties than the thrust had done.[2]

Trucks brought tents for us to put up. We had no experience in putting up tents, and every tent fell down two or three times before we managed to get it up. In the officers' quarter where I was, each tent had six to eight people in it. There were bigger tents for kitchens. It was summertime and they provided us with showers—pipes with holes in them. We had to take showers in front of each other, naked.

The food in the second camp was terrible. It was more varied than in the first camp—the vegetables were all right, I could eat them—but the meat was those bits of the cow that Jews don't eat, like the tail. They'd boil a tail for three hours, and there'd be nothing except some cartilage. I lived on bread and vegetable broth. When I came out I was quite thin.

Another thing I remember is the lice. It became so awful that they woke us up every morning half an hour earlier than the usual time with a bugle—we called it the 'lice bugle'— so we could clean ourselves. After a night of feeding on our blood, the lice were easier to get out. We'd sit next to each other, and look in each other's hair and armpits. In the end they brought DDT pumps with a hose, and we'd pump the powder everywhere on our bodies where there was hair. We got rid of the lice in the end, but it took weeks.

This camp had barbed wire all around it, watchtowers, gate, and guards. On the hilltop next to it were the offices—a big institution like that had to have offices for the commanders. When we went there the commander was somebody of no significance, but under him there was a security officer, and another who was in charge of the work gangs. The security officer turned out to be an Irgun man, Almog. We were afraid that he would be very fanatical, but Almog was gentle and civilized even though he was Irgun. I think that way he got on better with us, and was better informed, than when later somebody came in his place who was a Stern man. I think his name was Dr. Schneidman. This man always came into the camp on horseback, with his revolver, although this was against the rules. He would trot his horse among the thousands of prisoners.

His assistant was a sergeant, an Egyptian Jew who made friends with everybody because he spoke Arabic and cracked jokes *à l'égyptienne*. Later we became friends enough for him to take us to the nearest town, I think it was Herzliya. He'd take six of us at a time from the officer class, mainly Palestinians. We couldn't escape because we had uniforms with big blue diamonds painted on the trousers and the jacket, you could see them from kilometers away. He made it clear that we had to pay for him, and he would even let us drink beer. I don't know how he managed to take us; it must have been his own initiative.

An Egyptian officer, a squadron leader, with whom I was great friends, later wrote a book entitled *Kuntu asiran* [I Was a Prisoner of War]. In it he tells how a group of POWs came from the Jerusalem area, and the *homme de confiance* among them was a Palestinian, who distinguished himself in Jleel camp, and was again elected *homme de confiance*. He said that the Egyptian officers were angry because according to international law the highest-ranking officer should be the *homme de confiance*. The one of highest rank among the Egyptian soldiers was a Sudanese lieutenant-colonel, who was very sweet but quite spineless with the Israelis. They didn't want him to be *homme de confiance* so they said, "Yusif Sayigh seems to be a tough guy, better him than this other person." He goes on to say that he became friends with me from that moment. His name was Muhammad Annan. Later he became president of EgyptAir.

There were several very pleasant young Egyptian officers. Six or seven of them were airmen, and one was artillery. It turned out that five of these air force officers were downed on the same day because they had the wrong maps. They had flown over an Israeli airbase near Haifa, thinking it was a British airbase. The Israelis downed them one after the other. I spent a lot of time with them. They taught me chess—two were very good chess players—and I taught them economics. We played cards.

After we settled in the camps, and felt that there was no immediate danger of being killed—especially after we moved to the camp by the sea—there was a lot of talk about politics, especially with the Egyptians, Syrians, and Palestinians. The main subject of discussion was whether our side had a chance of winning the war. Most people extrapolated their situation as prisoners to their expectations of the outcome of the war. Here we were, thousands of prisoners—it meant that the Arab nation itself was defeated, itself a prisoner of war, unable to do anything. What shocked me, I remember clearly, was how these officers, instead of discussing this question in terms of balance of power and military preparedness, either consoled themselves by quoting verses from the Qur'an, or using religious clichés such as 'God protect us,' or 'God is great'; or they repeated expressions of bravado, that for sure we'd win. But everybody's morale dropped when the first truce was announced, and the Jews looked terribly happy. That was in July. The truce lasted for a number of weeks. We could tell that the Israelis were making very good use of it militarily, because the work gangs were forced to make trenches and fortifications, though prisoners of war are not supposed to be used in military efforts. Also those of them who had military experience could see new types of weapons; the crates of machine guns they were carrying had markings showing that they were quite different from the primitive types in use before. The Israelis were beginning to get weapons from Eastern Europe and elsewhere.

My own feeling was that the Arabs were wrong to accept the truce because essentially the Israelis wanted it to rearm, and make new plans based on the positions they had acquired. They were arming, and I had a feeling that our side was not, a feeling confirmed later by military people outside. There were many stories, for instance about the fall of Lydda and Ramleh.³ After these towns fell hundreds came to the camp. The Israelis picked up all the young men there and treated them as prisoners. These people told us how the Arab Legion had just left them to their fate, and moved eastward. That made me feel that we were not going to use the truce to get more arms, apart from the fact that we didn't have the money that the other side had to import arms. Moreover, the Arab governments, except for Syria and Lebanon, took orders from the British, whereas the Israelis didn't take orders from anyone—instead the British and the Americans supported them.

Executions

At that camp there were several incidents when the Security had information about prisoners having been fighters. Several times these men were shot and buried without even a religious ceremony. The officers would say that So-and-So had been shot while running away. There was one young man who knew that they had recognized him as a fighter, and was afraid that they would shoot him. I tried to save him from going on the work gangs by putting him to work in the laundry or the kitchen. But eventually they accused me of protecting him, and said they wanted him to work. He said goodbye sadly, went away, and never came back. When I asked about him, they said that he had tried to run away and was shot by the guards. So I took guards with me and went up to see Schneidman. I wanted to tell the Red Cross about this incident, but he wouldn't let me get in touch with them. I said, "It's my right under the Conventions." He said, "I'm not going to let you use the telephone."

The following day I went up again and saw the commander of the camp, a decent man, a bookseller in civilian life. When he realized that I'd read many English novels, he used to come and chat with me about books. Every now and then he used to lend me books from his shop in Tel Aviv—he was very human, the opposite of Schneidman. He allowed me to use his telephone. I talked to the Red Cross, and they came. I complained to them about this young man's death.

Eventually it reached Ben-Gurion himself. The Red Cross got authorization from him to dig up the body to see how he was shot. It was found that he was shot in the chest from the front, instead of from the back as would have been the case if he was running away. That doctor—his name was something like 'Moeur'[4]—told me after I was released that he had said to Ben-Gurion, "If you don't let us dig him up, I will suggest to our headquarters in Switzerland to pull out our mission and announce the reason." He was then the acting head of the Red Cross [in Israel]. So they gave in.

The Israelis gave the Red Cross assurances that this would not happen again. Schneidman was removed six weeks later. But before he was removed, he sent for me. I went to the gate, and told the soldier there that I wanted four guards to go with me. He said, "Why do you want four guards? You usually have two." I said, "I want four because I don't want to be tempted to run away." He gave me four guards, and I went up.

Schneidman said, "Look, we know each other well enough by now. If you are willing to give me your word of honor that you will not try to run away, you can come up any time you want without guards." I said, "To be killed by your soldiers pretending that I was running away? If you triple the number of guards, I'll be happier." He got angry, and said, "You are a troublemaker; you ought to know that we can punish you. I know from your record that you have five brothers and a sister. If you want to see them again, you'd better behave." Some Arab bravado came into me, and I said, "Since I have five brothers, one less won't matter much, there'll be others in my place." Actually I was worried that he might carry out his threat, but I conveyed that story to the Red Cross, and a few weeks later he was removed.

Escape Attempts

There were several attempts at escape. One was just before some Muslim feast. The prisoners were allowed to stay late outside the tents and sing religious chants. They told me beforehand that twenty-four of them were going to try to escape. I said, "It's very risky. It's up to you, but I'd hate to see you get killed." The nearest place to the camp was Tulkarm, about eighteen kilometers away. In eighteen kilometers there were dozens of chances of being met by patrols. But they said, "Twenty-four of us have sworn to go together and take the risk."

They had picked a watchtower where one of the barbed-wire fences had a little gap, so that a man could slip under it. I said, "But why right under the watchtower? Why not somewhere farther away?" They said, "Ah, that's deliberate because we want to make him drunk."

I said, "How can you make him drunk? He's way up there meters above you." They said, "We are going to chant. There are sixty of us, and we will take it in turns, fifteen at a time, to chant the same words, '*Allah hayy, Allah hayy, Allah hayy*,'[5] for hours." Sure enough—I was watching from my tent—I could see it all happening. The guard was very curious at first, watching and shaking his head, "What are these 'Africans' doing?!" Then his head began to droop. The others who did not escape that night told me they saw his machine gun fall against his thigh. He went to sleep. Then, while the others went on singing, the twenty-four who had decided to leave slipped under the wire.

Many months later when I got out I made inquiries. I found that only six or seven of the twenty-four escaped. The others were either caught or killed. According to the rules of war they should have been taken to a POW camp where security was higher. It's a rule that if a prisoner of war is caught escaping, he's ordered to stop, and only if he doesn't stop you shoot.

The second escape story involved many more people. It was not a real escape. A rumor circulated that a number of prisoners were going to be released because of bad health. Bad health was never defined. As we discovered later, a new security officer spread this rumor so that people would bribe him to list them among those worthy of being released. Ahmad Abdel Khalek was one of those who bribed him. I said to him, "You won't get away with it. It could be a trick. And even if it's not a trick, you won't get away with it." He said, "It's only fifteen pounds, I'm going to pay it." And he did. Just to complete the story, at the end, after we were released, Ahmad told me how they held him back for interrogation, as one of those who bribed that officer. The officer received five or six years in prison for having accepted bribes.

People came and said, "I have a hernia; I want to be on the list," or "My teeth are hurting"—this and that. The only interesting story is of the Egyptian officer, Annan, the one who wrote the book. He came to me and said, "I want to go out with the sick prisoners, but if they recognize me as an Egyptian officer they won't let me through."

The prisoners who were going to leave were allowed to change into ordinary shirts, so he said, "I need to borrow a *qumbaz*." I found him a *qumbaz* his size. He grew a mustache to change his face. Then he said, "I want my eyes to look smudged." I asked one of the work gangs to get some fig leaves, and told him to rub his eyes with them. We even gave him the name of somebody willing to give it. Two or three days later, there he was claiming to have trachoma, crouched with hundreds of others with hernias, or ingrown toenails, or whatever. They waited hour after hour for the buses to come, but nothing happened, and they were all ordered back to their tents. It didn't work.

But there were smaller groups that managed to escape. The ground wasn't rocky, it was agricultural earth, and they could dig under the barbed wire. They always managed to find tools. It was a big establishment, five thousand young men. They had to have huge kitchens, and to be able to repair things like shoes.

Winter

We stayed for months in that place until winter came. The tents were very bad, they leaked heavily. Two or three times under heavy rain the whole tent fell on top of us at night, with its big poles. We'd get up and clear ourselves and try to pick it up. I began to have severe pain in my back. In the end the pain was so bad that I couldn't move. Much later it was found to be a slipped disc, but then we didn't even know the term. In three or four weeks of awful pain, all they gave me was four aspirins, and those only on the last day before the Red Cross came to see why I was not contacting them. I couldn't move; I had to stay flat on my back. I used to pee in a tin, and the Sakkab boy would take it and pour it out. When I had to do the other thing, it would take me ten minutes of slow effort to get upright.

I didn't get the first letter from my family until three or four months after being taken prisoner. It was from my mother. She was always confident. She wrote, "I know God will keep me alive until I see you. Don't worry about me. I'm not going to die before you come out." I have the letters with me still. I wrote to them, but all we could write was a very simple formula, nothing that could be suspected of being a code.

After I became ill, they said, "You can't continue to be *homme de confiance*, since you can't move and look after the others." They decided to move me with thirty others to another camp. I was afraid that it would be a specially tough place, because they picked leading Palestinians to go, all activists like Daoud Jaber, a devil, who knew a lot about electricity and technical things. He spoke German perfectly because his father believed in German discipline and had sent him to the Schneller school. They moved us to a place halfway between Jleel and Atleet, which is near Haifa. We stayed there only for a few weeks. The only interesting thing that happened there was another attempt to escape. This time it was Daoud Jaber who was the leader. He had been a sergeant-major in the Jordanian army.

In that camp we were all in one huge room, like a dormitory. I asked them what the plan was—I couldn't go, my back was still bad— but Ahmad decided to go with them. The plan was that we'd all get into bed, and cover ourselves up to our chins, and that those who wanted to escape would stay in their clothes and shoes. Daoud Jaber was to short-circuit the electricity, which he did by scraping one of the bulbs in our room. All the lights in the camp went off.

But it was only two or three minutes before the guards rushed in. They realized that somebody had played around with the electricity, and stood by the doors with their guns in their hands. It was lucky for the people who wanted to escape because they would certainly have been pursued immediately and killed. We all pretended to be in bed, and when they came and made a noise, we said, "What's the matter? Why are you here?" They said, "What have you done?" The following morning, they came at dawn, and took out every bulb, and looked at it, and found the bulb that had been scraped to make the short circuit.

Nothing else eventful happened there. Then they moved us to another camp, to Atleet, which had been an army camp under the

British. By then, our number had gone up again. From five thousand we had been reduced to thirty; then in Atleet camp we found hundreds of prisoners. The *homme de confiance* there was a Bahai. I knew him from Tiberias; we had been friends there. But here he was a collaborator with the Israelis. When I discovered this I avoided him. I didn't want to challenge him because I was really tired. Being in continuous friction with security wasn't easy, and my back was still giving me trouble. I got no treatment for it at all.

By now, it was December '48 or early January '49. We used to get papers now and then, for example the *Jerusalem Post* (it was called the *Palestine Post* then), and we heard that there was another truce coming. So we expected to be released fairly soon. They began to prepare us for that. Life became quite routine, no surprises. Then my back got very bad, and I had to stay lying down.

In the last part of my stay in the big camp, I had a regular bed, like many other prisoners, with a mattress. They were taken from the villages, and had straw in them. Sometimes we'd get good blankets. I remember getting one that was six meters long. I used to fold it three ways, and sleep under it. Then I sewed it and turned it into a sleeping bag so that it would give me greater warmth all round, and put a sheet inside it—I managed to get a sheet as well.

One day, the commander of the camp came to me—I was in bed—and said, "I'm sorry that we ignored your back, but now we want to treat you. Here's a doctor who will give you an injection." I thought, "My God, they want to finish me off so I won't even be freed with the others"—because we were expecting it from day to day. I said to him, "No, I don't want an injection." They started struggling with me physically, to force me to be injected. I said, "Look, this is my ninth month here, and I haven't received a single injection. Now you remember to look after me? I don't want an injection. You're all my witnesses. If I die from this injection it means the Israelis have killed me." So they didn't give it to me. There were the other prisoners of war as well as soldiers watching.

While I was in the last camp I took notes on the Israeli lines of defense, thanks mainly to Daoud Jaber and others who went out to work, who told us things. Of course I had to hide these notes. I remember the very close shave I had one day when suddenly a large contingent of soldiers trotted in, and started searching the tents, beginning with the tent where I was. Whenever I finished writing the notes I would hide them. The edge of the tent had a folded section all the way round, like a pleat. I made a little pocket in it, and put the papers in. The guards went round touching this, all the way round, but they missed that little bit of about one foot where my notes were.

I decided then I couldn't leave them on paper, so I tore up a white shirt—by then we had received some shirts they brought from Palestinian houses they occupied—into handkerchief-sized pieces, and I wrote on them in outline the things that I wanted to remember and develop, information and ideas. This worked. Even if they searched—and they came again a few weeks later—they wouldn't find it because it didn't feel like paper, it was cloth inside cloth.

Two weeks before we were released—it was common knowledge that we were going to be exchanged as the armistice agreements were being signed one after the other—I undid the lining of my zip jacket—I always liked doing a bit of sewing—and slipped the pieces of cloth with notes into the right side and left side, and sewed them up. Two pieces of cloth remained. I used to wear old-fashioned underpants, made by my mother. They were a bit baggy, and that was fortunate because I could sew the pieces of cloth inside, under the testicles where there were two layers for protection. I went out with the notes on me. They searched us very thoroughly, body searches, but cloth doesn't crackle like paper so I got them out.

Release

We were put in buses and taken to Jerusalem. Ahmad had to stay behind, because of the inquiry. There at the Mandelbaum Gate were Abdullah Tal and Naseeb Boulos waiting for me, and many, many friends. They brought journalists to interview me, from Jerusalem and from Amman, because the story of my struggle with the Israelis had somehow reached them.

The interesting thing that I discovered later was that when we were in the first camp in Jerusalem, before the first cease-fire, the Jewish quarter of the Old City fell to the Jordanians. The Zionists had an enclave there and the Jordanians captured 1,200 Jewish fighters. It was quite something. Munir Abu Fadel[6] dashed to Amman to see the king. He said, "Your Majesty, 123 of our men are in the hands of the Jews. We have lists of their names from the Red Cross. They aren't giving them more than half an *ooqeeya*[7] of bread a day, whereas these Jewish prisoners are even getting live sheep, so they can kill them according to their kosher rules. And apples." Abu Fadel suggested an exchange of prisoners. The king said, "What! I won't exchange an Arab even for ten Jews. I will free my men with the power of the sword." So we stayed prisoners for nine and a half months, whereas the Jews were liberated soon after.

In Jerusalem I was interviewed by many journalists, foreign and Arab. Everybody was interested to know what the Israeli army looked like. For instance, I had a long sitting with Abdullah Tal in which I gave him all the information I got from the Egyptian officer and Daoud Jaber— people who could assess military things. I told him about the Israeli armaments and fighters, about their level of discipline and training.

Then Abdullah Tal said, "I want you to talk to the highest ranking British officer [in Jerusalem], who is commanding the Arab Legion." I went and talked to him. He said, "Are you a military person?" I said, "No, but I keep my eyes open." He grunted; you could tell from the beginning that it wasn't going to be a friendly meeting. He let me talk for a while and then he said, "What were people saying about Lydda and Ramleh?" I said, "Everybody said that if the British officers had not ordered the soldiers not to shoot, Lydda and Ramleh could have been saved." Upon that he stood up and said, "Thanks for coming to see me," and walked out.

One of the people I talked to in Jerusalem was Anwar Nusseibeh. By then he had lost a leg. While he was serving in the Nablus area he got a bullet in the thigh. The medical services there were very poor, they were slow in taking him to hospital, and they didn't have equipment. Gangrene set in and they had to cut the leg way up in the thigh. But he was still active, and his morale was high. I talked with him and analyzed the situation.

Naseeb Boulos took me to his apartment to stay with him for a few days. He made me shave off my beard. Then I went to Amman, and stayed there for a while to recuperate because I had lost a lot of weight, and my health was poor. I didn't want my family to see me like that.

While in Amman, I got out my notes on cloth, and started preparing my thoughts. Of the various Arab governments involved, the only one that seemed to have some heart, some toughness about it, was the Syrian government. So I decided to prepare a memorandum to send to the prime minister to give him the information that I had collected. When I suggested this idea to a few friends like Anwar Nusseibeh, they said, "Certainly there's no point in sending it to the prime ministers of Egypt or Jordan, or to Nuri al-Said."[8]

When I eventually got to Beirut, I prepared a long memorandum divided into parts: observations on Israeli military preparedness and what arms they had; observations by the officers around me and myself; and the feelings of people inside, how the prisoners of war saw the Israelis as less than 'supermen'—we were not as impressed by them as people outside were. I sent this memorandum to the prime minister of Syria, Jamil Mardem Bek, but never got any acknowledgment.[9]

Most people I met outside were terribly dispirited. "*Khalas*, it's finished"—that was the general feeling. They felt that we'd missed our chance mainly with the first cease-fire, but that with the second it was final. It meant we had lost the battle. Some people would say, "Don't worry. In five years' time we'll rearm, we'll do this and that," but these weren't many. There was a general loss of hope, a feeling that the Arabs were no good. If the political or military authorities in Egypt were ready, for a huge commission, to buy defective arms for their army, what could you expect?

When I came out of prisoner-of-war camp—I mention this as a sign of the mufti's generosity—he sent me 250 Palestinian pounds. He said, "I realize you are without work now and in need." The money came just in time. He didn't have much money either. I must say the man had many admirable qualities, though he was also a devil in a lot of things.

Reunion with the Family

When I was well enough, I took a plane to Lebanon. I had no passport, so Abdullah Tal gave me a letter, with my photo on it, saying, "To whom it may concern," that I had been a prisoner of war with the Israelis, and had just been released. I thought they'd let me into Lebanon on the strength of that. But it was February or March, and the plane couldn't get over Dahr al-Baydar. It was one of those planes with one wing on top of the other and one propeller. We were seven passengers in it, that's all it could take.

We returned to Amman, and I decided to go to Lebanon by road. In Syria, between Deraa and Damascus, some gendarmes stopped the bus to look at the passengers' papers. When they came to me, and I didn't have a passport, they asked my nationality. I said that I'm Syrian. "What's this paper you have?" I told them that I had been a prisoner of war. I thought that they would immediately pin a medal on my chest but they said, "A prisoner of war with Israel? You must be a spy." I said, "I'm not a spy; my papers are in Sweida. If you telephone the état civil office there, they'll tell you about me."

They said, "We belong to Deraa." I was taken down from the bus, and they made me hire a taxi to take them and me to Deraa. There they kept me overnight on a bench, under arrest. The next morning, they telephoned to Sweida, and asked for my cousin, Fareed

Ghorayeb. "Do you know somebody called Yusif Sayigh?" "Eh! Yusif Sayigh! He's my first cousin." To test him, they asked him, "What's his father's name?" He told them and said, "Of course he's Syrian. His registration number is such-and-such." After that they allowed me to go to Damascus to obtain proper papers, but all under guard. A gendarme came with me. I had to pay for him.

I spent a few days in Damascus, got a new passport, and traveled on to Beirut where my family was. I had heard in Amman that my family had left Tiberias after the Deir Yassin massacre. They stayed for a couple of weeks with a friend in Beirut who said to them, "Come and stay with us until you find a place that suits you." They stayed there for a few days, until they found an apartment at the end of the tram line. They stayed there a little over a year, and then moved to Ain al-Mreisseh where the family still lives today.

So when I got to Beirut I asked where my family was, and was given their address at the end of the tram line. My family knew that I had been released. They were expecting me by the hour. But I stopped first in the Place de Canons, to have a nice shave and a hair brush, so that I would not look too thin and worry them.[10]

It was a very moving meeting. My poor father—it was he who opened the door— hugged me. I had never in my life seen him cry until then. "Yusif, my son, is it really you?" My mother was waiting behind him saying, "Abdullah, enough, I want to kiss him too." The others gathered one by one—Tawfik, Mary, and Munir. Two of my brothers were abroad. Fuad was in Gaza; he went to work there before the fall of Palestine and stayed on. Fayez was in America—he went in 1947 for his doctorate. Anis was a boarder in Sidon, in the Gerard Institute.

11

"Life Will Never Be the Same without Her": Umm Yusif's Death, December 1950

The period 1949 to 1950 was one of changing direction or consolidation, and promotion in all our various careers. We pursued different careers, mostly on our own, without consulting my father. He would ask us one by one, "What are you thinking of studying?"—and we would give him our different answers. Fuad took engineering, and all of us felt that that was a good idea, because he liked it, and it was a practical thing that seemed to promise more than my business administration and certainly more than Fayez's philosophy. Fuad married in 1949, and in 1950 he came from Gaza to live in Lebanon. He took a job with Tapline as the engineer in charge of the construction of the pipeline that was being built from Saudi Arabia to Zahrani. He and his wife Clemence lived in Deraa, in Syria, and later in Kuneitra. But while he was in Deraa, an army officer, who was also an engineer, coveted Fuad's job, and he managed to dig up information that Fuad had a Syrian passport, and that he hadn't done military service. So Fuad was called to the army, trained, and became an officer. He served in the Kuneitra area, in the building of the *deshem* [fortifications]. They came to Lebanon in 1951 or 1952.[1]

Fayez picked on philosophy right from the beginning. He read a great deal of philosophy; he began to be interested in it as a teenager. He borrowed books, I think, from his school in Safad.

When he was ready to enter AUB he was only fifteen, and was not accepted because he was too young. So he came back to Tiberias, and I remember him borrowing books from Dr. Torrance, who had his father's library as well as his own. Then he began to buy books, and was always deep in them. He didn't talk to me about philosophy because I wasn't philosophical, but he talked a bit about theology with my father. Every now and then my father and mother would have a bright gleam in their eyes, and they'd say, "Maybe he'll go into theology and become a pastor." In fact he did go through a phase of piety, so they became even more hopeful, especially when they saw him reading the Bible. But I think he read the Bible as a philosopher would, as a book that had things like the "Sermon on the Mount." He got his PhD in philosophy in December 1950 from Georgetown University.[2]

Tawfiq had an interest in writing, also from the beginning. Later on he told me that he started writing poetry in Tiberias, but he never told us about it at the time. When his first collection of poetry appeared—it was called *Thalathun* because he published it when he was thirty—I remember saying, "What!? A collection of poems?" He said, "Yes, I have been writing these for years." I didn't know. I don't know if he talked more to Munir; they were close. Not to Fayez, I'm certain, because Tawfik used to feel upset by the way Fayez almost persecuted Fuad. He was very sensitive, probably the most sensitive among us. You could tell from his reaction to things happening, death, illness . . . you could see his lips vibrating as though holding back tears, but he didn't cry. The only time I remember seeing him being shaken by crying was when my mother died.

So Tawfiq chose literature, and I think my parents must have felt the same way as when Fayez chose philosophy—there goes another one who's not going to make money! It's true that they didn't care that much about money themselves but they wanted us not to feel the pressure that they had had. They wanted us to follow the simple life, but to be a little better off. They sacrificed a lot for us. I remember that when we had apples, which were a bit expensive in Palestine, unlike oranges, I can't remember how many times my mother said, "I don't feel like an apple today," in order for us to have more. She never bought herself anything new unless she was sure that all of us had new things, whether it was a shirt or a pair of shoes. But I remember my mother saying to us, as though answering a question in her mind, that you can make a little more money than your parents did and still be pious and virtuous. I remember how my father kept accounts, how every penny he spent he wrote down, every night; he had a little *mufakira*, a pocket diary in which he jotted everything down, day by day. Then he would add it all together into one monthly summary. That enabled them to control the spending.

After a period of unemployment, Tawfiq found a job as librarian of what later became the Kennedy Center, the United States Information Service (USIS) in Beirut. While there, he met someone called Marshal of the Rockefeller Foundation. Marshal used to come to visit AUB because the Rockefeller Foundation was an important contributor to the medical services, as well as giving fellowships to promising young professors or instructors to go and study abroad. He met Tawfiq because he used to go to the USIS, and they became friends. He knew that Tawfiq was writing poetry—which I didn't know at the time—and said he would try to find him a fellowship. This he did. It was a prestigious fellowship, called the "Rockefeller Foundation Fellowship for Creative Artists." That financed Tawfiq for two years at Harvard, where he was reunited with Jabra Jabra, whom he had known in Palestine, and Munah Khoury, who was studying literature. But Tawfiq insisted on not working for a degree. The Rockefeller Foundation did not encourage work for degrees, with the routine of courses and tests, because it meant deviation from creative work. After the two years there, Tawfiq came back, and the Foundation extended his scholarship. He spent a year—I don't know in what capacity, or with which college—in Oxford. Then he taught Arabic and literature for three years at Cambridge University. From there he moved to the University of London (SOAS), to teach literature.[3]

Mary refused to go to college. She didn't want to go through school discipline again. But it was also because she wanted to stay with my mother, and look after her, though there was always a maid to help her, and my father was at home most of the time.

In those years, 1949 to 1953, Munir was doing his medical training at AUB—a BA in medical sciences, and then four years of medicine. Right from the beginning Munir wanted to be a doctor. My mother used to encourage him. She'd say, "How about becoming a doctor and being my personal physician?" What made it easier for Munir to go into medicine was, first, that he was accepted for free by the Arab College, because of his high grades, and second, by the time he graduated, the mandate government promised to finance his university education the way they did with dozens of others who were at the top of the matric. He had to go outside because there was no medical school in Palestine, no college at all except law, and that was only a school of law. I can't remember if Munir was fully or only partly financed by the mandate government.[4]

Anis chose history. By that time I think my parents had given up hope, so they didn't make a fuss about it. History was not a money-maker either, but they were happy for him. He began university before my mother died.[5]

Though deep down my parents may have wanted some of us to go into business or something practical—or theology—[yet] they were proud of the fact that their six sons had chosen six different fields of study. It showed when people came to visit and they would ask, "What are your boys doing?" They were doubly happy because we were doing well. All of us got a certain amount of help from the institutions we studied at. But the 'constant' was my own contribution. Right from the second year of college I began to make enough money to help. My income was much better than my father's, so I probably contributed at least as much as my father. My contributions to the family ended in 1953 when I married.

If I was away from home, for instance in Jerusalem or Iraq, I sent a postal order to my father, but when I was living with the family I usually passed it to my mother. I felt embarrassed to give it to my father. Then when my mother died, I started giving it to Mary, who was in charge of housekeeping. By then my father was getting a reduced salary. I think that for two or three years after we arrived in Lebanon, he was receiving a retirement pension from the mission. They sent him a remittance every three months; it was about one-third of his salary before. From his property in Syria, he got small amounts depending on the season, from the sale of the wheat and 'adas—nothing much. Whenever he heard that his sisters were hard up, he would tell the agent to leave the money with them.

We began to be noticed, each in his field, when we began to write, or to lecture, or to enter into discussions. My mother began to feel that her children were doing all right. The sad thing is that she didn't live long enough to see us blossom. That came later. She saw Fuad marry—she wanted to see one or two of us marry before she died. I was the one on whom she put the most pressure to marry. Then she began putting pressure on Fuad. I remember once saying to her, "Here you are, always telling me to marry. How about your son Fayez, who already has a girlfriend?" She said, "Good for him!"

We all did well in college. I graduated with distinction. Fayez and Tawfiq both got first-class honors. Munir just missed a distinction, he had an average of eighty-four point something, but he needed to have eighty-five. At the doctoral level, the four of us who got doctorates almost had distinctions, but none of us quite managed. I was told that I was very near, and there was debate about it. After the defense of my dissertation, Professor Machlup told me that the reason they were slow coming out was not because they were discussing whether or not I'd pass, but whether or not I'd get a distinction. But I didn't.

I think I went into a career where I made a bit of a name. Fayez too. Fuad remained an engineer, and was successful with CAT company. They gave him a contract that was losing money and he turned it to a profit. He began having a bit of glamour, as somebody who could save a situation, and who was honest. But then his illness took him away. Tawfiq made a name for himself as a poet and as editor of a literary journal. Munir stayed as a physician with UNRWA, and ended up being the deputy head of medical services in Lebanon. Anis has also done very well as editor in chief of three journals that he established—and that led to renown—and as chief editor of the *Encyclopedia of Palestine*. So we six brothers have done rather well, except that we've been unlucky in terms of health, and four of us died rather young.

I think it was a cholesterol problem, though in Fuad's case it was rheumatic fever that he had when he was very young, which made his heart weak without us knowing it. In the case of Fayez, Tawfiq, and Munir it was cholesterol. My heart attack and Anis's (in 1989) were also due to cholesterol. In our family life we didn't feel pressure. It may be that every now and then there would be some tension, which would be a factor for stress, and affect our cholesterol. This is hindsight, looking back. The general tension in Palestine may have been a factor. But the fact that my mother was ill and we were very worried about her was more stressful. It wasn't poverty. We didn't feel poor. We didn't feel well-to-do like the Khourys, or the Sabbaghs, or the Tabaris, but we didn't feel poor. There were problems with money but they were never serious because they were overcome quickly. And now if you look at the harvest, the things that we've done and the books that we all wrote, my father down to Anis, it's quite a number.

My father began writing when we came to Lebanon. He wrote seven or eight books, I'm not quite sure how many. They sold very well among the faithful. He started by writing about the Jehovah's Witnesses, dissecting their dogma. He found them here in Lebanon, and was very annoyed because they were influencing many people— Protestants and non-Protestants—and converting them. My father was afraid this would have a snowball effect, so he started a campaign, along with a few people who felt the same way, like Bahjat Khawli's mother and Mrs. Sa'adeh, and a number of others. The Jehovah's Witnesses were dynamic and went from house to house distributing their tracts. They claim that their dogma is based on a proper understanding of the Bible, through the work of people who knew Aramaic—in other words, people who went back to the original texts. Where there is mention of Christ as God, they would say this word doesn't mean God, it means so-and-so. They're financed from America and very pro-Zionist. I remember having a hot argument with one of them in the Khawli house about Zionism.

The last of my father's books was written a few years before he died, called *Dhikrayati*, "My Memories." That book didn't circulate much, and I was the reason for that, because it had bits that would have created trouble, references to other sects that were too harsh. It could have led to court cases. He always published his books himself. He would give us copies, but he never asked us to read them before publication and give an opinion. When he wrote his memoirs, and it came out, I said, "I wish you had given me this one to comment on before you published it." I have thousands of copies in my office. He left them with me.

Anis has written at least five or six books. Tawfiq the same. Fayez, three or four books and many booklets, studies, analyses of politics related to Palestine. If you add all our books together, you might come up with thirty-five or forty books among us. Munir wrote a book with another person, but not under his name. It was on medical science in Occupied Palestine, published by the PLO Research Centre.

Fuad was the only one of us who was in a hurry to marry; whenever he saw a girl he liked, after seeing her for a few days he would propose. There were three such engagements before he married. He was handsome and likable, more popular than any of the other Sayeghs—with girls, but not only with girls. He was amusing, and very generous with his friends. When they went out, he'd be the first to put his hand in his pocket to buy a round of drinks. He was the most extrovert of us. He also stood out for his love of flowers and plants and animals. I remember how in Hawran he knew our sheep or goats, and could identify them when he was very young, no more than five or six. The flocks would come back—there was one shepherd for several families—and he could identify all our animals, one by one.

I remember the time we went to ask for the hand of his third fiancée, from a Haifa family, the N—s. Fuad was working in Haifa then, and came to know them. The father was a shopkeeper with what looked like a prosperous shop. Fuad came to Tiberias and told my parents. It was nearly summer, so we waited until we went to al-Bassa, and from there my parents and I and Fuad went to Haifa to ask for Fadia's hand.

It was very formal and stiff. They had put chairs on a big terrace in front of their apartment. On one side there were ten chairs for their relatives and us, and facing us there were two chairs like bishops' chairs, with a high back, for the engaged couple. They had to sit there. This was bad enough, but this formality continued until Fadia's family replied, "Yes, we'll be honored." I couldn't take any more, I said, "For God's sake, now that they're engaged why don't they kiss each other?" The terrace froze. My parents smiled, but her parents were shocked, they said, "*La, la! mish 'andna* [No, no! Not with us]." I said, "Instead of kissing secretly in the kitchen, why don't they kiss in front of us?" which made it worse. Fuad was the handsomest of us, dashing, not shy with women at all.

I've mentioned many lovely things about the family; we had many happy moments. But we had a lot of sadness too, in that four of my brothers died young. Fuad was only forty when he died. I think he would have lived much longer if there had been the money for him to go to hospital when he first had heart trouble, a mild heart attack, about a year before he died. He didn't stay in hospital long enough, just a few days. He didn't have enough money to stay. I wasn't aware of it, I didn't even know he was in hospital until Munir told me. I went to visit him, and he was very depressed. When I went to America in 1959, he came to see us off. I said to him, "Please don't come, it means a lot of waiting," but he insisted on coming and staying till the end. He got tired, so we made him sit down. When he hugged me, he said, "Yusif, I'm not going to last long. Look after the children." Then he started crying. He was the first to go. His son, Hani, was only a year and nine months old.

Tawfiq died in 1971, when he was forty-six. Then it was Munir in July 1975, and Fayez in December 1980. Fayez was the oldest of the four when he passed away aged fifty-eight; Munir and Tawfiq were both forty-six. Fayez was the first to have a heart attack, in 1952, but he was in the United States already and got very good medical care, because he had insurance. Fuad didn't. When he got ill, he was in between jobs, between CAT and CCC (Consolidated Contractors Company), so he couldn't benefit from the medical insurance of either. Tawfiq, as it appeared later on from his diary, was aware of something wrong with his heart, but he didn't want to go to a doctor. He had been saying—I think I mentioned it before—right from the time he was a teenager, "I'm going to die at thirty." He avoided doctors. Munir, on the other hand, had regular check-ups.

Life in Beirut

I was away when the family moved from the end of the tram line to Ain Mreisseh—I had gone to Jordan to buy a car, because cars were cheaper there. That's when I bought the Vauxhall.[6] The Arab Higher Committee sent me 250 dinars, and I signed promissory notes. I bought it from the Tannouses, and paid in monthly installments from my salary. Cars were the only things for which I was willing to go into debt.

My father was very active at that time. When he first came to Lebanon, at the beginning, he seems to have said to my mother, "What shall I do? I don't have a church or a congregation." She took the same position she always took, "*Allah bidabbir*.[7] You'll soon find a new congregation." And sure enough he did. He considered all the refugees who had come, even if they were Muslims, as part of his congregation. He went round visiting literally hundreds of families. Every day he walked at least five kilometers, from house to house, visiting, and it gave him a great deal of satisfaction. My mother was happy for him to do it. It was all volunteer work. He didn't have a post at all. He got a part of his salary from the Mission; they somehow found out his address, and began sending him quarterly remittances, bank transfers from Scotland. It was very little.

When I was still living at home with the family, I chipped in. When Fuad got his job with Tapline he began to help, but not regularly. He was already married. Every now and then he would send a remittance, a few hundred pounds, always with something special for Mary. As for Fayez, it wasn't until years later that he began to have a regular job. He was a local employee of the Lebanese embassy, a researcher with Charles Malek—in fact writing most of Charles Malek's speeches through which he became famous. He began to send a hundred dollars a month. Then when Tawfiq found a job he began to help a little. The same with Munir. So we were managing all right.

My father didn't only visit Palestinians in Ras Beirut; he went to faraway camps. He'd go to people he had known in Palestine, and from them he would come to know new people. In the case of Christian families he visited he would pray with them, and encourage them, give them hope that with faith in the Lord things would open up. My mother had to stay at home, but we received many, many visitors—mostly Palestinians whom we'd known before. We began to make new friends. Through Nora Hadawi,[8] my family came to know the Naseefs, and a cousin of Nora's, Khalaf, a Protestant and a lawyer. Sa'id Aql[9] used to visit on my account—I got to know him through the Maaloufs. He was a Ras Beirut figure more than an Ashrafiyeh figure in those days. Later he shifted. So there were visitors all the time. My father used to go out in the afternoons, so our visitors mostly came in the morning.

The Passing of Umm Yusif

The first death in the family was my mother's. She died on 13 October 1950, at the age of fifty-seven. My mother's death was very hard, not just because it was the first death in the family. What summed it up was Fayez's telegraph after he got our cable, saying, "God bless her, life will never be the same without her." The family felt shattered. We had assumed that she would live another twenty years with us. She ought to have been told in Tiberias to move and to walk. But when we came to Lebanon in 1948, it was too late to start her on exercising because her body wouldn't have been able to tolerate it. Her early death could also have been due to the fact that the family had to leave everything behind again in 1948, and become refugees once more. And my being taken prisoner of war, that must have been a terrible strain. When Anis was born in 1931 she lost a lot of blood; the doctor thought that must have weakened her. It's ironic that this was the only time she gave birth in hospital. The strongest in the family physically was my father; he died on 13th March 1974, aged eighty-nine.

My mother stayed at home all the time. She was getting medical attention through Dr. Bekamjian who lived near us in Ain Mreisseh. Dr. Bekamjian felt that at that stage my mother couldn't submit to new treatment, and that the best thing was for her to stay away from stress and not do physical work that might strain her. Umm Joseph visited often; she was doing odd jobs at the Shoueifat School, in charge of the laundry. She went on specific days when there'd be three or four women looking after the laundry machines.[10] She'd control the pieces of laundry that went into the machine and came out. Abu Joseph never worked. Relatives from Hawran also used to visit us.

Leaving Tiberias was a great shock for my parents, but they rarely mentioned it. People closed up about the Nakba. After my mother died I think it was ten or fifteen years before my father mentioned her name. My brothers and I used to introduce her name or her memory into our conversations as a way of keeping her alive, but he would frown and change the subject. It hurt him a lot. He was exceptionally attached to her.

I can't ever forget when Anis went to her room and found her dead. He didn't realize it because he'd never seen a dead person. He came to me—I was in my room, shaving—and he said, "*Yusif, ta' shuf Mama shu malha* [Yusif, come and see what's the matter with Mama]." When he said that, in that tone, I realized she must have died.

The strange thing is that that morning she had left bed, and when she met two or three of us in the sitting room, she said, "I don't think you have enough food to feed me today. I feel so well, with such an appetite." Mary said, "Shall I get you a tray ready?" She said, "No, I'm coming to sit with you at table." She went back to her room. Anis had a 7:30 am class, and when he went into her room to say goodbye, she was just lying there.

I rushed to my mother's room, without even telling my father, who was shaving. I found her with her eyes half closed, and she was a little bluish. She must have just died. I didn't even go to my room to put my shoes on, but ran barefoot to the Bekamjians around the corner, and shouted from downstairs, "Dr. Bekamjian!" I don't think I could have managed to get up the steps; my heart was beating so fast. She looked out, fortunately she heard me quickly. I said, "Please come down, please come to my mother." She realized immediately that my mother had passed away. She lowered her eyelids, and kissed her, and covered her face with the sheet.

12

Palestinian Politics

When I came to Beirut after being released from POW camp, I turned my political attention to one group only, the PPS, in the hope that it would be an important factor in Syria and Lebanon in creating enthusiasm for another round of fighting.[1] I must admit I was quite naive in thinking that there would be another round soon. With every year that passed, the Arabs were less ready for a second round. This was true for a number of years, until in the mid-sixties things began to change a little. For several years, up to 1956 and the attack on Suez, I went through a period of almost despair, feeling that there was not much we could do for Palestine because of the shameful carelessness of the Arab governments when Israel was establishing itself as a state.

A turning point came when I was going from Beirut to the Cedars, driving with friends. The radio broadcast news of the coup d'état in Egypt. Somehow all of us felt that this was a miracle, different from the coup d'état of Husni Za'im in Syria, which fizzled out quickly, and was followed by other coups.

You could feel that hope was coming back that something could be done about Palestine. But it was a hope that remained in the air, without anything solid to justify it, until 1956 when the Israelis attacked Egypt. They attacked to destroy Egyptian military power, after the news that

245

Egypt had bought war planes from Czechoslovakia. The British and French joined in the attack, which was the ignition of a plan to destroy the Arab world. The whole Arab world was electrified by those events, and Nasser emerged as the strongman of Egypt. As he began to take more of a pan-Arab attitude, people like me began to hope that he would concentrate on Arab affairs as much as Egyptian affairs. Indeed in his speeches and press conferences, he did focus on Palestine and Arab issues in general—liberation and development. The years from then until his death in 1970 were filled with expectations of Nasser. The 1967 war was a great setback. Our hopes that he would be a savior and somehow succeed in uniting the Arabs were dashed, especially that the first unity steps between Egypt and Syria were short-lived. Although Abdel Nasser kept his position in Arab minds and hearts, I think expectations of him began to recede at that point.

Before going further, I should indicate two things. First of all, what I felt when unity between Egypt and Syria was declared; and then how my first active association with Palestinian work after 1948 began. The unity agreement was declared in February 1958. As a Syrian passport holder, I felt that I ought to vote for unity. I went with a friend, a colleague from the university, Muhammad Diab. Muhammad was the son of one of the famous five partners of the Sharakat al-Khumsiyya, very capitalist in attitude, highly concerned with money, but I remember how excited he was, insisting that we should go in his car. They had put ballot boxes at Masna', so we stopped there and put our ballots for Nasser in the box, and returned. Nasser did not let us down. He went on holding our attention and feeding our hopes until 1967.

That early period was also fertile in new small movements, like the Tha'r [Revenge] group. It was the first form of the PFLP [Popular Front for the Liberation of Palestine]. They used to publish a magazine, *Shabab al-tha'r*. I knew the intellectuals among them, George Habash,[2] Wadi'a Haddad,[3] and Hani Hindi.[4] I didn't know any of the camp people then. That's also when Fatah was set up in secret, and one began to see glimpses of things being produced, but they did not mention who was running what. They used to come and talk to me about how something must be done, I think to sound me out. Probably I was too naive to notice that there was a purpose to their visits. I wouldn't have joined anyway; my experience with the PPS was enough to warn me not to join any secret organization, because if it's secret you can't know everything that's going on.

The fifties was a period of very little political activity for me. I was busy establishing myself academically. But in the early 1960s I was in Kuwait when Ahmad Shuqeiri visited the country.[5] At that time he was going around meeting people, preparing for the establishment of the Palestine Liberation Organization (PLO). I was one of the fifty or sixty people in the countries around Palestine whose opinion he sought. He was talking to groups, and forming his ideas. He invited me to breakfast in the government rest house; we walked around for a couple of hours, discussing what objectives and ambitions should be set, realistically, so that there would be some hope in the PLO, but not excessive expectations that might be dashed. I was chosen as a member of the first Palestine National Council of the PLO. There was no way of electing people then, it was Shuqeiri plus a small number of people around him who made the choice of members. He established three basic PLO institutions—the Palestine National Council, the National Fund, and the National Army.

It was the Arab League that gave Shuqeiri the authority to do this. It picked him for the job because Nasser approved of him, and by that time the mufti was discredited. Musa Alami, who might have been chosen, was not interested. I was quite closely associated with the mufti; I went on visiting him in Beirut, with Khalil Tabari or alone. Both the mufti and Shuqeiri had their bodies of followers, though Shuqeiri's following wasn't on the same scale as the mufti's. But the Arab countries didn't want the mufti to head the PLO. Perhaps the young officers around Abdel Nasser did not want to have anything to do with him because he was associated with Hitler and with defeat.

The mufti was able to stay in Egypt briefly after the revolution, but I think he felt that there was more freedom of action in Lebanon, and more Palestinians than in Egypt, so he came here. He couldn't go to Jordan because his relations with the king were very bad. He stayed up in Aley, and people would go to visit him. The government didn't object to his presence but they put conditions on him, such as not to be 'over-active.' His presence didn't frighten them in terms of security. There were figures in government who used to sympathize with Palestinians, in the early years.

One began to hear about Palestinian movements in the early sixties. In 1965, when Fatah made its first operation inside Palestine, everything came into the open—not totally open, but they allowed Arafat[6] to be known as Fatah's spokesman. The others put him into the limelight, and they stayed mainly in the dark. People knew about them, hundreds I'm sure, but I was not one of them. I've always been an independent. I think this was essentially because I refused the claim of any group to have the final truth. They all claimed that, beginning with the PPS and the Ba'th.

Second, they had so much infighting and struggles for power, and I hated that. I felt I was qualified intellectually to be in the small circle of leadership, but I knew I would never get into it because I hated fighting for positions. So I stayed out of things. I felt that all the leaders of these parties and movements had ulterior motives, and were not transparent. I didn't want to be involved. I knew most of the leaders of these movements—the PPS people of course. I got to know George Habash and Wadi'a Haddad in 1968, at the first meeting I attended of the National Council. I was also close to them through the Arab Cultural Club in Beirut, which Joseph Mughaizal headed all through the sixties.[7] I gave several lectures there that were published. Walid Khalidi was active in that circle then—he'd give one lecture a year. We used to joke that this was the one child that Walid conceives and gives birth to every year. Habash and Haddad were working more secretly. But there was Burhan

Dajani, Walid Khalidi, Husni Majzoub, and Mughaizal of course, Constantin Zureik, Halim Abu Izziddeen . . . . The Arab Cultural Club was important, though its lectures never had more than fifty or sixty people attending them, because it was a group that was firmly planted in the idea of Arab nationalism.

Joining the PNC and Forming the Planning Centre

I was one of the members of the first National Council that was to meet in Jerusalem in May 1964. I couldn't go because a few days before the start of the meeting, I had my heart attack. In '65, '66, and '67, the meetings were held in Gaza, I think. I meant to go to the '67 meeting in Gaza, but then the war started, so I missed it. The first meeting I went to was in July '68, in Cairo. It was during that meeting that I felt that new ideas should be put to the National Council. There was a new regime in the Council; the chairmanship of Shuqeiri had ended. He was forced to resign after '67, and there was a temporary takeover by the deputy chairman. New elections were held. I was proposed as chairman of the National Council, and people were working hard on me to accept. It was a strange combination of Wadi'a Haddad and Zuheir Alami.[8]

At the first meeting, the pre-election meeting, I made some interventions, and they sort of discovered me. Because I wasn't involved in any of the Resistance organizations, most people didn't know me. There were *fasa'el muqawameh* (Resistance factions) inside the Council, but they hadn't taken it over yet—that happened in '69. I was unsure about it because I was with the university; I didn't have a leave of absence. Besides, I didn't feel that I could take the politics—you have to be able to maneuver and plot. I noticed that there were many groups, with different ideas, different loyalties, and different politics.

I said no to being the candidate for the PNC chairmanship, though when Zuheir Alami, who was very influential in Fatah, and Wadi'a Haddad from the PFLP came to convince me to run, it looked as if I had a very good chance. But Abdel Mohsen Qattan wanted to run; he came to me and proposed that we shouldn't run against one another.[9] When they nominated me as a candidate in the meeting, I raised my hand and said, "I don't want to run." Abdel Mohsen got in. But in the end I accepted a position that forced me to take leave of absence from the university.

This was after I made the intervention that I had prepared. It seemed to me that the Resistance people were very disorganized, they didn't have ideas about processes, how to approach their aims. So I focused on the importance of planning. I said that even a small shop has to plan; it has to have what in economics we call 'cost effectiveness.' When as a fighting group you decide to attack a hill, or occupy a place, you have to consider whether the aim of the attack is worth the cost, the casualties. That means you have to plan. I elaborated on the idea of planning, and suggested the establishment of a planning center to prepare plans of various types—military, political, informational, financial. Later, when the actual center was established, I added a scientific plan.

There was applause from everybody there, and someone immediately asked for a resolution for me to become a member of the Executive Committee, and establish that plan. I tried to resist, because I wasn't eager to get into this thing. I thought I would just throw out the idea, and someone else would do it. But they said, "No, it's your idea, you must do it." I said, "I'm with the university." They said, "Take a leave of absence; try to free yourself." There was already an Executive Committee, and it was against the rules to add a member when it was not an election year. But they took a resolution; it was unanimous. The whole Council also took an open resolution to authorize the Executive Committee to allocate the funds that I estimated would be needed for the first year. Later the Executive Committee appointed me as director general of the National Planning Centre; and when they set up a board for it, I was made chairman of the board of the Planning Centre. That started me working intensively on Palestinian affairs for six years. It was a period of very intense activity, from '68 to '71 with the Planning Centre and '71 to '74 with the National Fund.

All the PNC sessions were held in Cairo up to 1979, when they moved to Damascus.[10] During these years of intense activity within the PLO, it was always in my mind that I was working in the broader Arab context. I always felt that unless the Arab world is mobilized effectively, behind and with the Palestinians, then we could not liberate Palestine. We still thought of liberating Palestine then; it was a thing it was possible to hope for.

So I became director general of the Planning Centre, and we started working on a plan. It took me a few months to find the personnel and make the rules and procedures. Then we started making plans in the different fields I mentioned. For that purpose I succeeded in mobilizing a total of thirty-eight people who helped with the planning from outside the center. These people were not all Palestinian; there were Arabs as well, like Constantine Zureik. I remember we cooperated with Lutfi Diab and Levon Melikian in preparing something on psychological warfare. People in the center such as Ibrahim al-Abed, Sa'id Hammoud, and Bassem Sarhan helped with the research. The plan was completed in 1969. At that time the PLO still had its head office in Amman.

My membership of the Executive Committee ended in February 1969, when Fatah and the other organizations joined it. Before, they had joined the National Council but not the Executive, so my term was brief, from July '68 to February '69. At the fifth PNC session in Cairo I had that very severe pain in my left shoulder, and it was so painful that I fainted at breakfast, in the hotel. Anis was there. It was the day of elections. They brought me a heart specialist, who later became the doctor of Abdel Nasser. The doctor brought his electrocardiac machine but he found nothing—it was my neck disc. They carried me to my hotel room. I stayed for a week there until the doctor allowed me to travel. So I missed the meeting, and people are not allowed to be elected in their absence. They wanted me to be re-elected to the Committee, but as I wasn't there I couldn't be. Kamal Nasser was elected instead.[11]

I stayed with the Planning Centre until 1971—three years. By then I felt that I had given it enough time. At the beginning, I took half-time leave from AUB; I couldn't suddenly leave the university, before they had prepared somebody to take my courses. But the year after I took full leave without pay.

The Last-minute Rescue

When the plan was completed, we ran copies of it for every member of the Executive, eleven or twelve people. Before taking them to Amman, I went there myself to arrange to have somebody meet me at the airport, because of the sensitive nature of the documents. They contained information on politics, our relations with Jordan, military planning—everything. I sat with Arafat and Abu Iyad, and told them that it was essential that someone should meet me, because the documents would be packed in cartons, and they would certainly open them at the Jordanian customs. I could end up in prison in south Jordan for at least ten years. We agreed on a date. Because I couldn't trust them to remember, we agreed on a code, so that I could remind them. I sent them this coded message saying that I would like to make a visit to Jordan, I'm coming on flight so-and-so, on such-and-such a date. They sent a message back saying, "*Ahla wa sahla*," which was supposed to mean that someone would be waiting for me.

When I got there, I didn't see anybody in the customs, when I was showing my passport. So I picked up my valise, and the three cartons that had eleven full copies, and I stood at the end of the queue. Our plane was the last plane to come to Amman that night so the queue wasn't a long one. The line got shorter and shorter. I hung around, pretending to be looking for a piece of luggage. When there were only three people left, the customs man said, "*Ya ustadh*, get closer! Why are you standing there?" I said, "When my turn comes I'll move." When my turn came, I left the cartons on the floor, and carried my bag, and

went over to him. He said, "I'm not interested in your bag, I'm interested in the cartons. Bring them over." I brought them, and he said,
"What do you have in there?" I said, "Books— economics, technical
things, nothing interesting." He said, "I'd like to look at them." So I
lifted one of the cartons and put it on the bench in front of him. I bent
and started undoing the knots one by one. I began to sweat. He said,
"*Yalla ya ustadh, 'ajjill*! [Come on, sir, hurry up!] This is the last plane,
I want to go home." I said, "I'm doing my best, but these knots aren't
easy to undo." He pulled a penknife from his pocket, and split open
the end of the rope. He was just on the point of opening the carton
to look in, and I was thinking of Rosemary and the kids, and how I
wouldn't be seeing them for God knows how long.

Then, suddenly, I felt hands pressing heavily on my shoulders,
and heard a voice saying, "Yusif! What are you doing here?" I turned
round, and there was Da'oud Zabani from Ramleh, who was with me
as a prisoner of war. We embraced warmly and I whispered to him,
"What a godsend!" He said, "What's the matter?" and turned to the
customs official—he talked to him with authority—"Why are you
holding him?" He said, "He has these documents here, I've asked
to see them." Da'oud said, "That's all right. *Yalla*, close up and call a
porter." A porter came and carried everything, and he walked with
me, all the way out to a taxi. When we were far from the customs
official, I asked him, "How can you do that?" He said, "I'm the head
of customs in the airport." I said, "God, if you only knew what I had!"
and I told him. I never saw him again; he died twelve years ago, of
cancer. I felt very sad when I heard of his death.

I went to the PLO office straightaway, because I knew they
worked late, and deposited the cartons, and raised hell. I told them,
"It's a miracle that I'm not already hanged." They said, "We forgot."
Everybody put the blame on somebody else. I couldn't sleep that
night, from anger and relief. I didn't stay to discuss the plan with
them because I wasn't a member [of the Executive Committee].
But I asked them to let me know what comments they had. They

said, "Of course." Back in Beirut, I heard nothing from them—one week, two weeks, three weeks. Then somebody told me that when it was time to discuss the plan and they saw that they had to read three hundred to four hundred pages—there was no executive summary, I wasn't aware of them in those days, but there was a table of contents—they just looked at the titles on the cover, and said, "We can't read these things, we haven't time." They turned to somebody who had a PhD from Cambridge, Hussam Khatib, and said to him, "You're an intellectual. Read this material, and give us a summary in four pages." He said, "What do you mean, four pages!? Look at the size of it!" Apparently one or two of them did read it all, but Hussam never undertook that task.

Later on, when the PLO was ousted, this material was in their offices, still undistributed, except for two or three copies taken by people who had the intellectual curiosity to read them. I didn't go to Jordan until ten years after that, in 1980. It was for the meeting of the ministers, in preparation for the economic summit. During that visit, Prince Hassan formed the Arab Thought Forum, and I was to be a member of the founding group who met in Aqaba for that purpose. In fact I didn't go because I was busy with the meetings of the ministers, giving an outline of a strategy for joint Arab economic action.

When Kamal Nasser met me on a visit to Beirut from Amman, I said to him, "I haven't received any feedback." He said, "Why are you so worked up about it?" I said, "Planning is important, you can't go on being disorganized, acting without thinking." He said, "I have to tell you what a member of the executive said—'*Thawra wa takhtit ma besir*' [Revolution and planning can't go together]." I asked him who had said this. He said, "Abu Lutf."[12] I was surprised, I thought he was an educated person; he had a master's in economics from AUC. I said to Kamal, "Tell him from me, that *thawra* comes from *thara*, 'to revolt,' not from *thawr*, 'a bull.' He laughed and said, "By God, I will tell him."

One more thing about the Planning Centre: when I decided to resign, I went to see Arafat —by that time they [the PLO] had been forced out of Jordan, and had arrived in Beirut, and he had set himself up in his empire in Fakhani. I went to tell him that I wanted to resign. He said, "You can't leave! You are the father of the idea, who else could take over?" I said, "You didn't show much interest in the Planning Centre's work. Why should it matter who becomes director? But I think Nabil Shaath would make a good director." He said, "Nabil Shaath! He is a full-time professor at the university, a full-time advertising advisor to the 7-Up company, and a full-time Fatah member. And you want to make him a full-time director of planning!" I said, "If he has been managing three full-time jobs, he might as well take on a fourth. I think he can devote time to planning." Arafat refused, and it took several days to convince him. He said, "I know Nabil Shaath better than you!" When he finally accepted I was relieved.

I decided to leave because I felt that if they did not take the plan seriously they couldn't take anything else seriously. The most important thing to do in the Planning Centre was to make a plan. What was the point in staying? They were just not interested. This was proved again at the end of 1970. At that time Hisham Sharabi[13] was beginning to make visits to the region after a long absence. I remember we sat there complaining about the way things were run, and the decision-making process, how poor it was. I said, "Why don't we invite the leaders to a *khulweh*, a secret meeting with no telephones?" Zuheir Alami was there, and he liked the idea, and Nabil Shaath, and of course Hisham liked it.

Hisham was coming with a halo around his head as a thinker, so we turned to him to prepare a very brief paper to justify the meeting and explain what it was meant to do, to optimize the efficiency of decision making, its credibility and effectiveness, and the importance of doing this. We began thinking of where to go, what hotel. But we couldn't do this in an open place. I said, "Why not our house in the mountains?"[14] So we contacted Abu Ammar [Arafat], and we decided whom to invite: Abu Ammar, Abu Iyad, Khaled al-Hassan[15]—I'm not sure if Khalil [Wazir][16] was there—Zuheir Alami, Nabil Shaath, Hisham, and myself. There were about fifteen or twenty people—all from Fatah except the independents—because I felt that Fatah was the seat of power in the PLO. If we could influence them it would be a good thing.

Abu Ammar accepted, and we made arrangements with a picnic restaurant to deliver food. We didn't want them to bring the food themselves, so we made arrangements to collect it. We stayed two nights up there holding these meetings. We borrowed a blackboard to make diagrams and graphs; we did it in a very modern way. Hisham delivered his paper and it was discussed. Abu Ammar said very little. There wasn't much enthusiasm except from those who actually thought of the idea—myself and the people who were with me. The others asked a few questions just to show that they were not asleep. The main thrust of our presentation was that Abu Ammar should not be left alone to take decisions. It was too serious to be left to him—"War is too serious to be left to the generals." We'd agreed without involving him that Nabil Shaath should stick to him like his shadow, and try to influence him, because he was persuasive and articulate. That was the thrust. We discovered later on that Abu Ammar had realized it. After the last meeting ended at about midnight, they went down in their cars. As they were leaving—I was saying goodbye to them outside the house—I heard Abu Ammar say to Zuheir, "Zuheir, I want to go with you." I thought it was security precautions, to change cars.

That night I began having terrible renal colic. I couldn't get up and drive home because my car keys and house keys were with Ahmad Jawad who had brought us food that evening, and kept them by mistake. The telephone up there wasn't working. In the morning, at about six o'clock, he came knocking on the door because he realized he had the keys with him. I was in severe pain. I said to him, "You came just in time." I dressed and told him to take me to the hospital, but first to take me to Zuheir Alami's office. We got there at about eight.

Zuheir was there. He said, "Do you know what Arafat said when he went down with me? He said, 'What are Yusif Sayigh and Hisham Shababi trying to do? To stick somebody to me? Nabil Shaath? Even if Nabil Shaath were my Siamese twin, I would operate and cut him off. I won't have anybody help me take decisions!'" Zuheir said to me, "All that work wasted!" That was the final thing that made me decide to leave the Planning Centre.

I called Rosemary from Zuheir Alami's office to say that I was on my way to the hospital. That's when the news of Tawfiq's death came. After I had got rid of the [kidney] stone, during my last two days in hospital, they told me. It was the end of the chapter of my association with the Planning Centre. Nabil Shaath took it over.

The first thing Nabil did was to move the Centre. When I was handing over, he made a long speech praising me, this brilliant idea, this beautiful organization . . . . The following day he called a meeting of the people who worked at the Centre. "*Khalas*," he said, "We are part of a revolution, and you are responsible young men and women. It would be beneath you and me if I ask you to come at 8 a.m. every day, and sign a book, and leave at 1 p.m., and come back at 4 p.m. Each of you has an assignment. Work on it at home; stay away for a week, two weeks. I trust you. When you are ready to discuss things with me, come over." He did that so nobody would notice that he was out most of the time. Then he moved the Centre to Fakhani, and the Planning Centre began a slow death. He started making opinion statements on events and sending them to Arafat. Then he began making cuttings from newspapers, foreign and Arab, and sending them day by day to Arafat.

The Story of the Missing Check

I think it was in '71 that Khaled Yashruti,[17] who was president of the Palestine National Fund, was killed when something fell on his head from a building he was supervising. There was a meeting soon after that, and they elected me as president of the board of the Fund. I was very reluctant, but they said, "You're an economist, that's the thing you should work on."

I served two terms there, and it was hell. Arafat was very difficult to work with. I was forced to work with him because our system was that we only gave allocations to institutions such as the Research Centre, the Planning Centre, the army. This meant that there would be big checks made every three months or every year as the case arose, within the budget. There was a budget that was approved by the National Council, and nobody could violate it, or go beyond it. According to the constitution of the National Fund, two people had to sign every payment order or check—the chairman of the PLO, Arafat, and the president of the National Fund, myself. Every now and then there would be an emergency or a new situation that required new funds. So there was a mechanism that permitted the introduction of sub-budgets for these purposes. This had to be done by the unanimous votes of four people—the chairman of the board, Chairman Arafat, the director general of the National Fund, Darwish al-Abiyadh, and a member of the executive committee concerned with that particular thing.

There were two kinds of trouble with Arafat. First, he would send people to my office with slips of paper saying, "Please pay this man ten dinars, or twenty dinars." I wasn't a cashier; I didn't have petty cash. Besides, every penny paid had to be within the budget. We had auditors; everything was absolutely organized. It got to the point where one day a man came and produced the back of a Bafra cigarette packet. Arafat couldn't find a piece of paper around, so he wrote on the cigarette packet, "*Al-akh* [Brother] Yusif, please pay this man twenty dinars." I said to him, "Arafat knows that this is not within the budget. Besides, we have to have two signatures." He said, "That's his signature and you have your signature." I said, "On this Bafra thing? Do you think I'm carrying dinars around with me?" He said, "But Arafat said that you can pay." I said, "No, I'm going to call Arafat with you here." I called Arafat, and I said "Why have you sent me this man?" Arafat didn't know the man was still there. He said, "I wanted to get rid of him." I said, "Give him money from Fatah. Do we pay the soldiers in Syria one by one?" The man left. I don't know what he did with Arafat.

The second kind of trouble was an event that opened my eyes to the possibility that Arafat might be receiving money for the Fund but taking it for Fatah. That was toward the end of my term—I was re-elected to the chairmanship of the board of the National Fund, and toward the end of that period, sometime early in '74, the trouble with Arafat turned into something bigger. It was more serious because it involved big money. One particular incident involved money that came from the Kuwait government for the PLO, equivalent to ten million dollars.

The first I heard about this sum of money was on a trip to Cairo, when I accidentally met the minister of finance of Kuwait in a coffee shop in the Hilton hotel, Abdel Rahman Salem al-Atiki, Abu Anwar. He saw me and hugged me—we were good friends—and he said, "You always complain when we meet that we're not giving money to the National Fund. I want to give you the good news that we decided in the Council of Ministers to give the Fund ten million dollars, a few days before my trip here." I said, "That's great news! I hope it reaches us." He asked, "Why do you say that?" I said, "Because it depends on who you sent it to. I haven't heard of it, neither by telex nor by telephone." He said, "No, you will be hearing. We sent it only recently."

A week passed and nothing happened. There was going to be a meeting of the Executive Committee, which I was attending as president of the National Fund. Before the meeting, I told three friends who were on the committee, Abdel Wahab Kayyali,[18] Ahmad Yemani,[19] and Zuheir Mohsen,[20] the story about my meeting with the minister of finance in Kuwait. I said that I hadn't heard about this money coming. It was a large sum, I should have heard of it. I said to them, "Why don't you say in the meeting that you have heard that the Kuwait government has decided to send this money, and ask me what has happened to it?"

They raised the question in the meeting. I said, "I've heard the same story"—I didn't say from whom I heard it— "but I haven't heard that it has arrived." Abu Ammar was in the meeting, and he didn't say a word. The following week, Arafat himself started by saying, "*Ya doctor!* Where is that money—the ten million dollars?! You haven't told us about it. You get money, and you don't tell us about it?" I said, "I haven't heard anything."

That made me decide immediately to take the plane and go to Kuwait. I visited the minister, and told him that I hadn't received the money. He said, "But I've signed the check." He picked up his phone and called Khaled Abu Sa'oud, a Palestinian, who was the director of his office. He said, "*Ya* Khaled, what happened to that money that we decided to send to the PLO?" Khaled said, "The check has gone. But don't you remember that the day after the resolution was taken, Arafat came to your office—somebody had told him about the check—and he said to you, in my presence, that it would make it easier for him to cash the check if you made it to the order of al-Qa'id al-'Amm li-l-Thawra al-Filastiniya, the general commander of the Palestinian revolution. That's how it was done. He put it in his pocket."

I said to the minister, Abu Anwar, "There's no such thing constitutionally as 'al-Qa'id al-'Amm li-l-Thawra al-Filastiniya.' There's the chairman of the executive, the president of the National Fund, the chairman of the National Council—nothing else." He said, "How could we know? We did it on trust. Surely it will end up in the National Fund?" I said, "No, mark my words, it won't end up in the National Fund." Then I asked him as a favor to give me the details of the check—the bank, number, and date. I put this information in my pocket and returned to Beirut.

The next meeting, again Abu Ammar said, "*Ya doctor!* We've asked you two weeks running about the money, where is it?" I said very coolly, "It's in your pocket." He said, "What! I'm not a thief," and he put his hand on his revolver. I knew he was not going to pull it out or shoot, he was just pretending to be very angry. Then he said, "I'm the chairman here, I won't be insulted in this way. I won't attend the meeting so long as Yusif Sayigh is in it." He got up and left the room. We were meeting in the apartment of Zuheir Mohsen in Hursh Tabet so, being the host, Zuheir followed him, and brought him back. He sat there and said, "*Ya doctor*, how can you insult me?" I said, "If you want to shout I can shout too." Everybody looked at me; nobody had ever spoken to him in that way. Even the opposition never spoke to him like that, never. They would argue with him, but they never raised their voices. He would raise his voice, but they never did. But I wasn't afraid of him.

He said, "How do you defend yourself for insulting me, for saying the check is in my pocket?" I said, "Let me tell you the story of the check." I told them the whole story. Then he relaxed and smiled, "Ah, that ten million dollars. That was not for the Fund, that was for Fatah." I said, "Because you said that it could only be cashed if it was in the name of the al-Qa'id al-Amm, which is yourself. But that's not true, it is our money." He said, "No, no, this is Fatah money." We never saw it. There was nothing we could do. The others members there felt shy and bent their heads. Even Abu Maher didn't support me. In Kuwait, they had gone back to the minutes, which clearly said that the payment should go to the PLO. I mentioned this in the encounter with Arafat, but he said, "No, you are wrong." He was an outright liar. By that time I was totally fed up, and decided not to let myself be re-elected to the post.

My term as chairman of the Fund was due to end in June 1974. Just before the meeting of the National Council that was to be held in July '74, people began to contact me saying, "We're going to re-elect you." I said, "No, nothing doing. I won't take it." They went on putting pressure, and in the end I realized that the best way out was not to attend the meeting at which the elections were held.

Before the meeting Arafat was telling everybody, "If Yusif Sayigh is president of the National Fund, I will not agree to be on the Executive Committee"—it was blackmail of course. I wrote a letter to the president of the National Council, Khaled al-Fahoum.[21] I sent the letter to him, and saw it placed on his desk. It said that I was going to absent myself from the election session because I didn't want to be re-elected, and the reason was that I couldn't get along with Arafat. They elected Walid Qamhawi[22] in my place. That was my last formal association at the executive level with the PLO. Of course I remained a member of the National Council.

Other Palestinian Institutions

My period of intense association with the PLO ended in June 1974. But during that period I had other activities with a Palestinian basis. At the beginning, between 1956 and 1974, I kept up relations with the mufti; I used to go up and visit him in Aley every now and then. On two or three occasions he asked Raja' al-Husseini to get in touch with me, because he wanted to discuss something.

Between '56 and '67, the mufti made an attempt to come back into prominence. He asked his supporters to organize a General Congress on Palestine, to be held in Beirut, in one of the camps, I think it was Bourj al-Barajneh. There was a preliminary session before it was formally opened, for the airing of ideas about what the Congress should do, and whether there should be a continuous mechanism for it. During that session it seems that Fayez made some impressive interventions. He was in Beirut that year, 1959, on a visit from America. So he was elected president of the Congress. This annoyed Hajj Amin [the mufti] very much, because he was hoping that one of his men, like Fares Sarhan or Khalil Tabari, would be elected, but it didn't go that way. That showed him that his standing among the masses was not what it used to be in Palestine.

Something that brought me to some prominence intellectually in the Arab world was my book on the Israeli economy, which was first published in 1963. It began as a series of twenty lectures that I gave in Cairo, and then it came out in book form from the Arab League. A second printing with updated material came out in 1966, published by the Research Centre in Beirut. That book is still talked about as the authoritative work in Arabic for the period it covered.

That period also witnessed the emergence of important institutions. One that preceded the establishment of the PLO was the Institute for Palestine Studies, which came into being a year before the PLO Research Centre. The Institute was the brain child of Walid Khalidi,[23] helped by Burhan Dajani, Sa'id Himadeh, and Issam Ashour. The other institution, the Research Centre, was the brain child of my brother Fayez. The Institute was set up in a very secretive way. There was a long period of preparation. Walid Khalidi is very thorough; he takes his time. He never told me what was happening although we were friends and neighbors.

I remember once going down to visit Walid, across the street, without phoning to say I was coming. We used drop in on each other in those days without formalities. They opened the door for me, and there was a group sitting there in an inner room, beyond the sitting room—Walid, Burhan, Issam, and a fourth person. They looked flustered when I came in and started talking about something else. I sensed their embarrassment and apologized for coming without announcement. Walid said, "*Ahla wa sahla*. Sit down and have a drink." I said, "No, thank you, I just wanted to say hello." I realized then that something was cooking. Later on, when the names of the members of the board appeared, it was obvious that their secrecy was so that neither Fayez nor I would know. We were never invited to be members.

I don't think it had anything to do with my old PPS affiliation. It was the quarrel between Fayez and Walid.[24] If not for that, I think Walid would ultimately have wanted me to be a member [of his board]. But that quarrel meant that he was not going to have any Sayigh. Walid's position was, "Why have two institutions doing research on Palestine?" He said to Fayez, "Why should a person like you agree to work with the PLO, to establish something that is not going to be independent? You will have pressures on you with regard to appointments and subjects to research." Walid accepted all along the role of a dignified advisor, *in camera*, to Arafat, but he never entered into open association, never attended a single National Council meeting.

I remember when I was appointed director of the Planning Centre I invited Walid for a drink, to tell him about this. We went to the Raouché. I said that I wanted us to cooperate. I respected Walid's ability and political analysis. He looked at me and said, "Yusif, *inta himar* [You're a donkey]." He laughed to lighten it, and I said, "I know I am a *himar* in some ways, but why in this instance?" He said, "You know that no matter what you plan, no matter how excellent your plan is, how intelligent, how relevant, unless Arafat himself is persuaded of it, it won't be followed. For it to be accepted by Arafat, it has to come from somebody who is very close to the center of power, which is Fatah. And you're not in Fatah. Even if you're a genius, Arafat will not take you seriously." I didn't pay much attention to him at the time because I'm an optimist. I thought that one can influence people by the power of ideas, of reason. No, I didn't take it to heart, or I would have resigned right away.

The feud between Fayez and Walid became very serious. Fayez stayed in Beirut at AUB for three years, from '64 to '67. He was a member of the first [PLO] Executive under Shuqeiri, along with Shafiq al-Hout,[25] Ahmad Sidqi al-Dajani, and a few others. It was a good group. But Fayez couldn't stay on as the director of the [PLO] Research Centre because it needed more time than he could afford as professor at the university. I don't think he took a leave of absence. It was summer when he was first elected as a member of the Executive—in fact, he was appointed by Shuqeiri. The first three-quarters of the year he was still at the university, at AUB, as well as being a member of the Executive Committee. The [Executive] meetings were every two or three weeks, so it wasn't difficult, he could attend them. He resigned from the Executive after a year. Later he left the Research Centre, because he couldn't cope with both the university and full time at the Center. Shuqeiri then appointed Anis [as director of the Center].[26] That feud poisoned relations between Walid and myself, and between Walid and Anis by extension, though there was no reason for Anis to be involved. Later Fayez was invited by the Kuwait government to be their spokesman on Palestine in America.

My Palestinian activism dropped between '74 and '84. That was a time when I left AUB and was trying to set myself up as an independent economic consultant. It also was a period of dashed hopes. The '73 war made it seem that the Arabs could stand up to Israel, but that hope collapsed when Sadat failed to make political use of the crossing of the Canal Zone. It became clear that he was playing an American game that he and Kissinger had designed together. Arab oil power that appeared first in '73 lasted throughout the decade and made the Arabs busy with their money, and less concerned with politics, especially Palestinian politics. As a Palestinian, I was depressed during that whole period.

Syrian–Jordanian Tension within the PLO

In 1984, while I was attending the Palestine National Council meeting in Amman, I made an intervention that angered Arafat very much. Prior to that meeting there had been a great deal of tension between the PLO and the Jordanian government, the king. Then somehow they got reconciled. So although before that there were all sorts of accusations against King Hussein, the PLO decided to hold its meeting in Amman. I was in Oxford that year, on an appointment with the Institute for Oil Studies and St. Antony's College.

The PLO contacted me by telephone to invite me to the meeting that was going to be held in Amman. They said, "Chairman Arafat wants to talk to you himself." He came on the line and said, "I want you to be here on Friday before the meeting starts on Saturday. You are one of twenty people who have been members of the Council all through from its establishment in '64, and I want to be photographed with the twenty of you." I knew that what he really wanted was to make sure that he had a quorum. Many—the Damascus people—preferred not to go. I myself planned to attend. In fact I telephoned Khaled al-Fahoum in Damascus from Oxford, saying I was going because I believe in criticizing from inside rather than the outside. He said, "I understand your position, but it will be misunderstood by many people."

Arafat persisted, in fact he sent the PLO representative Oweida from London to Oxford at midnight, to talk me into going. I told him it was impossible because I had to give a lecture at St. Antony's on Friday, and it's not every day that one gets that opportunity. I said I would leave on Saturday morning early, on the first plane going to Amman, and that since the Council would not begin until the afternoon, I would be able to make it. Oweida called Arafat from my house, and repeated to him what I had said. Arafat came on the line and put pressure on me, "I'll send my private plane for you. Or if you don't think my plane is safe, I'll send you Haseeb Sabbagh's plane to fetch you on Thursday. We'll have the photograph taken, and send you back to Oxford for your lecture, and then back again for the Council." I said, "I can't make all these trips in two days. I know you want me to be there because you are worried there won't be a quorum." He got angry at that, and I said, "On Saturday you'll see me there." In fact I was there on Saturday before the meeting was opened.

The council meeting opened on Saturday afternoon. Arafat, Khaled al-Hassan, Abu Jihad, and Abu Iyad met me warmly; they appreciated my coming all the way from Oxford to attend the meeting, as I had promised. The opening ceremony had speeches by many visitors who were not members of the Council. One of them was introduced as the head of the opposition in Syria, somebody whose name I had never heard before, and who was certainly not living in Syria. He got up and unleashed a ferocious attack against al-Assad, saying he was a traitor. I felt that that was not the kind of thing that should be said in PNC meetings. A guest should know how not to embarrass his hosts. When that man finished, I walked over to Arafat and told him, "You ought to have stopped him. This isn't the style we've been using in our meetings before." He said, "I'm democratic, I can't stop a guest from talking." I was very angry. I went back and prepared my notes for the meeting the following day, when I was set to make an intervention.

I started by saying that it was exactly twenty years since the establishment of the PLO. Even a small grocer makes accounts at the end of the year, to see whether he has made a loss or a gain. I think the PLO, as an important movement conducting a campaign of national liberation, ought after twenty years to stop and examine itself. One of the important things we should ask ourselves is, do we still have the aims we had in '64 when the PLO was established? If so, how much have we achieved? And if we haven't achieved most of it, why did we fail? What changes do we need to make, either in the aims or in the way we approach them? At least it would prove that we are capable of self-criticism, so that in the future we can move in a better directed way.

After this I said, "I want to end now on a totally different subject. In yesterday afternoon's introductory session, we heard very harsh things said against al-Assad of Syria, and the speaker was not stopped by Chairman Arafat. This is shocking. Let me remind anybody who is happy with this attack on al-Assad, that from the seventies onward we had very bad relations with Jordan. Yet here we are now meeting in Jordan, under the slogan 'Istiqlaliyat al-qarar al-filastini [Independence of the Palestinian decision].' I'm not sure that cursing Arab leaders is the best way of expressing our independence. Let me remind Palestinians of the Palestinian saying, 'Leave a place for reconciliation.' Our relations with Syria are passing under a dark cloud, but it's not as dark as the cloud under which our relations with Jordan have passed. We should leave room for reconciliation, not burn all our bridges." There was applause from a large body of the audience, and I went back to sit down.

Right after me Arafat went up, and said even more insulting things against Hafez al-Assad than the other man. He said, "I have here in my pocket a letter which Kamal Jumblatt, *Allah yirhamu* [God rest his soul], sent to Sadat"—Jumblatt and Sadat had both been assassinated by then[27]—"saying that Hafez al-Assad had tried to persuade him, Kamal Jumblatt, to turn the Druze areas in Lebanon away from Lebanon, and join them with Jabal al-Druze in Syria, to have a little state there with Kamal Jumblatt as head of it. But Kamal Jumblatt, noble man, refused. Instead he gave me the letter and I sent it to Sadat, *Allah yirhamu*." It was a falsification of course. He was always pulling things out of his pocket, and saying, "I have just received this cable." He went on to say that a man like this cannot but be called a traitor to the Arab cause and to the Palestinian cause.

After this, nobody except Khaled al-Hassan said a word to me, all through the remaining five or six days of the conference. Arafat wouldn't say hello when we met, Abu Jihad wouldn't say a word; they pretended I was a ghost. When I went back to Oxford, I called Khaled al-Fahoum, because I knew the meetings had been shown live on TV. He said, "Yes we saw it. I asked Abdel Halim Khaddam,[28] 'What did you think of Yusif Sayigh's intervention?' He said, 'Excellent, but he shouldn't have been there.'"

During that meeting in Amman, two people came and sat next to me. They were Abu Ala' [Qurei],[29] and Maher al-Kurd, Abu Ala''s assistant at SAMED[30] and the Department of Economic Affairs. Abu Ala' said, "Give us the text of your speech." I said, "I talk from notes." He said, "Never mind, write it in full, please, right now. We can photocopy and distribute it." They did that in a later session, which annoyed Arafat even more. They were part of the branch in Fatah that was not happy with what was happening.

That meeting was important for me because it influenced the direction of my work for several years to come, from '84 to '93. Abu Ala' told me then that the Arab Fund for Development had given the PLO some money for the Department of Economic Affairs and

Planning to engage capable economists to do studies. He said to me, "You're not at the university now?" I said, "No, but I don't want to be an employee." He said, "No, I'm going to ask you to do consultancy work." All that was in Amman, at that meeting, in a coffee break. He said that the terms of the grant from the Fund were that they would pay $250 a day for work, plus expenses incurred for actual work days. He said, "We would give you a retainer but on a job basis, not monthly. Our department has already commissioned several studies, and we want a capable, independent economist to judge their quality. You can do that. If you accept, we can make a contract now."

This arrangement continued for three or four years before I joined them [in Tunis]. We met again at a conference on industry in the Occupied Territories. I was elected chairman of that conference simply because at a preliminary meeting I had made some comments that caught people's attention, and the representative of UNIDO [United Nations Industrial and Development Organization] proposed me as chairman of the meeting. That was in '87 or '88, in Vienna. Abu Ala' tried from that time to attract me to go to Tunis, essentially to improve the quality of the work of his staff members. I told him, "Yes in principle, but I'm not free now. I'm writing something, and it will take time to finish."[31] In fact it took me two years to decide to go.

He asked me to do two important studies. One of them was an evaluation of the work of the Jordan–Palestine Committee for the Support of the Steadfastness of the Palestinians, which got money as a result of the Arab Summit in Baghdad. So I began going to Tunis every now and then, to get material, and to prepare my paper. It came out in book form, though it wasn't published—it was only for internal circulation.

Planning an Economy for a Future Palestinian State

In 1988, after the announcement of Palestinian statehood,[32] Abu Ala' asked me to prepare a study on the economic underpinnings of an independent Palestinian state. I finished that in late 1989, and made

some minor revisions after going to Tunis, and listening to comments. In that study, which was a long one, almost four hundred
typewritten pages, I said that my search for the economic underpinnings necessary [for a state] made me confident that a state was
feasible if certain conditions were satisfied. We should be prepared
from now, before statehood, to have a program for development.

Abu Ala' liked this idea very much. He invited seventeen people
from inside [Palestine]—economists, technicians, sociologists, engineers—to another meeting at UNIDO in Vienna, to sit and discuss
my vision of the program, how it should be undertaken, what its
assumptions should be. I wrote a memorandum of fifteen pages, which
was circulated to the participants, as well as to Abu Ala' and Maher
al-Kurd. There was unanimous support for the idea, but they made
it a condition that I should be in charge of producing the program.

At this point, early in 1990, Abu Ala' said that I must make the
decision to go and live in Tunis. I told him that I would go in July
and start work. But in April, I went there to address a meeting of
four hundred Palestinian businessmen. They felt it was essential that
I should present to them my study on the economic underpinnings
of the state, because of the declaration of statehood. They gave me
a whole session on the first day to make the presentation. Arafat was
chairing the meeting and heaped praise on me. We finalized arrangements for my moving, and I went back to Beirut. At the beginning
of July I returned to Tunis. They had provided a house for me. Later
the family joined me for the summer.

The program needed a great deal of preparation. I decided first
to make a list of capable experts who could help prepare sectoral
programs—agriculture, with its five or six sub-sectors, industry, tourism, government, and so on. I had recourse to the Palestine unit in
UNCTAD [United Nations Conference on Trade and Development]
in Geneva, and got from them a list of people inside Palestine with
whom they had been cooperating—from fifty to seventy names. I also
got lists from the economics department of the PLO, who also knew

many people. We also contacted people inside to ask them what names they could recommend. I ended up with around three hundred names.

Then came the political decision. I discovered that it wasn't enough for people to be technically qualified to participate. The final decision whether to take 'X' or 'Y' was a political decision. It was Abu Ala' who vetted the list—I don't know if it went beyond him to someone else. He would say, "We can't have this man, he's close to the Jabha al-Sha'biya [the Popular Front, short for the Popular Front for the Liberation of Palestine]." My answer was, "Then I won't accept that man because he is close to Fatah. This isn't a parliament; it's an intellectual undertaking. We have to have people who know about the economy, who have experience, intellectual integrity, and professional competence." In the end we settled on about 120 names out of the three hundred, and I prepared a letter introducing the idea of the plan. The first five pages were the same for everybody. If I asked somebody to write about tourism, the rest of the letter would specify this. If it was industry, something else. The whole letter was eleven pages long, five being common to all; the remaining six had to be done one by one.

It took three or four months to prepare the list and the letters; and it was eight months after the letters were received inside Palestine that the first sector project came back. That's why it took so long. I anticipated it would take from two to two and a third years, but it took almost three. Abu Ala' was very good all through; he didn't interfere in a single sector program. In fact he read only a few of them that I especially wanted him to read, either because they were very poor or very good. I had to discuss with him the program's basic assumptions, which were divided into four categories: first, political assumptions—how do we justify talking about a program of development for the West Bank and Gaza? It was on the basis of a certain understanding of autonomy, because the Madrid meetings were going on at that time, and there was already talk that all we could get was autonomy. Teams inside were preparing their concepts of autonomy with regard to laws, land, water, and so on.

So I stated our case for autonomy— the legal case, the natural rights case—if we could not have independence right away.

Then there were the demographic assumptions—what size of population were we talking about? How many of those displaced in 1967 would be allowed to go back? We had to make assumptions here. I assumed the return of a quarter of a million displaced persons. Nabil Shaath criticized me on this subject, saying that it wasn't patriotic to propose the return of only a quarter of a million; in his view a million should come back. But we were considering those displaced from Gaza and the West Bank in 1967. The 1948 refugees would have to wait until other developments were possible. I answered him that all I was saying was that the cost of return for a quarter of a million, or half a million, or a million displaced persons would vary. Then there was the territorial assumption—what area will be covered? Of course we assumed that it would be the whole of the West Bank and Gaza—and Himmeh!

From the study I had made on the economic underpinnings of a state, I felt that the Palestinians possessed the necessary human resources, trained and qualified, to run an efficient economy. This proved erroneous because of the way the Oslo agreement developed, but the human and material basics were there. There was enough land—if the land and the water came back to us. What was problematic was the financing of the program. At the meeting of businessmen, I remember turning to Abu Ammar, who was chairing the meeting, and saying to him, "Mr. Chairman, I would like to assure you that all of the economic underpinnings are there—except for the finance. You will have to look after that." What happened was just the opposite—the finance was available, but the human resources were not utilized properly.

The studies began to come in, and we found that on the whole those from inside were much below our expectations. When someone has a PhD, and is associate professor in a university, you expect a certain level of competence. Several of the papers were not up to this level. We gave the writers masses of time; the first paper came eight months after receipt of the commission. Once they were finished, the papers came in quickly—there was always somebody coming to Tunis from inside. It's true that we couldn't talk to each other every day about how things should go, but I communicated with them in writing. I met some of them at conferences, and could discuss specific points with them. Mahmoud Abdel Fadil[33] came from Egypt, and rewrote several of the papers. There were sixty-five people who helped from inside, and twenty-six from outside. Out of the twenty-six, four were non-Palestinians—three Egyptians, and one Tunisian.

Abu Ala' was the only arbiter. He depended on me to read every paper. I read all of them—water, immigration, refugees . . . . The only paper I didn't read was the one on security. The paper on water was prepared inside, and it was so poor that I had to rewrite it myself. It was a very tough period, and a very tough job, with a lot of work; I worked till 10 or 11 p.m. every night. That's when I began to have that pressure in my head. As I was going with Abu Ala' to a meeting in Paris, to meet the under secretary of political affairs, he said, "You must go and have a thorough checkup at the American Hospital. They have good services. Stay as long as necessary." I went, and they found nothing wrong with my head. It was overwork.

The Multilateral Talks

I finished the last of the work in the summer of '93, and I sent it from Oxford by special courier to Tunis to be typed. But during this period I wasn't only working on the plan. The multilateral talks had started according to the Madrid procedures.[34] In May 1992, there were five working groups, and I was asked to head the one on economic development and cooperation. Elie Sanbar headed the one on refugees. The Israelis, right from the beginning, said that they would not attend if I were head of the Palestine delegation. Abu Ala' stood by me, and made Abu Ammar take the decision to send me as head of the delegation whether the Israelis attended or not. They did not. It was in Brussels, that first meeting.

The Israelis boycotted the first refugee conference too. Their pretext was that Sanbar and I were both members of the Palestine National Council. Then the Israelis said, "You can keep Yusif Sayigh as long as he stays in the hotel, and meets with the members of the delegation, but doesn't attend the meetings." The PLO kept my name as head of the delegation, but announced that I was not attending because I was unwell. I was angry with this, because there I was in Paris and perfectly well. They appointed Zein Mayassi in my place. He was a disaster. The worst thing he did was when the journalists asked him, "How do you understand the movement of the bilateral talks and the multilateral talks? Is there any connection?" He said, "No, they are two separate things." All through the first meeting I was saying that these two parallel lines have to meet. There had to be success in the bilateral talks for the multilateral talks to be meaningful. You can't have economic agreements between governments that are in the state of war; they have to reach some kind of settlement.

I began my presentation at that conference by saying there are four principles. The first one is a peace acceptable to both sides. This is the horse that pulls the carriage, and has to precede any idea of cooperation. Second, cooperation requires give and take but the Palestinians were not in a position to give anything because our economy was so terribly underdeveloped. We had to have our land and our water returned to us before we could begin to cooperate. Third, we have to agree on what cooperation means. Cooperation must be equitable and voluntary; it's not something that a victorious party imposes on the other. I can't remember the fourth principle now. The point is that this was all contrary to the line the PLO was taking at the time. This was pre-Oslo, but Abu Ammar was already preparing himself for another kind of approach. According to Abu Mazen's book, they were already making contacts behind the scenes through some Israeli so-called academics.[35] My paper [at the Brussels meeting] was very well received.

The second meeting was in Rome. I went to it, but I didn't attend [the discussions]. I stayed there, and they would come and tell me that the Israelis had raised this question or that, and I would advise them what to do. An interesting incident occurred before the second meeting started. The head of the American delegation in all the meetings was a woman economist. She looked very unhappy with my presentation, and we entered into an argument. The chairman of the meeting was Portuguese, since Portugal was chairing the European Commission at the time. During the lunch break he came and put his arm through mine and said, "Come and sit at my table." Each table was for ten. There was a very intelligent young man from Oman, very impressive, who sat at the same table, and a few others. There were two empty chairs.

Then into the dining hall walks the head of the American delegation. She came to the chairman's table and said, "May I join you?" and took an empty chair. To start the conversation, she turned to the person next to her, who happened to be the Omani. His English was very good. When she heard him speak, she asked him where he had studied English. Then she looked at me and asked, "Where did you study, Dr. Sayigh?" I said, "Johns Hopkins University." Suddenly that grim face smiled. She said, "I'm a graduate of Johns Hopkins University, and my husband is teaching there now." I said, "Your degree is in political economy, isn't it?" She said, "Yes." I said, "So why were you arguing inside that you must divorce economics from politics?" She laughed, "That was inside."

The day before the start of the meeting, an invitation to tea came for our delegation. Abu Ala', who always came to these meetings because he had to keep Abu Ammar informed of what was happening, said that an invitation had come from the head of the American delegation—I forget her name now. She had said to Abu Ala', "Please make sure Dr. Sayigh comes as well." I went to the tea, because I wanted to face her. After tea, she said, "Can I have a word with you and Mr. Mayassi separately?" We went in, and I said to her, "I understand you supported the Israeli veto against me?" She said, "Yes. They said they would not attend if somebody who is a member of the National Council participates in the team even as a member." "But Mr. Mayassi is a member [of the Council], so why is he accepted? With due respect to Mr. Mayassi, he realizes that there is something illogical here." She said, "That's not a decision that I took."

A dinner was given that same evening in honor of the delegations taking part—there were about forty governments, and the Palestinians and the Israelis. Again the Portuguese host put me on his right. The American was on his other side and the Israeli [head of delegation] was opposite us. [The Portuguese] turned to me and said in a whisper, "I'm sorry that you aren't head of the Palestinian delegation, but we couldn't do anything. The Americans put their foot down, and the Israelis too—not even as a member of the delegation." This, he said, was on the highest orders from Israel. Abu Mazen says in his book *Through Secret Channels* that Rabin didn't want me or Elias Sanbar to be named as heads of delegation. To understand why, we have to know what was really going on in the multilateral talks. Politically, the central purpose was to produce an economic cake that would appeal to the Arabs so that they would make political concessions. I could see that. That's why my paper argued against that line. At the supper I said [to the American head of delegation], "I know my exclusion is because your delegation did not like my position paper." When we went out, Zein Mayassi understood the significance of my remark, and said, "*Wa ana himar ya'ni?* [You mean I'm a donkey?]" I said, "*La, inta mish himar* [No, you're not a donkey], but you have a different political line."

Even though it didn't express the PLO political line, my paper appeared as the position paper of the Palestine Delegation. I presented it in the first session. I wanted support from the Arab delegations for my position that it was premature to talk about economic cooperation before a political settlement had been reached. I succeeded in this with the Jordanians, after a face-to-face discussion.

The head of the Jordanian delegation was Fayez Tarawni, now the ambassador of Jordan in Washington. He saw my point, and asked me, "What do you want me to say?" I said, "Say that while cooperation is essential, it's premature. That's all I want from you." He said it, and got a black look from the American head of delegation.

But the coup was the Egyptians. I made friends with the head of the Egyptian delegation, a very capable woman, now ambassador to Japan, I think. I said to her, "It would be a shame if the Arab delegations talk in different voices. We need you, Egypt, our big sister, our leader. Shouldn't we coordinate?" She said, "Yes, why don't you invite us all to a meeting?" I said, "No. You invite us to a meeting." She was happy with this idea, and invited us. I said to her, "Let's you and I come to an understanding. Do you really believe that it makes sense to talk about cooperation, when only your country has a peace agreement with Israel, not the other countries? Couldn't you say it's premature?" She said, "Yes, I could say that." It seems that Cairo had given her some latitude.

Unexpected support came from the Saudi delegate, who came late to the meeting. He supported me fully in his intervention, and kept referring to my presentation. It's not really so surprising. Until now the Saudis say that they won't have anything to do with Israel until there is an acceptable settlement. After the meeting, I went to thank him, and he said, "Don't thank me, thank your late brother Fayez. I knew him well in America. I couldn't say anything against my conscience. I'd refuse to come here if I was told to say something else, but this is in line with my government's position."

The Americans had to show something for their work, so they proposed that we set up sub-committees to discuss areas [of cooperation] when the time comes. I intervened, "Mr. Chairman, don't you think this is running too far ahead of the events? We're still very far from a settlement. Let us concentrate on principles, let's define terms, what do we mean by cooperation?" The whole meeting went on like that, because of course the bilateral negotiations in

Washington were stalled. The Americans were not happy with me—no doubt everything was reported back to them.

All I could do from that moment on was to prepare the papers for our delegation, and the second and third delegations. The fourth meeting was after Oslo, and the veto on me was removed. I chaired the delegation again, but I took the same position as before. I did not say the same things, but when they came to discussing [cooperation], I continued to object. The European Commission, which always had the gavel for these multilateral talks—as a concession from the Americans—came up with a document that had thirty or forty projects that Palestinians and Israelis could go into together—plus some other Arabs—once there was a settlement. Jacob Frankel, the governor of the Central Bank of Israel, was the head of the Israeli delegation at that meeting. I wanted to respond to this proposal, so I addressed him: "Does it make economic sense to you, Dr. Frankel, to talk about specific projects now? We don't know how much money will be available once there is a settlement. We don't know who enters the settlement and who doesn't. Isn't it too early?" He said, "I agree. But"—of course there was a 'but'—"let us assume that there is an acceptable settlement, and talk about areas of cooperation, not specific projects. At least let us agree with the Europeans who want to divide these projects among themselves." I couldn't do more than dilute the thing. That was the last session I attended. It was in November '93, in Denmark.

Negotiations with the World Bank

After Oslo, Abu Ala' said to me, "Now is the time we need you, even more than before. You say the estimates of the World Bank are grossly insufficient for the infrastructure for the public sector"—it was $3 billion for ten years. In our program, which was finalized in July '93, I came to the conclusion that we needed $4.6 billion for seven years. Abu Ala' said, "Who can argue the case except you?" He got a letter from Abu Ammar addressed to the forthcoming meeting in

Washington, on September 20, seven days after the signing the Oslo Accords, that I would head a delegation of three, with Samir Abdallah and Muhammad Shtayeh. These two attended for one day, and then disappeared. I was fighting for $5 billion for ten years. There were forty countries there, but nobody said anything, the argument was entirely between me and the head of the mission of the World Bank, the one who headed the mission [to Palestine]. Altogether five World Bank missions went to survey the situation and examine the needs [of the Palestinian people].

The chairman of the meeting was an Indian, second in command after Caio Koch-Weser,[36] a vice president of the World Bank. I saw him writing something. He came over to me at the last meeting on the second day, and said, "Can you accept this formula, so that we can reach a conclusion?" The formula said, "After more careful examination of the needs of the Palestinians, and in light of the findings reported in the program for development that the PLO prepared, the figure will be upped from $3 billion to $4.8 billion for 10 years. For half of this, the United States government will seek pledges from the participants in the meeting to be held in a few days' time in Washington, on the basis of pledges up to $2.4 billion for five years." I was delighted with the results. The Israelis did not open their mouths at that meeting; they felt that this was an argument between the Palestinians and the World Bank—let it be played out between them. Immediately it was known outside, there was a flood of telephone calls. They wanted me for TV and for radio, but I had no time.

At this point a problem between the Americans and the Europeans appeared. Which of them was to head the liaison committee? Since not all the donors would be able to attend all the meetings, a liaison committee was to be formed of five or six major donors—Europe, America, and a few other countries. One day the first secretary of the Belgian embassy telephoned and said, "When can we get together?" We agreed on a time, he came, and said, "We in Europe are very eager to chair this liaison committee, because we are pledging $600 million as against the $500 million that America is pledging. We don't see why America should head the committee." I said, "I don't think it's fair to ask us, the Palestinians, who don't even have a state, to take sides in this matter and damage our relations with either of you." He accepted that, and later he telephoned me and said, "A formula has been reached whereby we'll rotate the chairmanship. You don't have to worry about the Palestinian role."

Two days after the World Bank meeting in which money was discussed, they contacted me and asked for a copy of the Palestine Economic Programme, and made three hundred and fifty copies. They said that they wanted me to give a lecture on the Programme to all the staff involved with Middle East affairs in the World Bank and International Monetary Fund. Every one of the participants would get a copy. I gave a number of short interviews, but I was really getting to a point of trembling with tiredness and stress. I was all by myself there.

Then Abu Ammar telephoned me. He said, "We're proud of you—*inta 'izna wa taj rasna* [you are our pride and crown]. You brought us one thousand eight hundred million dollars more than the World Bank wanted to give." I said, "It's not I, it's thanks to the acceptance of the Programme." He had never even read the Programme, though I sent him a copy. That was one meanness in Abu Ala'—I thought both of us would go and meet Abu Ammar, and take the Programme. But he took it by himself, to get the credit.[37]

I took this opportunity to tell Abu Ammar, "There are going to be two meetings for pledges to be made by the likely donor countries"—the countries who had taken part in the meetings had already indicated a willingness to pledge; there were around thirty-five to forty countries, some hadn't come yet—"one meeting will be on the 28th of September, I can handle that. But on the first of October, there will be a meeting which will be headed either by Clinton or by Gore, and the official participants of the meetings are all of ministerial rank except for myself. I want somebody to come from the

Executive." He said, "No, no. We don't need anybody else. Who can represent us better than you?" I said, "It's a matter of protocol. I'll be there if you want me to say something." He said, *"Inta bitkaffee* [You are enough]."

I went to the meeting of pledges. Before that I had had two meetings with the State Department, each three hours, with Dennis Ross,[38] Kurtzer, and Miller[39]—Indyk wasn't there—to discuss economic problems in Palestine as I saw them. They took a copy of the Programme, and made copies of it for the donor countries that were to attend the final meeting. The chairperson, Joan Spiro,[40] who was the U.S. under secretary of state for economic affairs, introduced me and said, "We'll give the first word to Dr. Sayigh. Please tell us about the Programme. We haven't all had the time to read it." I said, "This is a meeting for pledges. We [Palestinians] should pledge to use the money usefully, fruitfully"—everything I said then has been reversed.

Then on September 29th, at around nine o'clock at night, the telephone rang, and Nabil Shaath was on the line saying, "We've come because of the pressure you put on Abu Ammar"—though nobody can put pressure on Abu Ammar. Nabil and Yasser Abed Rabbo[41] had come for the meeting. I told them what had happened so far, what to say and what not to say, and advised them not to mention the conflict between the United States and the European Union about the chairmanship of the Liaison Committee. I told them that the Americans, especially Under Secretary for the Treasury Larry Summers, had tried hard to persuade me to take the American side. He had said, "I believe you will support our chairing this committee because we raised our contribution from $100 million to $500 million." I replied, "You raised from $100 million a year to $500 million for five years. We Palestinians may not be very advanced in science but we know how to do arithmetic. The Europeans are offering $600 million for five years." His face got red, and he changed the subject.

I told them [Nabil and Yasser] that this controversy had continued over the past week, and how the first secretary of the Belgian embassy came to see me in the hotel, to try and get us to vote in favor of Europe chairing this committee; and how I had asked him to leave us out of it because we are too small to stand up to a conflict with either party; and how he had accepted this formula. "Please," I said to them, "don't mention this in the meeting. Each delegation has only two minutes to speak, just to say 'We pledge so-and-so.' As a special favor the Palestinians have six minutes. We don't want to waste them on irrelevant issues."

I added "They don't want anybody to enter into politics. What is essential for us is to indicate our needs, and how we intend to satisfy them, through what institutions and processes." Immediately Yasser Abed Rabbo said, "No, I don't accept. We're going to talk politics." I said, "If you want to. But you won't have time for the other things for which you came, especially that when we Palestinians speak of politics we usually take at least half an hour for the introduction." He said, "No, no. I want to talk about Jerusalem, and about the four hundred Palestinians expelled to Marj al-Zuhur"[42]—they were then in Lebanon. I said, "I don't advise it, you won't have the time." He said, "Anyway, we have prepared a paper, and here it is. I would appreciate it if you would go over it and suggest changes." I said, "The meeting is tomorrow morning"—this conversation was on the morning of the 30th of September—"I don't think you have enough time to prepare a new paper. It's easier to delete things because the paper is very long."

I took the paper, and then I said, "Since we have only six minutes, I'd like to see how we can allocate the time. I suppose both of you will be saying something, but I would like to have a couple of minutes myself. I have lived with this whole operation over the last twelve days in Washington, I've had interesting discussions with people, and I think I know how to approach them, and how to justify the increased budget pledges." Then Nabil said, "No, Yusif, you and I will not say anything, Yasser Abed Rabbo will do all the talking. He and I come here as ministers, I as minister of finance, and Yasser as minister of foreign affairs." I said, "This is quite a surprise. You are not a member of the Executive Committee, so you cannot claim to be of ministerial status, unless you have been co-opted by the Executive Committee." He said, "I haven't been [co-opted] but I'm a minister." I said, "Finance is in the hands of Muhammad Nashashibi, so if it's the minister of finance who should come, it should be Nashashibi. As to foreign affairs, the minister of foreign affairs, Faruq Qaddumi, is currently in the United Nations in New York. Yasser is minister of information." Nabil said, "Never mind all that. It's in that capacity that we're here." I said, "All right, if you want to do all the talking, I will not sit like the 'delegate of Yemen'"—they used to say that about anyone who attends a meeting and doesn't speak, because the Yemeni delegate never said anything in the meetings of the Arab League.

Nabil said, "No, no, you will attend because you are a member of the delegation. I have a letter from Abu Ammar, I'll go and get it from the room." I said, "I believe you, Nabil. But nobody can force me to attend. I'm not an employee. I'm contracted to do a job that has nothing to do with these meetings. They are an extra that I'm doing. Luckily, in this extra, I got Palestine one thousand eight hundred million dollars more than the World Bank initially estimated. If you feel that I'm not entitled to say anything, I don't want to attend." He said, "Why shouldn't you? Write it down, and Yasser will include it in his speech." I said, "I'm not a speechwriter for Yasser." Nabil said, "But Yusif, when a prime minister or a president makes a speech do you think he writes it? Look at the last speech made by President Clinton; surely he didn't write that speech." I said, "President Clinton would have offered the job of speechwriter to somebody who would have accepted it. The job has not been offered to me, and I wouldn't accept it."

At this point Yasser Abed Rabbo got very red in the face, and his eyes bulged even more than they normally do, and he said, "*Ana ma bismah bi bahth al-mawdu‘* [I will not allow this subject to be discussed]." I said to him, "I argue things out with Abu Ammar himself, or with people even more important than Abu Ammar. I will never relinquish my right to argue. *Ma btismah* [You don't allow it]? That's a very authoritarian attitude." He looked at me and pointed his index finger straight in my face, and said, "*Na'am, li-innu ana as-sulta* [Yes, because I am the authority]."

I said to them, "If the two of you are that important, what am I doing here?" I got up to leave the meeting. They said, "No, no, you will be here tomorrow." I said, "No, no, I won't, tomorrow I'm taking a plane." Immediately I went out and made arrangements to change my booking. Instead of going to Tunis, I decided to go to Cairo, because there was a meeting there that I'd said I couldn't attend, but now I had changed my mind. I learnt later that many of the delegates at the meeting asked where I was. The pledges all went through, because they were already made. There had been a meeting on the 27th or 28th of September, a dress rehearsal for this final meeting, where delegates indicated what their countries wanted to pledge. But they had to have another meeting because not all the representatives had received instructions from their governments. The final pledges were made on October 1st, the day I left.

Struggle with Arafat around the Palestinian Economic Council for Development and Reconstruction

I returned to Tunis. Before packing up, I began campaigning for the signature of the order that Arafat had written establishing the Economic Council. The Economic Council was an idea that Antoine Zahlan[43] and myself developed; we went ahead and discussed the structure and functions of this council, and the name. It was to be called PEDRA—Palestine Economic Development and Reconstruction Agency (later changed to the Palestinian Economic Council for Development and Reconstruction—PECDAR). We worked late one evening, and Zahlan borrowed a computer from the office there, and stayed till two o'clock putting the final form into print in English. Abu Ala' took the document to Abu Ammar, who went through it and approved it verbally. What we wanted from Arafat was to sign this document. I had announced his agreement to the World Bank, and the Americans, and the European Community, and all the others involved, also in the meeting when I gave a lecture on the Palestine Economic Programme. So in Tunis I started trying to get Arafat to sign the document. All my contacts were through Abu Ala'; I didn't go and see Arafat myself.

Abu Ala' would come back every time a little more frustrated, because Arafat kept putting the thing off, saying he had to discuss it with the Executive Committee. Obviously, there were problems, and later on we realized, Abu Ala' and I, that the members of the Executive Committee wanted to become members of the board of governors of PEDRA. They realized it meant money and power. The importance of the board of governors came from the fact that we assigned all the important functions to it—choice of priorities in development, choice of projects, allocation of funds, supervision of work—all was in the hands of the board of governors. On top of the board of governors was to be an advisory council, consisting of fifty or sixty people. The idea behind it was to include in the council enough of the *abawat*[44]—the leaders, politicians, poets, notables, whatever—to satisfy and silence them, so that they would not block the work of PEDRA. We'd put them in the Supreme Advisory Council, headed by Arafat, but this council was to have no decision-making power. It would meet only once a year. All the powers were in the hands of the board of governors. We suggested a few names to be on the board—Abu Ala' to be head of the thing, that was our suggestion. Then there would be Antoine Zahlan, Taher Kanaan, Khalil Hindi, Ibrahim Dakkak, myself—I think we suggested seven names, and left it open for Arafat to add four or five more.

Our efforts to get Arafat to sign this document went on and on until halfway through October. At this point the World Bank contacted us in Tunis to say that the vice president would like to come, Caio Koch-Weser, along with the man who was in charge of the Middle East section, an Indian called Ram Chopra,[45] and Abdallah

Bouhabib,[46] who was in public relations for that division. A day was set for meetings between Arafat and this team, October 16th, at six-thirty in the evening. They came on the afternoon of October 15th, and got in touch with me, and said that in the morning they would be going to make a courtesy visit to the [Tunisian] minister of foreign affairs. But they wanted to talk to me before they met Arafat, so they asked me to lunch with them. I went, and I told them how to approach the subject, to make sure to insist on getting Arafat to come to the point, rather than going around and around. And to begin by congratulating him on the Oslo Accords. I said, "I don't think that the Accords call for congratulations to him personally, but he will expect that from you." We had a long session.

A little before the meeting, I learnt that Arafat was angry. He said, "These people have not come to see me but to visit the government." He was angry to the point of not sending a car to fetch them from their hotel. Of course they could take a taxi, but usually one sends a car to bring people who are your guests. I decided that I should go to the meeting room, and see him before they came, so that the atmosphere would not be poisoned.

I went in and said, "I hear that you're angry because you think they have come for something else, and you are on the margin. That's not true. They are coming to meet you, but they had to pay a courtesy visit, they couldn't ignore it." He kept quiet. At that moment his nephew, Nasser al-Qudwa, the representative of the PLO at the UN, came in. He had called for him. Arafat said to him, "I want you to attend the meeting, along with Yusif. But you are in your shirt-sleeves. Go and put on a tie and a jacket." Nasser said, "I don't have a tie or a jacket." Arafat rang the bell for one of the attendants and said, "Take him up to my floor and let him pick a jacket and a tie." Nasser went out and never came back to the meeting, he was so cross with his uncle. The next morning he said to me, "Does he think I'm a little boy! Why should I put a jacket on? These people are modern, they're not going to be impressed by a jacket and a tie."

We went to the meeting. They began by congratulating Arafat. Then they said, "Now that money seems to have been pledged, we want to say that we are very happy that your Department of Economic Affairs has designed something that we ourselves wanted to suggest, but we hesitated, because we didn't want it to look as though we are teaching people what to do. We were delighted to see our ideas coincide with those of the document that Yusif Sayigh has told us about. We want to congratulate you on having approved this. Now we need the approval in writing."

Arafat said, "It will be in writing at the right moment." They said, "We hope that we can take a written document signed by you before we return." He said, "No, it will take time. I have to check with my institutions." I had warned them about that. They said, "Of course, Mr. Chairman, you are entitled to time to discuss this with the Executive Committee." He said, "The Executive Committee, and there are other institutions"—looking very serious. They said, "How long will this take?" He said, "I can't tell you. A number of weeks, no doubt." They said, "Mr. Chairman, on November 4th and 5th there's going to be a meeting in Paris of all the donors, plus the World Bank, plus the Palestinians. We cannot have that meeting unless we have a written document in our hands on PEDRA, in writing and signed by you, and distributed to these people before they come to the meeting. Otherwise there won't be a meeting. If there is no meeting, there will be no flow of funds." He said, "Well, I'm sorry, but it will take time."

Before, when they said, "Let's talk business," Arafat interrupted them, "I want to tell you something. Kuwait owes me $106 million, and Saudi Arabia owes me"—the amount was even more—"and this money is mine. It's money that my people have paid, people employed in Saudi Arabia and Kuwait, deductions from their salaries." He went on and on about that, repeating himself. When he stopped for breath, Koch-Weser said, "Mr. Chairman, we're not here for that." Arafat said, "I know. But you must tell the Americans to put pressure on these Gulf countries." Koch-Weser told him, "I believe you have more influence with the American government than we have, why don't you do that? Please let's concentrate on our business."

It ended with Koch-Weser and Chopra repeating the same thing, "Mr. Chairman, there are three points we have to make very clear. First, it's essential that a mechanism is designed, namely PEDRA, to shoulder the various functions that we have mentioned. Second, the money will come from the donors directly to the projects, there's to be no stop on the way"—I had said to them before that if there's a stop, he can control where the money goes—"And third, it is the board that will determine the priorities and supervise the implementation of the projects, and all its operations should conform to the principles of efficiency, accountability, and transparency, as well as being subjected to internal and external audit. Nothing should be done under the table. These three points are essential if the donors are to be willing to put down their money. The money is big, Mr. Chairman, $2,400 million pledged for five years. Arafat said, "Yes, I will sign it." "When?" In the end, they said, "Mr. Chairman, if you won't give us a date, we have to tell you that the document must be signed and faxed to us by the end of October, so that we can circulate copies of it to the donors before the Paris meeting."

Toward the end of October I began inquiring whether he had signed the document, and Abu Ala' would say, "Not yet, there's a great deal of disagreement in the Executive Committee." He and I both realized that they didn't want PEDRA to control the direction of the flow of funds; they wanted to control it themselves. Some of them wanted to be members. Finally, by the 31st, I decided that if Arafat wasn't going to sign, it meant that we would have to tell [the World Bank] that there's no point in the meeting. I was supposed to leave for Paris on November 3rd, on a plane that took off in the afternoon, so that by the morning of the 4th I'd be ready for the meeting. By then Abu Ala' had gone to Washington; he was to come to Paris later. I made inquiries from people in the circle of Arafat, his advisors. I had a friend in the Economics Department who had a lot

of contacts there; he was my 'mole.' He would say, "No signature."
On the first and second of the month I began asking Abu Mazen, and
he said, "Nothing has happened."

On the third, at 10 a.m.—I was to leave for the airport at midday
because the plane would take off at 2 p.m.—I called Faruq Qaddumi, Abu Lutf, and said, "What's happened? I have to leave, but Abu
Ammar hasn't signed this document, and Abu Ala' isn't here." He
said, in the oratorical way he speaks in Arabic, "No, this document
hasn't been signed." I said, "It has to be signed if the money is to
come." He said, "This World Bank wants to ride our backs because of
this little money that they're giving us?" I said, "Are you joking? $2.4
billion dollars for five years isn't little." He said, "No, I'm serious.
We haven't signed. We may sign in a week, ten days . . . ." I thought
that there was nothing more I could do but check with Abu Mazen,
who is always gentle and polite. I told him what Faruq Qaddumi had
said. He laughed, "The money is important. But unfortunately last
night we met until after midnight, and there was a lot of argument
and shouting. The thing was still not signed when I went home." I
resigned myself to going to Paris without the document in my hand.

At noon I left the office, and because I was going by car to the
airport I had a driver to bring the car back. He started the engine,
and we began moving, when suddenly 'the mole' appeared and waved,
"Stop! Stop!" He ran to me and said, "Abu Ammar has just signed the
document. He has dated it October 31st instead of November 3rd,
but that's not the important thing. He has turned the structure you
prepared upside down. There's still an advisory body headed by him,
but he has moved all the functions that you put for the board of governors up to the advisory body. The departments under the board of
governors are kept as they are, and he has accepted your recommen-
dations for membership of the board of governors, but he has added
other people. And, finally, he has put himself as chairman of the board
of governors, as well as of the advisory body, and added two vice presi-
dents, Qaddumi and Nashashibi." I said, "This won't go through."

I took the plane to Paris, and went to the hotel where Abu Ala' and I were to stay. An hour or so later he telephoned to say that he had arrived. I went to his room, and I was still at the door when he said, "I have good news for you." I said, "I have bad news for you. What is your good news?" He said, "I've just telephoned Hakam Bal'awi"—the representative of the PLO in Tunis—"and he told me that Abu Ammar had signed the document as you and Zahlan designed it." I said, "Abu Ammar has signed the document, put the wrong date on it—that's unimportant—but he has turned it upside down." "What do you mean? You must be wrong." I told him what 'the mole' had told me. Abu Ala' said, "He must be mistaken. I have Hakam Bal'awi's version, I talked to him just after my arrival, and he said that everything is all right." About half an hour later the fax came from Abu Ammar, the document.

When the fax came, Abu Ala' devoured it, and his face went green. He said, "My God, you're right, not Hakam Bal'awi." I said, "Hakam was either telling you a lie, or was told a lie in the first place, or didn't understand the difference between this version and the version we gave to Abu Ammar to sign." He said, "What can I do? I can't fail to distribute it, because it has to be in their hands. But I can't defend it. I'll just distribute it and let them do what they want." He looked at me and asked, "Will you defend it?" I said, "No, of course I won't. You'll be lucky if I don't attack it in the meeting, as it stands now." He said, "You're lucky you are a professional consultant and not an employee."

The following morning we went to the meeting. Copies of the document had been distributed. Everyone was looking grim, and after the preliminaries the chairman of the meeting, who was the foreign affairs minister of Norway, Holst[47]—who died a few weeks after—began by saying, "We're surprised and shocked to receive this document. It is totally different from what we understood it would be from Yusif's presentation in Washington, when he announced the establishment of PEDRA. I would like to ask him now whether he is sure that what he told us then about the authority structure in PEDRA was what he designed?" I said, "Yes, but the present document is a reversal of the plan we made." He, and the World Bank and the Americans, said, "But you are a member of the board of governors"—the names were listed. I said, "I am a member of the board of governors in the document, but I won't take my seat." They said, "We must discuss this outside the meeting. Let's adjourn." The meeting was adjourned supposedly for half an hour. But it was two hours later that we met again.

All the donor countries were in that inner meeting—about forty countries—and the World Bank and the International Fund. I didn't know what went on inside, but they began inviting me to their offices. We were meeting in an old palace in Paris, and each delegation had an enormous room as an office. We the Palestinians, Abu Ala' and I, had a room as big as this whole apartment, the two of us sitting in there, no one else, because we were the delegation. Delegates would come in and ask for me, because Abu Ala' didn't say a word in the meeting, he decided to keep silent. All of them expressed their anger. They said, "Abu Ammar has certainly done the right thing if he doesn't want any money." It's true we got money in the end, but that was because the whole thing was changed again, completely, though it didn't go back to what we had designed.

The World Bank repeated what they said in the meeting. So did the members from the European Union. The Americans were the most outspoken. Joan Spiro said, "We want to express our displeasure and anger, and we have written a document." She read it out to me. It had seven points as to why they could not accept the formula that Abu Ammar had signed. We went to the open meeting, and this was declared. Then the meeting asked the chairman to see Arafat and tell him that the meeting refuses this formula, and that it has to go back to what it was before. There might be some minor changes, but the substance should remain as I had declared it verbally to them in Washington. This was on November 5th.

Abu Ala' and I went back to Tunis. At this point he was totally disgusted. He had been inflated by his 'success' in Oslo, where he was the chief negotiator. Now Abu Ammar was pulling the rug from under his feet through changing the formula for PEDRA, which was going to be a very powerful institution. He was annoyed by this. He saw that Abu Ammar had put himself as chairman and that he, Abu Ala', would have no power since the money would be channeled through Abu Ammar.

In fact Abu Ammar began right away, as soon as Abu Ala' got back, to clip his wings. For instance, Abu Ala' had been in charge of the overall coordination of the multilateral discussions. It was he who chose the teams for the five committees: the Economic Committee which I headed, the Refugee Committee which Sanbar headed, Water, Arms Control, and the Environment. But to win back Hani al-Hassan,[48] Abu Ammar took four of these committees and put them under al-Hassan, and put Abu Ala' in charge of Development and Cooperation, where I had been head. This made Abu Ala' more outspoken and more oppositional; he would curse Abu Ammar with people in the room. I took him aside, and said, "At least half these people are informers for Abu Ammar." He said, "I don't care. Let him do what he wants."

The stalemate did not last long. Just ten days after our return, on November 16th, the Norwegian minister of foreign affairs—Holst—came to see Abu Ammar, and stayed with him for hours. It was a very long meeting. A day or two after he left, a fax came from him to Abu Ammar, with copies to Abu Ala' and myself. I have it with me here. It was a long fax, six or seven pages—a letter and an attachment. The letter said, "Dear Chairman Arafat, I'm delighted that after our long discussion you've come round to seeing our point of view, and are ready to revise the structure of PEDRA. As you've agreed to this, I've taken the liberty to circulate this letter and attachment to all the donor countries, so they will know that we've reached an agreement"—of course he wanted to preempt Arafat [from taking further action]—"and so that there will be no misunderstanding, I'm attaching an outline of the structure and functions of PEDRA."

Four times in that document it said that the Advisory Council, chaired by Arafat, will meet once a year only, and that it has no decision-making power. And all the functions, all the decisions, are to be in the hands of the board of governors. We had had five or six categories of functions; they added one to it. The departments were all to operate under the board of governors. The chairman [of the board] was to be Qaddumi—they didn't suggest a vice chairman—the managing director would be Abu Ala', and the members were to be Antoine Zahlan, Khalil Hindi, Taher Kanaan, myself, and some others. They made no changes in the numbers, but they removed Arafat from the chairmanship [of the board of governors], and removed Abu Lutf and Zuhdi Nashashibi from being deputy chairmen. Abu Ala' and Abu Ammar, they said, would be a 'reporting point.' We wondered what they meant by that. Later someone explained that it is somebody to whom reports can go, 'c/c Arafat,' no more than that. Arafat was very, very angry; he closed himself in, and canceled all appointments. A week later, he put himself on his plane and went to Oslo to meet with Holst. But in between something happened.

I should explain that when the meeting in Paris was taking place, there were journalists and TV and news agencies all around. During the two hours of consultations, I happened to pass through the press room, and they grabbed me. It was the same question everyone was throwing at me, "How can you accept this formula which differs from what you announced earlier on, when you are a member of the board?' I said, "I'm not going to join the board." "Why?" I said, "Because the direction of the whole thing has been moved from the board of governors to an advisory council, and Arafat will be the chairman. Abu Ammar has designed it so that he will control everything. He has politicized an institution—PEDRA—which was meant to be developmental. Instead of respecting institutions, he's more interested in holding on to all the strings." This was all published.

A few days after our return from Paris, and the arrival of the letter from Holst, the correspondent of Reuters in Tunis telephoned me. He said, "We understand that Holst has sent a letter to Arafat. What are the main points? Are you aware of it?" I said, "I'm aware of the thing, but there are only a few minor changes." He said, "What are they? Who is the chairman now?" I said, "Farouq Qaddumi." "Not Arafat?" I said, "No, not Arafat." "Who is the deputy chairman? Nashashibi?" I said, "No, there is no deputy chairman." I didn't ask anybody for permission to speak to the press. I just threw caution to the winds; I couldn't tell them a lie and say everything was all right, or that the formula of Arafat was accepted. They had covered the meetings in Paris, so the press was aware of the issue. The Reuters man said, "How about the board of governors, has it got any new functions?" I said, "It has the functions that were taken away by Chairman Arafat." The correspondent sent a fax to Reuters, and they heard about it in Tunis.

That's when Arafat made a statement against me in an interview with a local journalist, saying, "It's a lie. I'm the chairman of the board, and Nashashibi is still deputy chairman." A member of Abu Ala"s department (Internal Affairs and Planning) was also made to write a piece criticizing me. Then I got a letter from Nashashibi, ten lines, saying, "I've read in the press the false information you gave them, and I don't understand how you have the face to fabricate such misinformation. Chairman Arafat is still chairman of the board of governors, and I'm still deputy chairman. I don't know in whose interest you're doing this"—he might have meant Abu Ala', or some foreign power. He ended by saying, "If I had known your real nature I would have acted differently toward you."

I wrote him a letter. Although he was in Tunis, I sent it to his desk and I faxed it to his office in Amman so that everyone would read it. I cut him to pieces. I took his letter, word by word, and said, "Let's see who was falsifying, you or me." I rubbed it in that he had been misled—"Obviously, Abu Ammar hasn't told you of the letter he received from Holst, which shows that he [Arafat] had agreed on the structure of PEDRA and its functions. You must be talking out of ignorance, because if you were aware of this, you wouldn't have sent me this letter." I added, "To make up for Mr. Arafat's failure to inform you, I'm attaching a copy of Holst's letter." He shut up totally after that.

When Arafat went to see Holst in Oslo, he didn't get what he wanted. He talked about orphans and widows, and he said, "I have to have authority." But after that they sent him another letter that kept Qaddumi as chairman, not him, and kept Nashashibi out; and the Advisory Council remained with no decision-making powers. So there was no change at all. They just added this item about 'reporting'—"Of course, Mr. Chairman, the board will send you reports about all its activities." Arafat agreed to Holst's formula simply because he wasn't going to recognize it.

Last Battles

So PEDRA remained more or less as it was planned, but on paper only. What happened was that the Israelis and Americans came to see Abu Ammar as necessary for them politically, and began to support him more and more, and to close an eye to his violations of PEDRA's rules and procedures. For instance, the World Bank sent a fat document on procedures: how to call for tenders for projects; limiting PEDRA to $25,000; only to authorize projects announced in advance, with a sealed tender; the functions of the various departments under the board of governors, and so on. All these regulations were violated. He began to interfere in appointments, as though he were head of PEDRA, or one of the members of the board of governors. But they [the Americans] kept quiet.

All their insistence at the beginning was on accountability and transparency—perhaps they meant it at the time—but in the end it was a question of politics; Arafat was their man, so they dropped accountability and transparency. He sat in on PEDRA's meetings as chairman. I said to Qaddumi one day, "Why do you allow it?" He said, "*Ya khayyi, bistihi minnu, rijjal kibeer wa* . . . [I feel ashamed (to confront him), he's an old man]."

Because Arafat was worried that PEDRA would become prominent and consolidate itself to a point where it would become difficult to dislodge it, he did two things. First of all, he began making quick tours to different countries, trying to get them to approve certain projects, to get the money himself. He would take with him second-raters who were around him. Then he established an Economic Advisory Committee that consisted of Khaled Salam[49] as chairman—an Iraqi Kurd who was not an economist—Umm Lutuf, who had no qualifications for that kind of job, Ha'el Fahoum, assistant to Qaddumi in the political department of the PLO, with a degree in political science, Marwan Abdel Hamid, a brother of Abul Hol, an engineer, and Akram Haniyeh, who is a short-story writer and journalist. This was the economic body, which was supposed to be a counterweight to PEDRA. It was a joke. He soon dropped the whole thing, but kept Khaled Salam.

Before I left Tunis there was an interesting episode. Arafat's office telephoned—it was the second meeting of PECDAR. I didn't go to the first one but Arafat made it a point that I should attend the second—he was heading every meeting. Though I was leaving they still invited me. I told Abu Ala' I wasn't coming. Abu Ammar insisted. He telephoned, and began by saying, "*Ya doctor!* *'Arafa al-habibu maqamahu wa-tadallala.*" This is half of an Arabic verse, which means 'The beloved one recognizes his status, so he becomes coquettish.' I answered him, "Chairman Arafat, I'm not being coquettish. I do not want to take part. I said it in public, I said it to the press, and I sent you a message to that effect. On grounds of principle, I refuse to take part." He said, "Come and tell us what these principles are." I said, "Only if you promise to give me half an hour to state my case without interruption." He said, "Okay." So I went. They had already started the meeting when I entered.

He wanted me there, because my name has some value. It is still on the board, although I sent him many faxes asking him to remove me. He wanted me for that particular meeting because he knew that I was leaving soon. When I got in, he said, "We are discussing the question of the establishment of a bank to finance development with a capital of five hundred million dollars, and I've been saying to the members here"—there were nine members, and Yasser Abed Rabbo was sitting there; he wasn't a member but he'd been visiting Arafat and stayed. There was a quorum, nine out of fourteen. There were two or three people from 'inside'—Sari Nusseibeh and Ibrahim Dakkak. Qaddumi was there of course, and Nashashibi. Arafat sat behind his big desk; he was chairing the meeting though Qaddumi should have been in the chair. Basically he was running PECDAR. That's what I said later in the evening when I got my chance.

He said, "They say they need time to study the idea. What do you think?" I said, "I think they are absolutely right." A few years ago, the Welfare Association had asked Edmund Asfour,[50] a distinguished Palestinian economist and a senior official with the World Bank, to prepare a proposal for the establishment of an industrial development bank. I said that what they needed now was a bank for general development. Asfour's proposal, which was well thought out and carefully written, was done well before Oslo, and there was a need for some changes in it. For instance, Asfour suggested that the headquarters should be outside Palestine, so that the board of directors could operate freely. Now the situation was different. Also the authority of the bank, its functions, should include other sectors—agriculture, industry, and tourism. I suggested that Abu Ala', who had a copy of this study, should photocopy it and distribute it to the members of the board, and allow them two or three weeks to make comments. These comments, with the opinion of a lawyer specialized in international law, should be sent back to Asfour to rewrite his study.

Abu Ammar said, "That will take many weeks." I said, "Yes, but it deserves it. It's five hundred million dollars." He said, "But this is urgent, I want it done right away. What you're saying is classical." I said, "I don't know what you mean by 'classical,' but it is correct. It cannot be done any other way. Let me put it to the test." I turned to the others, "*Ya ikhwan* [O brothers], if you had ten thousand dollars that you wanted to invest, would you invest it in a bank that was established in a twenty-four-hour meeting?" Of course nobody said "Yes." Yasser Abed Rabbo, of all people, said, "Dr. Sayigh is right." Ibrahim Dakkak agreed with him, and Abu Ala' said, "Yes, I have a copy of this, we can copy and circulate it." He didn't say I was right, but he implied it. Nobody else opened their mouth. Abu Ammar said angrily, "All right, if you don't like my way of doing things I will issue a decree." He took out a pen from his shirt pocket, and a piece of paper from the drawer in front of him.

I said, "Wait a minute! Before you write a decree, let me remind you that there is a procedure for the preparation of decrees. What the procedure specifies cannot be satisfied here. First of all, you are not on Palestinian land, you are in Tunis. Secondly, decrees usually refer to certain articles in the constitution, or the basic law. We haven't got one. Thirdly, in any government, if there is project 'X,' the minister in charge would propose it. It would be discussed in one or more meetings. When agreement is reached, the minister in charge will initial the thing, then the prime minister will sign on the strength of the minister's decision, then the head of state will publish it. There is a long process and none of the components of this process is satisfied here."

He kept quiet for a moment, then he said, "I have a solution. I'll issue two decrees." I said, "Mr. Arafat, if one decree is wrong how can two become right?" He said, "Wait a minute, wait a minute!"—with anger and impatience—"I'll issue a decree in my capacity as head of the state of Palestine, authorizing Yasser Arafat, in his capacity as chairman of the board, to issue a decree establishing the bank." I said, "I have an objection to this too. First of all, you cannot issue a decree in favor of yourself; things are not done that way. Second of all, you are not chairman of the board, Mr. Qaddumi is."

I went on, "This brings me to the reason I came here, as we agreed on the telephone. I'm coming here to tell you why I cannot serve. First of all, you don't observe constitutionality. Secondly, accountability is totally violated." He said, "What's this! Everybody is mentioning accountability." I said, "Yes. As head of PECDAR—you have placed yourself now as chairman of the board of governors—you will be accountable to yourself as head of the Advisory Council. You and the Advisory Council will be accountable to yourself as head of the Palestine National Authority, which is going to be formed when you enter Palestine. You and the National Authority will be accountable to the Executive Committee, of which you are the head. And you and the Executive Committee will be accountable to the head of the state, which is yourself. So you will be accountable to yourself on five levels."

I continued, "And when you act as chairman, will you take the opinion of the majority? If all the members of the board, thirteen of them, voted in favor of project 'X,' and you wanted project 'Y,' whose opinion would prevail?" He said, "*Tab'an ana* [Of course, me]." I said, "So democracy will not be respected either. Knowing you as director of the Executive Committee for years, I know that you always keep secrets in your pocket. Things will not be run with transparency. For all these reasons, and unless these reasons are removed, I will not take my seat. I consider myself not to be a member of the board. Good night." And I left.

That was late in November. I began to prepare to leave, and I left Tunis on December third.

13

"Bread with Dignity": Yusif Sayigh as an Arab Economist

Yusif's first notable book as an economist was *al-Khubz ma' al-karama* (Bread with Dignity).[1] He wrote it on a Dutch freighter as it transported the family from New York to Beirut after two study years in the United States: one as visiting research scholar at the Harvard Center for International Affairs and Middle East Studies Center; and a second as visiting research scholar at Princeton University.[2] Yusif recalled:

> It took us twenty-three days to arrive in Beirut. During that time I wrote a book, *al-Khubz ma' al-karama*, which won the prize of the Friends of the Book in 1961. Two chapters of it were pieces I had already published. One on development was called "The Invisible or the Visible Hand." It was published in the prestigious journal *World Politics*, and it drew attention there. The editor attended the seminar when I gave that paper in Princeton, and he asked me to have it to publish right away. And there was another chapter that had already been published somewhere. But I finished the whole book on the voyage. I used to write three or four hours every day, and then sunbathe.

Al-Khubz ma' al-karama prefigured all Yusif's later thinking and work as a development economist. Since it was never translated into

English, and is therefore inaccessible to most anglophone readers, I will give it some space here. The title he chose, "Bread with Dignity," highlights two crucial points in his thinking about development: that it must involve social justice; and that it must be suited to Arab national needs. 'Dignity' as an Arab value must go hand in hand with economic growth in Arab government policies. Development has to be social and egalitarian as much as economic; it has to "expand the dignity of workers of all sectors." Turning to the state of the Arab economies in the 1950s, Yusif saw the causes of underdevelopment in the legacy of colonialism, the primacy of the agricultural sector, the weakness of manufacturing, and the small size of the professional and administrative middle class.[3] For dynamic policies of economic and social development, Yusif looked to the public rather than the private sector, thus to an Arab political leadership that had to be mindful of its development responsibilities. Such a leadership must understand that political independence, economic independence, and social justice are interrelated. It had to be reformist, and to reject the status quo. Above all it had to deliver on the promise of social transformation. A constant thread running through all his writing, from *al-Khubz ma' al-karama* to *Elusive Development*, is his perception that popular Arab expectations for development and social justice are so high that the failure of leaders to respond will lead to an "explosion."

Yusif identified his model for development as 'Arab socialism.' In the late 1950s he hoped that Gamal Abdel Nasser would implement Arab socialism, and, on a visit to Egypt, presented him with a copy of his book. Thus from the beginning Yusif marked himself off from those economists who are only concerned with measuring economic performance or promoting economic growth. For him economics was always political, whether through positive programs for change, or, on the opposite side of the fence, through non-interference with the market. Though he was concerned with "catching up with the West," and advocated that Arab governments should pursue nationalist policies vis-à-vis control of resources, he never saw increasing productivity or gross national income as goals in themselves. Development must be social as well as economic, and it must be reformist: "the development process requires broad and deep transformation within all sectors of society and levels of government."

Such ideas might seem challenging to the Arab regimes of the period, but in the first decades after independence ideas of 'Arab nationalism' and 'Arab progress' offered a broad tent under which regimes and independent intellectuals could coexist. An optimist by nature, Yusif refused to view the Arab governments as structurally and irredeemably self-interested. He castigated them for their failures but remained convinced that they must in the end heed the voice of reason and nationalism. His statelessness as a Palestinian and his independence of political partisanship gained him a hearing from Arab leaders who would not have tolerated him if he had been a subject-citizen. Though he had joined the Parti Populaire Syrien as a student, by the 1950s he had distanced himself from it, alienated by its leader worship and ideological inflexibility, and, moreover, attracted by the wider scope of Arab nationalism. His concern for social justice brought him to the edge of the socialist camp, but though courted by the Ba'th party, he had seen enough of how political parties operate to avoid entanglement. This position made him acceptable to all the Arab regimes except Saudi Arabia, where he was barred from entry as a 'communist.'

Al-khubz ma' al-karama had a pervasive influence on other Arab economists. Dr. Khair El-Din Haseeb, Iraqi economist and founder of the Center for Arab Unity Studies, writes of it:

I first knew Yusif Sayigh as a reader, in Baghdad, when I read his book *Bread with Dignity* which was published by Dar al-Tali'ah in 1961. He was the first Arab economist, as far as I know, to emphasize the social dimension of Arab development, and I'm happy to say that he had a big intellectual influence on me. He, along with a visit I made to the Ahwar region of Iraq in 1957, left an intellectual imprint on my social orientation, visibly shaping my professional career in Iraq in the 1960s.[4]

Modern economics as a field of study and as a profession had been slow to develop in the Arab region compared with law, medicine, engineering, and commerce. The Business Administration Department at AUB was founded in 1900, and until 1950 basic economics courses were given within it. Among those who taught Yusif economics in the mid-1930s was Sa'id Himadeh, whom Yusif praised for his awareness of the importance of economic institutions.[5] Another AUB economics teacher who influenced Yusif was George Hakim, author of studies on land tenure and public finance, who left AUB for politics in the 1960s. But among the economists who influenced him as a doctoral student—Schumpeter, Myrdal, Rostow, Hagen, Adelman, Spengler—there are no Arab names. Commenting on the lack of Arab economic development studies, Yusif pays tribute to Himadeh's pioneering work in the thirties, but notes that the subject of development was not pursued by either Himadeh or his students.[6] Other Arab economists working in the post-independence period tended to focus on their countries of origin rather than on the region as a whole. Yusif's explanation of this limitation casts light on the state of economic knowledge at that time:

> Several reasons explain the failure of the many centres of higher learning in the region to make an attempt to study development in its wide regional context. Some of these were objective, such as the insufficiency of research material and the paucity of resources to finance travel and field-work. Some were subjective such as extremely limited familiarity with the Arab community of peoples and the weakness of interest in this wide community.[7]

Yusif's concern for broad Arab economic development coincided with a growing American and oil-company interest in the Arab region as a source of raw materials as well as a market for manufactured goods. Just two years before he joined it, AUB's economics department was separated out from business administration as a teaching and research unit under the impetus of Albert Badr[8] and A.J. Meyer. A Harvard scholar interested in oil, Meyer was probably the main conduit for funds from the Ford Foundation and the Technical Cooperation Agency that established the Economic Research Institute within the economics department in 1953.[9] Economic historian Cyrus Schayegh notes that "the very idea of institutes focusing on basic statistical-economic research and training—in *any* developing country—was conceivable early on after World War II because it was *this* sort of data and education that economists then deemed indispensable to Third World development."[10] Yusif's interest in the development of the whole Arab region, and his advocacy for its economic integration, was based in nationalism rather than 'developmentalism,' and in his perception of how colonialism had fragmented the Arab countries, and weakened their economies by tying them into unilateral exchange systems. But he also saw post–Second World War independence as creating possibilities for a new start. Working with AUB's Economic Research Institute gave him opportunities to travel and meet Arab economists in Egypt, Syria, and Iraq, with the aim of establishing a network of contributors to the *Middle East Economic Papers* that the Institute published between 1954 and 1969.

As an undergraduate at the American University in the mid-1930s, Yusif had no fixed ideas about a career, and was interested in architecture, literature, and law as much as in economics. His choice of business administration as his BA major was dictated by economic necessity rather than any love or talent for commerce. He says himself:

At that time, I didn't think much about a career; I didn't see myself becoming an economist. I didn't know what business administration would lead me to, and when—occasionally—I thought about it, it was only that it would give me a good job in a company. Economics as economics, or political economy, this notion wasn't in my mind at all, though when I first came across the French phrase '*économie politique*,' it caught my attention. This idea remained in me like a seed until much later, when I went to America to do graduate work, as a field I should specialize in. I was drawn to political science, but I realized that I couldn't put butter on my bread through that. I couldn't do law, though I would have liked to.

He had been guided to readings on socialism by one of his teachers, George Hakim, and was beginning to focus on Arab world economics in particular. In his own words:

The books that influenced me were the books that I read on political economy, socialism, and social systems. I was interested also in the economy of the Arab region, because Himadeh was an early structuralist. There is a great deal on institutions in his books, and the way institutions work. He brought in politics, always reminding us that these are economies working under mandates, therefore there are constraints. I began to notice these facts, through politicization in the party, and through my frequent contacts with Sa'adeh, which influenced me greatly.

The need to help educate his six siblings cut short any thoughts Yusif may have had of further study. Yet the interest he felt in political economy as a student stayed with him through a series of jobs, developing further after his return to Palestine from Iraq in 1940. Working in Jerusalem in the last years before the Nakba, he wrote a series of economic articles for the press, and was invited to write a paper on "Arab Land Hunger" for the Anglo-American Commission of Inquiry, in which he devised a weighted method for evaluating Arab landholding.[11] As general director of the Arab National Fund, he worked out a graded taxation system (see chapter 11). By this time he was recognized by the Palestinian political leadership as someone who combined nationalism with economic capability.

Early in 1949 Yusif was released from Israeli POW camp and joined his family in Beirut. He recalled:

When I got to Lebanon after being released from prisoner-of-war camp, I was offered a job by Charlie Saad, who was the head of a transport company. He knew my father because he was a Protestant, and a pastor's son. It was a miserable little job as part-time assistant accountant, but it gave me pocket money. I worked there until spring 1950, when Nassib Boulos, an old friend from Jerusalem days, told me that UNRWA, which had just started operations, had an Economics Department, and that the economic advisor was looking for a technical assistant. The economic advisor was an Englishman called James Baster. They offered me the job, and I took it because it gave me twice the salary I was getting from Saad, and also because it was in the field of economics. I wanted to be inside UNRWA, to see what it did and how it functioned.[12] By then I had decided on the advice of Albert Badr at AUB to do graduate studies in economics.

Yusif's work at UNRWA was the basis of his MA thesis "The Implications of UNRWA Operations," analyzing the economic impact of the refugees on the host countries.[13] After a year of combining work at UNRWA with economics coursework at AUB, Yusif left the Agency (where he was paid much less than his foreign secretary) to join AUB as an instructor. This was a period when Albert Badr was building up the economics department with Ford Foundation backing, creating the Economic Research Institute and its publications. Yusif recalls:

Albert's great supporter was A.J. Meyer who had just joined AUB. Meyer supported Albert in the idea of the setting up of the Institute, and that it should be under the economics department, not business administration. It was quite a coup for them, and not easy to achieve, because Sa'id Himadeh was powerful on campus, and highly respected. He wanted the Institute to be under both departments. But people like building their own empires; they don't want partners. I kept myself out of the controversy. I liked and admired Sa'id Himadeh very much, and I was aware of the arguments on both sides—Sa'id and Albert would take me for long walks on the campus to discuss the issue. But I made it clear to them that I was not going to take sides. I was a newcomer, I didn't know my way.

It was while Yusif was traveling in the Mashreq region in 1952–53 to locate Arab economists for the Institute that we met in Baghdad, where I was teaching English language and literature at the Queen Aliya College. To fill time during a long strike against the Portsmouth Treaty,[14] I had begun to work on a bibliography of books in English on development in Iraq. For several months Yusif and I exchanged long letters about the bibliography, with Yusif contributing many of the items. I was touched by his help. At the end of the summer term, on my way home, I stopped off in Beirut, we got engaged, and in October that year, 1953, were married by his pastor father in the Evangelical church. It was only later that I discovered that the entries he sent me for my bibliography were prepared by his research assistants at the Institute. This touch of the trickster didn't upset me. It seemed a natural part of the new world in which I was immersing myself, in all its exciting difference from postwar Britain.

Yusif describes the first stage of his 'take-off' as a professional economist in these words:

> When I became assistant director, I started doing research, and editing what came to be called the Middle East Economic Papers, a yearly publication that started appearing in 1953/54. As the first research item under the Institute, Albert Badr did a study of the national income of Lebanon, a pioneering work, with a team of researchers that included Salem Khamis, Asad Nasr, and others.[15] Later the same kind of study was done on Jordan. This put the Institute on the map, because the United Nations started using our figures. We also began to make studies of the economies of the region, with the idea that after building up a body of data with some analysis attached to it, we might publish a series of books. But we never reached that stage.

The first research project I undertook for the Institute was about Iraq. Albert asked me to do this because I had already gone to Iraq for UNRWA. I went to find information on the Iraqi economy, and to buy books—I came back with kilos and kilos of material. At the same time a new study was contracted along with a group of labor economists who were writing a study of the impact of the industrialization process on labor. There was Clark Kerr from California University (later its president); John Dunlop from Harvard University; Charles something-or-other from MIT; and Frederick Harbison from Princeton[16]—four very distinguished economists. For the Middle East, they wanted the Institute to undertake the studies. The data I was collecting in Iraq was for them. Later I wrote about labor and industrialization laws in Iraq.

By the first year of university work I felt myself already appreciated. In 1953, I was promoted to assistant professor. In those days there was no feeling at AUB that there were too many Palestinians.[17] On the contrary, we were thought of as an asset to the university. When a good Lebanese applied, he was employed. We were not taking jobs away from other people. We took jobs away from Americans rather than Lebanese. I remember asking Albert once, "Aren't you worried about employing me?" He said, "No. You're not replacing Lebanese or other Arabs. If the university doesn't develop local and Arab skills so as to replace Americans it will have failed."

Badr's tolerant attitude to the employment of Palestinians was not shared by all segments of Lebanese society. In 1951 Emile Lahoud, then minister of labor, issued a decree forbidding Palestinians to do any kind of work.[18] The right-wing Lebanese nationalist Kata'eb party campaigned hard against the employment of Palestinians in large foreign companies or institutions, including universities. There was a huge row in the National Assembly sometime in the mid-1950s as Kata'eb deputies tried to pass a law to this effect, while pro-Palestinian deputies such as Emile Bustani opposed them.[19] However,

AUB and its associate hospital continued to employ Palestinians until the 1980s when the insecurity created by Israeli invasions, the Civil War, and the Battle of the Camps, with its assassinations and kidnappings, pressured a large swathe of Palestinian professionals and businessmen into leaving Lebanon. Many had contributed to the Lebanese economy after 1948 through creating new forms of industry, for example filmmaking, or through developing already established services such as banking, tourism, and education.

Yusif continued:

Some time during 1953, a foundation in America called the Earhart Foundation[20] offered a fellowship to AUB worth $5,000, and said, "Pick someone promising for doctoral work in America." The economics department suggested me, and Albert and A.J. Meyer fought very hard for me to get it. . . . $5,000 was not such a big sum. I would have to pay more than half of it for tuition, and it would mean two years away from my job. In the end I managed to finish in one year and a term. Anyway, I got the fellowship, and in 1954 I went to the United States to do doctoral work.

I was thrilled by the opportunity to go to America, thanks to the fellowship, and by the idea that I was going to work for a PhD, and that I could finish the coursework in a year, or maximum a year and a half. I worked very hard for it. There were courses that were obligatory, but there were others that were optional. I picked the courses that concentrated on development, and on the relationship between economics, sociology, and politics. I was interested in the interdisciplinary approach to development, so I picked courses that led to that. There were a number of very capable professors at Johns Hopkins whom I had read in the literature before going to America—Simon Kuznets, Fritz Machlup, Evsey Domar,[21] an econometrician called Carl Krist, and Michael Posten, who taught economic history . . . . I worked very hard because I enjoyed the work there. Besides in America it's very competitive, the students were very sharp, much younger than I—I couldn't allow them to have better grades than me.

I began preparing for my dissertation,[22] and taking more courses in methodology to prepare myself for serious work and writing later on. I decided that I'd benefit if I stayed another term, to get more courses than the absolute minimum . . . . In that time I managed to write the first chapter of my dissertation. I'd already picked the topic, entrepreneurship, and designed the study, and got support for it from the Rockefeller Foundation. During that term I got interested in doing fieldwork on entrepreneurship, because the readings I made were all on developed countries, except for one study on Mexico. So I designed a research project. Then I thought, why not write to some foundation about it? I was encouraged in the idea by a visiting lecturer, somebody who worked with the World Bank with whom I became friends . . . .

The World Bank man said, "It sounds an interesting topic—why don't you try to get a grant for your research?" He gave me the name of the director of social research at the Rockefeller Foundation, an economist called Sidney Buchanan. I prepared a memorandum, and wrote a letter, and sent it to him in New York. By return mail he invited me to have lunch with him and talk about it. I went to New York, and over lunch he said, "I'll recommend this proposal to the board. I don't need any more details, I just want you to prepare a time and money budget." This I did later from Beirut. The thing was processed, and some months later they gave me a grant of $44,100.

Work on the project took the best part of two years, combined with full-time teaching at AUB. It was published under the title *Entrepreneurs of Lebanon: The Role of Business Leaders in a Developing Economy*, published by Harvard University Press in 1962.[23] In his choice of this topic Yusif wanted to challenge an idea prevalent in Orientalist views of the Middle East, that Islam, in contrast to Protestant Christianity, suppressed the spirit of economic enterprise. While not condemning the private sector, Yusif did not see it as capable of being the motor of the kind of development he advocated in *al-Khubz ma' al-karama*. On the contrary, it is evident from his discussion of the need for rational planning to enable the Arab region "to challenge the existing division of labour in the global economy" (1961, 110) that he saw the public sector as the primary instrument capable of achieving the goals he had laid down there as the crux of desirable development. Thus his next major study was *The Economies of the Arab World: Development Since 1945* and *Determinants of Arab Economic Development*.[24] Through its combination of data accumulation, analysis, and command of development theory, this study established Yusif as one of the leading Arab economists.[25] Funded by the Kuwait Fund for Arab Economic Development, the study marked a shift in Yusif's research support from American to Arab sources, a shift accelerated after leaving AUB by work with the Kuwait Fund, AOPEC, the Arab League, and the PLO.

A decade later, Yusif's other major study of Arab development was enabled by a study term at the Middle East Research Centre, Oxford, in 1985, when he wrote *Elusive Development: From Dependence to Self-Reliance in the Arab Region* (Routledge, 1991).[26] This was a period when it was hard even for an optimist to sustain the hopes that had inspired his earlier work. *Elusive Development* is more about shortcomings than achievements, focusing on Arab failure to develop agriculture and industry; insufficient rationality and planning in oil policies; faulty use of land and water resources; failure to improve the quality of education and to build a base of science and research; and *"the widening gap in income and wealth distribution among individuals, classes, and regions"* (1991, xiii; my italics).

In between these major books, he published another seven books in English, several small books in Arabic, forty-two articles in Arabic journals, and forty-four articles in foreign journals, always with the same mix of dogged empiricism, scholarship, and moral/political commitment. He was an unrepentant workaholic, always engaged, always carrying out multiple assignments.[27] Besides development, another of his main topics was oil, both as a potential motor of Arab economic development, and as irreplaceable resource which, mis-used, was corrupting the Arab will to develop through pervasive consumerism. In *Elusive Development* he wrote:

> the upsurge in Arab oil production and in the inflow of revenue from oil export during the 1970s have not led to commensurate invest-ment in the region at large. Instead, the relatively vast inflow of financial resources has, to a considerable extent, become an occasion for wasteful and misguided expenditure on ostentatious consump-tion, but likewise on the indiscriminate importation of over-priced capital goods and armaments. And it has also led to the build-up of enormous accounts in banks and investments in stocks and bonds in Western financial centres. (1991, 122)

From University Teaching to Independent Consultancy

Yusif's career as a teacher with AUB's economics department stretched from 1952 to 1974; during much of this time he held the chairmanship of the department. He is remembered by his students as an invigorating teacher who awakened their interest in the poli-tics of economics. His decision to take early retirement from the university in 1974 was dictated partly by the difficulties of travel for a full-time faculty member.[28] Undoubtedly the decline of the Economic Research Institute would have been another factor in his decision to leave AUB, since research rather than teaching had always been his major interest.[29] And by 1974 Yusif felt he could enjoy greater freedom and earnings as an independent consultant. A wealthy Palestinian friend helped him to open and equip an office, which became his base for a succession of policy studies. The most important of these was undoubtedly the two-part plan for Joint Arab Economic Action, commissioned by the Arab League, and approved by the eleventh Arab Summit in Amman (1980).

I remember Yusif's excitement during the period in which he was working on the Arab Economic Action plan, as well as the hum of activity in his office, controlled by the first of his two immensely competent secretaries, Sanaa Izzidin and Anwar Serhan. Arab economists Mahmoud Abdel Fadil, Georges Corm, and Mohammad Mahmoud al-Imam were involved in this project—finally published by the Arab League in three volumes—as well as twenty others who prepared specialist studies. At the time Yusif felt that their ideas for a joint Arab economic strategy had a chance of achievement. But Georges Corm recalls that during the 1980 Amman summit "the attention of the Arab heads of state was totally taken by the Iranian issue . . . and the quarrels between Syria and the rest of the members. I think Hafez Assad left the Arab League meeting before its closure. So there was no attention given to a plan of inter-Arab economic cooperation."[30] Commenting later on the non-implementation of the plan, Yusif attributed this to "the persistence of a number of deep-rooted cultural, political, and structural factors in Arab society, most particularly within the circles of political leadership and parts of the business community in which integration was not deemed desirable."[31] His analysis of this situation was political, that "most rulers are interested in power and how it can be captured and maintained, not in ideas of integration, collective self-reliance, or inner-directed development"; and that "(m)ost political parties and movements are likewise obsessed with political power."[32] During this period Yusif also did studies with AOPEC, the Kuwait Fund for Economic and Social Development, and for FAO on agriculture in the Arab world.[33] Palestinian economist Leila Farsakh notes his concern for agricultural production:

> At a time when development economists such as W.W. Rostow and others were stressing the importance of industrial growth in developing countries, Sayigh was emphasizing the importance of developing agriculture . . . he argued that agriculture played a central role not

just in providing food to the population but also in channeling savings and inputs to industry. Above all, agricultural growth was central to distributing wealth to the poor and thus creating a more equitable and just society. He had no qualms about advocating land reform and argued against relying just on market forces to induce agricultural productivity and welfare.[34]

The titles of the journal articles and books he published during this period of independent consultancy show his concerns and those of his Arab colleagues: Arab oil policies; Arab economic integration; Arab–European dialogue; the place of agriculture in the Arab world; and the Palestinian economy under occupation. As he tells in chapter 12, it was a series of meetings in 1989 with Ahmad Qurei, head of the PLO's Economic Department, that ended this phase of Yusif's work life and transferred him to another that was to be even more exciting and, ultimately, frustrating.

Conferences and Travel

The launching of Yusif's professional career coincided with growing international, and especially American, interest in the economics of the Arab region, and the beginning of conferences as a way of life. The conference format mixed academics with policy makers, and offered new chances for international travel. Yusif loved conferences, and much of his professional career took place within the conference framework, taking him not only to the countries of the Middle East but also to India, the Philippines, Mexico, Japan, many European countries, the United States, Canada . . . . He was an articulate speaker, equally fluent in English and Arabic, humorous, skillful in mediating between clashing points of view, so that he quickly became popular on the Arab and international conference circuit, whether the topic was development, manpower, oil, strategy vis-à-vis Israel, or Palestine. He believed that systematically collected information and analysis could lead to more effective government policies. A believer in economic planning, he was able to use a sabbatical year (1963–64) to produce a Five-Year Development Plan for Kuwait. Like his later plan for the PLO, this one seems to have been quickly consigned to a governmental bottom drawer, as indeed happened with most of the plans he made.

Yusif's career as a *conférencier* began soon after he got his PhD with an invitation from Ibrahim Hilmi Abdel Rahman, director general of the Planning Institute, an official body of the Egyptian government. Like the Economic Research Institute at AUB, the Planning Institute was financed by the Ford Foundation. Many of the early conferences were related to the region's economic develop-ment. As Yusif says, "There was a theory at that time that Islam was an obstacle to development. The man who expounded the theory with respect to the Arab region was Alfred Bonnet, an Israeli econo-mist." Yusif critiqued this theory both deductively and empirically, through his own work on Lebanese entrepreneurs. In the late 1950s, at a conference organized by the Center for Entrepreneurial History at Harvard, Yusif had an opportunity to demonstrate the falsity of Bonnet's premise to an audience of peers that included Gibb.[35]

At Harvard, Bonnet presented a paper in which he repeated some-thing he had said in a book on the economy of the Middle East, that because they are mainly Muslims, the Arabs can't be creative entre-preneurs because their religion orders them to pursue the known and avoid the unknown. He based this explanation on a verse in the Qur'an that says "*Al-amr bi-l-maʿruf wa-l-nahi ʿan al-munkar* [Com-mand what is right and forbid what is wrong]." The two key words are '*al-maʿruf*' and '*al-munkar*'—and this is where he made a terrible mistake. '*Al-munkar*' is something that's abominable—it has nothing to do with business or knowledge. He mistranslated it. Either his Arabic wasn't good enough, or somebody misled him. At that confer-ence I tore his theory to pieces. It wasn't hard. His whole theory was based on that one quotation.

When Yusif joined the PLO Executive Committee (1968–74), travel became harder, especially to anti-Palestinian countries. He tells an anecdote about a particular trip he made to Canada to present a paper at a conference on Arab oil:

I went to Canada in January 1974 on an invitation from Toronto University to give a paper at a conference on oil. I was then advisor to the OAPEC [Organization of Arab Petroleum Exporting Countries]. Of course the invitation mentioned the place and date of the conference. They said they would pay my ticket and accommodation, and that there would be no problem about my visa . . . . I telephoned the Canadian embassy in Beirut, and told them that I was invited to this conference. They told me to send them my passport with two photos. They said, "If your man can wait two hours, we'll give your visa to him right away"—it was that simple. When I telephoned them later to see if the visa was ready, they said, "How about leaving it until tomorrow?" Next day, I telephoned again. "Why don't we give you a ring when it's ready? There is a little delay, but nothing, no problem."

At that time, I was a member of the Executive Committee of the PLO. I realized that they must have found this out, and that the visa wasn't going to be a routine matter . . . it took six days for the visa to be granted. I went to Canada with Ali Atiqa.[36] We were together on the plane. When we landed we were taken to a little room, where there was an immigration officer . . . . Ali Atiqa gave him his passport, which was a diplomatic passport. The officer leafed through it, found the visa, stamped it, and gave him back his passport.

I had a special passport—all members of the PLO Executive Committee had special passports—issued by Syria. Relations between Syria and the PLO were good then . . . . I gave him the passport. Inside it was a letter of invitation, which said the purpose of the visit and all the financial details. The officer looked at the passport, then he said, "Why are you coming to Canada?" I said, "It's there in the letter. I'm coming to a conference, I'm invited by the University of Toronto." "What for?" I said, "There's a conference on oil, and I've been asked to give a paper on that subject, as the letter in your hand says." "Who is paying your expenses?" I said, "The letter also says that the ticket is paid by them"—in fact I had a PTA [Prepaid Ticket Advice]—"the ticket has been paid, and while I'm in Canada, I'll be the guest of the organizers of the conference." He kept leafing through the letter. "Will you leave Canada when the conference is over?" I said, "Yes, as my ticket shows"—I had also given him my ticket—"I'm leaving on such-and-such a date, via London." He kept silent for a while.

I said, "Look, these are not the real questions you want to ask, because all the information is there in the documents in your hand. There must be another question that you haven't yet put to me. What is it, so that we can finish with this business?" He said, "Why do you have a special passport?" I said, "Because I'm a special person." His face got red as a beetroot with anger. He took the stamp and stamped the passport and almost threw it at me.

The creation of pan-Arab professional associations was both an offshoot and stimulus of the conferences that punctuated Yusif's professional life as they did the cultural life of the region. Of the associations that Yusif was part of, the Centre for Arab Unity Studies (CAUS) was undoubtedly the most important. With Dr. Khair El-Din Haseeb, he was a co-founder of CAUS in 1974, and remained an active board member all his life.[37] Indeed, his last project, which he was never able to carry out because of the sharp decline in his health after returning from Tunis in 1994, was to study the mechanisms of the European Economic Community, on the premise that these might offer lessons for the Arab states. Other associations he helped to found were the Arab Thought Forum, the Economic Research Forum, and the Arab Society for Economic Research. During the last ten years, when poor health cut down on his work life, he continued to serve as chairman of the local board of the Welfare Association, a Palestinian funding organization formed by a mix of wealthy businessmen and intellectuals after the Israeli invasion of Lebanon in 1982, to assist local NGOs. This tribute comes from Faisal Alami, currently chairman of the Welfare Association in Lebanon:

> Dr. Yusif was a member of the Welfare Association Board of Trustees from its inception in 1983. He worked diligently to get support for Palestinians in the camps in Lebanon. His efforts led to an allocation of $50,000 per year in the late eighties, which he managed to increase to $250,000 in the mid-90s, when the Welfare Association Supervisory Committee was created. He chaired this Committee, and I was honoured to work with him from 1997, when I became a member of the Welfare Association. His efforts to grow and improve the program were continuous. Before every Board meeting he was ready to lobby for more support, leading to a doubling of the budget as a result of work done. In 2002 he proposed the libraries program for the camps, a program still running today. He was very thorough in reviewing project applications, and always related approval of funding to added value, efficiency and transparency. We learned a lot from working with him, and he is always missed.[38]

Oil and Development

The intertwining of economics with politics is nowhere better illustrated than in the constraints that the international oil companies laid upon the oil-producing countries in the early days that prevented the latter from turning oil into a resource for economic development. Down-line activities such as refining or petrochemical industry were ruled out in the contracts the internationals drew up with compliant Gulf state rulers. Moreover oil companies made sure that royalties were largely privatized, distributed through ruling families and their clienteles. Though some of the oil-producing countries, notably Iraq, managed to secure better deals in the 1960s, and, like both Iraq and Kuwait, to use oil royalties for investment in infrastructure and social services, yet much of Arab oil was siphoned off before Arab economies were able to benefit from it in terms of development, or store it for the future. It was here, moreover, that the disarticulation of the Arab region displayed its most negative effects, since, with the exception of Iraq, most Arab oil lay under countries with the smallest populations and the most autocratic rulers. Always a firm believer in regional economic integration as the only way to overcome dependency, Yusif saw oil as the potential basis of regional investment, labor mobility, and growth of the internal market. Yet he wrote about the 'grim side' of the oil boom years in *Elusive Development*, at a time when oil producers were facing a severe shrinkage in world demand (from 1982), targeting in particular "irresponsible over-production and depletion of a most valuable resource; short-sightedness in market expectations; inflow of easy money . . . gross misspending both in consumption and investment . . . and, on balance, development which in some basic aspects was patchy, misdirected, distorted, and sustainable only because of and during the inflow of substantial oil revenues" (1991, xi). Mismanagement of oil revenues was, in Yusif's view, a crucial factor in Arab state failure to achieve the goals for development that he had laid down thirty years before in *al-Khubz ma' al-karama*. He developed his critique in a number of essays and lectures.[39]

Like several of his colleagues, Yusif considered it unacceptable that the advanced industrial economies that reaped the greatest benefit from Arab oil should also be the main supporters of Israel. He is remembered as one of the first Arab intellectuals to propose that oil should be used as an instrument of pressure to bring about change in the policies of the United States and Europe toward the question of Palestine.[40] But he was just as sharp in criticizing the Arab states for the contradiction between verbal support for the Palestinian cause and failure to take Arab security concerns seriously. In particular he criticized the "huge outlay on armaments . . . [that] are not justified in any concrete or substantial way in action in the field."[41] This was all part of the consumerist mentality generated by the oil boom, and by "the dangerously erroneous view . . . that money . . . could buy development as well as national security."[42]

The balance sheet of Arab development that Yusif drew up in *Elusive Development*, his last major development book, published in 1991, points to a series of errors and weaknesses: a "painful underdevelopment of the two basic productive sectors" (agriculture and industry); poor management of oil and gas; under-utilization of land and water resources; growing economic inequality; failure to raise the quality of education; adoption of a consumerist culture; the brain drain; and the slow pace of regional integration. In addition he points to the "continued curtailment of freedom, encroachment on human rights, and severe limitation of political participation" (1991, xiii). What these failures add up to is "the vast reach and entrenchment of the state of dependence of the Arab region on the advanced industrial countries . . . and most heavily on the United States; a dependence that is manifest in economics, technology, culture, information, politics and security" (1991, xiii). Yet while the state of the Arab world at the end of the twentieth century had failed to reach the economic and political independence that Yusif laid out in *al-Khubz ma' al-karama* as both goal and condition of development, he did not allow himself to give in to despair: "The struggle [for transformation] may even necessitate far-reaching social and political re-structuring—indeed 'creative destruction,'" he wrote in *Elusive Development* (1991, 236); and his conclusion makes it clear that his purpose in writing this detailed analysis of economic and political failure is to pass on its lessons to future generations: "There is reason to believe that the young will refuse to inherit the gloomy future that the present, if not radically changed, would bequeath to them" (1991, 237). The truth of this prediction would become visible to all in December 2010.[43]

Writing on Palestine and a Palestinian Economy

While most of Yusif's work was on Arab economic development, Palestine was always a central part of his concerns, as a nationalist intellectual, scholar, and institution-builder. He wrote studies of the Israeli and Palestinian economies for the PLO Research Centre in Beirut, and was frequently invited to speak on the Palestinian issue, particularly after the emergence of the Resistance movement.[44] His personal experience of the colonization of Palestine combined with his political independence and command of detail made him a compelling speaker.[45] Long before his work as advisor to the PLO's Economic Department in Tunis he had written and lectured extensively on humanitarian and social as well as political and economic aspects of the Palestinian problem. Toward the end of the 1970s he was invited by the Economic Commission of West Asia (ECWA, today ESCWA) to design the framework of a study of the Palestinians in Lebanon. Undertaken by a Beirut-based research company called TEAM, the study was interrupted by the Israeli invasion of 1982, and published after the war in a limited edition, without ECWA's imprimatur. His early experience in Palestine as planner and institution-builder with the Arab Fund found new expression in the 1970s when he worked with the PLO to set up both its National Fund and Planning Institute. These stories as well as that of the national economic development plan are told in chapter 12.

His last, and surely in his view his most important, work was to prepare an economic plan for a future Palestinian state, the Programme for Development of the Palestinian National Economy for the Years 1994–2000.[46] This he did between 1990 and 1993, years spent living in Tunis, where the family would join him during the holidays. This was a period of intense work to fulfill deadlines, when he seldom left his desk before ten or eleven at night. The Plan involved commissioning studies from specialists in different aspects of the Palestinian economy, such as land, water, commerce, manufacture, and so on. Contacts with scholars inside Occupied Palestine were hard to sustain before the advent of email. Not all the contributions were up to standard, and Yusif spent a great deal of time rewriting them. Overwork caused bad migraines, for which Abu Ala' sent him to Paris for a medical check-up. By sticking fiercely to his three-year schedule, he was already writing up the final version of the plan by the summer of 1993.[47] Though he worked quite closely with Ahmad Qurei during the preparation of the plan, Yusif was completely unaware of the Israeli–Palestinian talks taking place in Oslo that summer, in which Qurei was the main PLO negotiator. His final months in Tunis were spent in a vain struggle to prevent Arafat from monopolizing control of the funds that began to flow in from international donors after the signing of the Accords. Partly this took the form of an institutional blueprint that would have set up a system of checks and balances. Named the Palestinian Economic Council for Development and Reconstruction (PECDAR), Yusif worked on this with Antoine Zahlan and Khalil Hindi.[48] Yusif also used his membership in Executive Committee meetings to challenge Abu Ammar head-on. This story is also told in chapter 12. After failing to find support either from other members of the Executive Committee, or from the international bureaucrats who visited Tunis after the Oslo Accords, Yusif resigned from PECDAR and returned to Beirut, deeply disappointed by the turn he saw the Palestinian national leadership taking.

The stress involved in finishing the Programme on schedule, combined with the frustration of foreseeing its neglect in the hands of the national leadership, brought on a series of health crises that spoiled his last years, leaving him incapable of travel or sustained mental work.

Post-2008: Revival of Relevance

Ignored by the leadership that made up the post-Oslo National Authority, Yusif's Palestine Development Programme has been rediscovered by a younger generation of economists critical of the National Authority's laissez-faire liberalism, dependency, and failure to achieve growth or welfare. The Programme had emphasized the primary necessity of creating an independent national economy, one that would "correct the distortions and imbalances . . . created by over a quarter of a century of Israeli occupation";[49] the West Bank and the Gaza Strip were to be integrated economically with the aim of lessening the gap between them in employment opportunities and income; a third imperative was "involving the beneficiaries of development in the design of sector programmes." The PEP starts from recognition of the damaging effects of Israeli occupation as a prerequisite to rehabilitation, leading to the reclamation of land and water rights; independent decision-making particularly in regard to expansion and diversification; control over licensing and permits; national banks and a national currency; free trade exchange with Arab countries; and investment in physical and social infrastructure. Without a dynamic reversal of the effects of occupation, development will remain elusive and Palestinians disempowered. Thus the Programme gives priority to the building of a strong public sector—"the civil service and basic public institutions which have to be ready and able to run the 'business of government.'" The banking sector needs to be reorganized, and development banks established. Agriculture needs regeneration, and employment openings created for the labor force. Dependence on the Israeli economy must be reduced through "expanded relations with the Arab region in the areas of trade, financial flows into and visits to Palestine." The basic assumption of the PEP is that the Palestinian Authority "will be able to exercise the right of economic and social decision-making and the implementation of related decisions," an assumption that has not been fulfilled. Insofar as a Palestinian public sector exists, it focuses on securitizing Israel rather than achieving Palestinian well-being. Economic dependence on Israel is now compounded by dependence on the EU.

In 2009 the independent think tank MAS (Ma'had al-Siyasat al-Iqtisadi al-Filastini)[50] established an annual event named "The Yusif A. Sayigh Development Lectures," designed to open up economic thinking in Palestinian society by inviting internationally known economists to lecture in Ramallah.[51] MAS's opening statement pays tribute to Yusif's work as a "scholar and patriot whose critical mind was devoted to the cause of his people" and whose Palestinian Development Programme "remains today a visionary document which best summarizes the challenges of building a sovereign national economy freed of occupation."[52]

The Authority's economic policies have come under increasing attack since the appointment as prime minister of Salam Fayyad, an ex-banker who worked with the IMF before his involvement with the National Authority as finance minister from 2002 to 2006, and as prime minister from mid-2009 to April 2013. However, it is not Fayyad's economic policies alone that have generated critique and anger, but rather the continuing subjection of the Authority to Israeli–U.S. control. Scholars, students, workers, and ordinary people have not been slow to voice their anger. Palestinian economists Raja Khalidi and Sobhi Samour are scathing in their critique of the NA for its dependency and neoliberalism:

> It is ironic that the all-important "local ownership" of neoliberal reform, as manifested in the PA statehood plan, comes at a time when the global financial crisis has led to a legitimacy crisis for—if not of— neoliberalism. An economic policy framework under revision by its designers seems an odd choice to deliver development to a damaged and fragmented economy like that of the occupied Palestinian territories . . . . Soft physical borders cannot protect Palestinian national security, and soft economic borders can only perpetuate Palestinian dependence on Israel and allow personal prosperity for some but communal impoverishment for all.[53]

Yusif was a determined opponent of the idea promoted by the United States that 'economic peace' could pave the way for a political settlement, seeing this as no more than a sweetener to the pill of capitulation on national issues. He fought this idea tenaciously at all the conferences he attended as head of the Palestinian economic delegation to the Madrid talks, in spite of an Israeli campaign to remove him as head of delegation.[54] He would have agreed with Khalidi and Samour in their criticism of the Authority's failure to build up a strong public sector. Like them he would surely have advocated "economic resistance" in place of continuing dependency, and called for a "participatory process of development policy-making" and "active trade policies designed to diversify Palestinian trade markets and products as a means of reducing overwhelming dependence on trade with and through Israel" (2011, pp. 18–19).

Recalling Yusif's ideas, Leila Farsakh cites growing poverty, unemployment, and income inequality as evidence of the NA's failure to achieve national economic and social aims. Farsakh remarks that "Palestinian economic growth since 1993 has been marked by major fluctuations and unsustainability. Palestinian real GDP per capita income in West Bank and Gaza in 2007 was 30 percent lower than in 1999. Poverty touches 49 percent of Gaza and 25 percent of the West Bank in 2007"; and adds that "although real GDP grew by over 6 per cent in the West Bank and by nearly 25 per cent in the Gaza Strip since 2009, it has been mainly fueled by international assistance, which amounted to over 20% of GDP. Poverty rates still stood at 33.7 per cent in the Gaza Strip in 2010, where over 71 per cent of the population receives some form of aid."[55]

The faith Yusif expressed in Arab youth and "their restlessness and concern for human rights, democracy, and development"[56] has been more than justified by the 'Arab Spring' and the 'Ongoing Intifada' in Palestine. Yusif would have been delighted by the interest in his ideas newly shown by a younger generation of Arab economists, particularly those of Palestine. This would have compensated him for the neglect his plans suffered during his lifetime. For sure, his continuing influence is not based on his ideas alone, but more on the kind of human being he was and the kind of economics he advocated—humanist, political, and egalitarian. The American economist Sara Roy[57] has put this best, and it is fitting that Yusif's memoirs should end with her tribute:

Yusif Sayigh was that rare scholar who combined great intellect with uncompromising principle. His work was never confined to understanding *what is* but to articulating, without fear, *what can and should be*. Yusif was, in the most profound sense of the word, a social scientist, one whose science always insisted on a vision of the world that was just and humane, that embraced possibility and transmitted hope.[58]

Notes

Notes to Introduction

1 The house was still there when I visited Tiberias in 1981 but had been converted into a Chinese restaurant.
2 Ironically Anis was the only one of the Sayigh children to be born in a hospital. The others were all delivered through the 'birthing chair' with the help of a midwife.
3 The gap in age between Yusif and his next sibling Fuad is visible in the photo of the four brothers taken in Sweida (second page of plates, top)
4 These sessions were recorded between December 1996 and February 1997.
5 'Klashin' is the colloquial form of 'Kalashnikov,' the gun that Palestinian guerrillas used.

Notes to Chapter 1

1 The name Kharaba probably comes from *khirbet*, meaning 'a ruined village.' High grain prices in the mid-nineteenth century caused the resettlement of deserted villagers in the Hawran plain, as Damascene merchants invested in the grain trade. Kharaba was one of several Christian villages in the Jabal al-Druze area of Hawran.
2 The Gerard Institute was founded in 1881 by American missionaries. The Sidon Girls' School was founded even earlier, in 1862. Both schools were owned and run by the American Presbyterian Mission until 1959, when they were taken over by the National Evangelical Synod. In 1985 they were united in one school.
3 Mary Maxwell Tennessee Ford was an heiress who ran her own Presbyterian mission. She built two houses in Palestine, one in Safad, the

other in Tiberias. This is where the Sayigh family lived later. She also built many village schools.

4   See Hanna Abu Rashed, *Jebel al-Druze* (Cairo: Zeidan Public Library, 1925); Birgit Schaebler, "Rebels, Shaykhs and State(s)," lecture series *Zokak al-Blat* (Beirut: Orient Institute, 1998).

5   Anis Sayigh thinks that Abu Yusif was ordained in the late 1920s, after the Druze uprising. But Yusif does not speak of leaving al-Bassa to go to Jerusalem.

6   One of the ways an oral life story differs from an autobiography is that the author cannot edit mistakes or inconsistencies. Yusif never knew his grandmother so it's natural that he might give two different versions of the date of her death.

7   This happened during the Druze uprising against French rule. Yusif describes it later in this chapter. See Hanna Abu Rashed, *Huran aldamiya* (Cairo: Zeidan Public Library, 1926); also Schaebler, "Rebels, Shaykhs and State(s)."

8   For a description of peasant life in the early twentieth century see André Latron, *La vie rurale en Syrie et au Liban: étude d'économie sociale* (Beirut: Imprimerie Estholique, 1936).

9   A long shirt or dress, worn in the countryside.

10   *Qumbaz* and *thawb* both designate the cotton shirts (*dishdasha*s) that boys wore in villages in the Arab east.

11   Long cotton shirt worn by boys in rural Syria.

12   *Amariddeen* is made by cooking apricots and drying them in sheets. *Halaweh* is made from sugar and sesame paste.

13   The main products of Kharaba and the villages close to it were wheat, legumes, and livestock. Though rainfall was scarce, the land was rich alluvial soil, famous for its grain harvests. Hawran was one of three main areas of Syrian wheat production: Sa'id Himadeh, *Economic Organization of Syria* (Beirut: American Press, 1936), 75.

14   This pastor, Antoun Hamwi, was married to one of Abdallah Sayigh's older sisters, and it was in their home that Abdallah grew up after being orphaned. Pastor Hamwi was like a father to Abdallah, and it was possibly through his influence that he decided to become a pastor (source: Anis Sayigh).

15   According to Anis Sayigh, his father owned a piece of land there—if at all—and not the whole village.

16   Abu Yusif says nothing about his childhood in his recollections *(Dhikrayati)*; but Yusif undoubtedly imagined him as unhappy because he was an orphan and had never experienced a mother's love.

17 I pressed Yusif to speak about these subjects because I was surprised after we married by how many foodstuffs he hated. As to health, he was always plagued by a sensitive stomach, slipped disks, and heart problems. In spite of this he remained a doer and a work enthusiast until the end of his life.

18 *Ayran* is *laban* to which water and a little salt have been added to make a cold drink.

19 A dish made of lentils, rice, and onions.

20 A type of kerosene stove.

21 Paper-thin Arab bread baked on an iron dome.

22 Low wooden table used for serving food when people are sitting on the floor.

23 *Taba(q)* were discs woven from wheat straw with colorful patterns that were used as mats for serving food. They were typical of the mountain regions of Syria and Jordan. See Johannes Kalter, *The Arts and Crafts of Syria* (London: Thames and Hudson, 1992), 110. Kalter has photographs of some fine examples (108). Abu Trab Abd al-Majeed, *Asrar al-Mihan* (Damascus, 1987), 145–46, says that housewives make them using local dyes.

24 Baggy trousers once worn by men in rural areas of Lebanon and Syria, today mainly by mountain Druze.

25 *Keffiyyeh*: a head scarf, black or red checkered, worn mainly by rural men. *I'qal*: the cord that holds the *keffiyyeh* in place.

26 Mary Abi Ad (Yusif's sister) remembers her mother as always elegant and neat, even though her dresses were homemade and simple.

27 Sultan al-Atrash was the leader of the Druze uprising. He raised the revolt in July 1925, after a Druze delegation to the French authorities was detained. Al-Atrash scored several military successes at first, and joined with nationalist leaders in Damascus in an alliance to end the French mandate. But in 1926 the French brought reinforcements from Morocco, and by April had reoccupied Jabal al-Druze. See Schaebler, "Rebels, Shaykhs and State(s)"; also Robin Bidwell, *Dictionary of Modern Arab History* (New York and London: Kegan Paul International, 1988), 128.

28 Yusif may not have known, or may have forgotten, the reason for his father's trip to Damascus, but according to the story that Abu Yusif told Clemence (one of his daughters-in-law), he went with the Orthodox bishop to try and get protection for the Christian villages in Jabal al-Druze. Clemence also remembers Abu Yusif telling her that the incident that sparked the Druze uprising was when the French

authorities summoned all the Druze *mashayekh* ('sheikhs') to Sweida and, once they were assembled, produced a photographer, announcing their intention of photographing the *mashayekh* and sending the photo to France as evidence of Druze support for French rule.

29   *Shmaliyeh* means 'woman from the north,' that is, from northern Palestine. Umm Yusif had no relatives in Kharaba, which was probably one reason why she was not happy there.

Notes to Chapter 2

1   The Sayighs lived in al-Bassa (Palestine) from 1925 until 1930, before moving to Tiberias. But for many years after the move the family continued to return to al-Bassa in summer. This is why at times in this chapter Yusif describes the village as he remembered it as a young boy, at other times as an adolescent.

2   There was a story about this marriage that Yusif didn't tell me and maybe didn't know. I heard it from his mother's cousin, Umm Joseph, in Dbeyeh refugee camp, Lebanon. When his grandfather from Batroun asked to marry the nun (Umm Yusif's mother), her father the priest at first refused. The man from Batroun emptied a sack full of gold at the priest's feet. According to Umm Joseph, this display immediately removed all obstacles to the marriage.

3   An unusual name, Mbadda' means 'the early one,' that is, first born.

4   Even in Ottoman times, al-Bassa had a public elementary school for boys and one for girls as well as a private secondary school: Yusif Haddad, *al-Mujtama' wa-l-turath fi Filastin: qaryat al-Bassa*, third printing (Los Angeles, 2002), 289. The village developed into a local educational center that served the surrounding area. Late in the mandate, a secondary school with classes up to matriculation was established, al-Eskofiyyeh, connected to the Greek Catholic church. After 1948, several refugees from al-Bassa set up schools in Lebanon.

5   The *mijwiz* is a double reed flute: see Anis Sayegh and Hashem Abdulhadi, *al-Mawsu'a al-filastiniya* , vol. one (Damascus: Hey'at al-Mawsu'a, 1994), 28. *'Ataba* is a traditional genre of Palestinian song popular all over Bilad al-Sham. According to Nimr Sarhan its name comes from the way it expresses affection and lament over changing fortune, which is why it often starts with '*Ouff!*': *The Encyclopedia of Palestinian Folklore* (Amman: al-Dustour, 1989), 69.

6   In late Ottoman times, al-Bassa was part of the same *sanjak* as South Lebanon, but was transferred to Palestine after the First World War by agreement between the British and French Mandate authorities.

Haddad gives a brief history of al-Bassa in English at the end of his book, including, "Antiquities were found inside and outside the village. Inside were the remains of an ancient village, mosaic floors, cisterns, and rock-hewn tombs." A Christian burial place excavated in 1932 contained coins and glass dating back to the fourth century AD (Haddad, *al-Mujtama' wa-l-turath*, 290).

7   This land was known for many years in the area as 'Ard Sitt Afifeh.' The British government took it in the early 1940s for a military airport, which the Israelis later appropriated. The British continued to pay rent for it for some years after 1948 (source: Anis Sayigh).

8   Crushed olive stones compressed to make fuel.

9   The women of al-Bassa used to gather on the rooftops toward the end of summer to make their stocks of vermicelli (*sha'riyyeh*) or dried figs (*quttayn*) together. It was a sociable event common to villages of the region, but in al-Bassa—and only there—women brought their adolescent children of both sexes, who mingled easily and naturally together in a party-like atmosphere (source: Anis Sayigh).

10   Jad, Abu Joseph, was one of the sons of Hanna Boulos, one of al-Bassa's *mukhtar*s. Later he married Yusif's cousin Layya. After 1948, Umm and Abu Joseph lived in the refugee camp of Dbeyeh and it was during visits with them that I learned about al-Bassa.

11   Lamps that fed from a gas container.

12   Residence of a Catholic or Orthodox priest, usually within the church precincts.

13   Matthew 3: 7.

14   *Hanayina* is a diminutive of *hanuna*, meaning 'an affectionate woman.'

15   The *sandook al-'ajab* "is a story box which has elements of picture story telling in a peepshow setting. It is the center of an entertainment act, performed by a wandering singer-artist-storyteller who recites one or more folktales or commentaries. . . . On the outside the box is usually profusely decorated with colorful pictures, prints, folk motifs, and decorations." Moa'taz Dajani, "Sculpture Inspired by *Sandouk al-'Ajab*, the Traditional Arab Storybox," BA thesis, State University of New York, 1981.

16   "Look and watch and see, see the battle out in the open, Abu Zaid al-Hilali is riding his black horse."

17   Later there were many cafés and restaurants at Musherfeh, and it became a favorite stopping point on the way between Palestine and Lebanon. Sarafand in south Lebanon was another place to stop on this well-traveled route because of its fish restaurants (source: Anis Sayigh).

18   *Kibbeh* is minced meat mixed with softened burghul wheat and spices to make a hollow ball that is filled with minced meat, chopped onions, and nuts, and then fried.

19   *Mooneh* refers to food provisions prepared at the end of the summer and kept in storage for winter.

20   Shukri Freiwat is briefly mentioned in Anton Shammas's prize-winning novel *Arabesques* (Berkeley: University of California Press, 2001), which is partly about the village of Fassuta, close to al-Bassa, and like it in many ways.

21   When Anis Sayigh knew al-Bassa, the mayor was Tawfiq Jibran, a wealthy farmer who had married a woman of the Sanbar family from Haifa. One of their sons, Jibran Jibran, was rich and extravagant enough to buy Clark Gable's car.

22   Yusif's cousin Mbadda', mentioned earlier, came to be called 'Abu Michel' after he married and had a son called Michel.

23   Munir Abu Fadel was a Lebanese man from Ayn Anoub who became head of general security in Palestine and the highest Arab officer serving the mandate. When Yusif was taken prisoner of war, Abu Fadel did his best to get him released (source: Anis Sayigh). After 1948 he became a deputy in the Lebanese National Assembly and later, as a Greek Orthodox, its deputy speaker.

24   Literally, *hadha ajr 'andkun* means 'This is payment for you,' with the idea that being charitable to Boutros would invoke God's protection for Yusif and his brothers.

25   "Curse you! [literally, "May your religion burn!"] Why the hurry? Calm down. Take breath."

26   In 1943 Umm Yusif and Abu Yusif were forced to sell the family house to help pay university and school fees. It was at the time when Fuad, Fayez, and Tawfiq were in, or ready for, university and Mary was at boarding school in Beirut. Munir and Anis were soon to go to boarding school in Jerusalem (source: Anis Sayigh). Anis remembers that the sum paid for the house was 600 Palestine pounds, and that his mother was very sad.

Notes to Chapter 3

1   The Gerard Institute is mentioned in Roderic Matthews and Matta Akrawi, *Education in Arab Countries of the Near East* (Washington, DC: American Council on Education, 1949), 486.

2   In June 1930, three Palestinians were hanged in Acre prison by the British authorities: Fuad Hejazi (from Haifa), Muhammad Jamjoum,

and Ata al-Zayr (from Hebron). They were accused of having taken part in the massacre of Jews in Hebron and Safad during the Wailing Wall 'disturbances' of 1929.

3   Rushdi Maalouf became a poet and journalist, writing a popular column in *al-Jarida* and establishing his own newspaper, *al-Safa*. He died in 1980.

4   Yusif remained a lover of novels all his life. As a young man he tried his hand at short-story writing.

5   Except for swimming, Yusif was not a sports lover, though he did do exercises to improve his physique. At a time when there was a craze for sports throughout the Arab region, linked to nationalism and the growth of a Westernized elite, his family represented an older, more sedentary style of middle-class life probably based in inland provincial towns.

6   The Zeins were a prominent Shi'i family with a feudal estate in Kafr Roman, south Lebanon. The father of Yusif's friend Izzat, Yusif Zein, was speaker of the National Assembly for several years.

7   These three were from well-known Sidon families. Maarouf Saad became a popular political leader and supporter of Arab nationalism. His assassination by Army snipers while leading a demonstration in defense of Sidon fishermen (1975) was a factor that led to the Civil War.

8   Yusif speaks about 'Muslims' and 'Christians' without the Sunni–Shi'i distinction, as would be the case today. There seem to have been no Druze students at the Gerard Institute in Yusif's time—possibly they went to the National School in Aley or to Souk al-Gharb. When Anis Sayigh attended the same school some fifteen years later there were Druzes, but in other ways the school's multi-sectarian character had diminished, with fewer Sunnis, and Christians only from south Lebanon.

9   Naseef al-Yaziji and Boutros al-Bustani were distinguished Lebanese scholars who led the revival *(nahda)* of Arabic language and literature in the mid-nineteenth century. They also assisted in the translation of the Bible into Arabic (published 1865). See Kamal Salibi, *The Modern History of Lebanon* (London: Weidenfeld and Nicolson, 1965), 143–45.

10   In Arabic grammar, *kana* and twelve other 'sisters' are used to modify verbs, for example in indicating the time at which an action takes or took place.

11   Beshara Trabulsi came from Mashghara in the Bekaa. He remained a close friend until emigrating to Brazil in the 1960s.

12   Kamel Mroueh, also from a distinguished Shi'i family, founded the newspaper *al-Hayat*, and wrote editorials for it. He was assassinated in May 1966 at a time of sharp Saudi–Egyptian conflict that spilled over into Lebanon.

13   Emile Bustani was born in 1907 in Dibbiyeh, a village near Sidon. He was an orphan with extraordinary intelligence and energy, who worked his way through university in Lebanon and America, and eventually became one of the biggest Arab contractors in the Middle East. He was elected to the Lebanese parliament in the early 1950s, and might well have become president if he had not been killed in 1963 in a plane crash. See Desmond Stewart, *Orphan with a Hoop: The Life of Emile Bustani* (London: Chapman Hall, 1977).

14   The Protestant church Yusif mentions here is near Riad al-Solh Square, opposite the Serail.

15   The eastern side of the Bourj (Beirut's central square) was the 'red light' district, an area of licensed prostitution. It was destroyed during the Civil War.

Notes to Chapter 4

1   Mary (Yusif's sister) remembers that they used to put a table outside and eat their meals between rows of carnations, *otra*, and *ful*. *Otra* is a scented geranium, or pelargonium; its leaves can be used in jams and sweets.

2   This was Sheikh Taher Tabari, mufti of Tiberias and leading member of the Tabari family. Mustafa Abbasi gives more details on the Tabari and other notable families of Tiberias in his "The End of Arab Tiberias: The Arabs of Tiberias and the Battle for the City in 1948," *Journal of Palestine Studies* 37, no. 3: 6–29.

3   The Arabic word, *yateem* (pl. *aytam*), means a child who has lost his or her father.

4   Hajj Amin al-Husseini, grand mufti of Jerusalem and president of the Arab Higher Committee, established at the beginning of the Great Revolt in April 1936. See Philip Mattar, *The Mufti of Jerusalem: Al-Hajj Amin al-Husayni and the Palestinian National Movement* (New York: Columbia University Press, 1988).

5   Kafr Bir'em is a village in the hills of Upper Galilee, close to the border with Lebanon. In 1948 its inhabitants were ordered to leave for two weeks, and have never been allowed to return. See http://www.birem.org/

6   The Rutenberg concession gave Pinhas Rutenberg, a Zionist industrialist, the monopoly over supplying electricity to all of Palestine except Jerusalem. The British government awarded the concession in 1921,

before assuming authority as mandate: see J.N.M. Jeffries, *Palestine the Reality* (Westport, CT: Hyperion, 1976), 427–41.

7   When Yusif told me about his affairs with Jewish women, I asked him if he hadn't felt a contradiction between his sex life and his Arab nationalism. He said that it was almost impossible in those days to have an affair with an Arab woman. But he added a tinge of nationalist ideology by saying that sleeping with Jewish women was a way of 'getting back' at the enemy.

8   According to Wikipedia, the Maccabi football club was founded in 1913 in Haifa. Palestinians formed their own All-Palestinian League for Football in 1924, and took part in the World Cup in 1934.

9   On the Scots Mission and the Torrance family, see Michael Marten, "Imperialism and Evangelization: Scottish Missionary Methods in Late 19th and 20th Century Palestine," *Holy Land Studies* 5, no. 2 (2006).

10   In the British education system in effect in Palestine at this time, 'matriculation' referred to the examinations taken at the end of secondary school. 'To graduate with matriculation' meant to earn high enough marks on these examinations to enter university.

11   Anis Sayigh tells a slightly different story. He says that the Arab College had a very small intake (a total of ninety pupils in only four levels), and only accepted boys with the highest grades in each school. He was accepted on the basis of his grades, but refused admission because the college had a rule that not more than two brothers from the same family could be admitted. It was an elite government school, and none of its students ever failed matriculation.

12   I asked Anis if his mother managed to love and care for all her children equally, or whether, as is usually the case with large families, some felt neglected. He said that if any of his siblings suffered, it was Tawfiq, the sad one, the poet, who predicted his early death. He died in 1971 in the United States.

13   This passage underlines the importance of education for the Sayighs as a family, and the sacrifices made for it. Yusif took great pride in his siblings' achievements. I think this made him underestimate the psychological and health effects of continual pressure on them all to do well in school. Their getting educated was not quite as smooth as Yusif describes. Both Fayez and Tawfiq took jobs between school and university because of lack of money to pay fees.

14   Fayez was to become one of the best spokesmen for the Palestinian cause in the United States. He was the first of the brothers to suffer a heart attack (1949) but survived until 1980.

15   Literally, 'light-blooded,' used of people who are not boring, easy to get along with.

16   Haseeb Sabbagh founded the CCC construction company in 1945 in Haifa. After 1948 he was joined by his brother-in-law, Sa'id Khoury, and Kamil Abd al-Rahman. CCC did well in Iraq, Saudi Arabia, and the other Arab Gulf states. Haseeb was famous for his generosity and patriotism, and did much to help refugees. See Mary-Jane Deeb and Mary E. King, eds., *Hasib Sabbagh: From Palestinian Refugee to Citizen of the World* (Lanham, MD: University Press of America, 1996).

17   Hanan Mikhael became famous as a spokesperson for Palestine. She was chosen as one of the Madrid conference negotiators (1991), was elected to the Palestine Legislative Council (1996), served briefly as minister of higher education in the National Authority government, and set up a human rights organization, Miftah (the Palestinian Initiative for the Promotion of Global Dialogue and Democracy).

18   Wadi'a Khartabil was Lebanese, from a Beirut family that contained several feminists. Soon after going to Palestine, she was elected as chairwoman of the Tulkarm branch of the Arab Women's Association.

19   'Tegarts' were round, fortress-like buildings built by the British during the Great Revolt to protect government installations. They were named after Sir Charles Tegart, an expert in anti-guerrilla warfare who was brought to Palestine in 1936.

20   Anis Sayigh tells a variant to this story, which suggests its stereotypical character: Khartabil was walking behind two men when he heard them tell about a hidden tin of gold; he went immediately and dug it up.

21   PPS stands for 'Parti populaire syrien.' This is the way the party founded by Antoun Saadeh is usually referred to in Lebanon, rather than as the Syrian Social Nationalist Party (SSNP).

Notes to Chapter 5

1   Charles Malek (1906–87) was an eminent Lebanese thinker, a diplomat at the United Nations, and one of the drafters of the Bill of Universal Human Rights. Later he taught philosophy at AUB.

2   Albert Hourani (1915–93) was "one of the most prominent scholars of Middle East history of the 2nd half of the 20th century" (Wikipedia). He helped prepare the Arab case for the Anglo-American Committee of Inquiry.

3   Constantin Zurayk (1909–2000), educated at Princeton, was one of the fathers of modern Arab nationalist thought. See Aziz al-Azmeh,

Qunstantin Zurayk: 'arabi li-l-qarn al-'ishrin (Beirut: Institute of Palestine Studies, 2003).

4   Antoun Sa'adeh (1904–49) was founder/leader of the Parti populaire syrien (PPS) (1932). He spent much of his life in jail or in exile, harassed by the French mandate government because of his opposition to a Lebanese state. See Labib Zuwayya, *The Syrian Social Nationalist Party: An Ideological Analysis* (Cambridge, MA: Harvard University Press, 1966). Sa'adeh taught briefly at AUB, before Yusif arrived there.

5   Riad al-Solh was the first prime minister of Lebanon, and an architect of the unwritten National Pact between the dominant Maronite and Sunni sects on which Lebanese independence was based.

6   Sa'id Taqqedin was a well-known Beirut figure and philanthropist in the 1930s, and president of the AUB Alumni Club for several years. It was he who helped Fuad, Fayez, Tawfiq, and Munir get loans to go through the university.

7   Yusif lived with the Maalouf family during his last two years at AUB and while working with Socony. He was joined there by Fuad and Fayez when they came to AUB in 1936 and 1937. Fawzi Maalouf remembers that "they were like our brothers." The youngest of a family of seven, he also remembers that the Maaloufs took a larger house to be able to accommodate everyone. Antoun Sa'adeh ('Uncle Antoun') lived across the road and came to lunch most days (Fawzi Maalouf, 1 November 2006, Beirut).

8   Flat bread spread with *zaatar* (dried thyme) and olive oil.

9   Carob molasses with sesame paste.

10   *Amid* means 'dean.' The PPS was a strongly hierarchical party, somewhat like an army, and its ranks were named after state or university positions.

11   For a list of Himadeh's studies see chapter 13, note 5.

12   Al-Urwa al-Wuthqa was an AUB cultural association founded in 1918. It was closed after the 'events' of March 1954, when AUB students demonstrated against the Baghdad Pact. The security forces reacted harshly, killing one student and seriously wounding another (Yusif Shibl, *Main Gate* 5 (3), Spring 2007).

13   May Ziadeh (1886–1941), born in Nazareth, educated in Lebanon, resident in Cairo, was a famous literary figure in the early twentieth century. She has been called "a pioneer of oriental feminism." See Rose Ghurayyib, "May Ziadeh (1886–1941)," *al-Raida* 47 (1989).

Notes to Chapter 6

1   Marcel Carton was kidnapped in Beirut in March 1985 by Islamic Jihad, and released three years later.

2   Though Yusif was the first Sayigh to join the PPS, Fayez was the one who rose highest in the party until his conflict with Sa'adeh in 1947. According to Anis, it was Fayez who taught him and Munir to do the PPS salute when Anis was aged five or six. Anis never actually joined the PPS, though he was closely associated with it, and was eventually expelled for not attending meetings. Tawfiq went to take the oath, but was repelled by the darkened room lit with a candle, and withdrew at the last minute. Fuad and Munir never joined.

3   By 'self-educated' Yusif probably meant that Sa'adeh had not studied at university.

4   Hisham Sharabi, a leading Palestinian intellectual, was born in Jaffa in 1927; joined the PPS in 1947; became a professor emeritus in history at Georgetown University; edited the *Journal of Palestine Studies* for many years; and died in January 2005.

5   'Respected leader! Long live the leader!' 'Long live, long live the leader! Long live, long live, long live. He's building life for Syria! He is our leader! Long live the leader!'

6   In July 1949 Sa'adeh declared a revolt against the Lebanese government. The revolt failed, and Sa'adeh fled to Damascus.

7   Husni Za'im, an army officer, seized power in a bloodless coup d'état on 11 April 1949, backed by the United States and possibly assisted by the PPS. This is doubtless why Sa'adeh counted on Za'im to protect him.

8   Two more coups followed Za'im's in 1949: the first by Shishakli and Hinnawi, army officers close to the PPS; Shishakli was motivated by anger at Za'im's betrayal of Sa'adeh— he is said to have handed Za'im's bloodstained shirt to Sa'adeh's widow. Shishakli took over the presidency in December 1949. In November 1951 he restored military rule, banning all parties. He was overthrown in February 1954.

9   Michel Aflak founded the Ba'th Party with Saleh Bitar in 1947.

Notes to Chapter 7

1   Nairn, the first overland bus service between Beirut and Baghdad, was set up by Gerald and Norman Nairn, two New Zealanders who served during the Second World War in the Middle East.

2   Tikrit had been a great city in Mesopotamian and later times, possessing a fortress and a large Christian monastery. Salah al-Din (Saladin)

was born there (so was Saddam Hussein, in 1937). It was destroyed by the Mongols in the thirteenth century.

3   Rashid Ali Gailani (1892–1965) was an Arab nationalist, several times prime minister, who opposed British hegemony over Iraq. He negotiated with the Axis powers during the Second World War and sent a force against the British base of Habbaniya in 1941. When the uprising failed he took refuge in Saudi Arabia.

4   'Excuse me for mentioning it, but my wife was sick.'

5   Iraq was occupied by the British army during the First World War, and put under British mandate by the League of Nations in 1920. The British imposed the Hashemite monarchy, provoking a Kurdish and Shi'i rebellion that was brutally suppressed. The British mandate ended in 1932, leaving Iraq nominally an independent constitutional monarchy.

6   Both were prime ministers at different times.

7   Ghazi (1912–39) was the oldest son of King Faisal, who ruled briefly (1933–39). He was an Arab nationalist, and his death in a car accident in 1939 was said by nationalists to have been engineered by the pro-British politician Nuri al-Said.

Notes to Chapter 8

1   The black and white checkered *keffiyyeh* was the headscarf worn by rural men that became a symbol of solidarity with the insurgents in 1936–38.

2   "In some of the villages that were close to urban centers, the Jewish troops followed a policy of massacres in order to precipitate the flight of the people in the cities and towns nearby. This was the case of Nasr al-Din near Tiberias." Ilan Pappe, *The Ethnic Cleansing of Palestine* (Oxford: OneWorld, 2006), 110.

3   Suleiman Naseef was one of the owners of the Himmeh concession, and also general manager.

4   In Egypt, Suleiman Naseef, together with Fares Nimr and Yacoub Sarouf, formed a 'Party of the Seven' calling for the independence of Lebanon. It was thought that the British supported it.

5   Wooden slippers used in wet areas such as bathrooms.

6   Anis Sayigh tells another version, that Grossman, the hotel owner, was anti-Jewish, and that his hotel had a notice on its door: "No dogs or Jews." According to this version, he committed suicide because of German defeat in the Second World War. Grossman's widow married again, a British army officer. A grandson, Sebastian Hope, wrote a book about the hotel and his grandfather: *Hotel Tiberias: A Tale of Two Grandfathers* (London: Harper Perennial, 2004).

7   This campaign, called 'Operation Exporter,' did in fact take place,
     though unreported at the time. Churchill pushed the campaign, fear-
     ing that the Germans might use Vichy French Mandate Syria and
     Lebanon as a springboard for attack against British-controlled Egypt.
     Allied troops invaded Syrian and Lebanon on 8 June 1941, advancing
     from Palestine and from Iraq. The campaign ended in the defeat of
     Vichy French forces under General Denz on 10 July. General Catroux
     was placed in control of Syria and Lebanon, recognizing their inde-
     pendence on behalf of General de Gaulle and the Free French. Among
     those who accompanied the Allied troops was Asmahan: see Sherifa
     Zurhur, *Asmahan's Secrets: Woman, War and Song* (Austin: The Center
     for Middle Eastern Studies, 2000), 113–31. See also Muhammad al-
     Taba'i, *Asmahan tarwi qissataha* (Cairo: Ruz al-Yusuf, 1965).
8   General Edward Spears wrote about her: "She was and will always
     be to me one of the most beautiful women I have ever seen . . . . She
     bowled over British officers with the speed and accuracy of a machine
     gun. Naturally enough, she needed money, and spent it as a rain cloud
     scatters water," quoted in Zurhur, *Asmahan's Secrets*, 125.
9   Keith-Roach Pasha was a mandate official about whom Yusif only
     remembered that he loved being called 'Pasha.' There is a recent
     memoir: Edward Keith-Roach and Paul Eedle, *Pasha of Jerusalem:
     Memoirs of a District Commissioner under the British Mandate* (London:
     I.B.Tauris, 1994).

Notes to Chapter 9

1   Fuad Saba established the first auditing company in Palestine, per-
     haps in the Arab region. He was also a member of the Arab Higher
     Council. His photo can be seen with other AHC members in Walid
     Khalidi, *Before Their Diaspora: A Photographic History of the Palestinians
     1876–1948* (Washington: Institute for Palestine Studies, 1984), 197.
2   Izzat Tannous (1896–1969) was born in Nablus. He was a medical
     doctor who represented the Palestine Arab Higher Committee at
     the United Nations General Assembly during the British mandate,
     and headed the Arab Higher Committee delegation to the United
     Nations in the 1950s.
3   Awni Abdel Hadi was born in 1889 in Nablus, a lawyer educated in
     Beirut, Istanbul, and the Sorbonne. In 1924 he became one of the
     chief spokespersons of the Palestinian Arab nationalist movement,
     and later was general secretary and first elected president of the Pal-
     estine Istiqlal (Independence) Party.

4   Sami Taha was leader of the Palestine Arab Workers' Society
     (appointed 1946), and a member of the Arab Higher Committee.
     He was assassinated in September 1947. The mufti was suspected of
     ordering his assassination.

5   Anwar Nusseibeh (1913–86) studied law at Cambridge University.
     After 1948 he was elected to the Jordanian parliament and later
     became Jordanian ambassador to the United Kingdom.

6   Anwar al-Khatib (1917–93) was mayor of Jerusalem in the late 1950s; a
     member of the Arab Socialist party in the early 1960s; Jordan's ambas-
     sador to Cairo in 1963; and governor of Jerusalem from 1967 to 1970.

7   Jamal al-Husseini (1892–1982) was a member of the Arab Higher
     Committee from 1936 to 1937, and its representative to the United
     Nations from 1947 to 1948. He was exiled by the British to Rhodesia
     in the 1940s.

8   Musa Alami (1897–1984) was born in Jerusalem; graduated in law
     from Cambridge University; served as secretary to the High Com-
     missioner; took part in the 1936–39 revolt with the mufti. After 1948
     he stayed in Palestine and founded the Arab Development Society to
     educate orphaned boys in Jericho. See Geoffrey Furlonghe, *Palestine is
     My Country: The Story of Musa Alami* (London: John Murray, 1969).

9   Darwish Mikdadi taught at the Arab College of Jerusalem.

10   Ahmad Shuqeiri (1907–80) was born in Akka (Acre); studied at the
     Jerusalem Law School and at AUB; and became first president of the
     PLO (1964–67).

11   Albert Hourani (1915–93), prominent Arab historian, founded the
     Arab Office in London to carry out Palestinian advocacy. See Walid
     Khalidi, "Albert Hourani, the Arab Office and the Anglo-American
     Committee of 1946," *Journal of Palestine Studies* 35, no. 1 (2005). Cecil
     Hourani is Albert's younger brother, also a noted scholar.

12   Walid Khalidi, born in Jerusalem in 1925, is an eminent Palestinian
     historian. Educated at London and Oxford universities, he was the
     initiator of the Institute for Palestine Studies in Beirut (1963). Burhan
     Dajani was an economist and a co-founder of the Institute for Pales-
     tine Studies.

13   Abdel Qadir al-Husseini (1907–48) participated in nationalist
     demonstrations from the age of thirteen; was dismissed from AUB
     for political activities; was founder and leader of Jaysh al-Jihad al-
     Muqaddas (1930); deported from Egypt 1932; became a leader of the
     resistance in the 1936 revolt and the 1948 fighting; and was killed at
     Qastal on 8 April 1948.

14   Yusif must have meant Dr. Hussein Fakhri Khalidi (1895–1966), a medical doctor who became mayor of Jerusalem (1934–37). He founded the Reform Party in 1945, and was a member of the Arab Higher Committee, the only one who stayed in Palestine throughout the war of 1947–49.

15   Jabra Ibrahim Jabra (1920–94), distinguished novelist, poet, and translator, was born in Bethlehem. After 1948 he lived in Iraq. His autobiography *The First Well: A Bethlehem Boyhood* is available in Arabic and English.

16   Sami Hadawi (1904–2004) was in charge of land taxation under the mandate government; he was an able statistician and author of several books on Palestine. Among the most valuable is *Village Statistics 1945: A Classification of Land and Area Ownership in Palestine* (Beirut: PLO Research Centre, 1970).

17   This was in Beirut in the 1970s. See chapter 12.

18   National Committees were established in Palestine in towns and villages at the beginning of the General Strike in 1936, and again between 1946 and 1948.

19   Nabil Shaath was a close advisor to PLO chairman Arafat, and served as the Palestinian Authority's first foreign minister from April 2003 to February 2005.

20   The Jaysh al-Inqadh al-'Arabi [Arab Salvation Army] was composed of Arab volunteers led by Lebanese-born Fawzi Qawuqji, with Syrian backing. It entered Palestine before the British withdrawal on 15 May.

21   For a biography of the mufti, see Philip Mattar, *The Mufti of Jerusalem* (Columbia University Press, 1988).

22   French military expression for 'general staff.'

23   Apart from Yusif's description, I haven't found any reference to Abu Dayyeh in Palestinian sources such as PASSIA (the Palestinian Academic Society for the Study of International Affairs).

24   The All-Palestine Government was established by the Arab League in September 1948, with Ahmad Hilmi Abdel Baqi as prime minister and Jamal al-Husseini as foreign minister. It was recognized by most Arab states except Transjordan, enjoying brief sovereignty over the Gaza 'Strip,' and issuing passports until 1959, when it was annulled by Abdel Nasser. See Avi Shlaim, "The Rise and Fall of the All-Palestine Government in Gaza," *Journal of Palestine Studies* 20 (1990).

Notes to Chapter 10

1   The International Red Cross had a large delegation in Palestine during 1948 headed by Jacques de Reynier.

2   Wikipedia has it that the Iraqi forces reached Natanya before withdrawing to Jenin. However, this would not have cut Palestine in half. A comprehensive Palestinian history of the conflict of 1947–49 has not yet been published.

3   Lydda and Ramleh were all-Arab towns near Jaffa. The Israelis began to attack them on 8 and 11 July, forcing their populations to leave, and closing off all exits except to the east, where there were mountains and no roads. Many died on what was later called 'The Death March.' See Michael Palumbo, *The Palestine Catastrophe: The 1948 Expulsion of a People from Their Homeland* (London: Faber and Faber, 1987): 126–38.

4   The IRC delegate whose name Yusif tried to remember was probably Dr. Emile Moeri, a frequent visitor to the detention camps. See Salman Abu Sitta and Terry Rempel, "The IRC and the Detention of Palestinian Civilians in Israel's 1948 POW/Labor Camps," *Journal of Palestine Studies* 43, no. 4 (2014): 11–38.

5   This chant—'God lives'—is used in Sufi ceremonies to induce trance.

6   Munir Abu Fadel was a Lebanese who had been employed by the British mandate in the police force. Later he returned to Lebanon, was elected to the National Assembly, and served briefly as deputy speaker.

7   A measurement of weight equivalent to 200 grams.

8   Nuri al-Said (1888–1958) was an Iraqi politician during the British mandate and the Hashemite monarchy, and served fourteen times as prime minister. He was known in Iraq and the Arab region for his pro-British stance.

9   Years later, in 1984, in Oxford, Yusif met Salma Mardem Bek, Jamil's daughter, and learned from her that she was working on her father's papers to prepare a doctoral dissertation on the period when he was prime minister. She told him that among all the papers, there was this one memorandum, written by hand, to which her father had attached a note saying that the author must be an intelligent and patriotic young man.

10   Mary Abi Ad (Yusif's sister) remembers that when he came home from POW camp he was very thin, and still suffering from back pain that made him unable to walk properly.

Notes to Chapter 11

1   By then Fuad and Clemence's daughter Hala had been born, giving Umm Yusif the happiness of having a grandchild.

2   Fayez Sayegh (1922–80) got his PhD in philosophy at Georgetown in 1949; became an outstanding keynote speaker on Palestine; taught

at Yale, Stanford, AUB, Oxford, and Macalester College; and wrote many books in Arabic and in English, for example, *Zionist Colonialism in Palestine* (Beirut : PLO Research Centre, 1965) recently excerpted in *Settler Colonial Studies* 2 (1): 2012.

3   Tawfiq Sayegh's (1923–71) main publications were: *Thalathun qasidah* (Beirut: Dar al-Sharq al-Jadid, 1954); *Al-Qasida K* (Beirut: Dar Majallat Shi'r, 1960); *Mu'allaqat Tawfiq Sayigh* (Beirut: al-Mu'assasa al-Wataniya li-l-Tiba'a wa-l-Nashr, 1963); and *Adwa' jadidah ala Jibran* (Beirut: al-Dar al-Sharqiya li-l-Tiba'a wa-l-Nashr, 1966). See also Mahmoud Chreih, *Tawfiq Sayegh: Biography of a Poet in Exile* (London: Riad al-Rayyes Press, 1989).

4   Munir Sayegh (1929–75) worked as a doctor with UNRWA after graduating from medical school with distinction in 1954; he was promoted to the post of deputy chief of the Arab doctors at UNRWA; known for his dedication, hard work, and good relations with the refugees, he wrote a book under a pseudonym entitled *Science and Scientists in Israel*.

5   Anis (b. 1931) studied history and political science at AUB and Cambridge; taught at AUB in 1958 and Cambridge from 1959 to 1964; was director of the Palestine Research Centre from 1956 to 1976; headed the Institute of Higher Arab Studies in Cairo in 1968; edited the Palestinian Encyclopedia from 1978 to 1993; established and edited three cultural journals; published several studies, among them *Lubnan al-ta'ifa, al-Fikra al-'arabiya fi Misr, al-Hashimiyin wa qabdat Filasti*, and his autobiography, *Anis Sayegh 'an Anis Sayegh* (Beirut: Dar al-Rayyes, 2006).

6   Yusif said 'the Vauxhall' because this was the car he had when I stopped off in Beirut on my way home from Baghdad to England.

7   Literally, '*Allah bidabbir*' means 'God will manage,' but surely Umm Yusif meant 'God will help us.'

8   Nora Hadawi was Albert Badr's sister and married to Sami Hadawi (see chapter 9, note 16).

9   Sa'id Aql, born in Zahleh in 1918, was a Lebanese poet and nationalist.

10   Abu and Umm Joseph were Yusif's mother's relatives who lived in al-Bassa, mentioned in chapter 2. In Lebanon they lived in Dbeyeh camp, about twenty kilometers north of Beirut, with other families from al-Bassa. Umm Joseph worked in domestic labor, as many refugee women did in the early years; she died shortly before the outbreak of the Civil War (1975). Dbeyeh was overrun by Christian militias in 1976.

Notes to Chapter 12

1   Yusif and I agreed that Palestinian politics should have a chapter to itself. The recording filled four tapes of sixty minutes each. These sessions took place between December 1996 and February 1997.

2   George Habash (1925–2008) was born in Lydda, won a scholarship to study medicine at AUB, and co-founded the Arab Nationalist Movement in 1951 with Wadi'a Haddad; he also established with Haddad a clinic for poor Palestinians in Amman and established the PFLP in 1967, remaining its secretary general until 2000 when he resigned, citing health reasons. He died on 26 January 2008.

3   Wadi'a Haddad (1937–78), born in Safed, graduated in medicine from AUB in 1952; worked as a doctor in Amman with Habash; was imprisoned for three years in Jordan; took up commando action from 1963; died of leukemia in 1978.

4   Hani Hindi is Syrian; he fought in Palestine in 1948; was a co-founder of the Arab Nationalist Movement; a minister in the UAR government; a co-founder of the PFLP; a researcher at the PLO Research Centre in the early 1970s; and published his MA thesis on the Jaysh al-Inqadh.

5   Ahmad Shuqeiri (1907–80) was born in Acre; studied law at Jerusalem Law School; was a member of the Istiqlal Party, and of the Arab Higher Council (1946–48). After 1948 he worked with the Arab League and the United Nations; was Palestinian representative to the Arab League (1963), and first president of the PLO (1964–67).

6   Yasser Arafat (1929–2004) was born in Cairo to a Palestinian father from Gaza. He entered university in 1947 but left to fight beside the Muslim Brethren in Gaza in 1948. After the war he studied civil engineering in Cairo, and served as first president of the General Union of Palestinian Students. In 1957 he went to Kuwait, where Abu Iyad and Abu Jihad were already working; they began building Fatah. In 1962 Arafat moved to Syria and began recruiting for the PLA; became chairman of the Palestine National Council in 1969; returned to Palestine after the Oslo Accords as chairman of the Palestine National Authority; and was besieged for the last years of his life in his headquarters in Ramallah when Ariel Sharon re-invaded the West Bank.

7   Joseph Mughaizal (1924–95) was born in Tibnin (South Lebanon); he was a leading lawyer and a pioneer in the struggle for democracy, secularism, and human rights; presided over the Arab Cultural Club from 1960 to 1972; founded and headed the Democratic Party in 1969, and the Lebanese Association for Human Rights in 1985.

8   Zuheir Alami was from a well-known Jerusalem family; he was an
     engineer; joined Fatah; became a member of the PLO Executive
     Committee; and was in charge of the National Fund before Yusif.
9   Abdel Mohsen Qattan was born in Jaffa in 1929; he began studying
     political science and economics at AUB in 1947 but had to switch
     to business to support his widowed mother and younger siblings; he
     went to Kuwait in 1951, worked briefly in government, then founded
     his own construction company; he remained a staunch nationalist and
     philanthropist, giving generously to Palestinian causes. In 1999 he
     launched the Qattan Foundation in Ramallah, one of the leading cul-
     tural and educational institutions in the Arab world.
10   Apart from the first session held in Jerusalem and the third in Gaza,
     all early PNC meetings up to 1979 were held in Cairo (though there
     was an extraordinary session in 1970 in Amman). But the move to
     Damascus only lasted for the fourteenth and fifteenth sessions. In
     1983 it was held in Algiers and in 1984 in Amman. The PNC has met
     once after Oslo, forced by Netanyahu to repeat the annulment of the
     PLO's charter, in Gaza in 1998.
11   Kamal Nasser (1925–73) was born in Gaza to a Birzeit family;
     educated at Birzeit school and AUB; wrote poetry; studied law in
     Jerusalem and worked as a journalist; was elected to the Jordanian
     parliament as a Ba'th member; expelled from the West Bank by the
     Israelis in 1967; edited *Filastin al-thawra;* served on the PLO Execu-
     tive Committee 1969–71; was assassinated in Beirut in 1973 by an
     IDF commando unit led by Ehud Barak.
12   Abu Lutf (Faruq Qaddumi) was born in 1931 near Qalqilya; he was
     an early member of Fatah and headed the PLO Political Department.
     A critic of the Oslo Accords, he remained in Tunis when the leader-
     ship returned to Occupied Palestine.
13   See chapter 6, note 4.
14   In 1968 Yusif used a windfall to buy land in Ain Anoub, in the western
     Chouf mountains, and we built a house there just before construction
     costs skyrocketed. It was long before the Lebanese law forbidding
     stateless foreigners (that is, Palestinians) to own property.
15   Khaled al-Hassan (1928–94) was the eldest of the three al-Hassan
     brothers; he was born in Haifa and joined Fatah in 1962; was the
     main architect of the PLO's foreign policy; and advocated an Israeli–
     Jordanian–Palestinian confederation.
16   Abu Jihad, Khalil Wazir (1935–88), was expelled in 1948 from Ramleh
     to Gaza. He co-founded with Arafat the first Fatah cell in 1957 and was

responsible for clandestine organization and anything else to do with
the occupied territories after the assassination of Kamal Udwan in April
1973. He was assassinated by an Israeli death squad in 1988 in Tunis.

17   Khaled Yashruti (1937–70), from Acre, was an engineer. He first
joined the Ba'th, and then became a leading member of Fatah in
Lebanon.

18   Abdel Wahab Kayyali (1939–81) was born in Jaffa, grew up in Lebanon, and joined the Ba'th party; he graduated from AUB in 1968;
became a leading member of the Arab Liberation Front (pro-Iraqi);
a member of the PLO Executive Committee from 1973, heading the
Educational and Cultural Affairs department; took a PhD from SOAS
in history, with a thesis published in Arabic, English, and French (*Palestine: A Modern History* [London: Croom Helm, 1979]); established
the Third World Centre for Research and Publishing in London; and
was assassinated in 1981 by unknown agents.

19   Ahmad Yemani, Abu Maher, was born in the Galilean village of Sohmata
and expelled in 1948 to Lebanon; he first lived in Bourj al-Barajneh
camp, becoming a noted educator and member of the Arab Nationalist
movement; later, he became a leading member of the PFLP.

20   Zuheir Mohsen was the leader of al-Saiqa in Lebanon.

21   Khaled al-Fahoum (1923–2006) was born in Nazareth; he studied
chemistry at AUB; fought in 1948 and was expelled to Syria; joined
the PLO in 1964 and attended the first PNC; was its speaker from
1971 to 1984; and was involved in Syrian–Palestinian dialogue.

22   Walid Qamhawi was born in Nablus in 1924; he studied medicine
at AUB, graduating in 1947; during 1948 he worked in Nablus with
the Iraqi Red Crescent; he joined the ANM in the early 1950s; was
arrested intermittently; became a member of the first PLO Executive
Committee; became a leader of the Palestine National Front; helped
establish the Maqasid hospital in Jerusalem after 1967; was perma-
nently deported in 1973 (allowed to return in 1993); and was head of
the PLO National Fund from 1974 until 1981.

23   See chapter 9, note 12.

24   The quarrel arose from their competition to be first to establish a
Palestinian research center.

25   Shafiq al-Hout was born in Jaffa in 1932; left for Lebanon in 1948;
got an MA in psychology from AUB; worked in teaching and journalism; attended the first PNC meeting in 1964; was appointed PLO
representative in Beirut from 1964 until 1993 when he resigned in
protest against the Oslo Accords; occasionally represented the PLO

at UN meetings, and served on the PLO Executive Committee until 1993; and published (in Arabic) *Twenty Years with the PLO: Memoirs* (Beirut: Dar al-Istiqlal li-l-Dirasat wa-l-Nashr, 1986).

26   Anis Sayigh was director of the PLO Research Centre from 1966 to 1976. He resigned because of Arafat's continual interference.

27   Kamal Jumblatt was assassinated in March 1977 and Anwar Sadat in October 1981.

28   Abdel Halim Khaddam was a Syrian politician who served as foreign minister from 1970 to 1984, and was in charge of the 'Lebanon file.' He resigned in 2005, and went to Paris, from where he attacked Bashar al-Assad and the Syrian regime.

29   Abu Ala', Ahmad Qurei, was born in 1937 in Abu Dis (near Jerusalem); he joined Fatah in 1968; became director of the PLO's investments and economic institutions; led the Palestinian delegation in negotiating the Oslo Accords (1993); was elected deputy for Jerusalem; became speaker of the Legislative Council; and has headed several ministries in the PNA.

30   SAMED (the Palestine Martyrs' Works Society) was a productive economic institution established in Amman in 1970 by Fatah, and became part of the PLO. It was headed from its inception by Abu Ala'. Transferred to Lebanon in 1971, it provided employment for many Palestinians and Lebanese.

31   At the time Yusif was engaged in writing *Elusive Development: From Dependence to Self-Reliance in the Arab Region* (London: Routledge, 1991).

32   Palestinian statehood was declared at the Palestinian National Council meeting in Algiers, November 1988. It was recognized immediately by more than twenty countries.

33   Mahmoud Abdel Fadil, an Egyptian economist.

34   Initiated after the first Gulf War by the United States, the Madrid conference gave birth to a set of multilateral negotiating teams to discuss water, security, arms control, refugees, the environment, and economic development. By 1996 they were stalemated by the 'peace process.'

35   See Mahmoud Abbas, *Through Secret Channels: The Road to Oslo* (London: Garnet, 1997).

36   Caio Koch-Weser, a German-Brazilian economist specializing in developing countries, was World Bank regional vice president for the Middle East and North Africa between 1991 and 1995. In 2000 he was Europe's candidate for the post of director general at the IMF but was blocked by Bill Clinton.

37   The Palestine Economic Programme was not published but remained
     in Tunis, with the PLO. Credit for its authorship is given to Abu Ala'
     by PASSIA.
38   Dennis Ross was counselor at the Washington Institute for Middle
     East Policy and envoy to the Middle East under presidents Clinton
     and G.W. Bush.
39   Probably Daniel Kurtzer, former U.S. ambassador to Israel, and
     Aaron David Miller, senior advisor on Arab–Israeli relations to the
     State Department under the last three presidents.
40   Joan Spiro, under secretary of state for economic affairs in the first
     Clinton administration.
41   Yasser Abed Rabbo, born in Jaffa in 1945; he took an MA in econom-
     ics and political science at AUC (Cairo); co-founded the DFLP with
     Nayef Hawatmeh (1968); headed the PLO's department of Informa-
     tion and Culture from 1973, and occupied the same post with the
     PNA (from 1994). He was one of the first to propose the 'two-state
     solution'; was expelled from the DFLP Politburo in 1991; and formed
     FIDA (a breakaway from the Democratic Front).
42   In December 1992 the Israeli authorities expelled 415 mainly Hamas
     Palestinians to Lebanon. The Lebanese government refused to let them
     into the country so they remained encamped in Marj al-Zuhur, a true
     'no-man's-land' near the border, infested with snakes and scorpions.
43   A.B. Zahlan was born in Haifa in 1928; taught physics at the Ameri-
     can University of Beirut; is an activist, science policy consultant,
     author of books on manpower, technology transfer, and the 'brain
     drain'; founded the Royal Scientific Society (Amman), where he set
     up a 'brain bank' of Palestinian professionals; and was invited to Tunis
     by Abu Ala' in 1993 to write projects for retraining Fatah cadres.
44   *Abawat* ('fathers') is the generic term for the leadership of Fatah, who
     adopted this rural naming style as part of their appeal to the people.
45   Ram Chopra, an Indian economist, was the Middle East director of
     the World Bank's MENA region.
46   Abdallah Bouhabib was Lebanon's ambassador to the United States
     1983–90; he worked in the World Bank 1976–83 and 1992–2001.
47   Johan Jorgen Holst (1938–94) was foreign minister of Norway during
     the Oslo negotiations.
48   Hani al-Hassan was born in 1937 in Haifa and joined Fatah in
     1963. He and his brother Khaled were critical of Arafat for back-
     ing Saddam Hussein during the first Gulf War, and also for the
     secret Oslo negotiations; he returned to Palestine in 1995; became

a member of the PLO Central Committee, and served briefly in the
PNA as minister of interior.

49   Khaled Salam, an Iraqi Kurd, also known as Mohammed Rashid,
started out in Palestinian politics as a photographer for Palestinian publications in Syria and Cyprus in the 1970s; became a protégé
of Khalid al-Wazir, who appointed him editor of the *Sawt al-Bilad*
newspaper; joined Arafat's inner circle sometime before Abu Jihad was
assassinated in 1988; and served as Arafat's financial adviser.

50   Edmund Asfour was born in Haifa in 1926; he studied economics;
was associate professor at AUB; senior economist at the World Bank
(1969–87); wrote *Backdrop to Tragedy: The Struggle for Palestine*, with
William Polk and David Stamler (Boston: Beacon Press, 1957); and in
1992 wrote "Development Finance and Leasing Company and Industrial Development Fund in the Occupied Territories in Palestine" for
the Welfare Association, Geneva.

Notes to Chapter 13

1   Because we didn't manage to do a recording session on Yusif's career
as an economist this chapter is composed from different sources:
fragments from the memoirs and publications; correspondence with
economist colleagues; and my own recollections. For their help and
encouragement I would like to thank Drs. Raja Khalidi, Leila Farsakh,
Sobhi Samour, and Ziad Abu-Rish; also Drs. Khair El-Din Haseeb,
Marwan Iskandar, and Sara Roy for their tributes and answers to my
questions. Special thanks to Ziad Abu-Rish for supplying me with an
English digest of *al-Khubz ma' al-karama*.

2   *al-Khubz ma' al-karama: al-muhtawa al-iqtisadi al-ijtima'i li-l-mafhum
al-qawmi al-'arabi* (Beirut: Dar al-Tali'a, 1961). The full title in English is: *Bread with Dignity: The Socio-Economic Component of the Concept
of Arab Nationalism.*

3   It was perhaps too early in the 1950s to see dependence on the export
of crude oil as a factor that would lower the economic productivity
of the whole region, increase inequality, and cause unsustainable patterns of consumption.

4   Khair El-Din Haseeb, "Fi ta'bin Yusif Sayigh: 'aql iqtisadi 'arabi
ra'id," *al-Mustaqbal al-'arabi* 25 (2004): 6.

5   Himadeh wrote *The Monetary and Banking System of Syria* (1935); *Economic Organization of Syria* (1936); *Economic Organization of Palestine*
(1938); *Effects of Land Tenure on Land Use and Production in the Near
East* (1955), as well as editing several collected volumes.

6   *The Economies of the Arab World: Development since 1945* (1978), 12.
7   *The Economies of the Arab World*, 12.
8   Albert Badr (1912–2010) was an outstanding Lebanese economist who taught at AUB for twenty-five years before emigrating to the United States. He devised a system of making realistic estimates of the national income of countries too poor to have statistics.
9   A.J. Meyer, associate director of the Harvard Center for Middle East Studies from 1957 until his untimely death in 1983, taught economics at AUB in the early 1950s.
10   Schayegh continues, "an economic research institute in the Arab East was believed to be best located at AUB because of that university's position as a double hub. It was the region's educational center, with a correspondingly broad network of contacts; and its exceptionally strong personal, financial, and scientific American connections turned it into a pivot between the U.S. and the Arab East." "The Man in the Middle: Developmentalism at the Beirut Economic Research Institute between the U.S and the Middle East, 1952–1967," lecture delivered at AUB, 8 May 2013.
11   This paper was condensed for presentation with others to the Commission. No copy of the original paper appears to have remained.
12   Yusif began to realize through his work in the economics section of UNRWA "that UNRWA, as its name suggests, was interested . . . to see how the refugees could be absorbed and possibly resettled—in other words '*tawteen*.' . . . . Of course I was hostile to the idea of any resettlement of the refugees outside Palestine, and I had long arguments with Baster on this issue."
13   Published under the title *The Economic Impact of the Arab Refugee Problem on Lebanon, Syria and Jordan* (Karachi: Pakistan Institute for International Affairs, 1955), the study remains a basic reference on the numbers, destinations, origins, skills, and capital transfers of the refugees.
14   Signed in 1948 between Britain and Iraq, the Portsmouth Treaty reaffirmed British control over Iraq, arousing continual protests.
15   Salem Khamis and Asad Nasr were brilliant Palestinian mathematicians who taught in the economics department at AUB in the early 1950s. Nasr went on to work with Middle East Airlines. Khamis became chairman of the mathematics department at AUB from 1955 to 1958, then joined the Food and Agriculture Organization (FAO) as an expert statistician. His main work was helping developing countries to improve their food and agriculture statistics, writing many scientific research papers. He was known for his support of the Palestinian refugee camps.

16   Clark Kerr (1911–2003) specialized in industrial relations; he became
      chancellor of the University of California, Berkeley. John Dunlop (1914–
      2003), a Harvard economics professor, specialized in labor relations,
      and served as secretary of state for labor under Gerald Ford. Frederick
      Harbison specialized in labor management. That four such eminent
      economists were supporting AUB's Economic Research Institute under-
      lines U.S. interest in the economics of the Arab region at that time.

17   By the mid-1950s deputies belonging to the Kata'eb party began
      to attack the employment of Palestinians in large companies and
      institutions.

18   Suheil Natour, "The Legal Status of Palestinians in Lebanon," mim-
      eograph (1984): 5.

19   Bustani had operated as a contractor in pre-1948 Palestine, and
      his construction company CAT employed a large number of
      Palestinians.

20   The Earhart Foundation was founded in 1929 by Harry B. Earhart,
      an oil magnate. The Foundation supports "free enterprise scholars,"
      and contributes to the American Enterprise Institute.

21   Simon Kuznets (1901–85) was a Nobel prize-winning economist
      whose work on national income and gross national product helped
      launch 'development economics.' Fritz Machlup (1902–83) was an
      Austrian American economist whose key work was on the produc-
      tion and distribution of knowledge in the United States (1962). Evsey
      Domar (1914–97), a Polish-American economist, was co-author of
      the Harrod-Domar model of economic growth.

22   Yusif's dissertation was entitled "Entrepreneurship and Development:
      Private, Public and Joint Enterprise in Under-developed Countries,"
      and was the basis of his study on entrepreneurs in Lebanon, eventu-
      ally published as a book.

23   Reviewed by Nimrod Raphaeli, *Administrative Science Quarterly* 9, no.
      2 (1964); and Terence J. Byre in *Bulletin of the School of Oriental and
      African Studies* 27, no. 2 (1964).

24   Both volumes were published in 1978 by Croom Helm, London.

25   Reviewed briefly in *Foreign Affairs* 656, no. 4 (1978); by Louis Turner
      in the *Third World Quarterly* 1, no. 1 (1979); and by M.J. Grieve in the
      International Journal of Middle East Studies 25, no. 2 (1993).

26   *Elusive Development* was reviewed by Fred H. Lawson in the *Interna-
      tional Journal of Middle East Studies* 25, no. 2, May 1993.

27   During Yusif's last year in Tunis as economic consultant to the PLO,
      I asked him whether it wouldn't be pleasant to retire there. He was

then seventy-seven years old. He looked at me in horror: "I have no plan to stop working" was his only comment. His work mania was surely a product of his desire to correct the dire mismanagement of Arab economies and polities, and a lifelong belief that he could do so through 'constructive criticism.'

28   AUB regulations in that period prohibited travel during term time, and obtaining exceptional permission was difficult.

29   Schayegh describes the rise and fall of the Economic Research Institute in his paper "The Man in the Middle," 2013.

30   Personal communication, 12 July 2013.

31   "Arab Economic Integration: the Poor Harvest of the 1980s," in Michael Hudson, ed., *The Middle East Dilemma: The Politics and Economics of Arab Integration* (Taurus, 1999), ch. 11.

32   Yusif Sayigh, "Arab Economic Integration."

33   Published as a monograph under the title "The Place of Agriculture in Economic Integration and Regional Cooperation in the Arab World," FAO, Rome, 1983.

34   Leila Farsakh, "Yusif Sayigh's Contribution to Arab Economic Integration," Ma'had al-Abhaath al-Siyasat (Palestine Economic Policy Research Institute, 2009), brochure.

35   H.A.R. Gibb (1895–1971), distinguished scholar of Islam, moved from Oxford to Harvard in 1955 and later became director of the Harvard Center for Middle East Studies.

36   Secretary general of OAPEC.

37   Dr. Haseeb writes: "The planning of CAUS was agreed upon in the summer of 1974, when myself and Saadoun Hamadi were in Lebanon, and I was at a Broumana hotel, where our meetings took place . . . together with Yusif, Bashir Daouk, Walid Khalidi, and Burhan Dajani. The draft statement about setting up the CAUS was drafted during these meetings. The statement was published in March 1975" (personal communication, 26 December 2012).

38   Personal communication, 4 June 2013.

39   See "Arab Oil Policies: Self-Interest versus International Responsibility," *Journal of Palestine Studies* 4, no. 3 (1975); "Oil in Arab Development and Political Strategy," in Naiem Sherbiny and Mark Tessler, eds., *Arab Oil: Impact on the Arab Countries and Global Implications* (New York: Praeger, 1976); "The Social Cost of Oil Revenues" in *Energy in the Arab World* (Kuwait: Arab Fund for Economic and Social Development and Organization of Arab Petroleum Exporting Countries, 1980).

40 Dr. Khair El-Din Haseeb supports this recollection and cites several of Yusif's works: *Siyasat al-naft al-'arabiya fi al-sab'inat: fursa wa-mas'uliya* (n.d.); "al-Siyasat al-naftiya al-'arabiya: bayn al-maslaha al-dhatiya wa-l-mas'uliya al-duwaliya," *Qadaya al-'Arab; al-Naft al-'arabi wa-l-qadiya Filastin fi al-thamaninat* (n.d.); "al-Mustaqbal al-iqtisadi li-buldan Majlis al-Ta'awun al-Khaliji," *al-Mustqbal al-'arabi*.

41 *Elusive Development*, 142.

42 *Elusive Development*, xii.

43 A reviewer of *Elusive Development* comments, "In an era of cascading capitalism, Yusif Sayigh offers a welcome alternative vision for the future" (Lawson, *International Journal of Middle East Studies*).

44 For example: *al-Iqtisad al-Isra'ili* (Beirut: Markaz al-Abhath, PLO, 1966); *Towards Peace in Palestine* (Beirut: The Fifth of June Society, 1970); with Sami Hadawi, *Palestine in Focus* (Beirut: PLO Research Centre, 1970).

45 Yusif's speech "Towards Peace in Palestine," delivered to the Council of Arab British Understanding in London, was published by CAABU as a pamphlet in 1970. "The Palestinian Economy under Occupation: Dependency and Pauperization," published in the *Journal of Palestine Studies* 15, no. 4 (1986), grew out of a symposium on "Economic Development under Prolonged Occupation," held at St Catherine's College, Oxford University, 3–5 January 1986. "The Role of the Palestine Liberation Organization," 1988, was given at a seminar organized by the United Nations Committee on Palestinian Rights in Berlin; "The Intifada and the Balance of Power in the Region" was a paper given at the Fourth Euro–Arab Dialogue in Bari, 1988; "Development Strategies for the Palestine Development Programme" was a paper given at the ECCP Nengoot Conference, Brussels, 1992; "Why Palestine is not the Proving Ground for Regional Cooperation: Strategies for the Middle East One Year after Autonomy" was a paper given at the Conference on Regional Cooperation: Institution-Building in the Middle East for Free Trade in the Mediterranean, Cairo, 1995.

46 Department of Economic Affairs and Planning, PLO, Tunis, July 1993, referred to in chapter 12 as the Palestine Economic Programme. The plan was thereafter practically ignored by the newly emerging National Authority.

47 Overtaken by the Oslo Accords, the Plan received little Palestinian attention. But for a gender critique see Rita Giacaman, Islah Jad, and Penny Johnson, "For the Common Good: Gender and Social Citizenship in Palestine," *Middle East Report* 198 (1996).

48 Antoine Zahlan was born in Haifa, Palestine, in 1928; he became
    professor of physics at the American University of Beirut, and a sci-
    ence policy consultant. His latest book is *Science, Development and
    Sovereignty in the Arab World* (New York: Palgrave Macmillan and the
    Centre for Arab Unity Studies, 2012). Khalil Hindi was born in 1944
    in Tantura, Palestine; gained a PhD from Manchester University,
    UK, in electrical engineering, in 1976 and a DSc in management
    sciences and systems management from Brunel University in 2000;
    taught at Manchester University, 1988–98, at Brunel University, UK,
    1998–2002, and at the American University of Beirut as professor of
    engineering science and as associate dean, 2002–10; and was elected
    president of Birzeit University in 2010.

49 All quotations in this paragraph are from the Executive Summary of
    the *Programme for the Development of the Palestine National Economy for
    the Years 1994–2000* (Tunis, July 1993).

50 MAS was set up in Jerusalem in 1994. See: http://www.mas.ps/2012/
    about_mas

51 To date the following have lectured: Jome Kwame Sundarum (2009);
    Mushtaq Husain Khan (2010); Issam Shahrour (2011); and George
    Abed (2012).

52 Quoted from MAS's initial brochure, 2009.

53 Raja Khalidi and Sobhi Samour, "Neo-Liberalism as Liberation: The
    Statehood Program and the Re-Making of the Palestinian National
    Movement," *Journal of Palestine Studies* 40, no. 2 (2011).

54 Yusif said of the multilateral talks launched at Madrid in 1991:
    "Politically, the central purpose was to produce an economic cake that
    would appeal to the Arabs so that they would make political conces-
    sions." See chapter 12, page 276.

55 Leila Farsakh, "Colonialism and Development in the West Bank
    and Gaza: Understanding the Palestinian Economy in the Light of
    Yusuf Sayigh's Writings," in Rochelle Davis and Mimi Kirk, eds.,
    Palestine and Palestinians in the 21st Century (Bloomington: Indiana
    University Press, 2013).

56 *Elusive Development*, 237.

57 Sara Roy is an economist at Harvard, author of numerous studies
    on the economy of Gaza, among them *The Gaza Strip: The Political
    Economy of De-development* (1995, 2001, 3rd edition 2013); *Failing Peace:
    Gaza and the Palestinian–Israeli Conflict* (2007); and *Hamas and Civil Soci-
    ety in Gaza: Engaging the Islamist Social Sector* (2011, 2013).

58 Personal communication, 25 September 2012.

Glossary

'adas	lentils
ahla wa sahla	welcome!
'Akka	Arabic for the city name Acre
amariddeen	apricot paste
'amid (pl. *'umada*)	dean (a position in a state or party hierarchy)
'anab	grapes
'arees	bridegroom
argileh	water pipe
'aroos	bride
arzal	tree house
asraniyeh	a snack; a picnic
'ataaba	lament, a style of singing
ayn	well or eye
ayran	a cold drink made by mixing yogurt with water
baklawa	originally a Turkish delicacy of fine-layered pastry, ground nuts, and syrup
baseeta	it's okay, it doesn't matter
bateekh	watermelon
bayyara	plantation
bekaffi	enough!
bsat (pl. *bsut*)	rug
dabkeh	type of dance
dama	checkers
damer	vest made of thick material
deshem	fortress, fortifications

359

dibs a'nab	grape molasses
dibs kharoub	carob molasses
dunum	a measure of land (about a quarter of an acre)
eid (pl. *ayyad*)	(religious) feast
fatayer bi-s-sabanikh	pastry with spinach filling
faza'a	a spontaneous collective rush to defend something or someone
fira'	branch
fukhar	pottery
ful	native gardenia
fuul	fava beans
gallabiya	a long shirt or dress
halaweh	a confection made mainly of sugar, sesame paste, and nuts
haloum	Turkish delight (the original term in Arabic was *rahat halqoum*)
hawsh	an enclosed yard
hayat	life
himar	donkey
i'qal	the black cord worn around the head to attach a scarf
'izba	country house
jam'a	university
jawahari	jeweler
jaysh	army
jukh	velvet
kaymakam	governor of a district
keffiyyeh	head scarf of checkered black or red worn mainly by rural men, sometimes by women
khafeef al-damm	literally 'light-blooded,' easy to get along with, fun to be with
khafifha	go easy! lighten up!
khalas	it's finished, it's over
khallee	let him!
khayt massees	strong thread
khubz	bread
khubz saj	paper-thin Arabic bread baked on an iron dome
khulweh	secret meeting
khuruj	saddlebags

kibbeh	a dish made of ground meat and crushed wheat
kibdeh wa fasheh	raw liver and lung
klashin	a Russian-made machine gun (Kalashnikov) used by Palestinian fighters
klaysheh	a pastry made with dates
koosa mahshi	stuffed zucchini
kulliyyeh	college
laban	yogurt
labneh	cream cheese made from yogurt
lahm mishwi	barbecued meat
lizza'yat	pancakes
mabrook	congratulations!
macaron	an old-fashioned Arabic cake
madas	homemade shoes worn by farmers
madkh	village water pool
manousheh (pl. *mana'eesh*)	hot bread spread with oil and *zaatar*
mansaf	a festive dish of baked lamb and rice with sauce
mansoob	words that end with an 'a' *(fatha)*
marfu'	words that end with a 'u' *(dammi)*
mijwiz	double reed flute
mjaddara	a dish of lentils, rice, and onions
mooneh	winter food stores
mudir	director
mudiriyyeh	directorate
mufakira	a pocket notebook
mujahideen	guerrilla fighters
mukhtar	a local official mediating between village or neighborhood and the state
muraabi'	sharecropper
mutawassita	intermediate level (school)
mwafak	may you succeed!
nafs	soul, spirit
nareet	crushed olive stones compressed to make fuel
ontosh	a priest's residence
ooqeeya	a measure of weight equal to 200 grams
otra	a scented geranium
oud	Arab lute
PPS	Parti populaire syrien, or Syrian Social Nationalist Party

qassees	pastor or priest
qumbaz	a long shirt or dress
quttayn	dried figs
reeh	wind
saaha	village square or center
samneh	fat made from sheeps' tails
sanjak	Ottoman administrative district
sankari	plumber
satora	meat chopper
sayegh, *sayigh*	goldsmith
shabab	young people
sha'riyyeh	thin pasta used with rice or in soups
sheikh (pl. *mashayekh*)	religious figure or senior man
shirwal	baggy trousers
shursh	shirt
sidra or *sidara*	a military cap worn in Iraq
sitte krozeh	a silky material
subbeir	prickly pears
taba[q]	a flat, round tray made of colored woven straw
tabliyeh	low table
tabooleh	a salad of crushed wheat and finely chopped parsley, tomato, and onion
taheeneh	sesame paste
tajbeer	bone-setting
tanjara (pl. *tanajer*)	saucepan
ta'reefeh	smallest coin in Palestine
thara	to revolt
thawb	a shirt or dress
thawr	bull
thawra	revolution
titjalla	to make something glitter, mainly used of brides
tric-trac	backgammon
tubb 'arabi	Arab medicine
ub'ab	wooden slippers worn where there is water
ustadh	honorific term mainly used for (or to) teachers
walad (pl. *awlad*)	child, children
yahya	long live!
yakhneh	a stew of meat and vegetables

zaatar	typically a mix of dried wild thyme, dried sumac, and sesame seeds
za'eem	leader
zahr al-laymoun	orange blossoms
zajal	extemporized poetic event, usually outdoors
zebeeb	raisins

Yusif Sayigh's Publications

Books in English (chronological order)

1. *The Economic Impact of the Arab Refugee Problem on Lebanon, Syria and Jordan*. Karachi: The Pakistan Institute for International Affairs, 1955.
2. *Entrepreneurs of Lebanon: The Role of the Business Leader in a Developing Economy*. Cambridge, MA: Harvard University Press, 1962.
3. *Economics and Economists in the Arab World*. Monograph. Beirut: The Economic Research Institute, 1964. (Translated into Arabic; see item 2 in Arabic books.)
4. *Jordan: Country Report*. Co-authored with Edmund Asfour. Mediterranean Development Project Series. Rome: FAO, 1967.
5. *Palestine in Focus*. Editor. Beirut: Palestine Research Centre, 1968.
6. *The Determinants of Arab Economic Development*. London: Croom Helm, 1978. (Translated into Arabic; see item 11 in Arabic books.) To be reissued in 2014 as a volume in Routledge Library Editions: The Economy of the Middle East.
7. *The Economies of the Arab World: Development since 1945*. London: Croom Helm, 1978. (Translated into Arabic; see items 7 and 10 in Arabic books.) To be reissued in 2014 as a volume in Routledge Library Editions: The Economy of the Middle East.
8. *The Arab Economy: Past Performance and Future Prospects*. Oxford: Oxford University Press, 1982. (Translated into Arabic; see item 8 in Arabic books.)
9. *Arab Oil Policies in the 1970s: Opportunity and Responsibility*. London: Croom Helm, 1983, for the British edition; Baltimore, MD: The Johns Hopkins University Press, 1983, for the American edition. (Translated

into Arabic; see item 9 in Arabic books.) To be reissued in 2014 as a
volume in Routledge Library Editions: The Economy of the Middle East.

10. *The Place of Agriculture in Economic Integration and Regional Cooperation in the Arab World.* Monograph under the author's name. Study
prepared for the Food and Agriculture Organization of the United
Nations (FAO). Rome: FAO, 1983.

11. *Elusive Development: From Dependence to Self-reliance in the Arab
Region.* London and New York: Routledge, 1991. (Translated into
Arabic; see item 13 in Arabic books).

12. *Programme for Development of the Palestinian National Economy for the
Years 1994–2000: Executive Summary*; chapters 1, 2, and 3 written by
Yusif A. Sayigh, and chapter 4 by Ali Nassar. Tunis: Department of Eco-
nomic Affairs and Planning, Palestine Liberation Organization, 1993.
(See items 14 and 15 in Arabic books, respectively, for Arabic texts of
the full "Programme" in two volumes, and of this Executive Summary.)

Articles and Essays in English (chronological order)

1. "Arab Land Hunger in Palestine." Monograph forming part of *The Arab
Case*, submitted in 1946 by The Arab Office, Jerusalem, to the Anglo-
American Committee of Enquiry into the Palestine Problem.

2. "The Development of Cotton Cultivation in Syria." In *Quarterly Bulletin of
Economic Development* (UNRWA Quarterly, Beirut; Spring 1951).

3. "Underemployment: Concept and Measurement." *Middle East Economic
Papers, 1956* (1956).

4. "Lebanon: Special Economic Problems Arising from a Special Structure."
Middle East Economic Papers, 1957 (1957).

5. "Management–Labour Relations in Selected Arab Countries: Major Aspects
and Determinants." *International Labour Review,* June 1958. (Also in
the other languages in which the Review appears).

6. "Towards a Theory of Entrepreneurship for the Arab East." *Explorations in
Entrepreneurial History* (1958).

7. "The Place of Agriculture in Economic Development." *Land Economics*
(1959).

8. "Dilemmas of Arab Management." *Middle East Economic Papers, 1960*
(1960).

9. "Development: The Visible or the Invisible Hand?" *World Politics* (1961).

10. "Development and Democracy." In *The Development Revolution: North
Africa, the Middle East, South Asia*, edited by William R. Polk, 119–28.
Washington, DC: The Middle East Institute, 1963.

11. "Government Economic Policies and Inducements for Capital Formation."
    In *Capital Formation and Investment in Industry*, 287–300. Istanbul:
    The Economic and Social Studies Conference Board, 1963.

12. "The Middle East—Economic Geography and Development." In *Collier's
    Encyclopedia*, vol. 16, 156–62, 1963. Revised version in *Collier's Ency-
    clopedia*, 1968 and 1970 editions.

13. "The Modern Merchant in the Middle East." In *Markets and Marketing as
    Factors of Development in the Mediterranean Basin*, edited by C.A.O.
    van Nieuwenhuijze, 53–70. The Hague: Mouton & Co., 1963.

14. "Cultural Problems and the Economic Development of the Arab World." In
    Religion and Modern Asia, edited by Robert N. Bellah, 56–73. The Free
    Press, Collier-Macmillan, 1965.

15. "Population Growth, Capital Formation and Economic Growth in the
    Middle East." In *Proceedings of the Second World Population Confer-
    ence*, vol. 4. Belgrade, 1965.

16. "Towards Peace in Palestine." Speech delivered in London, 1970. Pub-
    lished by the Fifth of June Society, Beirut (and as a pamphlet by the
    Council for the Advancement of Arab–British Understanding, London).

17. "Problems and Prospects of Development in the Arabian Peninsula." *Inter-
    national Journal of Middle East Studies* 2 (1971). Also in *The Arabian
    Peninsula: Society and Politics*, edited by Derek Hopwood. London, 1972.

18. "Arab Oil Policies: Self-interest versus International Responsibility." *Jour-
    nal of Palestine Studies* 4, no. 3 (1975). (Translated into Arabic; see
    item 14 in Arabic articles).

19. "Oil in Arab Development and Political Strategy." In *Arab Oil: Impact on the
    Arab Countries and Global Implications*, edited by Naiem A. Sherbiny
    and Mark A. Tessler. New York: Praeger, 1976; a revised version in *Oil,
    International Politics, and Development in the Middle East*, edited by John
    Duke Anthony. Washington, DC: American Enterprise Institute, 1975.

20. "Arab Economic Integration and the Alibi of Sovereignty." Paper given at
    the Eleventh Convention of the Association of Arab-American Univer-
    sity Graduates, Minneapolis, Minnesota, 27–29 October 1978. (Also
    published in Arabic in *al-Mustaqbal al-Arabi* 6 (1979); see item 17 in
    Arabic articles).

21. "A Critical Assessment of Arab Economic Development, 1945–1977." Paper
    given at the Seminar on Population and Development, Amman, Jordan,
    18–30 November 1978, under the sponsorship of the UN Economic Com-
    mission for Western Asia. Published in *Population Bulletin* 17 (1979):
    32–45. (Also published in Arabic; see item 18 in Arabic articles).

22. "The Economic, Social, and Environmental Implications for the ECWA Region of Present and Future Trends in International Relations." In United Nations Economic Commission for Western Asia (ECWA) and UN Environment Programme (UNEP), *Development Problems and Environmental Issues in Western Asia*. Proceedings of the Regional Seminar "Alternative Patterns of Development and Life Styles in Western Asia" and the United Nations Environment Programme, 219–40. Beirut, January 1980. (Appeared also in Arabic; see item 22 in Arabic articles).

23. "The Integration of the Oil Sector with the Arab Economies." Paper given at the Oxford Energy Seminar, Oxford University, September 1980. Published in *OPEC Review* 4, no. 4 (1980): 20–41 (Also published in Arabic; see item 24 in Arabic articles).

24. "The Social Cost of Oil Revenues." Paper given at the First Arab Energy Conference, sponsored jointly by the Organization of Arab Petroleum Exporting Countries and the Arab Fund for Economic and Social Development, in Abu Dhabi, UAE, 4–8 March 1979. Published in *Energy in the Arab World*, vol. 1, 323–41. Kuwait, 1980. (Also published in Arabic; see item 20 in Arabic articles).

25. "New Framework for Complementarity among the Arab Economies." Paper given at the Sixth Annual Symposium of the Center for Contemporary Arab Studies at Georgetown University, Washington, DC, "Arab Resources: The Transformation of a Society," 9–11 April 1981. Published in *Arab Resources: The Transformation of Society*, edited by Ibrahim Ibrahim, 147–67. London: Croom Helm, 1983. (Also published in Arabic; see item 24 in Arabic articles).

26. "Arab Economic Development and the Critical Triangle." *Middle East Economic Survey* 26, supplement to no. 3 (1982). (Résumé of an essay in Arabic; see item 26 in Arabic articles for full text).

27. "1973–83: An Unusual Decade." In *The Arab Economies: Structure and Outlook*, 9–31. Bahrain and London: Arab Banking Corporation, rev. ed., 1984. (Published in Arabic simultaneously; see item 29 in Arabic articles).

28. "Arab Economic Strategy in a Changing World Oil Market." *Third World Quarterly* 6, no. 1 (1984). (Published in Arabic simultaneously; see item 27 in Arabic articles).

29. "Europeans and Arabs: Motives, Issues and Obstacles in a Dialogue." In W.F. Van Eeklen and Yusif Sayigh (with comments by Mohammed Bedjaoui and C.A.O. van Nieuwenhuijze), *Europeans and Arabs in a*

Dialogue (the first in a series of lectures on "Euro-Arab Dialogue Lectures" sponsored by Lutfia Rabbani Foundation, The Hague, 1985), 24–39.

30. "The *Intifada* and the Balance of Power in the Region." Paper given at the Fourth Euro-Arab Dialogue, sponsored jointly by the Italian Institute for International Affairs and the Arab Thought Forum, Bari, Italy, 6–8 November 1988.

31. "The Palestinian Economy under Occupation: Dependency and Pauperization." *Journal of Palestine Studies* 15, no. 4 (1986): 46–67. Reprinted in *The Palestinian Economy: Studies in Development under Prolonged Occupation*, edited by George T. Abed, 259–85. London and New York: Routledge, 1988. (Also published in Arabic; see item 35 in Arabic articles).

32. "The Role of the Palestine Liberation Organization." Paper given at a seminar organized by the United Nations Committee on Palestinian Rights, 25–28 April 1988, in Berlin, GDR, Document no. CRP/SEM/88/11.

33. "The Arab World Perspective, and the Diplomatic Role of the Arab Governments Involved in the Quest for a Palestinian State." Address given at the School of Foreign Service, Georgetown University, Washington DC, 9 March 1990. (Published along with two other addresses given in the same series).

34. "Towards a New, Structured and Formalized Arab–Japanese Economic Relationship." Paper given at the Second Arab–Japanese Dialogue sponsored by NIRA (National Institute for Research Advancement) of Japan and the Arab Thought Forum, Jordan, and held in Tokyo, 23–25 September 1991. Published in *Arab Japanese Dialogue*, 129–48. Tokyo: Arab Thought Forum and NIRA, National Institute for Research Advancement, 1993.

35. "Arab Economic Integration: The Poor Harvest of the 1980s." Paper given at the Georgetown University's Center for Contemporary Arab Studies Seventeenth Annual Symposium on "Arab Integration: A Critical Evaluation," 9–10 April 1992. Published in *Arab Economic Journal*, 48–83. Cairo: Arab Society for Economic Research, 1993.

36. "Development Strategies for the Palestine Development Programme." Paper given at the ECCP Nengoot Conference on Palestinian Development for Peace, Brussels, 28 September–1 October 1992.

37. "Historical Review of Research on the Arab Region and the Lessons It Teaches." Keynote speech given at the First Annual Conference on

Development Economics, held by the Economic Research Forum (ERF) for the Arab Countries, Iran and Turkey, Cairo, 4–6 June 1993. Published by the ERF in *Forum* (newsletter).

38. "Why Palestine is Not the Proving Ground for Regional Cooperation: Strategies for the Middle East One Year after Autonomy." Paper given at the Conference on Regional Cooperation: Institution Building in the Middle East for Free Trade in the Mediterranean, organized by the Research Group on Europe at the University of Mainz and the Bertelsmann Foundation in Gütersloh, Cairo, 21–23 June 1995. (To be published in the forthcoming *Proceedings* of the Conference).

39. "The Arab Economics on the Threshold of the Twenty-First Century." Paper given at the Fifth Congress of the International Association of Middle East Studies and Aal al-Bayt University, Amman, Jordan, 10–14 April, 1996. (Arabic translation published in *Arab Economic Journal* 6 (1996); see item 42 in Arabic articles).

40. "The Emerging Arab Economic Cooperation: Assessment of Achievements and Results." Paper given at a seminar on "Unleashing Market Forces and Building Cohesion: The Emerging Economic Cooperation," organized jointly by Frederich Nauman Foundation (Germany) and the League of Arab States (Cairo, Egypt), in cooperation with the European Union (EU), Association of South East Asian Nations (ASEAN), and South Asian Association of Regional Cooperation, Cairo, 15–16 March 1998.

41. "Towards a Meaningful Euro–Arab Economic Partnership." Paper given at the Arab–European Economic Partnership Conference held by the Arab Society for Economic Research and the Chambres de Commerce Franco–Arabes, Paris, 17–18 March 2000.

Books in Arabic (chronological order)

1. *al-Khubz ma' al-karama: al-muhtawa al-iqtisadi al-ijtima'i li-l-mafhum al-qawmi al-'arabi*. Beirut: Dar al-Tali'a, 1961.

2. *al-Iqtisad wa-l-iqtisadiyun fi al-'alam al-'arabi*. Beirut: Ma'had al-Dirasat al-Iqtisadiya, 1964. (Also published in English; see item 3 in English books.)

3. *al-Iqtisad al-isra'ili*. 2nd ed. Beirut: Palestine Liberation Organization, 1966.

4. *Nazra thaniya fi al-iqtisad al-lubnani* (with Muhammad Atallah). Beirut: Dar al-Tali'a, 1966.

5. *Istratijiyat al-'amal li-tahrir Filastin*. Beirut: Dar al-Tali'a, 1968.

6. *al-Naft al-'arabi wa-qadiyat Filastin fi al-thamaninat.* Beirut: Mu'assasat al-Dirasat al-Filastiniya, 1981.

7. *Iqtisadat al-'alam al-'arabi: al-tanmiya mundhu al-'amm 1945. Vol. 1: al-Buldan al-'arabiya al-asyawiya.* 3 vols. Beirut: al-Mu'assasa al-'Arabiya li-l-Dirasat wa-l-Nashr, 1982. (Translated from the English; see item 7 in English books.)

8. *al-Iqtisad al-'arabi: injasat al-madi wa ihtimalat al-mustaqbal.* Beirut: Dar al-Tali'a, 1983. (Translated from the English; see item 8 in English books.)

9. *Siyasat al-naft al-'arabiya fi al-sab'inat: fursa wa-mas'uliya.* Beirut: al-Mu'assasa al-'Arabiya li-l-Dirasat wa-l-Nashr, 1983. (Translated from the English; see item 9 in English books.)

10. *Iqtisadat al-'alam al-'arabi: al-tanmiya mundhu al-'amm 1945. Vol. 2: al-Buldan al-'arabiya al-afriqiya.* 3 vols. Beirut: al-Mu'assasa al-'Arabiya li-l-Dirasat wa-l-Nashr, 1984. (Translated from the English; see item 7 in English books.)

11. *Muqarrarat al-tanmiya al-iqtisadiya al-'arabiya.* Beirut: al-Mu'assasa al-'Arabiya li-l-Dirasat wa-l-Nashr, 1984. Vol. 3. 3 vols. (Translated from the English; see item 6 in English books.)

12. "al-Muqawwimat al-iqtisadiya li-dawla filastiniya mustaqilla." Study carried out for the Palestine Liberation Organization. Limited circulation only, 1990.

13. *al-Tanmiya al-'asiya: min al-tab'iya ila al-i'timad 'ala al-nafs fi al-watan al-'arabi.* Beirut: Markaz al-Dirasat al-Wihda al-'Arabiya, 1992. (Translated from the English; see item 11 in English books.)

14. *al-Barnamij al-'amm li-inma' al-iqtisad al-watani al-filastini li-l-sanawat 1994–2000,* 2 vols., edited by Yusif Sayigh. Tunis: Palestine Liberation Organization, 1993.

15. *al-Barnamij al-'amm li-inma' al-iqtisad al-watani al-filastini li-l-sanawat 1994–2000, al-mulakhas al-tanfidhi.* Executive summary in four chapters. Chapters 1–3 by Yusif Sayigh. Chapter 4 by Ali Nassar. Tunis: Palestine Liberation Organization, 1993. (Also published in English; see item 12 in English books.)

16. *al-Tanmiya al-'arabiya: min qusur al-madi ila hajis al-mustaqbal.* Amman: Muntada al-Fikr al-'Arabi, 1995.

Articles and Essays in Arabic (chronological order)

1. "Tijarat Filastin al-kharijiya: muqarana wa-tahlil," in *al-Dalil al-iqtisadi li-Filastin,* Jaffa, 1946.

2. "Mushkilat al-ard fi Filastin," in *al-Abhath*, magazine published by the American University of Beirut, Summer 1948.
3. "al-Iqtisad al-isra'ili fi al-mizan," in *al-Taqrir al-iqtisadi al-'arabi*, December 1961, pp. 60–85.
4. "Nahw sigha 'arabiya li-l-ishtirakiya," in *al-Abhath*, January 1962, pp. 524–49.
5. "Alam al-numuw al-'arabi," in *Hiwar*, January 1963, pp. 40–53.
6. "al-Ishtirakiya al-'arabiya: hisab al-arbah wa-l-khasa'ir," in special annual issue of *Annahar*, December 1965, pp. 1–33.
7. "Shakl al-tahdith wa-jawharihi fi al-mujtama' al-'arabi," in *Hiwar*, nos. 24–25 (1966), pp. 101–11.
8. "Tamwil al-inma' fi al-buldan al-namiya," in *al-Mawarid al-maliya wa-l-inma' fi Lubnan*, pp. 29–92. Beirut: Nadwat al-Dirasat al-Inma'iya, 1968.
9. "al-Ta'bi'a al-iqtisadiya wa-l-nidal al-qawmi," in *al-Thaqafa al-'arabiya*, nos. 7–8 (1968), pp. 250–65.
10. "Istratijiyat inma' Lubnan," in *al-Istratijiya al-siyasiya li-inma' Lubnan*. Beirut: Nadwat al-Dirasat al-Inma'iya, 1968.
11. "al-Naft al-'arabi fi istratijiyat al-mujabaha al-'arabiya al-isra'iliya," in *Shu'un filastiniya*, no. 16, December 1972.
12. "Tajrubat al-takhtit fi al-'alam al-'arabi," in *Watha'iq wa-abhath mu'tamar Ittihad al-Iqtisadiyin al-'Arab al-rabi'*, part 1, pp. 41–62. Paper presented at the 4th meeting of the Union of Arab Economists, held in Kuwait, 17–20 March 1973.
13. "Filastin bayn al-tahrir wa-l-taswiya," published as a series of articles in *Annahar* newspaper, 11–14 December 1973. Also published in a single booklet.
14. "al-Siyasat al-naftiya al-'arabiya: bayn al-maslaha al-dhatiya wa-l-mas'uliya al-duwaliya," in *Qadaya al-'Arab*, April 1975. (Also published in English; see item 18 in English articles.)
15. "al-Tanmiya al-'arabiya: injasatiha, qadayaha wa tatalu'atiha," in *al-Naft wa-l-ta'awun al-'arabi*, no. 1 (Summer 1975), pp. 54–67.
16. "Dawr al-naft fi al-tanmiya," in *Asasiyat sina'at al-naft wa-l-ghaz*. 3 vols. Vol. 2, *al-Dirasat al-qitisadiya*, pp. 255–80. Kuwait: OPEC, 1977.
17. "al-Indimaj al-iqtisadi al-'arabi wa dhari'at al-siyada al-'arabiya," in *al-Mustaqbal al-'arabi*, no. 6 (March 1979). Translation of a paper presented in English at the 11th meeting of the Association of Arab-American Graduates, held in Minneapolis, Minnesota, 27–29 October 1978. (See item 20 in English articles.)

18. "Taqyim naqdi li-l-tanmiya al-iqtisadiya al-'arabiya 1945–77," in *al-Nashra al-sukkaniya*, no. 17 (December 1979). Paper presented at seminar entitled "Population and Development" convened in Amman, Jordan by the United Nations Economics and Social Commission for Western Asia (ESCWA) on 18–30 November 1979. (Also published in English; see item 21 in English articles.)

19. "al-Maham al-iqtisadiya al-'arabiya li-nihayat al-qarn al-'isrhin," in *al-Naft wa-l-ta'awun al-'arabi* 5 (3) (1979). Lecture delivered on 5 February 1979 in Abu Dhabi at the invitation of the Ministry of Culture and Communications, UAE.

20. "al-Taklifa al-ijtima'iya li-l-'a'idat al-naftiya," in *al-Taqa fi al-watan al-'arabi*. Vol. 1, pp. 389–406. Kuwait: OPEC and AFSED, 1980. From the 4-volume proceedings of the first conference convened by the Organization of the Petroleum Exporting Countries (OPEC) and the Arab Fund for Social and Economic Development (AFSED) in Abu Dhabi, 4–8 March 1979. (Also published in English; see item 24 in English articles.)

21. "Istratijiyat al-tanmiya fi al-'alam al-'arabi," in *Dirasat 'arabiya* 16 (7) (May 1980): 3–28.

22. "al-Athar al-iqtisadiya wa-l-ijtima'iya wa-l-bi'iya li-l-ittijahat al-hadira wa-l-muqbila fi al-'ilaqat al-duwaliya 'ala mintaqat al-lajna al-iqtisadiya li-Gharbi Asya," in *Mashakil al-tanmiya wa qadaya al-bi'a fi Gharbi Asya*, pp. 311–41. Beirut: n.p., 1980. Proceedings of the regional seminar "Alternative Patterns of Development and Life Styles in Western Asia" convened by ECWA and UNEP. (Also published in English; see item 22 in English articles.)

23. "Indimaj qita' al-naft bi-l-iqtisadat al-'arabiya," in *al-Naft wa-l-ta'awun al-'arabi* 7 (3) (1981). (Also published in English; see no. 24 in list of publications in English.)

24. "Itar jadid li-l-takamul bayn al-iqtisadat al-'arabiya," in *Shu'un 'arabiya*, no. 10 (December 1981). (Also published in English; see item 25 in English articles.)

25. "Istinzaf Isra'il natijat al-sira' al-'askari," in *Shu'un filastiniya*, no. 4, September 1981.

26. "al-Tanmiya al-'arabiya wa-l-muthallath al-harij," in *al-Mustaqbal al-'arabi*, no. 41 (July 1982). (Also published in English; see item 26 in English articles.)

27. "Azmat al-naft al-rahina wa mustaqbal al-iqtisadat al-'arabiya," in *al-Mustaqbal al-'arabi*, no. 59 (January 1984). (Also published in English; see item 28 in English articles.)

28. "Afaq al-tanmiya al-iqtisadiya al-'arabiya fi al-thamaninat," in *al-Mus-taqbal al-'arabi*, no. 65 (July 1984).

29. "1973–1983: ashar sanawat farida," in Arab Banking Corporation, *Iqti-sadat al-duwal al–'arabiya: bunyatiha wa-afaqiha al-mustaqbaliya*, pp. 9–28. Bahrain and London, n.p., 1984 (revised ed.). (Also published in English; see item 27 in English articles.)

30. "al-Mustaqbal al-iqtisadi li-buldan Majlis al-Ta'awun al-Khaliji," in *al-Mustaqbal al-'arabi*, no. 87 (May 1986).

31. "Nahw tanmiya mustaqilla fi al-watan al-'arabi," in *al-Tanmiya al-mus-taqilla fi al-watan al-'arabi: buhuth wa-munaqashat al-nadwa al-fikriya al-lati nazzamaha Markaz Dirasat al-Wihda al-'Arabiya*, pp. 907–30. Beirut: n.p., 1987.

32. "Nahw i'adat tawjih al-tanmiya al-'arabiya," in *al-Ta'awun* 2 (7) (July 1987), pp. 107–22.

33. "Fi al-iqtisad al-siyasi wa-l-ijtima'i li-idarat al-tanmiya al-'arabiya," in *al-Mustaqbal al-'arabi* no. 114 (August 1988).

34. "al-Taswiya al-siyasiya fi al-ufq al-tarikhi li-l-qadiya al-filastiniya," in *al-Mustaqbal al-'arabi* no. 113 (July 1988) and in the Centre for Arab Unity Studies, and the Society of University Graduates, Kuwait, *al-Qadiya al-filastiniya fi arba'in amman: bayn darurat al-waqi' wa tumuhat al-mustaqbal*, pp. 462–79. Beirut: n.p., 1989.

35. "al-Iqtisad al-filastini taht al-ihtilal: al-istilab wa-l-ifqar," in Centre for Arab Unity Studies, *al-Iqtisad al-filastini: tahadiyat al-tanmiya fi zil ihtilal madid*, pp. 265–390. Beirut: Centre for Arab Unity Studies, 1989. (Translated from the English; see item 31 in English articles.)

36. al-I'timad al-jama'i 'ala al-nafs: al-mu'awwiqat wa-l-aliyat—ma' tarkiz 'ala al-waqi' al-'arabi," in the Centre for Arab Unity Studies, and the Arab Society for Economic Research, *al-I'timad al-mutabadil wa-l-takamul al-iqtisadi wa-l-waqi' al-'arabi: muqarabat nazariya*, pp. 263–92. Beirut: n.p., 1990.

37. "Mustaqbal al-tanmiya al-'arabiya wa dawr al-qita'ayn al-'amm wa-l-khass fiha," in Centre for Arab Unity Studies, *al-Qita' al-'amm wa-l-qita' al-khass fi al-watan al-'arabi: buhuth wa-munaqashat al-nadwa al-fikriya al-lati nazzamaha Markaz al-Dirasat al-Wihda al-'Arabiya bi-l-ta'awun ma' al-Sunduq al-'Arabi li-l-Inma' al-Iqtisadi wa-l-Ijtima'i*, pp. 739–64. Beirut: Centre for Arab Unity Studies, 1990.

38. "Dalalat al-tahawwulat al-jidhriya fi majmu'at al-buldan al-ishtirakiya al-urubiya bi-l-nisba ila al-watan al-'arabi wa-qadiyat Filastin," in *al-Mustaqbal al-'arabi*, no. 150, August 1991.

39. "Manzur al-Sharq al-Awast wa-dalalatihi bi-l-nisba ila al-'Arab," in *al-Mustaqbal al-'arabi*, no. 192, February 1995, pp. 4–21.

40. "al-Tanmiya fi Filastin: al-furas al-ihtimaliya wa-l-mu'iqat al-fi'liya." Paper presented at seminar on "Restoring Construction and Development to Palestine," convened in Cairo by the General Secretariat of the Arab League and the Palestinian al-Ta'awun Association, 7–9 November 1995.

41. "Muwjibat al-bahth fi mawdu' 'Mashru'at al-takamul al-badila fi al-watan al-'arabi,'" in *Waqai' al-mu'tamar*. N.p.: n.p., 1997. Originally a paper presented during the opening proceedings of the third meeting of the Arab Society for Economic Research, 14–16 November 1995, in Beirut.

42. "al-Iqtisad al-'arabi 'ala masharif al-qarn al-hadi 'ishrin," in *Buhuth iqtisadiya 'arabiya*, no. 6 (Winter 1996). (Translated from the English; see item 39 in English articles.)

43. "al-Bu'd al-iqtisadi li-l-sira' al-suhyuni/al-isra'ili–al-filastini," in *Majal lat al-dirasat al-filastiniya*, no. 36, Autumn 1998, 64–94.

44. "Kayf wa mata yusbih 'naft al-'Arab li-l-'Arab' haqqan?," in *al-Mustaqbal al-'arabi*, no. 255, May 2000.

45. "al-Imkaniya al-iqtisadiya al-isra'iliya, in *al-Dirasat al-asasiya* (September 2000), one of two volumes published as part of the proceedings of a conference entitled "al-'Arab wa-muwajahat Isra'il—ihtimalat al-mustaqbal: nahw istratijiya wa-khittat 'amal" convened by the Centre for Arab Unity Studies in 10–13 March 1999.

Index